Good News for Common Goods

Good News for Common Goods

Multicultural Evangelicalism and Ethical Democracy in America

WES MARKOFSKI

OXFORD
UNIVERSITY PRESS

OXFORD
UNIVERSITY PRESS

Oxford University Press is a department of the University of Oxford. It furthers
the University's objective of excellence in research, scholarship, and education
by publishing worldwide. Oxford is a registered trade mark of Oxford University
Press in the UK and certain other countries.

Published in the United States of America by Oxford University Press
198 Madison Avenue, New York, NY 10016, United States of America.

CIP data is on file at the Library of Congress

ISBN 978-0-19-765970-0 (pbk.)
ISBN 978-0-19-765969-4 (hbk.)

DOI: 10.1093/oso/9780197659694.001.0001

Paperback printed by Marquis, Canada
Hardback printed by Bridgeport National Bindery, Inc., United States of America

For our daughters, Kaia and Sasha, and a better world

Contents

Figure and Tables

Acknowledgments

I would first like to thank the hundreds of individuals, groups, and organizations across the country who generously shared your lives, time, insights, struggles, and passions with me through the research process. You educated me in ways I could not have imagined before embarking on this project, and I continue to learn from you even as I hope this book brings your experiences and voice into productive conversation with broader audiences near and far.

This work has benefited greatly from the insight of many individuals who have provided feedback and insight on parts of the work at various stages, including in no particular order Rich Wood, Ruth Braunstein, Korie Edwards, Phil Gorski, Mustafa Emirbayer, Stephen White, George Marsden, Joseph Ewoodzie Jr., Jack Delahanty, Grace Yukich, Jeff Guhin, Janelle Wong, Gerardo Marti, Matthew Engelke, Brad Fulton, Brian Steensland, Andrew Lynn, Julian Go, Pamela Oliver, and the anonymous reviewers at Oxford University Press among others. I received more helpful feedback from panelists, participants, and audience members while presenting parts of the work at Columbia University's Institute for Religion, Culture and Public Life; the University of Connecticut Humanities Institute; the Indiana University Consortium for the Study of Religion, Ethics, and Society; Carleton College's Humanities Center and Faculty Research Seminar; and Annual Meetings of the American Sociological Association and Society for the Scientific Study of Religion. This feedback has saved me from many errors and omissions; I bear full responsibility for those that remain.

I am fortunate to work and learn alongside a wonderful group of colleagues and students at Carleton College, including in particular the students, faculty, and staff of the SOAN department. Thank you also to Cynthia Read, Theo Calderara, and all of the fine individuals at Oxford University Press who helped bring this work to publication. Many thanks as well to Scott Bessenecker, Jeremy Kroening, Justin and Anne Markofski, Abby Witter, Halena and Josh Ernst, Dan Markofski, and Sue and Matt Peterson for additional feedback, debate, and love through it all.

It is a great gift to share life with a family of artists, musicians, and writers who every day embody and create beauty. Neel, thank you for traveling with me across the watershed of another Big Adventure. I can't wait to see what's around the bend, for you and for us. Kaia, my writing and reading partner, thanks for cheering me on to the finish line and filling our home with your beautiful music, voice, and light. Sasha, mom's artist partner, thanks for all your gifts of art and love, and for always pointing out all the birds, deer, and sunsets outside Riverbend that you know I love.

This work was supported by the Louisville Institute Dissertation Fellowship and Sabbatical Grant for Researchers funded by the Religion Division of Lilly Endowment, the University of Wisconsin—Madison Graduate School, the Society for the Scientific Study of Religion, Carleton College's Hewlett Mellon Fellowship, and the Carleton College Humanities Center. Excerpts from "Secular Evangelicals: Faith-Based Organizing and Four Modes of Public Religion," "Reflexive Evangelicalism," and "The Public Sociology of Religion" are reprinted with permission.

Soli Deo gloria.

Introduction

Collaboration for Common Goods

Evangelicals and Others Seeking Justice and Power Together

On the topic of American evangelicalism, one is reminded of a question posed two millennia ago by the educated elite of another troubled nation confronted with rumors of strange happenings in remote, looked down upon regions of their land: "Nazareth! Can anything good come from there?"[1] For many today, the question might be, "Evangelicalism! Can anything good come from there?" The question is particularly pointed with respect to white evangelical Christians living in the United States, whose views of politics and public religion are often quite different from those of evangelical Christians living outside the United States,[2] and from Black, Asian, Hispanic, and Indigenous evangelicals living in the United States.[3]

It is easy to look at "the 81 percent"—the number that has come to represent white evangelicals' overwhelming (and enduring) support for Donald Trump in the 2016 (and 2020) presidential election—and write off American evangelicalism as a hopeless and uninteresting "monolithic bloc"[4] of dogmatic religious conservatives, white Christian nationalists, and Fox News loyalists bent on destroying all pluralist, democratic, and egalitarian advances in the world today. But, as the title and content of this book suggest, that would be a mistake.

It is true that "81 percent" is a big, consequential number that should not be ignored or explained away. Indeed, recent years have seen an avalanche of scholarship seeking to understand Donald Trump's robust appeal to white evangelical voters in the United States.[5] However, the overwhelming focus of public depictions and academic accounts concerning white evangelical support for Trump in particular—and right-wing partisan politics in general—obscures the fact that the field of American evangelicalism remains a complex, dynamic, contested, and diverse religious field that belies its representation as nothing more than white Christian nationalists or the Republican Party at prayer.[6]

Good News for Common Goods. Wes Markofski, Oxford University Press. © Oxford University Press 2023.
DOI: 10.1093/oso/9780197659694.003.0001

I have spent much of the past fifteen years studying the cracks and fissures lying underneath the apparent monolith of conservative evangelical Christianity in the United States, focusing on minority perspectives and populations in the American evangelical field: new monastic and emerging evangelicals,[7] "Red Letter Christians" and the evangelical left,[8] progressive and cosmopolitan evangelicals,[9] evangelical people of color,[10] NAE and *Christianity Today* evangelicals,[11] and other evangelicals occupying a "contradictory cultural location" between the religious right and secular left.[12] How do these evangelicals engage diverse social others across boundaries of race, class, gender, sexuality, politics, and religious difference? With what spirit and purpose do they enter the public arena? And what lessons can they teach us about evangelical Christianity and ethical democracy in America?[13] This book is about these "other evangelicals,"[14] and about new ways to think about how diverse religious and secular Americans can, do, and ought to interact with one another as members of a common democratic social and political community.

I will argue, based on extensive original sociological research and participant observation among multicultural evangelicals across the country, that the varieties of public religion practiced by evangelical Christians in the United States are not always, and need not always be, bad news for nonevangelicals, people of color, and those committed to advancing ethical democracy in the United States. Like all human endeavors, this work is messy, imperfect, contested, and incomplete. But that does not negate its interest or importance for those concerned about the future of democracy in America.

* * *

On a brisk November Sunday morning in the gritty immigrant working class community of East Boston, I watch as dozens of parishioners make their way out of a venerable stone-and-spire Catholic Church to join their neighbors celebrating in the street. Against impossible odds and in the teeth of a multiyear corporate lobbying campaign costing north of $3 million dollars, a grassroots coalition of concerned community members and local faith communities had miraculously mobilized their neighbors to reject a referendum proposal for a $1 billion dollar resort casino development in East Boston. The mood in the street and on the makeshift stage—where seven Black, white, and Hispanic faith and community leaders waited their turn to address the growing crowd—was giddy. "We want to thank you for this amazing victory, that we have won with the help of God!" the priest began, first in Spanish and then in English, as local television cameras rolled. The crowd cheered and waved their picket signs—"THANK YOU!! EASTIE," "¡¡GRACIAS!! EAST BOSTON," "casi<u>NO</u>: Vote NO on Nov. 5!"—before quieting for the next speaker: "Four years ago, when we started fighting this casino, people said we didn't have a chance. . . . We went up against a billion-dollar company and made them spend millions of dollars to try to figure out who we are and sell their casino to us. But because of each and every one of you beautiful, talented faces and all your hard work, we won!"

The "David versus Goliath" nature of East Boston residents' campaign against the meticulously planned, lavishly funded, and slickly marketed casino project—which enjoyed self-tailored legislation and unanimous backing from powerful state and local politicians deluged in $16 million of casino lobby money—made the casino fight a major news story.[15] The New York Times, The Wall Street Journal, The Boston Globe, and other news outlets chronicled the parry and thrust between anticasino East Boston residents and the powerful casino lobby.[16] The story gained steam when one of the most prominent names in the gaming industry was forced to pull out of the project three weeks prior to the casino referendum over allegations of unsustainable debt and unsavory ties to the Russian mafia.[17] When the underdog anticasino coalition actually pulled off the upset to defeat the referendum— whose success was such a foregone conclusion that local politicians had already begun spending millions of dollars of city budget reserves in anticipation of future casino tax revenue—it was such a shocking blow to casino interests that religious and nonreligious observers alike reached for biblical language to describe Eastie residents' stunning victory.[18]

The victory, however, was short-lived. Just as it appeared that David had slain Goliath—that participatory democracy and political self-determination had scored a stunning victory over corporate power and pay-to-play government—the ground shifted under David's feet. Quite literally in fact: while East Boston residents defeated the casino referendum, residents in neighboring Revere voted yes on the proposal, which in effect allowed casino proponents to simply shift the location of the casino development a few acres north and carry on with their plans as if the East Boston referendum had never happened. East Boston residents were dismayed, telling The Boston Globe that public officials and casino developers "need to take no for an answer."[19] The message resounded in the street in the shadow of church spires: "No means no! No means no! . . . They think they can just move everything over to Revere," thundered a community leader to the sign-waving, racially diverse crowd, "but we're not gonna stop. While they've been playing checkers, we've been playing chess. Back in September we started collecting signatures to repeal the state casino law. So please sign your name to the petition at the right of the stage." More cheering and sign-waving followed as people lined up to sign the petition, "The people of Boston didn't ask for a casino. The mayor, the state senator, the gaming officials asked for this casino. We didn't start this fight. But we're gonna take the fight to them!"

The East Boston anticasino coalition did indeed "take the fight to them" in the form of a statewide referendum proposal to repeal a 2011 law that paved the way for gaming industry expansion in Massachusetts. East Boston community leaders joined an emerging statewide coalition of faith leaders and another anticasino group to organize support for the referendum.[20] A small network of evangelical East Boston residents who had become active in the anticasino fight in Eastie joined the fray in an effort to mobilize evangelical pastors and campus leaders to the repeal effort:

> To be perfectly honest with you, I had no intention of getting involved in this big old casino fight. The reason I got involved is because a casino was trying to force its way into our neighborhood in East Boston. And against all odds, working hand in hand with our friends and neighbors, with pastors and people of faith, and with our friends of no faith at all, we beat the casino in our town. The press actually called it a David vs. Goliath victory. It was an extraordinary journey. And along the way I learned a lot about casinos. I learned about how they prey on the poor. I learned about how casinos always increase crime, addiction, and bankruptcy in communities. I learned about how even though casinos promise so many jobs,[21] what they actually do is suck the life out of the local economy. They take more jobs than they ever provide. That is why I'm urging you to now join us in this fight, because we seriously can make a difference. . . . So come on people! Help us in this David vs. Goliath fight against a predatory industry that is trying to buy its way into our towns and into our communities.[22]

Outspent nearly 100–1 by the casino lobby, the repeal effort was unsuccessful.[23] The Massachusetts Gaming Commission, however, decided to award the only Boston-area casino license to a competing bid rather than to the East Boston-Revere project. There would be no major casino development in East Boston.[24]

For the many East Boston faith leaders who joined the anticasino fight, gratification came from more than just their improbable victory and the preservation of casino-free neighborhoods. Even while the outcome was in doubt, the priests, pastors, and imams of East Boston celebrated the empowering and unifying effects of the community's struggle for political self-determination:

> God can take something bad and turn it into something good, and today something good is happening. Because of this casino, for the first time that I can remember—in the seven years I have been here—we are united in ecumenical, interfaith community. We are united because we want the best for East Boston.[25]

In Neighborhood Solidarity, an informal group of evangelical faith leaders and neighborhood residents joined Catholic, Muslim, Mainline Protestant, Pentecostal, and non-religious leaders in common cause for what they understood to be their neighborhood's common good:[26]

> *Muslim imam:* "These people coming here with their filthy money to try to ruin our lives, and our children's lives, we're not gonna allow them, are we?"[27]

> *Catholic priest:* "We know the collateral damage that will come from this casino, and we don't want it. We say, no."[28]

> *Evangelical pastor:* "The casino is not good for families. It is not good for marriage. It is not good for the Gospel."[29]

> *Evangelical college minister:* "This casino fight enabled us to work side by side with the pastors of our town for the good of our community. And that fight is still bearing fruit in the streets of East Boston right now."[30]

For evangelical residents of East Boston like Tim, joining the casino fight was a way to "do something missional in our community," one that, "didn't take too much thought or exegesis really to see that a casino . . . makes God's house [referring to the neighborhood] into merely a sort of marketplace, one in which people are being taken advantage of." Along the way, they found satisfaction in being provided the opportunity—or from a grassroots democracy perspective, the necessity—of developing collaborative relationships across race, class, religious, and partisan political lines to fight for democratic self-governance and the common good of the community they held in common.

* * *

Across the country in greater Los Angeles, I witnessed a remarkably similar struggle—albeit on a smaller scale—between outside corporate interests and residents of a low-income, predominantly Latino neighborhood over the proposed development of a new regional waste transfer station. On a hot February afternoon in L.A.'s inland empire, I joined sixty faith and union leaders, community organizers, and neighborhood residents affiliated with Together for Justice—a faith-based community organizing coalition—in a neighborhood walk and canvassing effort to inform local residents about the proposed development and encourage them to contact their city councilman to voice their opposition. I was paired up with a passionate white-haired Jewish man from a local synagogue and listened as we were given our marching orders from a megaphone-wielding white woman standing on top of a picnic table outside the local elementary school:

> The flier that we want to leave for everybody is our main information—which we have in English and in Spanish—that emphasizes the main things we object to in this project. One is that the building of this waste transfer station is within one mile of nine schools. We think that's horrendous in terms of the implications for kids and their health. . . . There's cancer risk for too many nearby residences, and it's a violation of air pollution standards that have been set by the Air Quality Management District [AQMD] for our health: the noxious levels, which are those tailpipe emissions, are three times over the level set [by the AQMD], and that kind of violation is something that is not acceptable to us. The other thing is we're fine with processing our own trash, but we don't want to process the region's trash! We don't want to be Trash City—the center of trash for this region. So we object that this plant would serve not only Pomona but eleven other cities and that it's located in the poorest and already most-polluted part of our city. We think that's an undue burden on people that are already burdened by so much other waste processing in that area.

Naomi, the woman with the megaphone, was a neighborhood resident, mother, and evangelical ministry leader who brought fifteen members of her church to the canvassing effort. Naomi was one of several principal organizers of the Don't Trash Pomona campaign. After giving further instructions, she handed the megaphone to a teachers' union leader and then to a local Indigenous Mexican American man who sent the group out with a word and a song:

> [This waste facility project] is gonna be affecting an Indigenous community here in Pomona, primarily people of color from historically oppressed peoples. So we would like to honor you. We ask you to walk in beauty, to walk gently, to speak gently, to speak from the heart. This is a Spirit Walking Song, a Chumash song from here in Southern California, it's about 4,000 years old, and it's asking the spirit—whether it be Allah, whether it be Moses, whether it be Jesus—to come and enter our hearts, enter our feet, so we can walk with a good spirit.

Several Indigenous men proceeded to perform a powerful undulating chant and drumbeat before concluding with a benediction of sorts to the clapping crowd:

> Native American songs are usually sung four times, but we sang it twice to honor you, since you're going to be walking in pairs [*crowd laughter*]. I walk in the path of Christian compassion . . . but the morality of Indigenous peoples, especially the people that live in Pomona, is to be mindful of the Seven Generations. Every decision we make: how does it affect the seven generations that have yet to come? And that's the way we're supposed to think as human beings today. So walk in beauty. Thank you.

Naomi thanked the men and dispersed the group into the streets.

For Naomi and her fellow evangelical churchgoers, the waste station struggle served as an eye-opening crash course in local politics, corporate malfeasance, grassroots democratic organizing and the struggle of "relational people power against organized money": unveiling the "power structure of the city" (David, white evangelical) and "really weird, weird, icky stuff . . . like the incestuous relationship between political and economic power and the families that have been here forever. You know: everybody on the same boards . . . deal-cutting in the back, things like that" (Naomi). Naomi and David spoke of their corporate opponents' "long-term entrance strategy" to curry favor in the community for the waste station proposal, a "ten-year plan" involving major donations to the local Boys and Girls Club and other neighborhood nonprofits, financial contributions to city council members, and even placing company trucks in the city's Christmas parade. Naomi, David, Linda, and their fellow evangelical waste station opponents were appalled when the company handed out pro-waste station t-shirts to local homeless persons in an effort to boost their presence at a public hearing that drew hundreds of project opponents to city hall, "misleading the most vulnerable people" and creating a "super awkward situation. . . . We're like, where are your scruples?" (David).[31] Linda (white evangelical) was one of many who gave testimony at the public hearing:

> It has been exciting to be a part of it. Because I feel like part of the neighborhood, trying to prevent something that's going to hurt people from happening. Especially the poorest neighborhood in Pomona. They know they'd never put [the waste transfer station] in Claremont. . . . So the justice aspect of that is enough for me. I can see Jesus walking around that property and looking at those children, shaking his head at the Pharisees or the money changers or whatever. I can see it. And if it goes in, I can see him weeping.

As a local resident, Jesus follower, and secular nonprofit director who worked closely with children and families in the affected neighborhood, Linda felt compelled to give testimony and get involved in the organizing effort despite acknowledging that "it takes a lot of meetings to do community organizing, which is hard for me" and that she "never in a million years thought I would be up in front of any kind of government anything."

Just like the casino fight in East Boston, the waste station struggle took Linda, Naomi, and their fellow Don't Trash Pomona advocates on a roller coaster ride of triumphant victories and disheartening defeats. They deluged city hall with thousands of letters from community members opposed to the project, held public hearings and informational meetings that gathered hundreds, wrote op-eds and organized canvassing efforts, and got one planning commissioner to recuse himself for publicly endorsing the project before any public hearings had been held, which was a violation of local government policy.[32] They rallied forty local businesses, community groups, and religious congregations in public opposition to the project alongside more than fifty local pastors, academics, educators, nonprofit leaders, and small business owners. The unprecedented public pressure convinced half of the city planning commission to reject the proposal, a major victory for Don't Trash

Pomona. However, the decision was overturned on appeal to City Council, allowing the project to move forward despite ongoing public opposition.[33] A lawsuit filed against the city to block the project on environmental grounds was dismissed, effectively ending the fight. Still, Naomi and her fellow advocates took some solace in the fact that their efforts forced the company behind the project to make several important concessions, including reducing the proposed number of waste tonnage to be processed at the plant by one-third, guaranteeing that all company trucks would be run on compressed natural gas rather than diesel, capping the number of noncompany owned diesel trucks allowed to enter the facility each day, and eliminating an on-site diesel refueling station:[34]

> You're out of the realm of ideals when you're in politics. It's almost entirely by its nature about compromise. . . . You realize we may get some of what we want and not all of it. Is that okay? Is that better than nothing? Yeah, it's better than nothing. That practical side of the political—there isn't much in my [evangelical] background that prepared me for that.

They also celebrated how the campaign mobilized unprecedented levels of public participation and involvement in local decision-making; developed and deepened relations across race, class, and religious lines; and taught them valuable lessons about their city, their faith, the democratic process, and themselves.

* * *

In Atlanta I witnessed a different type of democratic civic engagement: the slow, less visible, consensus-building work of community development in contrast to the dramatic, sometimes contentious, back-and-forth work of democratic community organizing. In an urban café owned and managed by Peachtree Community Development Association (PCDA), I say thank you to the young, pink-haired barista, her heavily pierced face and lips smiling widely as she reaches over the counter to hand me my drink. I find a small café table and sit down. At the moment I am the only white person in the café—the barista, small group of adolescent males, and several solitary working men pounding away on their laptops—are Black. The youth are engaged in a vigorous debate about how some disputed past event went down, with one looking cautiously around while telling his expletive-fond friend, "Don't swear!" as his friend insistently fires back, "He did that shit!

I mean stuff!" The café is a well-frequented community gathering place that draws neighborhood youth, local working professionals, and old heads from the neighborhood who work, share information, relax, and debate politics and local issues in the old Black barbershop or British pub tradition.

I spent nearly four months hanging out and meeting people at this café in a historic African American neighborhood in Atlanta while conducting research as a participant observer with PCDA and other groups in the city. These conversations offered a multigenerational window into neighborhood relations and concerns—a window whose scope and clarity were frequently enhanced by inside information and local knowledge from Alicia—the café's vibrant and beloved head barista, manager, and Black neighborhood resident who generously shared her knowledge and networks with me during my stay. Alicia later points me to a table where two men—one Black and one Latino—are locked in a friendly but intense debate over the root causes of racial inequality in America. "Wes, you should stay here and eavesdrop!" she tells me, "They're in here debating and discussing deep stuff like this all the time." "He's really educated," Alicia says of the older African American gentleman, "Knows his information. Always wearing African shirts. Dresses real nice." The Latino man is making an economic argument about the causes of inequality, while his Black interlocutor emphasizes family background and the historic legacy of racial oppression. Alicia and her friend Bethany—a young, white evangelical woman who lives nearby and works with the housing arm of PCDA—side with the African American gentleman. A group of Black male teenagers and a middle-aged white man working on his laptop pause occasionally to listen in on the conversation. A bit later Ayesha, another friend of Alicia and Bethany, enters the café and joins us as the conversation turns to how everyone ended up living nearby. Bethany nods in agreement as Ayesha explains how she "came here alone and fell in love [with the neighborhood]. Now this is home." Ayesha, a former Black Muslim who now describes herself as "spiritual," elaborates: "The Universe brought me here. So I guess my Self brought me here, which is the Universe." Bethany chimes in, "God brought me here." Ayesha and Bethany then proclaim "we're all so connected!" as they proceed to explain a series of friendship and family ties between them. By all accounts they are genuine friends.

However, later on after Bethany leaves, Ayesha begins to name some problems she has with PCDA's work in the neighborhood, problems which suggest that perhaps people in the neighborhood are not always "all so connected" after all. We talk while looking through the café's large, modern windows at an old run-down gas station across the street, which occupies a highly visible space at the apex of the two bisecting diagonal roads forming the symbolic entrance to the neighborhood. The gas station no longer pumps gas, but it still functions as a small convenience store, neighborhood hangout, and food vendor for a particular population of long-time neighborhood residents: mostly thirty- to fifty-something African American men and their people. It had served as a food vendor, that is, until the white non-profit business manager of the café decided, after much anguished deliberation and discussion, to call city hall to report the property for selling cooked food without a permit. Soon thereafter the unlicensed food vendor was shut down. Ayesha found this act unconscionable:

> I know the guy over there who was [selling food]. He's a felon, probably multiple counts, recently out of prison, was in for like fifteen or twenty years. So now he has his own business: he alone buys the food, he alone makes the food, he alone sells the food, that's what he does. He has to feed his family and he has no other options. Do you want him doing that for money? Or do you want him banging down your door? Is that Christian, to call the cops on this guy? Feels just like self-interest to me: like you just out to get yours. . . . It takes away from what you are doing in the neighborhood. And that's *really* not helping you at all, on any front.

From Ayesha's perspective, calling city hall to shut down this "competitor" to the Christian nonprofit café's own food service business was both unwise and unjust: "I mean, why would you even, why would you do that? I wouldn't want enemies like that, ever."

Ayesha also gave voice to a handful of neighborhood residents' stinging perceptions of the multiracial community development association's work in the neighborhood: "They help women and youth, and lighter-skinned people, but not men. Not those who really need help." She went on:

> The old and the new in this neighborhood: they don't meet. There's conflict. They [the "old"] won't come in here [to the café]. But why not go in there? There are some people who don't go over to that store right there. They wouldn't walk in that door. And it's like: you wanna help? That's where you gotta go, cause that's really where it is. That's where all the people who are influential, all the ones in the neighborhood who have a say so and can get you where you need to go, they are all there. And it's not to go and sit in there, because they are not gonna let you sit in there, but why not just, you

know, shop? They sell water and juices and chips and stuff. Just go in and say, "Hi. I'm just here to pick this up." You know, and after you keep doing that enough times, they understand.

Ayesha's words—along with the neighborhood's symbolic and spatial geography, where a run-down former gas station (frequented mostly by a group of underemployed middle-aged men and their personal networks) sits directly across the street from a more modern building that houses the café, slick professional coworking space, neighborhood thrift store, bike shop, and meeting space for church and community gatherings (frequented more often by women, youth, older persons, working professionals, and newer residents)—dramatize the struggles and conflicts between old and new or middle class and low-income neighborhood residents that inevitably arise in the context of urban gentrification and community development work.[35]

The café itself was a microcosm of these complicated relationships and undercurrents, where conversations among customers and workers throughout the week generated unpredictable collisions and convergences of cultures, dispositions, and concerns arising from various elements within the community. One morning I came into the café to hear Sheri—a Black barista and neighborhood resident—telling some customers about the drive-by shooting she had found herself in the middle of on her way to work one day. "Two cars just opened fire on each other," she said, describing how she nearly got caught in the crossfire, "they obviously didn't care if they hit anyone." Sheri sped ahead and ran into the side of a car, and then a street curb, in an effort to get away from the gunfire. When the police arrived, Sheri said they gave her a hard time for jumping the curb and sideswiping a car. "The cops were not empathetic," she fumed, to which a customer responded, "That's the *Atlanta police* for you [emphasis original]!" The conversation turned to broader issues of the lack of police responsiveness in their neighborhood and Black neighborhoods in general:[36]

Sheri: "If you can help someone, help them! There was a break in two houses down last week, but it takes forty-five to sixty minutes to even get a response from the police."

First Black male customer, complaining about apathetic police response and indiscriminate treatment of Black neighborhood residents: "When we get

riots in our neighborhoods, cops just say, 'Calm down or we're going to ar-
rest everyone.' They're lazy! Think we're all criminals."

For the other Black male customer at the counter, Sheri's experience elicited
a negative reaction about the neighborhood itself: "This is my second time
living in this neighborhood, and I'm trying to move out. I go to the ATM on
the first of month for my check and everyone's out there: 'Lend me a dollar,
lend me a dollar'" [*shakes head ruefully as he makes his way to the door*].
Sheri and the first customer vigorously disagreed with the man, defending
the neighborhood and its many virtues. The customers moved along. A few
minutes later, Sheri approached Dave—the white evangelical nonprofit business manager of the café and thrift store—to talk about posting fliers and
food menus at the big recycling center down the block in an effort to get the
word out about the café's new lunch service. Two customers engaged in a
sports debate. Someone mentioned church. Here, conversations about gun
violence, police malpractice, and anti-Black racism were part of the everyday
routine, existing mundanely alongside conversations about business, work,
school, family, and faith.

While interpersonal trust and social capital can be in short supply in economically disadvantaged communities—not least across race and class
lines—the café functioned as an effective "third space" where conversations
were continually sparked among age/race/class/religion diverse neighbors;
public issues were discussed and debated; neighborhood governance
meetings were held; local art, poetry, and music were continually on dis-
play; and well-compensated jobs for neighborhood residents were created.[37]
In combination with its affiliated thrift store, housing programs, bike shop,
coworking space, food co-ops, and multi-ethnic church, PCDA and its
neighborhood affiliates and partners have invested significantly and often
effectively—yet not without conflict—in efforts to combat racial and economic inequity and bridge pernicious race and class divides that have long
plagued democracy in America.

* * *

Whereas PCDA in Atlanta has been partnering by invitation with disadvantaged neighborhoods for nearly forty years, Neighborhood Partners in
Portland is a relative neophyte, having launched as an independent nonprofit organization (out of an influential evangelical megachurch) less than
a decade ago. Still, Neighborhood Partners quickly became the go-to expert

for asset-based community development (ABCD) training in Southeast Portland and beyond, drawing nonprofit, neighborhood, city government, public school, and faith leaders from around the city for intermittent day-long training seminars in ABCD strategies for collaborative and partici-patory community transformation. During one special training event set up exclusively for a large faith-based housing nonprofit in Canada at that organization's request, we visited a local conservative Baptist church where Neighborhood Partners had brokered a partnership between a long-standing ecumenical night ministry for homeless individuals and four local evangel-ical churches looking for ways to get involved in the community. One as-pect of the partnership involved each church hosting a monthly breakfast that served approximately seventy people. Kent—founder and executive director of Neighborhood Partners—winced as he recalled the objectifying and "othering" language one pastor used while giving instructions at the first monthly breakfast hosted by his church. "He kept referring to all the home-less guests at this breakfast as 'you people': like, 'You people' stand over there while we serve you food. 'You people' can sit over there. We hope 'you people' enjoy our breakfast. I was so angry I was shaking," Kent told us, "I wanted so badly to stand up and tell this guy, 'Stop! Sit down! You're killing us!'"

One year later, however, things had started to change. The Baptist church began regularly hosting a preexisting worship gathering involving about thirty homeless persons that was itself led by a recently homeless individual. After staying away for several months so the "churches would take more and more ownership" of the partnership, Kent returned to the monthly breakfast to find one of his friends, a homeless man named Pete, serving food along-side church volunteers with several other homeless guests. And rather than isolating themselves behind the counter while serving food to "those people," church volunteers mingled and ate breakfast right alongside everyone else. Kent was thrilled:

So the whole organization was changing in how it was postured. But Pete in particular, I was just watching him. I stayed for the church service after the breakfast on Saturday. Pete was singing worship songs. He was leading worship at the church. And then on top of that, they told me that the church had invited him to do special music a few weeks earlier. And he did. He went and sang at their Sunday morning service. Not the homeless church on Saturday, but the main service. And because of that, they asked him to lead worship for VBS [Vacation Bible School] for an entire week. Yeah.

I just, it was very emotional to me on multiple levels. You know: Pete is transforming. And the church is transforming. And the way that [the ecumenical homeless ministry] operates with all the other churches is changing the way those lay people, those volunteers, those ministers, are engaging their neighborhood. Just fabulous. That was very cathartic.

Kent and his fellow Neighborhood Partners ABCD trainers constantly hammer home the difference between doing things "for" economically disadvantaged people in often condescending one-way service-oriented relationships versus doing things "with" them in reciprocal relationships of mutual respect and benefit. Kent counted this conservative Baptist church as one of Neighborhood Partners' unlikely success stories.

After hearing more about the work from several volunteers, pastors, and Frank—director of the ecumenical homeless ministry—the conversation spontaneously turned toward a critique of long-standing evangelical styles of social engagement. "For seventy-five years the evangelical community has left 'Relationship' for 'Tellers' [by which he meant they had abandoned authentic two-way relationships for one-way evangelistic and moralistic modes of public engagement]," Frank declared. Kent chimed in that evangelical churches needed to move "beyond proclamation to demonstration" of the gospel. Later in the day, after hearing more about Neighborhood Partners programs and partnerships in the community—including a presentation by the non-Christian executive director of a local housing nonprofit with whom Neighborhood Partners had developed a strong working relationship—one of the Canadian visitors steered the conversation back to what is, for many evangelicals, the million-dollar question: "But are people coming to Jesus?" The question kicked off an extended discussion in which Kent argued it was important to work with people "who were not interested in church" and that nobody should "have to be a Christian" to gain access to basic services or gain recognition as equal partners in community life, while at the same time affirming that, when appropriate, "you need to speak [about the gospel] too."

Proclamation and charity-oriented approaches to poverty and public engagement have long dominated white American evangelicalism.[38] While trying to train evangelical churches and others to move away from one-way "ministry to" or "service for" paradigms to more collaborative, participatory, and reciprocal modes of engagement, Neighborhood Partners still worked with organizations that operated in the old model. The four local churches described above first worked together under the auspices of a free one-day medical clinic for underinsured community residents organized by Neighborhood Partners in 2009 with the help of another local faith-based nonprofit called Healing Hands. These free one-day medical clinics are led by coalitions of neighborhood churches across the city—almost all of them evangelical—which mobilize volunteers and donations from local churches and businesses to provide free medical, dental, and chiropractic care to un-insured and underinsured neighborhood residents, undocumented and otherwise. In 2014, Healing Hands facilitated nearly twenty free one-day medical clinics involving approximately 200 churches, 3,500 volunteers, and $475,000 of free medical services provided to over 4,500 people across the city.[39] Healing Hands and its partner churches are unabashedly evangelical; their free medical and dental clinics are "designed to show the love of God to neighbors who are underinsured and in need."[40] Although firmly rooted in the charity-oriented "ministry to" tradition of evangelical public engage-ment, Healing Hands takes a different approach with respect to gospel proc-lamation: proselytizing at the clinics is strictly off limits.

In this regard, Healing Hands' medical clinics are similar to Serving the City's even larger efforts to mobilize Portland evangelicals for public service. In the summer of 2008, a group of pastors representing fifty leading evangel-ical churches across the Portland metro area organized by Patrick—senior executive of a large international evangelistic ministry based in greater Portland—met with Portland's mayor to hash out a plan to mobilize 15,000 church volunteers to work on areas of public need identified by the city. After a few more meetings with the group, the mayor and city officials selected hunger, homelessness, health care, the environment, and partnerships with public schools as the five primary "areas of service that would make sense" for Serving the City's volunteer efforts to focus on (Patrick). By the end of 2008, 26,000 volunteers from over 400 evangelical churches had participated in 278 city-designated volunteer projects: including public school mainte-nance and beautification projects, services to the city's homeless population, and free meals and mentoring support for low-income students, among other projects. According to public school district records, Serving the City volunteers working in sixty-eight public schools saved budget-strapped school districts nearly $500,000 in landscaping and labor costs in the first year of the program.[41] Evangelical churches involved with Serving the City raised an additional $100,000 which they donated to public school efforts to reduce dropout (or pushout) rates.[42] One large church partnered with a major corporate donor to raise nearly $200,000 to begin rebuilding the athletic facilities of an underfunded local high school serving low-income students of color.

Originally conceived of as a one-time event, Serving the City became an annual collaboration mobilizing over 25,000 volunteers annually from 500 evangelical churches. This "unexpected partnership" between evangelical churches and public officials in a proudly progressive city and one of the nation's first openly gay mayors attracted significant local and national media attention as an example of a "new face of American evangelicalism."[43] By all accounts, the partnership exceeded expectations. But many public school and city officials were initially skeptical of the arrangement, and for good reason. One of the keys to the partnership is a strict agreement not to prose-lytize. In the words of one public school principal won over by the initiative after initial opposition rooted in church-state separation concerns, "They are not in the hallways passing out tracts, they're not proselytizing, but they're simply asking, 'What do you need? And how can we help?' "[44] Or, as Patrick put it, "The reason this works . . . is that we've agreed to play by the rules," practicing public "service with no strings attached."[45]

Whereas Serving the City and Healing Hands stand in a long line of charity- and service-oriented American evangelical approaches to engaging poverty and inequality—albeit with a more socially reflexive approach to gospel proclamation across different contexts[46]—Christians for the Common Good (CCG) exists to mobilize evangelicals and other Christians in support of social justice–oriented public policy at the state level. Since its founding in 2006, CCG sponsored or cosponsored successful state legisla-tion on over a dozen bills on issues ranging from criminal justice reform to expanded health care coverage for children and low-income adults, earning a reputation for "punching above its weight class" among state legislative rep-resentatives, as one legislator put it.

I spent six months participating in regular legislative committee meetings in which CCG staff, board members, and volunteers discussed potential policy recommendations and legislation to support during Oregon's short spring legislative session in 2012. During this period the committee focused its attention on health care advocacy for undocumented immigrants and other underinsured populations, defending the earned income tax credit and antipoverty programs threatened by Great Recession era budget shortfalls, joining an emerging coalition of anti-death penalty groups in Oregon, and ongoing anti-human trafficking efforts. Because of the short legislative ses-sion, restrictive budget climate, and limited organizational capacity due to recent staff turnover and funding issues, the committee was initially unsure whether CCG would get behind any specific bills in the upcoming legislative session.

By the time the legislative session arrived in February, however, I drove down to Salem with two committee members to give testimony in support of a CCG developed bill calling for the expungement of criminal records for people under the age of eighteen charged or convicted of prostitution. Two of us sat in the audience at a house judiciary committee public hearing as Mindy—a twenty-six-year-old white evangelical CCG member who had a primary role in advancing the bill—gave testimony on behalf of Christians for the Common Good before the committee. She began:

> Christians for the Common Good (CCG) unites Christians to seek God's justice in Oregon. We base our personal and public values on the life of Christ as taught to us in the Bible and advocate for policies which reflect this care for the poor, the oppressed, and the most vulnerable. Our main focus areas are poverty, health care, care for the environment, and human trafficking. As an Oregon resident and human trafficking head of the CCG legislative committee, I worked with community stakeholders and Representative [X]'s office in developing House Bill [XX]. The representative will speak more about the specifics of the bill.
>
> Fighting for victim rights has been a passion of mine for many years. During my undergraduate studies in human services, I interned for a year at a County Victim's Assistance Office where I case managed a plethora of sex abuse, child abuse, and domestic violence cases. I saw both the short and long-term distress and obstacles—including unjust conviction—that victims faced in being able to move forward with their lives after victimization. Seeing these stories compelled me to commit myself to making structural transformation occur in the criminal justice system.

Mindy went on to cite statistics on the prevalence of human trafficking and sex victimization of minors in Oregon and the United States, told stories of individuals unable to find employment as a result of prostitution convictions when they were under the age of eighteen, and argued it was inconsistent for the state to treat youth who were under the age of consent as criminals rather than underage victims of sexual exploitation.

After hearing testimony from other individuals and organizations in support of the bill, a member of the house judiciary committee thanked

Mindy and the bill's legislative sponsor and proceeded to give an impas-
sioned impromptu speech to fellow committee members along the lines of
Mindy's testimony—a promising development for bill supporters. After the
public hearing ended the three of us went office-to-office as Erin—a CCG
staff member—handed out postcards and spoke to both Republican and
Democratic Party legislative staffers about the proposed legislation. The bill
was unanimously passed by both the Oregon House of Representatives and
Senate and signed into law one month later, adding another minor chapter to
Christians for the Common Good's list of legislative success stories.

* * *

Four cities, eight groups and organizations, four distinct examples of multicultural evangelicalism in action.[47] Here we see evangelicals engaging
racial difference and inequality (the subject of Chapter 2), poverty and economic inequality (Chapter 3), and religious, cultural, and political difference
(Chapter 4) in ways that extend beyond traditional evangelical approaches
to American politics and public life.[48] We also see evangelicals participating
in four distinct strategies of public engagement—faith-based community organizing (in Boston and Los Angeles), community development
(in Atlanta and Portland), transpartisan political advocacy (in Portland),
and public service collaborations (in Portland)—that hold some measure
of promise for contributing to the advancement of ethical democracy in
America under the right conditions.

But how much promise, exactly, might more widespread evangelical participation in such practices hold for the future of ethical democracy in America? How do these individuals and groups practice—or fail to
practice—social reflexivity across different types of difference (race, class,
religion, politics, gender, sexuality, etc.), and to what effect?[49] How might
we increase critical understanding, communication, and collaboration for
common goods across deepening social inequality and division? And what is
ethical democracy, or multicultural evangelicalism, anyway?

In search of answers to these and related questions, I spent twelve months
conducting full-time participant observation research while living and
working alongside faith-based community organizing, community development, political advocacy, and public service groups in Portland, Atlanta,
Los Angeles, and Boston, observing multicultural evangelicals in action and
interaction across a wide range of public and private settings, studying their
organizational records and histories, and conducting over ninety in-depth

interviews with race, class, gender, and religion diverse activists, community leaders, neighborhood residents, and others. A detailed description
of research methodology and the organizations, people, and places where
I conducted my research can be found in the Appendix, "The Exceptional
Case Method." I provide a brief overview of the book's organization and each
of its chapters below.

Overview of the Book

I have tried to write a book that will be of interest and use to sociologists
and scholars of religion and democracy, as well as to religious practitioners,
journalists, community leaders and nonprofits, activists and organizers,
students, and general readers interested in the challenges of pluralism, inequality, and difference in American public, political, and religious life.[50]
General readers and practitioners will likely find Chapters 2 through 6,
along with the concluding chapter, to be of particular interest, along with
portions of Chapter 1. Scholars and specialist readers will be interested in
the whole of the book, with Chapter 1, Chapter 6, and the Appendix being
of perhaps special interest. Chapter 1 introduces key terms and concepts
from the book's title and argument—such as ethical democracy, multicultural evangelicalism, common goods, social reflexivity and reflexive evangelicalism, and pragmatic postsecular pluralism among others—in relation
to relevant academic debates and research in sociology, theology and religion, social and political philosophy, and democratic theory. Chapter 6
draws together key ethnographic findings to introduce an original four-fold
typology of the practice of different types of social reflexivity across difference and their relevance for ethical democracy. While the typology emerged
from empirical research on multicultural evangelicals, it offers a potentially
generalizable framework through which to investigate the practice of different types of social reflexivity across other groups, identities, or settings.
The Appendix lays out my research methodology, empirical cases, and the
theoretical and normative logic of the *exceptional case method* I deploy in
this book.

Chapters 2 through 4 investigate how multicultural evangelical individuals
and groups engage racial difference and inequality (Chapter 2), poverty
and economic inequality (Chapter 3), and politics, culture, and religious

difference (Chapter 4) across different social settings, organizational types, and geographic locations in the United States. While each chapter focuses on the subject matter described in the title, there is also significant overlap between each of these chapters in light of the intersectional nature of how different types of social identity and difference relate to social, economic, and political inequality in the United States.[51] For example, Chapter 2 (centered on race) contains sections that address poverty and economic inequity, Chapter 3 (centered on poverty and economic inequality) contains a section on "gentrification with justice" that addresses racial dynamics of gentrification along with intersectional analyses of race and class drawn from interview data, and Chapter 4 (centered on political, cultural, and religious difference) contains sections that address socioeconomic inequity and racial justice issues along with different types of religious and cultural difference. In this sense, the organization of the book reflects sociological theory in recognizing the significance of specific dimensions of difference for structuring inequality, while also attending to the intersectional and contextual processes and structures (such as racial capitalism) that drive categorical inequalities of varying types.[52]

Chapter 2 introduces *strategic relocation*—the intentional, invitation-based practice of moving into disadvantaged contexts in order to live, learn, and participate with residents in projects of social empowerment and transformation—as a particular example of racial integration of interest to theorists and practitioners of racial and ethical democracy.[53] Drawing on ethnographic, interview, and organizational document data from Atlanta and elsewhere, the chapter investigates the practice and experience of strategic relocation in relation to work and community economic development, housing and gentrification, and education and youth development from the perspective of local residents and strategic relocators alike. It also investigates dynamics of racially integrated workplace and religious organizations, experiences of racial inequity in policing and law enforcement, and other topics. The chapter concludes with a discussion of the benefits, limits, and conditions of strategic relocation—and racial integration more generally—in relation to other necessary interventions for racial justice and democracy in the United States.

Chapter 3 investigates a range of multicultural evangelical initiatives and organizations aimed at addressing poverty and economic inequality across the United States: from innovative food co-ops in Atlanta to asset-based community development projects in Portland, and from broad-based community organizing efforts in Los Angeles to housing and community development in Atlanta. It also describes how multicultural evangelical interview respondents answered questions about the biblical view of poverty and inequality, and whether or not Christians, churches, or the government should be active in efforts to reduce poverty and economic inequality in the United States. The chapter examines debates and discourse over the "deserving" and "undeserving" poor; bottom-up versus top-down, autonomous versus collaborative, and internal versus external strategies of social change; the government or church's role in poverty alleviation and economic redistribution; and charity-based "service for" versus collaboration-based "partner with" approaches to combating poverty and economic inequality in various geographic and organizational settings. It concludes with a comparative description and assessment of different multicultural evangelical strategies of engaging poverty and economic inequality.[54]

Chapter 4 shifts attention to how multicultural evangelicals navigate political, cultural, and religious difference and disagreement in organizational practices and public life. It introduces postsecular "particularist pluralism" as one preferred mode of public religion among multicultural evangelicals engaged in multifaith community organizing and political advocacy work in Los Angeles and Portland.[55] The chapter describes in detail CCG's advocacy and lobbying efforts in the Oregon legislature, drawing on participant observation, interviews, organizational records and other documents to investigate CCG's health care, antipoverty, and environmental legislation and education efforts. The case highlights key issues involving evangelical and mainline Protestant relations, partnership with religious and secular others, issue selection and voting prioritization in evangelical circles, navigating political partisanship and divisive culture war issues, and various organizational funding and mobilization challenges that face progressive-leaning evangelical advocacy organizations. A final section examines multicultural evangelical approaches to gender and sexuality from the perspective of women holding leadership positions in Portland- and Atlanta-area faith-based organizations.

Chapters 5 and 6 turn attention to reflexive evangelicalism and the practice of various types of intellectual humility and social reflexivity across difference, along with their implications and relevance for ethical democracy and evangelical Christianity in the United States.[56] Chapter 5 begins by examining multicultural evangelical approaches to evangelism and religious

difference across various public and private settings, followed by interview data on whether or not multicultural evangelical research participants
supported collaboration with religious and secular others while pursuing
social change objectives, and why. In the chapter's middle sections, multicultural evangelical interview respondents discuss whether and how
their views of politics, poverty and inequality, and race had changed since
coming to their current geographic or organizational settings. The chapter
concludes with research participants' self-reports of the practical and theological reasons behind their practice of strategic relocation, how their
experiences had changed them and their views on important issues, and how
these learning experiences map onto pragmatist theories of action and ethical democracy.

Chapter 6 dives more deeply into how multicultural evangelical
experiences of learning, growth, and change through intentional experience and action alongside diverse social others exemplify postsecular
pragmatist theories of action and democracy, and explores further the relationship between humility and conviction, scripture and experience, and
faith and reason in social reflexivity and ethical democratic practice. The
chapter defines and gives examples of the four distinct modes of social reflexivity I observed while conducting ethnographic research across multiple
settings with multicultural evangelical groups and organizations across the
country: namely, segmented reflexivity, transposable reflexivity, deep reflexivity, and frozen reflexivity. Individuals and groups practice *segmented reflexivity* when they think and interact flexibly and self-critically with respect
to one type of social difference but not others, whereas they practice *transposable reflexivity* when they think and interact flexibly and self-critically
across multiple domains. Individuals and groups practice *frozen reflexivity*
when they think and interact self-critically, but partially and inflexibly, with
respect to identities, groups, and settings in which they are involved. *Deep
reflexivity*, by contrast, is reliably recursive and fallibilist, involving iterative
capacity for flexible and self-critical thought and action while recognizing
the inescapably partial and fallible nature of human understanding and action across difference. Though emerging from research on multicultural
evangelicals, these concepts offer a potentially generalizable framework applicable to other groups and settings.

Finally, in the concluding chapter, I summarize the book's main findings
and arguments concerning reflexive and multicultural evangelicalism, the
relationship between multicultural and other varieties of evangelicalism, and

make my closing arguments for a postsecular pragmatist approach to pluralism and ethical democracy in the United States, one with potential to help us better navigate the persistent existence of deep difference and disagreement in our pursuit of ethical democracy and common goods in American public and political life.

1
Good News? Common Goods?
Multicultural Evangelicalism?
Ethical Democracy?

The title of this book contains a number of deceptively familiar terms whose precise meanings, in isolation and relation to one another, map the contours of its content and argument. "Good news," "common goods," "multicultural evangelicalism," and "ethical democracy" all have particular meanings that speak to important concepts and prior work—on democracy, multiculturalism, evangelicalism, and the common good—and to the different ways this book aims to challenge and build on relevant debates and research in sociology, theology and religion, social and political philosophy, and democratic theory. I discuss these and other key concepts (social reflexivity and reflexive evangelicalism among them) and their particular usage in this book, below.

Good News

The name *evangelical* is derived from the Greek word εὐαγγέλιον, transliterated as *euangelion* (*evangelium* in Latin), which means "gospel" or "good news." What is this good news? In the orthodox Christian tradition, it is the good news that, "Jesus, the crucified and risen Messiah, is Lord."[1] For early Christians, the manifold accomplishments of Jesus of Nazareth's life, death, and resurrection for the forgiveness of sin and reconciliation of the world to God were "good news" not only for Jewish people, or for Christians, or for people of any specific racial or ethnic group, or those who followed a particular moral or religious code, or those seeking justice and freedom from Roman imperial oppression.[2] The εὐαγγέλιον was good news for the entire world.

In particular, it was good news for the poor, marginalized, outcast, and oppressed. Famously, as recorded in the book of Luke, when Jesus made the

Good News for Common Goods. Wes Markofski, Oxford University Press. © Oxford University Press 2023.
DOI: 10.1093/oso/9780197659694.003.0002

inaugural appearance of his public ministry in the village of Nazareth in Galilee to announce the central aims of his religious project, he read a quote from the prophet Isaiah in the Hebrew scriptures:

> The Spirit of the Sovereign Lord is upon me, for the Lord has anointed me to bring good news to the poor. He has sent me to comfort the brokenhearted and to proclaim that captives will be released and prisoners will be freed. He has sent me to tell those who mourn that the time of the Lord's favor has come. (Isaiah 61:1–2, NLT)

He then rolled up the scroll, said, "The Scripture you've just heard has been fulfilled this very day!" (Luke 4:21, NLT) and proceeded to tell provocative stories of God healing and restoring poor and sick racial-religious outsiders that foreshadowed his own ministry (and nearly got him killed by his audience).[3]

Evangelical *means* good news—not just for Christians or Jews, not just for sectarian religious believers or moral traditionalists, but for the entire world—particularly (but not exclusively) for the poor and oppressed, the sick and sinners, the dominated and marginalized. This definition of the term evangelical is both subjectively and objectively meaningful in that it accurately captures both the self-understanding of the evangelical Christian tradition (a tradition known for prioritizing the gospel or good news) and the semantic content of the label (*evangelical*) that has come to denote this tradition.[4]

In the contemporary United States, however, the word evangelical is not typically associated with good news. It is, far more frequently, associated with bad news—particularly for the poor and marginalized, the dominated and disadvantaged. It is often associated with bad news for those who do not adhere to evangelical understandings of humanity, nature, or the divine, or for those who do not belong to the nation's dominant (white, Christian) ethnoreligious group—whether at home or abroad. Through decades of culture war politics culminating in the age of Trump and its aftermath, evangelical Christianity in the United States has become associated with virulent forms of ethnoreligious nationalism,[5] sexism and heterosexism,[6] and arrogant or fearful intolerance of the many racial, cultural, moral, and religious "others" with whom evangelicals share common citizenship and humanity.

As such, there are certain modes of white evangelical public and political engagement—many of which occupy dominant positions in the American evangelical field today—that are decidedly not "good news" for any reasonably defined notion of the "common good."[7] White Christian nationalism, for example, actively seeks to delimit racial and religious minority groups' freedom and access to important social and political goods (such as citizenship, voting rights, and nondiscrimination protections) based on racial and religious categories of belonging,[8] while many religious right positions on gender, sexuality, and the politics of "family values" arguably do the same to women and sexual minorities.[9] Other evangelical practices and strategies of public engagement—such as aggressive proselytization and inflexible evangelism prioritization, or sectarian withdrawal from pluralistic public settings and civic institutions, or conspiratorial undermining of legitimate scientific and governmental knowledge and authority—are also unlikely to be experienced as good news for nonevangelical citizens or contribute to the "common good" under reasonably defensible definitions of the term.[10]

In this book I will argue, however—based on extensive original sociological research with multicultural evangelicals across the country—that the varieties of public religion practiced by evangelical Christians in the United States are not always, and need not always be, bad news for nonevangelicals, people of color, and those seeking a more equitable, pluralist, and participatory democratic social order in the United States.[11] More specifically, I will show how evangelicals—like other religious and secular moral communities, both liberal and conservative—can and do work with diverse race, class, religious, moral, and cultural others to achieve common good solutions to public problems,[12] and that they can do so without abandoning their own distinctive convictions and identities (or demanding that others do so).[13] As we will see, like all other human and political projects, this work is messy, imperfect, and incomplete. But that does not negate its interest or importance for those concerned about the future of ethical democracy in America. Before elaborating on these claims further, it will first be helpful to discuss more precisely what I mean by "common goods."

Common Goods

The common good is a powerful idea, one that has for centuries inspired religious and secular philosophers, theologians and religious leaders, political movements, public servants, and ordinary citizens to imagine and pursue a form of democratic politics that prioritizes the fair treatment and welfare of all over narrowly cast individual or group interests. It is found in the writings of Plato and Aristotle,[14] in Locke and Rousseau,[15] and in the secular political philosophy of John Rawls and Michael Walzer.[16] It has deep roots in Christian Thomist and Catholic social thought, finding philosophical expression in Jacque Maritain[17] and Alisdair MacIntyre[18] and religious expression in papal encyclicals such as *Caritas in Veritate* and *Laudato Si*. It has purchase in Islamic political thought and jurisprudence, and in the prominent Jewish concept of *tikkun olam* found in the Mishnah and midrashim.[19] It is ubiquitous in contemporary Alinsky-Cortes-style multifaith community organizing movements in the United States and the United Kingdom.[20] Not least for our purposes, it is the language by which prominent evangelical activists,[21] authors,[22] and theologians[23] have challenged white evangelicals in the United States to abandon hyperpartisanship, ethnoreligious nationalism, and culture war politics in favor of an alternative "politics of the common good."[24]

I witnessed this firsthand in my own ethnographic research across the country. In Atlanta, for example, Black evangelical leaders drew on MLK mentor Rev. Howard Thurman's *The Search for Common Ground* to guide Peachtree Community Development Association's bridge-building work across racial, religious, and political divides.[25] In Portland, a multiyear apartment complex outreach initiative cosponsored by evangelical organizations Neighborhood Partners and Serving the City encouraged participants to think of themselves as "people of faith, working with people of goodwill, for the common good."[26] Kent, Neighborhood Partners' founding director and lead asset-based community development trainer, told gathered volunteers that this involved having "no preconceived notions of what the common good is going to be" in any given situation, because their goals were to "listen" to residents' own understanding of their gifts, assets, and motivations for organizing and seeking change in their setting. Rather than seeking to "solve problems" according to their own preconceived values and understandings, Kent reminded evangelical participants their job was to work "*together with*" (emphases original) diverse apartment complex residents to build consensus around shared projects developed by and for residents themselves.

Christians for the Common Good (CCG) similarly framed its organizational mission in terms of the common good, describing themselves as a "network of Christian citizens, rooted in the Word, active in the public arena, boldly proclaiming the fulness of Christ's vision for humanity, empowered to work together to shape public policy for the common good."[27] Founding board members defined the common good as a "common life that provides or promotes for *all* the general economic, social, cultural, and political conditions of human flourishing" (emphasis original), and defined CCG's mission as "maximizing the common good and justice."[28] We will hear much more about how Neighborhood Partners and CCG attempted to put these ideals into practice in Chapters 3 and 4, respectively.

The compelling ideal of the common good for the practice of a truly democratic politics can be clarified by considering its opposites—that which it stands opposed to. It is opposed to the reduction of democracy to interest-group politics,[29] in which competing factions seek to assert their own groups' particular interests or values on the entire body politic in a power-based struggle over influence, without regard for the interests, values, or consequences of the imposition of their preferred policies and projects on their political opponents, with whom they share common citizenship and humanity. By groups, I mean any interest, identity, or value-based collectivity of persons at any level of organization—religious groups, racial or ethnic groups, political parties, social movements, organized corporate interests, neighborhood associations, etc.—that assert public or political claims based on particular interests, identities, or values they hold in common. A politics of common goods does not deny such groups exist or that they often have competing or divergent interests that deserve expression and fair hearing in the public and political arena.[30] Nor does it deny the legitimacy of agonistic democratic struggle among competing groups or parties.[31] It simply opposes the reduction of democratic politics to nothing more than power-based struggles between competing factions over finite political, social, economic, natural, or cultural-symbolic rights, recognition, and resources. It asserts that democratic politics—as the regulative dimension of the democratic civil or public sphere[32]—can and ought to be more than a zero-sum Machiavellian struggle between competing persons and groups seeking to assert their Nietzschean will-to-power over one another.[33] Rather, the politics of democratic societies can and ought to involve an aspirational moral dimension involving common commitment to a just and equitable distribution of rights, recognition, and resources for all members of a commonwealth.

The ideal of the common good can also be clarified by considering how various influential philosophical, political, and religious traditions have defined and applied the term. Consider the 2015 encyclical *Laudato Si*, in which Pope Francis calls for an international, intergenerational response to global

environmental degradation and inequity that draws heavily on the long tradition of common good thinking in Catholic social thought. "The climate is
a common good, belonging to all and meant for all,"[34] *Laudato Si* asserts, before proceeding to address the challenge of climate change and its unequally
distributed consequences under a common goods framework:

> Climate change is a global problem with grave implications: environmental,
> social, economic, political and for the distribution of goods. It represents
> one of the principal challenges facing humanity in our day. Its worst impact
> will probably be felt by developing countries in coming decades. Many of
> the poor live in areas particularly affected . . . There has been a tragic rise in
> the number of migrants seeking to flee from the growing poverty caused by
> environmental degradation. . . . Sadly, there is widespread indifference to
> such suffering, which is even now taking place throughout our world. Our
> lack of response to these tragedies involving our brothers and sisters points
> to the loss of that sense of responsibility for our fellow[s] upon which all
> civil society is founded.[35]

Contrasting interest-group from common good politics, *Laudato Si* argues,
"There are too many special interests, and economic interests easily end up
trumping the common good and manipulating information so that their
own plans will not be affected,"[36] lamenting,

> These situations have caused sister earth, along with all the abandoned of
> our world, to cry out, pleading that we take another course. Never have we
> so hurt and mistreated our common home as we have in the last two hun-
> dred years. Yet we are called to be instruments of God our Father, so that
> our planet might be what he desired when he created it and correspond
> with his plan for peace, beauty and fullness.[37]

Note the combination of general/universal and particular/religious language adopted in this text, which represents a common feature of common
good thinking among theologically exclusivist or particularist religious
communities that we will return to.[38]

Laudato Si draws on Vatican II in defining the common good—a "central
and unifying principle of social ethics"—as "the sum of those conditions of
social life which allow social groups and their individual members relatively
thorough and ready access to their own fulfilment":[39]

Underlying the principle of the common good is respect for the human person as such, endowed with basic and inalienable rights ordered to [their] integral development. . . . The common good calls for social peace, the stability and security provided by a certain order which cannot be achieved without particular concern for distributive justice; whenever this is violated, violence always ensues. Society as a whole, and the state in particular, are obliged to defend and promote the common good. In the present condition of global society, where injustices abound and growing numbers of people are deprived of basic human rights and considered expendable, the principle of the common good immediately becomes, logically and inevitably, a summons to solidarity and a preferential option for the poorest of our brothers and sisters. . . . this option is in fact an ethical imperative essential for effectively attaining the common good.[40]

Much like the difference principle in political philosopher John Rawls's theory of justice as fairness,[41] Catholic social teaching articulates a preferential option for the "least advantaged members of society"[42] as an imperative of scripture and common good politics alike.[43] Note, in both cases, that commitment to a universal "common good" rooted in "respect for the human person as such" does not require treating everyone exactly the same, but allows for a certain kind of preferential treatment for the poor or "least advantaged."[44]

In the secular philosophical and political tradition, the "common good" refers to objects or entities, whether:

material, cultural or institutional—that the members of a community provide to all members in order to fulfill a relational obligation they all have to care for certain interests that they have in common. Some canonical examples of the common good in a modern liberal democracy include: the road system; public parks; police protection and public safety; courts and the judicial system; public schools; museums and cultural institutions; public transportation; civil liberties, such as the freedom of speech and the freedom of association; the system of property; clean air and clean water; and national defense.[45]

More than just a shared set of buildings or institutions, the common good also constitutes a "model for practical reasoning among the members of a political community" which, in a constitutional democracy, "takes for granted

that citizens stand in a 'political' or 'civic' relationship with one another"—
a relationship involving reciprocal rights and responsibilities toward one's
fellow citizens.[46]

In the liberal secular tradition of Rawls and Habermas, a constitutionally
democratic state must remain neutral with respect to alternate conceptions
or competing perspectives of what the "common good" may mean to any
given political community. Rather than being imposed by the state or a
subset of citizens holding particular substantive views of the good that are not
shared by the rest of the body politic, in the liberal democratic tradition the
"common good" must be deliberatively negotiated and agreed upon through
universally accessible rational reflection and communication that does not
privilege the reasoning, identity, beliefs, or substantive morality of any particular individual or group of citizens, whether based on racial, ethnic, religious, linguistic, gender, sexual, regional, or class-based commonality and
difference.[47] In the liberal secular tradition, the neutrality requirement has
often been interpreted as requiring the exclusion of "thick" or particularistic
religious language and reasoning in democratic discourse, deliberation, and
decision-making, because such language ostensibly violates the neutrality
principle by introducing forms of authority and communication that are not
universally accessible or agreed upon by all.[48]

In practice, however, liberal secularism has proven to be neither unas-
sailably "rational" nor "universal" in its attempts to negotiate different types
of difference in the public and political arena, as an ever-growing chorus of
critics from both left and right have persuasively demonstrated.[49] Whether
uncovering majority-privileging bias against racial minorities,[50] religious
minorities,[51] women and sexual minorities,[52] or religious persons in general,[53] the philosophical, sociological, religious, and political critics of liberal secularism have become legion. Any viable reconstruction of the liberal
democratic tradition and the idea of a common good must take these critics
into account.

One way to do so is to turn from philosophy to practice: to learn from
existing experiments in democracy in which diverse social groups and organizations are attempting to enact "ethical democracy" and forge a new
"politics of the common good" across race, class, religious, and cultural
divides.[54] Such is the approach taken by faith-based or broad-based community organizing movements—such as Faith in Action (formerly PICO)[55]
in the United States or London Citizens (an Industrial Areas Foundation
[IAF] affiliated coalition)[56] in the United Kingdom—and their intellectual

interpreters.[57] In these grassroots democratic coalitions, labor unions, local businesses, public schoolteachers, and secular nonprofits work together alongside racially diverse Jewish, Muslim, Buddhist, Catholic, and Protestant communities of faith in "collaborative pursuit of the common good."[58] For many of these coalitions, common good language is the dominant frame through which diverse citizens mobilize and coordinate collective action in the midst of deep differences:[59] "It's Jews, Muslims, Christians, students, trade unionists, and many others working together for the common good. It's inspiring."[60]

Rather than denying difference or making a priori exclusions of particular religious or secular communities or communicative practices, these coalitions feature distinctive modes of communication and identity construction that are incommensurate in abstraction but united in collective, practical action:

> In London Citizens, there is no translation between "public reasons" and "private" religious languages, nor this there a process of hybridization whereby different discourses are merged with one another. Rather, different language worlds stand side by side, sometime[s] collide and sometimes overlap. . . . The process of overlapping in London Citizens is one in which explicit "religious" language and beliefs are present alongside and feed into "secular" public reason.[61]

In combining diverse secular and religious modes of practical reasoning and communication, grassroots democratic organizing coalitions attempt—often successfully—to enact "a genuinely plural construction of secular space in which faithful speech, along with other kinds of language, [is] part of the *sensus communis*"[62]—the common sense through which diverse citizens forge relationships and organize partnerships to exercise power democratically in pursuit of common goods.[63]

The turn to practice is also a hallmark of the American pragmatist tradition of democratic social theory. Bretherton's description of the "pluralistic pattern" of a common life politics, in which "no single tradition of belief and practice sets the terms and conditions of shared [democratic] speech and action"—whether secular or religious—and in which the practical, experimental, collective, open-ended development of democratic projects and the pursuit of common goods by diverse citizens is a "negotiated, multilateral endeavor" aligns closely with pragmatist theories of democracy and with the central argument of this book. This pragmatic postsecular pluralist approach to democratic politics is reflected in the title's reference to common goods (plural) rather than common good (singular), as it is in Bretherton's subtle shift away from conceptualizing democratic organizing in terms of a "politics of the common good" in favor of the "politics of common life."[64] Such a shift places emphasis on the practical, contextual, place-based, people-centered nature of democratic life in pluralist societies: on "democracy as a form collective problem solving"[65] among diverse citizen-neighbors who share membership in a common "community of fate"[66] in their neighborhood, city, nation, or world.

The difficulty in defining a single, shared notion of the common good in the midst of "deep difference" also underlies legal scholar John Inazu's move from a singular "common good" to "common ground" conceptualization of American democratic citizenship.[67] For Inazu, the more we attempt to reach singular consensus on the meaning and application of higher order principles such as justice, equality, or the common good, the more impossible our task becomes—particularly as we move from microlevel community and neighborhood settings to macrolevel metropolitan, regional, and national settings; and from identity- or value-based communities of choice to place- or nation-based communities of fate. Inevitably, in deeply diverse societies such as the United States, demands for consensus at higher levels of abstraction (common good, justice, equality) and aggregation (city, state, nation) lead to "suppressing or excluding dissenting or unheard voices,"[68] and as such can easily become antidemocratic tools of majoritarian domination over racial, religious, or moral-cultural minorities.[69] Rather than a single common good, therefore, our deep differences require us to search for "common ground"—practical convergences of shared interests and mutual concerns that encourage and sometimes require us to build relationships with people who "differ from us in important and often insurmountable ways" in order to solve public problems or achieve some desired end.[70]

Inazu's metaphor of finding common ground in the midst of deep difference or disagreement is made concrete in the "re-neighboring" work of place-based community developers and activists, grassroots organizers, and related modes of civic action.[71] As Bretherton observes,

> In addition to the shared commitment to concrete issues of mutual concern, a shared commitment to a particular place provides further grounds for common action. Different [secular and] faith traditions will have

different overarching visions of the good life and often very different beliefs and practices; but simply by sharing the same mutual ground, they necessarily have a shared investment in the good of that place. . . . A common commitment to place can foster a common commitment to the people who live there, despite their differences. Added to the mutual material interests that emerge within particular places there is also what we might call a "convivial interest": if we are going to be sharing space with people, we have an interest in maintaining friendly relations with them. Through a common commitment to shared places (a place-based interest) and local people (a convivial interest), a shared story of belonging and a shared social and political life can emerge.[72]

There is no necessary limit on the scale of a practical, place-based, people-centered, project-oriented politics of common life;[73] while practicing "re-neighboring" and finding common ground across is difference is "perhaps more attainable at the local level,"[74] it may be enacted by citizens of nation-states (or earth-inhabiting persons and creatures) just as well.[75]

Multicultural Evangelicalism

The title's reference to multicultural evangelicalism has two meanings, one empirical and one normative. Empirically, this book focuses on a particular type of evangelicalism—*multicultural evangelicalism*—rather than on American evangelicalism in its entirety. In its ideal typical form,[76] multicultural evangelicalism is marked by several characteristics. First, it is multiracial.[77] While American evangelicalism as a sociological and political category is often understood to be synonymous with white conservative Protestant Christianity, multicultural evangelicalism is multiracial in demography and intention. As such, multicultural evangelicalism rejects and is incompatible with white nationalism, whether explicit or implicit. Second, it practices a nonexclusivist mode of public religion that accepts the legitimacy of other religious, secular, and moral-cultural identities and communities in American public and political life.[78] As such, multicultural evangelicalism rejects and is incompatible with Christian nationalism, and with any notion of "Christian America" that would exclude, subordinate, restrict, or marginalize the perspectives and presence of nonevangelical, non-Christian, non-Judeo-Christian, or nonreligious persons and communities. Third and related, multicultural evangelicalism is internally diverse—theologically, culturally, and politically—in demography, culture, and intention. This is true of the American evangelical field as a whole;[79] it is even more true of multicultural evangelicalism.

There are other terms that could be used to describe the population of evangelicals on which the research in this book is centered. *Cosmopolitan evangelical* is one of them.[80] In *Faith in the Halls of Power: How Evangelicals Joined the American Elite*, sociologist Michael Lindsay distinguishes between cosmopolitan evangelicals, who tend to be "well educated, well read, and more likely to live in urban centers," and populist evangelicals, "the faithful masses you might see profiled on cable television," who are more likely to be working-class residents of rural and suburban areas.[81] Cosmopolitan evangelicals have come to hold influential positions in politics, business, media, academe, entertainment, and the arts, and they tend to hold views that reflect their positions in being "less sectarian" and "more engaged with [nonevangelicals] than populist evangelicals."[82] As such, "their views are more nuanced, and their rhetoric is less bombastic than evangelical populists":[83]

> These are well-educated men and women who read both *The New York Times* and *Christianity Today*, and who are wary of the evangelical masses' penchant for polarizing rhetoric, apocalyptic pot-boilers, and bad Christian rock.[84]

Populist evangelicals, on the other hand, and populist evangelical movement leaders, have constituted the dominant conservative evangelical mainstream since the early twentieth century and are most likely what one thinks of when hearing the term in evangelical in the United States:

> Evangelical populists look like most populists in that they respond well to mass movements, bumper-sticker theology, and sound bites. . . . They were the evangelicals that rallied behind Jerry Falwell, Pat Robertson, and the Moral Majority in the 1980s.[85]

As defined by Lindsay, populist evangelicals became strong Trump supporters during the 2016 presidential campaign after some initial hand-wringing, while cosmopolitan evangelicals have been generally opposed to Trump.[86]

The term cosmopolitan evangelical has several things to recommend it, not least how it captures many aspects of the individuals and groups I got to know while conducting research for this book across the United States. These evangelicals lived in urban centers, were frequently well-educated, and often held positions of influence in their neighborhoods, cities, and workplaces. They were also positively engaged with nonevangelicals and deeply invested in projects that pushed back against Christian Right and exclusivist modes of evangelical public religion. Consider this episode from my ethnographic fieldwork. In November 2011, *Christianity Today*—the flagship periodical of evangelical Christianity in the United States—launched a new multiyear initiative called "This is Our City" aimed at cultivating a new type of urban evangelical public engagement. I was conducting research in Portland—where *Christianity Today* launched the initiative—and was invited to attend an evening gala where senior executives and writers formally introduced the project. Listening to the eclectic program of inspirational speeches, poetry readings, video vignettes, and live interviews while mingling in informal conversation with the accomplished and enthusiastic guests around the room, it was immediately striking how badly these evangelicals wanted to be seen as trusted participants and partners, rather than disengaged or combative culture warriors, in the civic life of their city.[87]

The term cosmopolitanism also bears significant resemblance to multiculturalism in contemporary social and political theory, to the extent that some theorists consider them synonymous.[88] Both cosmopolitanism and multiculturalism affirm difference and oppose the rote imposition of a single group or tradition's standards or ways of living onto others.[89] However, cosmopolitanism often carries connotations of globalism, urbanism, and a certain type of detached and universalist "cosmopolitan habitus" akin to a "suave world traveler,"[90] evoking a "polished, sophisticated, and urbane individual who is both worldly-wise and broad-minded."[91] As such, there is a certain elitism in the term cosmopolitan that I do not wish to invoke, because it fails to capture both the sensibilities of my research participants and the overarching argument of this book. Multiculturalism, on the other hand, avoids these connotations while placing emphasis on pluralism and taking difference seriously and constructively—rather than lightly or destructively[92]—in confronting the challenges and opportunities of democracy amid deep difference.

Another challenge with the cosmopolitan/populist designation is that "populist evangelicals" are far more politically heterogeneous than suggested by stereotype.[93] Nor does a cosmopolitan/populist divide best explain white evangelical support for Trump in the 2016 US presidential election. As Yale sociologist Phil Gorski aptly noted, "The divide between Trump and #NeverTrump evangelicals was vertical, not [only] horizontal. It did not run between the masses and the leadership but cut through both."[94] Finally, given its urban (and urbane) connotations, adopting the cosmopolitan/populist designation would exclude rural and suburban evangelicals whose identities and perspectives align with multicultural evangelicalism, even if their proportional numbers are smaller than those of evangelicals (such as those featured in this book) who live in larger metropolitan areas.

Progressive evangelical is another term that could be used to the describe the population of evangelicals on whom this book is centered. It too has merit. Not least, it is a familiar term of self-designation for evangelical left activists and their chroniclers, who hearken back to nineteenth and early twentieth century progressive-era politics and the evangelical politicians and social movement leaders at the front of abolitionist, pacifist, and women's suffrage movements across the United States.[95] As Dartmouth historian Randall Balmer and Brantley Gasaway note,

> Nineteenth-century American evangelicals . . . participated in progressive and sometimes radical campaigns to end slavery, redress economic injustice, promote women's rights, reform prisons, enhance public education, and promote peace.[96]

Highlighting this legacy, contemporary movement leaders such as Tony Campolo, Lisa Sharon Harper, Shane Claiborne, and Jim Wallis often refer to themselves as progressive or "19th-century Evangelical[s] born in the wrong century."[97] Moreover, in addition to the subjective and historical resonance of the term progressive evangelical, there are contemporary political resonances as well. Multicultural evangelicals often take recognizably left-liberal or progressive positions on topics such as racial justice and inequality, poverty and economic inequality, gender equality, environmental protection, immigration, foreign policy, and religious pluralism.[98] Many progressive evangelicals also take progressive or center-left political positions on culture war topics involving LGBTQ+ and abortion rights, although these areas are generally more contested.[99] As such, the term progressive evangelical also has as many things to recommend it.

However, while illuminating in many ways, the term progressive evangel-ical also has its challenges, including some noted by evangelical movement leaders themselves. When a group of high-profile evangelical left leaders and allies decided finally they could no longer identify as "Evangelical" because of its overwhelmingly right-wing political connotations, they landed on the term "Red Letter Christians" after having considered and rejected the self-designation of "progressive evangelical."[100] As Tony Camopolo notes in *Red Letter Christians*, "We did not want to call ourselves 'progressive Evangelicals,' because that might imply a value judgment on those who do not share our views."[101] It also does not speak directly to the multiracial aspect of multi-cultural evangelicalism, which also complicates the descriptor "progressive" in the term progressive evangelical. Progressive evangelicals are "progres-sive" in the nineteenth century sense to the term, and on many issues they are "progressive" in the contemporary sense of the term—not least regarding issues of racial justice and inequity.[102] But not all. As noted above, while all progressive evangelicals criticize Christian Right approaches to the politics of sexuality and the family, many remain opposed or ambivalent about unre-stricted abortion rights under a "consistent ethic of life" standpoint that weds progressive economic, environmental, racial, and global justice perspectives to pro-life protections for the human rights of fetuses.[103] Along with many white evangelicals, Black, Asian, and Hispanic evangelicals are particu-larly likely to hold more conservative standpoints on gender and sexuality compared to white secular progressives.[104]

There are also important stylistic differences between certain elements of contemporary American progressivism and the evangelicals who are the subject of this study. Rather than a strident, self-righteous "secular funda-mentalist" politics of progressive purity that mocks and harasses opponents, turns ideologically diverse allies into enemies, stigmatizes religious per-sons, and brooks no dissent, multicultural evangelicals tend to accommo-date a broader diversity of religious and political perspectives within their communities and organizing networks.[105] As such, this diversity of ra-cial, cultural, theological, and political identities and perspectives is better captured by the multicultural rather than progressive designation.

So, multicultural evangelicalism, not cosmopolitan or progressive evan-gelicalism. It remains to clarify briefly what I mean by *multiculturalism*.

The academic literature on multiculturalism runs deep and wide, with important contributions from social philosophers, political theorists, legal scholars, sociologists, and political scientists.[106] This literature can be organized along a spectrum, with strong multiculturalism on one end and weak multiculturalism on the other. Strong multiculturalism demands affirmation, cultural self-determination, and positive valuation of group differences as a matter of justice, particularly those that diverge from majoritarian group norms and identities.[107] Strong multiculturalism is associated with the "politics of recognition" and "identity politics" perspectives that challenge Western political liberalism's claims to universalism and neutrality while prioritizing the rights and claims of marginalized minority groups: such as Muslim immigrants in Europe, racial and ethnic minorities in the United States, and LGBTQ+ persons around the world.[108] Weak multiculturalism, on the other hand, dodges issues of power and inequality while limiting public discussion and political deliberation concerning deep differences to "superficial engagement and surface agreement" about the positive value of diversity in its various forms.[109]

This is the "American multiculturalism" of the corporate "diversity expert," involving "motley celebrations of diversity, multicultural sensitivity training, and American history textbooks featuring favorable depictions of the achievements of Americans from different shores."[110]

Strong multiculturalism suffers from a performative contradiction in that it fails to provide adequate grounds for moral critique and political judgment of antidemocratic minority groups[111]—such as white supremacists and ideological or religious extremists—whose views most would not want to bestow with affirmative recognition or positive valuation.[112] Weak multiculturalism suffers from acknowledging only "apolitical, non-contentious differences between people," resulting in a milquetoast public philosophy that "eschews difficult discussions of institutional racism, of economic, material, and educational inequalities across racial divides, of restitution and reparation for past injustices committed against people of color, and so on."[113] My use of the term rejects both the strong and weak varieties of multiculturalism in favor of a robust, yet circumscribed,[114] commitment to pluralistic recognition and positive negotiation of deep difference—including heightened attention to how group-based differences in the distribution of cultural, economic, and political power can sustain "durable inequalities" that call for an ethical democratic politics of redistribution and distributive justice across difference.[115]

The last task of this section is to set multicultural evangelicalism in the larger context of the American evangelical field as a whole.[116] This is a tricky task, for a variety of reasons. The first has to do with race. Unlike the global evangelical field, American evangelicalism has historically been a predominantly (though decreasingly) white religion: partly due to demographics, partly due to conceptualization.[117] Regarding demographics, as described by the Public Religion Research Institute:

> Fewer than two-thirds (64%) of all evangelical Protestants are white. Nearly one in five (19%) are Black, one in ten (10%) are Hispanic, and six percent identify as some other race or mixed race.[118]

Asian American and Hispanic evangelicals together make up roughly 13 percent of all evangelicals in the United States.[119] Moreover, American evangelicalism, like the population of the United States as a whole, is becoming less white and more racially diverse.

> Young evangelical Protestants are far more racially and ethnically diverse than previous generations. Only half (50%) of evangelical Protestants under the age of 30 are white, compared to more than three-quarters (77%) of evangelical Protestant seniors (age 65 or older). Twenty-two percent of young evangelical Protestants are Black, 18% are Hispanic, and nine percent identify as some other race or mixed race.[120]

As such, although evangelicals as a whole constitute 26 percent of the American population, the number of white evangelicals in the United States is in decline—to 17 percent of the population in 2018—despite the fact that white evangelicals constitute roughly 25 percent of the American electorate.[121] Regarding demographics, evangelicalism in the United States has been predominantly, though decreasingly, white.

From the perspective of standard sociological conceptualizations and political polling, evangelicalism in the United States appears even more to be white. It is standard practice for sociological surveys and research to construct "Black Protestantism" as a separate religious category distinct from "evangelicalism," even though roughly two-thirds of Black Protestants are evangelical or "born-again" by self-identification and religious belief and behavior.[122] This practice is not arbitrary: there are good reasons to distinguish between Black and white evangelical Protestants given the well-documented and "established principle that for African Americans, differences across Protestant affiliations pale in comparison to structural and cultural similarities resulting from the legacy of racial discrimination and inequality."[123] To give just one of many possible examples, no less than 75 percent of Black evangelical Protestants are Democratic Party supporters—despite religious beliefs and behavior that align closely with white evangelical Protestants—which is in line with overwhelming Democratic Party support among Black Protestants and African Americans in general.[124] In this, Black and white evangelicals are mirror opposites of each other. Political surveys and exit polls likewise routinely disaggregate white evangelicals from Black, Asian, and Hispanic evangelicals; the former make ubiquitous headlines for their overwhelming support for Republican Party politics, the latter rarely make headlines.[125]

This combination of measurement choices and underlying demographics results in a restricted view of the American evangelical field, one that has "never been fully accurate, but it's increasingly becoming less accurate," namely, "The default image that most people have in their heads is of politically conservative white evangelicals."[126] While understandable given the political significance and dominant position of conservative white evangelicals in the field, it has become far too easy and common to reduce American evangelicalism into caricature, and to ignore the significant and growing racial, cultural, and political diversity and complexity of evangelicalism in the United States.[127] Combined, evangelical people of color and white evangelicals who identify as politically liberal or Democratic Party supporters constitute between one-third and one-half of the total evangelical population in the United States, depending on measurement choices.[128] Moreover, younger evangelicals are increasingly likely to belong to this category,[129] and a significant proportion of white conservative evangelical voters have views that align with particular multicultural perspectives on race, pluralism, policy, and public religion in the United States.[130] Despite the dominance of politically conservative white evangelicals in the field, multicultural evangelicalism constitutes a significant and growing population in the United States, one that ought to be of particular interest to those concerned about the future of ethical democracy in America.[131] To that end, this book deploys an exceptional case method to empirically investigate cases of multicultural evangelicalism in action across the United States, and to put this original sociological data to work in constructing normative arguments, theoretical analyses, and ethical reflection concerning the relationship between varieties of evangelical Christianity—multicultural evangelicalism in particular—and ethical democracy in the United States.[132]

Ethical Democracy

Democracy, in the classical American pragmatist and republican traditions, is concerned as much with cultural dispositions and relations among individuals and groups in public life as with legal and political structures.[133] "The democratic spirit," Jane Addams admonishes us, "implies that diversified human experience and resultant sympathy which are the foundation and guarantee of Democracy."[134] Under conditions of pervasive pluralism and inequality, ethical democracy requires society's members to actively cultivate cognitive and embodied habits of "mixing on the thronged and common road where all must turn out for one another, and at least see the size of one another's burdens," lest "we grow contemptuous of our fellows . . . and not only tremendously circumscribe our range of life, but limit the scope of our ethics."[135] The classical American pragmatist and republican traditions remind us that ethical democracy cannot flourish without an "underlying democratic culture" in which citizens cultivate skills, habits, and institutions conducive to democratic practice in public and political life.[136]

This tradition has been taken up and built upon by contemporary social philosophers such as Elizabeth Anderson, who advances pragmatist theories of democracy in arguments for racial justice and integration in *The Imperative of Integration* and elsewhere. Anderson contrasts her characteristically "thick" pragmatist conception of democracy as a "membership organization, a mode of government, and a culture" with "thin" conceptions focused narrowly on formal legal and political procedures and institutions:

> In stressing the cultural dimension of democracy, I oppose conceptions of democracy that focus on its governance structures alone: a universal franchise, periodic elections, majority rule, transparent government, the rule of law. Such conceptions foster the illusion that laws alone make a democracy, even in the absence of interaction among citizens across group lines. It tends to stress a decision rule, handing victory to the majority, at the expense of norms of equality that form the essential background condition for majority decision making to fulfill democratic ideals.[137]

For Anderson and Addams, the pursuit of ethical democracy requires attention to culture and publics alongside law and politics, all of which require "interaction among citizens across group lines"—sometimes cooperative, sometimes competitive, never violent or antagonistic—in order to have any chance of approaching democratic ideals in spirit and substance.[138]

In focusing attention on the "cultural and institutional underpinnings of democratic life,"[139] the American pragmatist conception of democracy is consistent with a long tradition of democratic theory and practice reaching back to the founding of the American republic and beyond.[140] To speak of ethical democracy, then, is to speak of a "thick" conception of democracy concerned with the dispositions, practices, and relations among ordinary citizens and civic institutions no less than the policies, rules, and practices surrounding election cycles and partisan politics. In both the classical republican and pragmatist traditions, it is the former which sometimes govern the latter.[141]

Nor is this broader conception of democracy limited to the classical pragmatist and republican traditions. Durkheimian social theorist Jeffrey Alexander builds on Addams and Dewey in pointing to the cultural, emotional, and moral constitution of the democratic civil sphere. In place of narrow, formal, instrumentalist, cynical, and reductively materialist notions of democracy, Alexander echoes Addams, Dewey, and Anderson in pointing to the "idea of democracy as a way of life."[142] For Alexander, the "suprapolitical base" on which democracy rests, and without which social justice is impossible,[143] is the democratic civil sphere: "a world of values and institutions that generate capacity for social criticism and democratic integration at the same time,"[144] which in turn relies on "the ideal of a broadly humanistic solidarity"[145] involving "feelings for others whom we do not know but whom we respect out of principle."[146] Like the early American pragmatists, Alexander combines empirical research and normative argument in an attempt to construct a "realistic social theory of democracy" that is simultaneously practical and principled, "hard-headed" and hopeful, realistic but not reductionist, empirical but not empiricist, aspirational but not utopian, idealizing but not naïve.[147] Such is also the aim and method of social theorist Erik Olin Wright's magnum opus *Envisioning Real Utopias*, which moves beyond strict Marxian orthodoxy to build an empirical and normative case for the desirability, viability, and achievability of more deeply egalitarian and participatory forms of economic organization and social democracy, or democratic socialism, across all levels of economic, social, and political organization.[148]

Sociologist Richard Wood coined the term "ethical democracy" to articulate the practice and vision of democratic organizing in the tradition of Saul Alinsky and Ernie Cortés—grassroots laboratories of diversity and democracy that have become known as the field of broad-based or faith-based community organizing.[149] As the title of Jane Addams's classic book on the subject suggests, linking democracy and social ethics lies at the heart of the American pragmatist tradition represented by Jane Addams and her collaborators.[150] As such, ethical democracy's broader theoretical and historic lineage includes but goes beyond the field of contemporary broad-based or faith-based community organizing. Below I describe and extend several features of this empirically informed normative type of democracy that are of central importance to the arguments made in this book.

First, ethical democracy combines elements of both participatory and representative democracy, without which democratic accountability and stakeholder principles of democratic governance are impossible.[151] In this case, participatory democracy (or deep democracy) involves "the cultivation of grassroots democratic organizations via face-to-face [or 'one-to-one'] relationships," through which ordinary citizens and stakeholders identify problems, deliberatively weigh solutions, hold leaders accountable, and organize "relational power" to accomplish goals through democratic political participation.[152] Representative democracy, on the other hand, recognizes the necessity of selecting representative leaders and working with political officeholders at all levels as legitimate means of collective political decision-making. When working properly, representative democracy selects leaders who effectively represent the cultural and sociodemographic diversity and interests of citizen stakeholders, and who are "held to accountability by participatory process[es]."[153]

Second, ethical democracy involves an approach to politics and public life that combines the instrumental rationality of power and ("enlightened") self-interest with the value rationality of deep moral commitments derived from both secular and religious sources.[154] Rather than compelling people to leave their deepest ethical or religious commitments at the door, ethical democratic institutions are simultaneously "moral communities" and "power organizations":[155] they embrace communication and reflection about the underlying moral or religious motivations of their diverse partners and constituents, and they explicitly draw on these traditions to frame goals, address opposition, and mobilize support for their activities.[156]

Third, ethical democracy aims to combine multiculturalist commitments to group rights and representation with universalist commitments to liberty and justice for all.[157] This is a difficult balance—with no preset solution—requiring constant communication, contestation, and compromise in our multiracial, multicultural, multifaith world. On the multiculturalist side, ethical democracy rejects strictly individualist, rationalist, and procedural accounts of democracy that promote formal equality or justice (such as ostensibly "color-blind" racial politics) at the expense of substantive equality or justice.[158] On the universalist side, ethical democracy rejects strong multiculturalist arguments for unassailable group separatism and self-determination that denies the possibility or desirability of cross-group solidarity and integration while refusing to subject all groups—whether minority or majority—to mutual social and ethical critique.[159] On the terrain of race, the pragmatist argument for racial justice and integration becomes "racial democracy":[160] ethical democracy's answer to racial domination, "color-blind" universalism, and the reductive "identity politics" of strong versions of "left multiculturalism."[161] On the terrain of religion, it becomes a "post-secular" democracy committed to "mutual recognition" and "complementary learning processes" among diverse religious and secular citizens alike.[162] Democracy cannot be ethical without making room for positive expression of our deep differences, and without also attending to how these differences often mark the boundaries along which pernicious and persistent inequalities among us track.[163] Nor can democracy be ethical without attending to goods that are common among us; without forging the solidaristic bonds, commitments, compromises, and collaborations across difference on which the possibility of justice relies.[164]

Fourth, rather than imposing a fictive (and biased) ideal of nonexpressive, disinterested, formally articulate, universally accessible rational communication in the public and political arena, ethical democracy recognizes the empirically ubiquitous and normatively legitimate presence of love and anger, passion and performance, image and emotion—of diverse communication styles, experiential standpoints, cultural codes, and embodied performances of politics that challenge nonsociological and nonrepresentative constructions of ideal democratic practice.[165] As Alexander notes, poking the bear of (white, male, educated, elite) liberal Western philosophical tradition, "The public has never been a dry and arid place composed of abstract arguments about reason."[166] We must acknowledge, as Anderson argues while building her pragmatist case for empirically realistic nonideal democratic theory, "We are not nearly as rational, self-aware, and self-controlled as we imagine ourselves to be."[167] We must also acknowledge how abstract, formalized notions of democratic deliberation "may unduly narrow our conception of democratic communication to the kinds of relatively sober talk that take place in a congressional hearing or around a negotiating table."[168]

> Often, however, bringing matters to the attention of the public requires communicating with loud voices, in large numbers, with theater, drama, and symbolism. It may require disrupting the normal routines of citizens so that they sit up and listen. This is why the right to mass public assemblies and demonstrations is such a critical feature of democracies. Restricting communication to quiet rooms governed by norms of subdued and polite conversation can be a means the powerful use to suppress the communication of grievances.[169]

Accepting the legitimacy of reason *and* emotion—of deliberative *and* disruptive democratic communication alike—ethical democracy does not make a priori exclusions or rules regarding the substance or style, tone or tenor, of legitimate participation in the public or political arena.

Fifth and finally, in its embrace of pluralism and (partial) critique of the rationalist-individualist presuppositions of liberal political theory, ethical democracy incorporates elements of the agonistic conception of democracy developed by Belgian political theorist Chantal Mouffe, William Connolly, and Bonnie Honig among others.[170] In contrast to a technocratic liberal understanding of democracy involving the rational harmonization of competing interests through deliberative negotiation and consensus building, Mouffe advances a theory of "agonistic pluralism" that recognizes the inevitability of substantial difference and conflict in every democratic political order while aiming to channel ineradicable conflicts toward non-destructive ends.[171] As in Alexander's civil sphere, agonistic pluralism asserts that every attempt to construct an inclusive "we" in sociopolitical life "requires as its very condition of possibility the demarcation of a 'they.'"[172] "The crucial issue then," Mouffe recognizes, "is how to establish this us/them distinction . . . in way that is compatible with the recognition of pluralism."[173] Mouffe's solution is the construction of democratic norms and institutions that turn potentially antagonistic conflicts between "enemies" into agonistic conflicts among "adversaries":

> Conflict in liberal democratic societies cannot and should not be eradicated, since the specificity of pluralist democracy is precisely the recognition and legitimation of conflict. What liberal democratic politics requires

is that the others are not seen as enemies to be destroyed, but as adversaries whose ideas might be fought, even fiercely, but whose right to defend those ideas is not to be questioned. . . . What is important is that conflict does not take the form of an "antagonism" (struggle between enemies), but the form of an "agonism" (struggle between adversaries).[174]

Depending on the issue at hand, diverse citizens or groups may be aligned as adversaries who "fight against each other" to assert incommensurate or incompatible visions of freedom, equality, and the good life, but in practicing agonistic democracy, "they do not put into question the legitimacy of their opponents right to fight for the victory of their position" (or the legitimacy of unfavorable outcomes adjudicated through established procedures and norms of democratic institutions).[175] In this, agonistic pluralism resembles Inazu's vision of confident pluralism and echoes James Davison Hunter's warnings against both the denial of difference and the extremes of culture war politics in the United States.[176]

On one point, however, Mouffe's theory of agonistic pluralism and democracy requires sympathetic but critical reconstruction in order to align with the vision of ethical democracy outlined here. Like Habermas before his post-secular turn, Mouffe affirms an a priori exclusion of religious standpoints and discourse from legitimate agonistic struggle and democratic political life.[177] In fact, Mouffe's position is even more problematic, in that it excludes—as "non-democratic forms of identification"—not just religion, but all "forms of politics articulated around essentialist identities of a nationalist, religious or ethnic type," along with other "confrontations over non-negotiable moral values, with all the manifestations of violence that such confrontations entail."[178] In other words, Mouffe resolves all the truly difficult political conflicts arising from deep religious, moral, national, and racial or ethnic difference and disagreement by fiat, defining them out of existence and participation in legitimate democratic struggle altogether. Given the breathtaking sweep of the exclusions—which also happen to be just the sort of differences that can give rise to the most intractable sorts of democratic conflict[179]—it is difficult to see just what differences might be left that would genuinely threaten to turn agonistic adversaries into antagonistic enemies.[180] It is also difficult to see how such an arrangement can rightly be viewed as ethically democratic (not to mention sociologically realistic), assuming we grant standard democratic commitments to self-determination and inclusive participation to *all* citizens (even those who frame their democratic participation in terms of "identities of a nationalist, religious or ethnic type"),[181] which "empowers them to be the authors of laws to which as its addressees they are subject."[182]

In conjunction with a robust common good politics, then, ethical democracy also calls for an agonistic politics of confident pluralism without enmity—assuming we move from a restricted to inclusive definition of agonistic politics.[183] Our agonistic struggles must always be checked by and contained within broader universal human and democratic solidarities in order to prevent their devolution into zero-sum antagonistic struggles with essentialized enemies against whom we become willing to perpetrate symbolic or physical violence. For as Alexander notes, "It is not only difference and antagonism [or better, agonism] that sustain democracy, but solidarity and commonality."[184]

Ethical Democracy and Existing Democracy

It is likely clear by now that ethical democracy bears only passing resemblance to democracy as it actually exists in the United States (not to mention other purportedly democratic nations). The practitioners and theorists of grassroots democracy are certainly aware of this reality. Democratic activists and theorists lament the extent to which contemporary American "elections are, for the most part, exercises in mass manipulation."[185] Others speak of the "three demons that bedevil American society": obdurate racism and racial inequity, corrupting and unjustifiable levels of economic inequality, and elite-driven political polarization that have rendered our governing institutions ineffective, detached, and self-serving—unwilling or unable to address the concerns and interests of the vast majority of ordinary Americans.[186] Unchecked corporate interests, unrivaled flows of money into politics, unrepresentative political and economic elites, and ever-eroding protections for shared public goods, services, spaces, and ideals undermine democratic participation and accountability.[187] Ongoing inequities in access to good jobs, schools, positions, homes, neighborhoods, health care, public services, markets, police protection, and legal justice across different types of categorical difference undermine democratic ideals of fairness and equal opportunity, the "positive freedom" of classical republican theories of democratic citizenship.[188] When one contemplates the gulf between existing and ethical democracy, it is tempting to fall into cynicism.

Of course, the idea that democracy is an illusion—that it serves only as cover for elite domination through capital and empire, heteropatriarchy and white supremacy—is not a new one.[189] Existing democracy is not ethical democracy; our only option is to work to make it more so. Giving up—by sliding into the seductive grip of hopeless resignation, smug cynicism, or authoritarian strongmen who promise to "protect our values" and save us from our (real or fictitious) enemies, for example, or pursuing inchoate utopian revolutionary or communalist dreams that aim to overthrow or opt out of our flawed democratic social and political institutions—only serves the enemies of ethical democracy.[190] Given the state of our union and world, we are not in position to afford such luxuries.

Good News for Common Goods

"That is all very well," one might ask, "but what does any of this have to do with evangelicals and democracy in America?" What does it mean to assert that multicultural evangelicalism can be good news for common goods and the practice of ethical democracy? It will take the entire book to answer this question fully, but it is possible to make some preliminary remarks here.

The first thing to note is that there is robust support in the evangelical community, born out in the empirical sociological research that is the subject of this book and others, for a *pragmatic post-secular pluralism* that combines an agonistic politics of particularist pluralism with a pragmatic politics of common goods in keeping with ethical democracy. This support, moreover, is deeply rooted in the particularistic religious convictions of the Christian evangelical tradition—in widely held evangelical views of scripture, theology, and practice—such that evangelicals need not cease to be evangelicals or abandon their attachment to the "good news" of Christ's life, death, and resurrection and its social and political implications in order to participate in good faith in ethical democratic projects and the pluralistic public sphere.[191] This is good news for evangelicals who desire to act and be recognized as members in good standing of the pluralistic common life of their neighborhoods, cities, nations, and world, but who have felt trapped by anti-democratic and anti-pluralist interpretations of the public implications of biblical faith.[192] It is also good news for non-evangelicals who care about advancing the cause of ethical democracy in the United States, for at least two reasons: first, evangelicals are far more likely to be motivated to participate in multifaith, multiracial, multicultural ethical democratic projects on the basis of their own particularistic religious convictions than on secular political or nonreligious grounds, and second, because evangelicals constitute a significant proportion of the US population and electorate (one that is not going anywhere anytime soon). Notwithstanding the hopes and erstwhile predictions of secularization theorists and "radical secularists" on the one hand,[193] or religious revivalists on the other, we can neither deconvert nor convert our way out of all that ails democracy in America.

As mentioned previously in the section on "Common Goods," arguments in favor of democratic pluralism and common good approaches to politics and public religion among evangelical theologians, pastors, movement leaders, grassroots activists, and flagship institutions abound.[194] These are not fringe positions or perspectives. The National Association of Evangelicals, for example, along with one of its former presidents, highlight "Influence for Good" and a "New Evangelical Partnership for the Common Good" at the top of their agendas.[195] Prominent evangelical theologians, pastors, and movement leaders write books describing their "lifelong quest for common ground,"[196] the importance of "mobilizing for the common good,"[197] and "how the gospel brings hope to a world divided" through a commitment to the "(un)common good."[198] Award-winning Reformed evangelical historian George Marsden points to the "principled pluralism" of The Center for Public Justice as one of many resources available to "theologically traditional Christians" for "moving beyond culture-wars thinking and either-or simplicities . . . regarding religion and public life."[199]

Marsden's example, The Center for Public Justice, rejects religious nationalism and antigovernment libertarianism while foregrounding political pluralism and common good politics at the center of its advocacy mission:

> The Center argues for the high calling of government, whose responsibility is to uphold justice for all citizens in the political community (in our case, the republic of the United States). Government's calling is to protect and enhance the common good—the wellbeing of the commonwealth—and not just to protect individual freedom or to make room for private purposes. We advocate equal treatment of people of all faiths, because the political community should be a community of citizens, not a community of faith. . . . And we advocate strong public protections of the civil rights of all citizens.[200]

Against the antigovernment libertarians and white Christian nationalists in their midst, the "other evangelicals" have been vigorously contesting Christian Right hegemony and anti-democratic impulses via "expanding the vision of the common good" in American evangelical religion and public life for decades.[201]

Two formulations of the evangelical position stand out, both of which affirm political pluralism and common good approaches to public and political engagement as authoritative for faithful evangelicals, one of which aligns closely with the pragmatic post-secular pluralist approach to ethical democracy advanced here. Christian theologian Luke Bretherton notes that these formulations form two distinct yet "interrelated and symbiotic forms of civic life," both of which are consistent with "faithful witness" for Christians in general, and evangelical Christians in particular.[202]

The first formulation, corresponding to what Bretherton calls a politics of hospitality or "hospitable politics," "relates to the situations in which religious groups are the initiator and lead in generating shared action and a faithful form of secularity."[203] An evangelical politics of hospitality centers action rooted in the particularistic communities and convictions of the evangelical faith tradition while affirming multifaith, multiracial, and multicultural projects in the public and political arena. In *A Public Faith: How Followers of Christ Should Serve the Common Good*, Yale theologian Miroslav Volf makes the theological case that, "Christians, even those who in their own religious views are exclusivist, ought to embrace pluralism as a political project," based on traditional evangelical interpretations of scripture.[204] Arguing forcefully against all forms of religious totalitarianism and political exclusivism, Volf develops a distinctively Christian and evangelical definition of "human flourishing" and "the common good," one that is overlapping but distinct from other secular or religious definitions, while arguing:

> The way Christians work toward human flourishing is not by imposing on others their vision of human flourishing and the common good but by bearing witness to Christ, who embodies the good life. . . . In a pluralistic context, Christ's command . . . entails that Christians grant to other religious communities the same religious and political freedoms that they claim for themselves. . . . Any form of imposition of a social system or of legislation allegedly based on God's revelation must be rejected. To affirm freedom of religion is to reject any form of religious totalitarianism and to embrace pluralism as a political project.[205]

Seeking an "alternative both to secular exclusion of religion from the public sphere and to all forms of 'religious totalitarianism,'"[206] Volf's evangelical argument advocates for political pluralism and the right of all secular and religious groups to "insert themselves as one voice among many to promote their own vision of human flourishing and serve the common good."[207]

The second formulation, outlined in Marsden's *The Outrageous Idea of Christian Scholarship*,[208] corresponds to what Bretherton calls the "the politics of a common life," in which "no single tradition of belief and practice sets the terms and conditions of shared speech and action" in the public or political arena, and in which the means and ends of democratic process are a "negotiated, multilateral endeavor."[209] This is an antifoundationalist position in keeping with pragmatist theories of democracy, an affinity that Marsden recognizes and welcomes as amenable to evangelical affirmation.[210] Marsden cites William James's essay "What Pragmatism Means" as a "helpful image of how liberal pluralistic society ought to work,"[211] which is,

> like a corridor in a hotel. Innumerable chambers open out of it. In one you may find a man writing an atheistic volume; in the next someone on his knees praying for faith and strength; in the third a chemist investigating the body's properties. In a fourth a system of idealistic metaphysics is being excogitated; in a fifth the impossibility of metaphysics is being shown. But they all own the corridor, and all must pass through it they want a practicable way of getting into or out of their respective rooms.[212]

Marsden proceeds to describe James's "pragmatic liberalism" as "quite congenial" to his own position—one rooted in evangelical Christian faith and scholarship—that "in a pluralistic society we have little choice but to accept pragmatic standards in public life."[213]

Marsden is concerned, however, to preserve the deep pluralism of Jamesian pragmatism as opposed to the "absolutized" pragmatism he attributes to the "spiritual descendants of John Dewey," which he (reasonably) argues is illiberal toward religious persons.[214] Too often, Marsden argues, liberal culture has sought to "absolutize the pragmatic method," turning pragmatic virtues such as "tolerance, openness, dialogue, [and] agnosticism" into new "commandments," the absolute values of a new inviolable secular religion:

> John Dewey recognized the potential religious functions of such a liberal polity and even attempted to promote it as "a common faith."[215]

So absolutized, liberal pragmatism has little tolerance for traditionalist religions that challenge the pragmatic absolutes.[216]

The resulting antifoundationalist foundationalism, in which an absolutized pragmatic method is elevated to the status of a secular religion that sets the terms for public discourse and democratic politics, violates pluralism by imposing a single vision of the common good onto the entire democratic polity while making unjustified a priori exclusions of persons or communities who voice dissenting or alternative positions on religious or other non-pragmatist grounds.[217]

Social Reflexivity and Reflexive Evangelicalism

Finally, unlike some dominant conservative expressions of white evangelical Christianity in the United States, multicultural evangelicalism is a *reflexive evangelicalism*, both structurally and culturally. Structurally, it is reflexive in its embrace of religious, cultural, and ethnoracial pluralism as central to the American democratic project. Culturally, it embraces the practice of social reflexivity across different types of difference in American public and political life. Drawing on the classical American pragmatist tradition of Jane Addams and John Dewey, sociologist Paul Lichterman first developed the concept of *social reflexivity* to help explain why some religious groups he observed while conducting ethnographic research in the upper Midwest were able to build two-way bridges across difference while others struggled to do so.[218] In Lichterman's conceptualization, groups practice social reflexivity when they "welcome reflective talk about [their] concrete relationships in the wider world."[219] "By engaging in that reflective talk," Lichterman found, "groups can open up possibilities for bridges across social differences."[220] Lichterman's pragmatist-inspired concept of social reflexivity calls attention to how culture in the form of group customs and communication can help or hinder efforts to establish relatively durable ties across social differences—or what is known as "bridging social capital" in the neo-Tocquevillian literature on democracy and public life.[221]

Whereas Lichterman's original conceptualization focuses on the communicative practices of groups, I define social reflexivity more broadly as people's capacity to think and interact flexibly and self-critically in relation to diverse social others and situations.[222] This expanded definition is in keeping with Addams and Dewey's original vision and, as we will see in Chapters 5 and 6, offers significant payoffs in our ability to describe and analyze how efforts to bridge social differences, and thereby advance ethical democracy, relate systematically to different types of socially reflexive practice across social groups and situations.[223]

Practicing Ethical Democracy

Ethical democracy starts with people. It begins with a recognition that every person and participant in the *demos* is a creature of intrinsic dignity and worth. There is no single human tradition from which this recognition derives or on which it rests.[224] Different traditions have developed different ways of signifying this recognition. Some speak of human dignity,[225] others human rights,[226] human capabilities,[227] human flourishing,[228] the oneness of being, or the *imago Dei*. Some traditions view them as God-given, others as self-evident to reason or spiritual reflection, still others as the product of social compacts and negotiation. Ethical democracy draws on these traditions in recognizing the full rights and responsibilities of citizens (broadly construed) of all identities and traditions without restriction, striving to ensure their participation in public and political life be as inclusive and equitable as possible in both process and outcome.[229] Organized people, not organized money; democracy, not oligarchy, are the means and ends of this striving.

In its vast diversity of identities and traditions, the *demos* is in fact a *demoi*, a plurality of peoples, each of whom shares in the common life of their neighborhood, city, and nation. The *demoi* of ethical democracy is not a herd, a mass, an undifferentiated aggregation of persons whose manipulated majoritarian will-to-power sets the conditions and meaning of public life and political process.[230] Power is necessary, but so, too, is principle. Ethical democracy is a world of people and principle alike. It is principled in its insistence on minority rights, personal liberties, and political pluralism; its resistance to tyrannies of the majority; and its recognition and inclusion of multiple traditions of justice, rationality, ethics, and discourse in public and political life.[231]

As embodied creatures, people interact with one another in shared places. We are bounded physical entities, not free-floating minds or spirits, as even the most otherworldly of our religious traditions recognize about our present form. People must share places with one another, at various levels of scale, ascending from neighborhood, town, and city to nation-states and our shared planet earth. How we share these places matters. Ethical democracy recognizes shared responsibilities and rights across difference in each of these places, for both insiders and outsiders, interacting across all levels of scale. Public life and collective decision-making through democratic politics belongs to all the people of a place, not one particular group or tradition among them.

Ethical democracy is also, finally, practical. It does not seek absolute agreement on first principles, or demand consensus where there is none. Conversely, it does not overthrow the rights of majorities nor aim to silence dissenting voices or minority perspectives. It pursues, but does not expect, perfect justice. It seeks consensus across difference with full equality and inclusion while recognizing its absolute unattainability, accepting the practical necessities and limitations of democratic governance. Against the puritanical zeal of uncompromising ideologues across the political spectrum, it registers the "tragic dimension" of the ethical democratic project, that "democracy is a method of finding proximate solutions to insoluble problems,"[232] while refusing cynical resignation and self-defeating escapism. In the midst of deep differences, with a thin yet strong layer of shared principles held together by diverse underlying motivations and discursive justifications, we find common goods to pursue across varieties of scale. Sometimes for us, sometimes for others; always principled, never blindly partisan. Focused on practical achievements and creative problem-solving rather than abstract agreements and zero-sum power struggles, we address common concerns: public health, education, infrastructure, personal security, economic opportunity, cultural and aesthetic expression, environmental stewardship, family obligations, and personal freedoms.

When we can't find agreement, we resolve our differences through the agonistic politics of pluralism, resisting antagonism and eternal enmity. Sociologically, we recognize the presence and possibility of antagonism in democracy: the ever-present temptation to demonize, dehumanize, and delegitimize our political adversaries as unfit for public life, unworthy of respect or recognition, and unqualified for political participation or public office on the basis of their divergence from identities or values we hold dear. Ethically, we fight for our beliefs and interests while recognizing our common citizenship and humanity—even with those whose values or standpoints we vehemently oppose—acknowledging their right to full and equal participation in public and political life. Sociologically, we recognize the emotional appeal and instrumental utility of antagonism: to treat our political opponents not as adversaries—whose practices differ and whose views we may abhor (let us not pretend), but whose basic dignity and voice as citizens and humans require recognition—[233] but as enemies to be exterminated or excommunicated from public life. Ethical democracy resists its siren song.

Starting with people, who share places, recognizing plurality and accountable authority, committed to principles—some shared, some not—seeking practical solutions to public problems and collaborative constructions of common goods amidst the backdrop of agonistic pluralism: such is the nature of the ethical democratic project. It remains to explore exactly how multicultural evangelicals across the United States embody, or fail to embody, ethical democratic approaches to racial difference and inequality, poverty and economic inequality, and political, cultural, and religious differences—the task to which we now turn.

2

Engaging Race and Inequality

Racial justice is an essential component of ethical democracy; no democracy can be ethical without it. This chapter explores multicultural evangelical approaches to engaging racial difference and inequality, with a particular focus on the practice of strategic relocation, a practice that brings racially diverse evangelicals and nonevangelicals into close interpersonal and institutionalized intergroup contact for the purpose of social change. As such, strategic relocation provides an excellent window into multicultural evangelical approaches to racial difference, inequity, and division in the United States. It also allows us to learn from individuals and groups involved in what Harvard sociologist Orlando Patterson calls the "ordeal of integration," whose challenges and costs are too often disproportionately experienced by people of color.[1] Strategic relocation attempts to recognize and shift the burden of these costs. This chapter investigates multicultural evangelical attempts to address racial inequity and division through grassroots community development and organizing initiatives in the areas of housing, neighborhood governance, jobs, economic opportunity and redistribution, education, policing, youth development, and racially integrated public and religious organizations and settings.

Strategic relocation is worth investigating for a number of reasons. First, it is a practice in keeping with pragmatist notions of racial and ethical democracy, one that directly tests pragmatist and sociological arguments about the benefits of racial integration and experiential learning for the advancement of racial equity and ethical democracy.[2] Second, strategic relocation is a hallmark feature of institutionalized multicultural evangelical attempts to address racial and economic inequity dating back to the civil rights movement in the 1950s and 1960s.[3] It thus provides an effective lens through which to explore relatively widespread multicultural evangelical beliefs and practices concerning racial difference and inequality in the United States.[4] Third, strategic relocation directly involves multicultural evangelicals in controversial and contested arenas of gentrification, local governance, neighborhood identity, integration, and racial justice with extreme significance

Good News for Common Goods. Wes Markofski, Oxford University Press. © Oxford University Press 2023.
DOI: 10.1093/oso/9780197659694.003.0003

and import for the practice of ethical democracy in the post-2020 American racial landscape. Fourth and finally, studying strategic relocation through ethnographic methods provides an up-close look at multicultural evangelical efforts to bridge differences and practice social reflexivity with respect to racial difference and inequity.[5] In Chapter 6, findings from this chapter will be combined with subsequent chapters to analyze how multicultural evangelicals and others practice different types of social reflexivity across racial, economic, cultural, religious, political, and gender lines. As I discuss at length in the conclusion of this chapter, strategic relocation is by no means the only, nor always the best, way for individuals and groups to pursue racial justice and ethical democracy. It is, however, one way—one that I argue can in fact contribute to the advancement of racial and ethical democracy under the conditions and qualifications discussed throughout the chapter.

Finally, while I have no intention of advancing a binary Black-white view of racialization in the U.S.,[6] the bulk of the chapter focuses on Black-white relations in light of demographic makeup of the primary empirical case under investigation. Peachtree Community Development Association (PCDA), a faith-based community development nonprofit organization in Atlanta, has practiced strategic relocation in pursuit of racial and economic equity for over forty years. Starting with PCDA in Atlanta and moving on to other multiracial contexts in Los Angeles and Boston, this chapter explores multicultural evangelical approaches to racial inequality and division across a wide range of public and private, formal and informal, religious and nonreligious, organizational and interpersonal contexts and settings.[7]

In the Neighborhood

"We used to do this all the time in the neighborhood back in the day," Ms. Deborah told the group as we gathered to kick off the inaugural neighborhood association progressive dinner. Ms. Deborah, a sixty-five-year-old Black woman and life-long neighborhood resident, conceived of the progressive dinner idea and pitched it to residents at a neighborhood association meeting. Like many of Ms. Deborah's suggestions, the idea was quickly adopted. Ms. Deborah enjoyed community-wide authority and respect as official neighborhood historian and sought-after storyteller, recalling life in the neighborhood with her eight siblings before segregation and after. Several dozen neighborhood residents were gathered—roughly split between Black and white participants—to partake in the festivities. Others joined the group as the evening wore on. Five households in different parts of the neighborhood—all walkable but somewhat distant—had volunteered to host. Each person received a single red plastic cup to bring with them for drinks between houses, a waste-reduction strategy and sign of event participation. The sun shone brightly with a hint of evening shadows as we meandered through the neighborhood laughing and chatting between houses together, our bright red cups reflecting golden evening sunlight. People broke off here and there into small groups of animated conversations that shifted lazily in size, composition, and pace along the way. Some neighborhood kids tagged along, interacting playfully with each other and several Black and white progressive dinner participants who ran PCDA's summer youth program. A designated photographer took pictures for posterity. Talk flowed freely and easily between all participants, with no signs of strain or unease between different ages or identities.

As we walked through the neighborhood, we encountered several other social gatherings: backyard barbecues, horseshoes, a birthday party with explicit hip hop lyrics set to loud thumping bass that temporarily drowned out conversations as we passed by. Some residents—all Black—watched the group curiously, some nodded or called out greetings, while others paid us no mind. Our group, like the neighborhood association gatherings, contained a slight overrepresentation of white folks in comparison to the neighborhood at large, in which approximately four of five residents are Black. As we walked, Ronald, the thirty-something Black male who served as current president of the neighborhood association, joked with Jared, the neighborhood association's current vice-president—a white, gay man and former intern with a PCDA-related ministry—about teaching Jared how to play various old-school domino games with Ronald's sons so that Jared could shock unsuspecting folks with his knowledge in a hypothetical future visit to the Georgia countryside. Jared's house was one of the progressive dinner host sites, where we enjoyed sweet tea vodka and lemonade cocktails in his dark, atmospheric home decorated with candles, tiki torches, world art, and a "gay haiku" coffee table book. When Jared heard about my research, he pulled me aside for a minute to point out, "This works because we're just neighbors. We don't 'evangelize' or 'proselytize.' We're just neighbors."

At Tanya's house—another simple, sharply decorated PCDA-restored house similar to Jared's—we were treated to an appealing spread of appetizers, fruit, and drinks on artfully prepared picnic tables and benches indoors and out. Tanya, a single Black woman in her thirties, was hosting despite her house having been broken into the previous week, an event that generated a fair bit of discussion without dominating the conversation. Property crime was by far the largest source of criminal complaints in the neighborhood, with cars, copper pipes, small electronics, jewelry, and cash—or, in Tanya's case, her electric meter ("they do that to stop the alarm," someone said later) and other small items—being common targets. Activity usually spiked in the summer, when local drug dealers recruited neighborhood youth with no jobs and time on their hands to make some quick cash. Progressive dinner participants debated police response and presence in the neighborhood, with a mix of negative and positive views. Other debates were equally animated, such as where to find the city's best barbecue, or the best spots for Jamaican, Thai, and soul food. These debates were held among Black and white guests and hosts over eggplant zucchini lasagna, turkey meatballs, watermelon, southern greens, "south Atlanta grown pesto wheels," salads and other items, with a mixture of alcoholic and non-alcoholic drink options.

I spoke at length with a dynamic young Black couple about their lives and reasons for moving into the neighborhood the previous year. Both were young professionals—with full-time jobs and an infant son—who told me they moved into the neighborhood to take advantage of tax breaks for new homeowners after the Great Recession, to be closer to downtown, and because they had found this neighborhood affordable. I had another long conversation with a Black man in his early thirties who had lived in the neighborhood for five years with his wife and young children. He was a software designer who traveled frequently for work, largely to China but also elsewhere, who was excited about reaching a stage of not needing to travel as much. Everyone spoke positively about the neighborhood and its prevalence of active, engaged residents while acknowledging neighborhood problems with sighs, shrugs, short quips, and silences.

It was dark by the time we reached the last stop of the evening, an old house whose weather-beaten, paint-chipped façade was transformed into glory by smartly arranged white lights and candles that illuminated several grand wide porches in the southern style. A blond white woman greeted us at the door alongside an orange-robed Buddhist monk from East Asia, whom we learned was staying at the house for a month while offering reiki to some of its residents, most of whom were artists or writers. An impressive dessert spread awaited inside—strawberries, gelato, cheesecake, wine, coffee—along with live music on keyboard and djembe offered up by a tall, white, long-haired man conspicuously wearing a white toga-like robe. Art covered the walls of each room, including a giant original oil painting of a nude female mermaid-like figure in brilliant colors. It was the only house of its type in the neighborhood.[8]

In Local Governance

The progressive dinner event was hailed as a "grand success" afterwards by Ronald and others at the subsequent neighborhood association meeting, confirming participants' real-time impressions and comments.[9] People spoke of planning another progressive dinner in the future. Weeks prior to the event, I had attended the monthly neighborhood governance meeting where Ronald, the organization's president, announced the dinner and introduced Tanya as its lead coordinator. Both were Black neighborhood residents, as were half of the association's elected officers. The meeting was attended by approximately forty neighborhood residents, a majority of whom were Black. Besides the progressive dinner, other topics of discussion included the need for better street signage in light of a recent accident involving a bike-riding neighborhood youth being hit by a car, application updates for several small community grants, an announcement of free health assessments available at a nearby community development run health clinic, a citizens advisory group and bylaw change report, acknowledgement of new neighbors and longtime resident milestones including the pastor of a Black Baptist church in its thirty-seventh year in the neighborhood, and beautification committee reports on upcoming volunteer clean-up days for discarded tire piles and the local park. Other social committee events were also mentioned, such as an upcoming hot dog fest with cornhole and the recently completed second annual "Southern Fried Kickin'" kickball tournament fundraiser. Residents also listened and responded with questions to a law enforcement officer's monthly crime report on recent activity in the neighborhood (mostly property crimes), about which Jared (vice president) queried towards the end of the meeting, "I'm frustrated by the policing reports. Anyone else?" Several hands went up along with a number of verbal affirmations. "I'd like to help them help us a little better." A multiracial group of residents got up to speak with Jared on the topic as the meeting adjourned.

Monthly neighborhood association meetings were generally well-attended, where Black and white neighborhood residents led by Black and white elected neighborhood officials came together to plan events, interact with city and law enforcement officials, discuss issues, welcome new residents, hear from committees, raise concerns and complaints, and try to solve shared problems. Led by African American presidents for as long as anyone could remember, neighborhood association leadership had transitioned from an old guard group of long-time residents who initially invited PCDA into the neighborhood, to a younger group of Black and white young professionals who owned homes and had lived in the neighborhood for many years. Several officials—including the president—had no affiliation with PCDA, while others had current or past involvement with PCDA. Only highly invested, long-term white strategic relocators had ever held office in the neighborhood governance association, and never as president. Those associated with PCDA maintained an engaged but constrained presence at the meetings, aiming to "keep the peace" by deferring to established Black neighborhood leaders and staying out of the president's chair. They also "tried to tame a little," as Deb put it, the voices of a few white "artist-types" (such as the hosts of the last stop on the progressive dinner) who had recently come into the neighborhood because they had "found a good deal, were kind of on that gentrification train, and wanted to make it a cool neighborhood." "Not in a controlling way," Deb noted, "but just like, Let's not let that be the dominant voice. Because those are the voices that sometimes start to dominate." We will revisit the race and class dynamics of neighborhood association leadership and involvement in Chapter 3.

In Religious Organizations

Like the neighborhood association, PCDA's leadership council was racially integrated and led by a Black man, Leonard (coexecutive director, soon to be executive director), who took the lead at director's meetings and spoke frequently at training events, along with Deb (white female, chief operating officer), Richard (white male, retired founding director), Deanna (Black female, director of education and youth programming), and Jack (white male, director of housing). Nick, the white coexecutive director, was in transition out of the organization and largely absent. During one leaders' meeting, Leonard began by giving a PowerPoint presentation he had prepared for a PCDA board meeting, which gave an overview of PCDA's work and current priorities. He started with a slide showing PCDA's mission statement:

Our mission is to create healthy places in the city where families flourish and God's shalom is present.

- *Dignity*: We practice equality, believing that every voice matters and that all people are made in the image of God.
- *Empowerment*: We practice friendship with a guiding adage, "Never do for others what they can do for themselves."
- *Neighboring*: We practice local living, believing that poor and privileged need each other, doing life together, raising families together.

"All our work is community centered," Leonard said, "our foundation was built on one family moving into a neighborhood. We believe Christian community development starts from this premise: 'Who is my neighbor?'"

In asking "Who is my neighbor?" Leonard was quoting from the biblical story of the Good Samaritan in Luke 10 (verse 29), in which an expert in Jewish law "wanted to justify himself" in response to Jesus's assertion that the way of salvation—and "all the law and the prophets" (Matthew 22:37-40)— were summarized by two simple commands: First, to "Love the Lord your God with all your heart and with all your soul and with all your strength and with all your mind," and second, to, "Love your neighbor as yourself" (Luke 10:27). In the story, a Jewish priest and Levite—men of privileged gender, racial, and religious standing in ancient Israel—ignored and passed by a man robbed and beaten on the side of a road, while a Samaritan man, whom many at the time viewed as racially and religiously inferior, stopped, cleaned the man's wounds, carried him to an inn in the next village, and paid for his stay while he recovered. Challenging his privileged interlocutors, Jesus presented the Samaritan man as hero of the story, reversing racial, religious, socioeconomic, and moral hierarchies of the day.

Leonard proceeded to describe the "strong injustice," "oppression," "abandoned kids," and race-based economic disadvantage in the neighborhood, giving examples of PCDA's commitment to identify and support "risk-taking" leaders from the community—people who "want to work in the 'perceived' worse places, while also *challenging* that perception." He spoke about the organization's education and training work with "denominations, ministry leaders, and heads of state" around the nation and world, aimed at helping them "start from a different place" than what is common among white-dominated religious and political institutions. "What someone believes deeply effects their work among the poor," Leonard noted, "If I believe these people are lazy and have nothing to offer, I'll treat them that way." What is needed instead is a starting point of "investment and equity," with a goal "to make dignity, empowerment and neighboring across cultures ordinary." He spoke about the many young Black female and male leaders emerging through PCDA's youth, economic development, and housing programming who will soon "be part of this table, part of the board." Leonard drew on African American theologian Howard Thurman—whose book, *Jesus and the Disinherited*, Leonard was reading at the time—noting, "Thurman was multicultural, but he was shunned by both sides in the [19]30s."

Leonard also discussed the enormous challenge of breaking cycles of intergenerational poverty—particularly in racially oppressed African American communities—requiring both changed structures and changed life and "work ethics" enabled by equitable access and "exposure" to education, resources, and real opportunity for meaningful advancement and growth. "It takes two generations to break the string," Leonard said, drawing on personal experience and research on intergenerational poverty, to move from deep poverty to equitable flourishing, with significant support and equitable investment, under current conditions.[10] As he discussed PCDA's attempts to combat racialized intergenerational poverty and disadvantage, Leonard discussed "three streams" of responses: those focused primarily on life and work ethic; those focused on structural and neighborhood transformation through education, job creation, and community development (which he called "recovery"); and those focused on "hard core" struggles involving addiction, mental illness, violent victimization and criminality—all of which occur under the auspices of "injustice" and "oppression" suffered by Black Americans. When Pastor James—the white sixty-six-year-old founding director of The Food Co-op (Chapter 3) who sometimes attended PCDA leadership meetings and training events—asked Leonard,

> How does this relate to the church? The community of believers? We've left the old models of "just evangelism," partly because there's nothing to evangelize people *to*! The church has completely conformed to culture. How do we raise up articulate, life-giving churches?

Leonard responded, "The church is really good at the first stream. Not the recovery stream. We're doing the recovery stream. But we don't know how to deal well with the third stream. We don't have a lot of expertise about that around this table." Deanna interjected, "[A former PCDA staff partner] worked with abused Black women," and with "victims of trafficking. But we don't have that piece now. It requires specialized skills." Based on my ethnographic observations, these appeared to be apt assessments of PCDA's work.[11]

As Leonard wrapped up this part of the meeting, Deanna, Pastor James, and others expressed appreciation for Leonard's powerful presentation to the board. After a pause to gather his thoughts, Pastor James added:

> This is good kind of work. To see what's at the center of what we do. I feel so foolish saying this, but: It's gotta be the work of the Lord. What needs to be so clear, what we've got to be guided by, is the Holy Spirit and prayer. We all believe this. We have to be careful, when we get successful, not just to follow the plan.

Leonard responded, "I agree," and Pastor James quickly replied, "I hope you don't hear this as criticism!" Leonard assured him that he did not, and the meeting moved on to a report from "White Dave," director of economic development, who discussed the previous week's break-in at PCDA's café. "They got the iPad," Dave said, "but it was minimal. It happens. I'm thankful that nothing's ever happened to a person in the store." Dave went on to discuss plans for Alicia and Sheri, two Black women from the neighborhood who helped manage PCDA's café and thrift store, to take on management of day-to-day operations in the store. "We're working to get the money to pay them as managers," Dave reported, "I think it'll take about six months." Deanna and other directors added reports and updates before the convivial, high-energy, openly deliberative group adjourned.

Strategic Relocation and the Imperative of Integration

Chapter 1 of this book introduced the idea of racial democracy as a category of ethical democracy. In *The Imperative of Integration*, pragmatist social philosopher Elizabeth Anderson draws on social-scientific research and nonideal political theory to develop a sometimes flawed yet forceful argument for the necessity of racial integration in US schools,[12] neighborhoods, workplaces, governing bodies, and public institutions for the advancement of racial democracy.[13] Racial integration, Anderson argues, is "an imperative of justice and an ideal of intergroup relations in democratic society."[14] Why?

Sounding themes from Tilly and others, Anderson argues for a relational theory of group inequality that "locates the causes of economic, political, and symbolic group inequalities in the relations (processes of interaction) between groups, rather than in the internal characteristics of their members or in cultural differences that exist independently of group interaction."[15] If, as Anderson argues, exploitation-enabling segregation is one fundamental cause of durable group inequalities (such as Black-white inequality in the United States),[16] it follows that dismantling unjust group inequalities requires new norms and practices of racial integration under ethical democratic conditions, both logically and sociologically.[17]

To prove her point, Anderson marshals a vast array of social-scientific evidence concerning the negative effects of ongoing institutional, interpersonal, and residential racial segregation in the United States, and, conversely, how racial integration with justice can reduce inequality without thereby erasing racial identities or subordinating the racial cultures of minority groups through arbitrary assimilation to majoritarian norms of "whiteness":[18]

> Segregation is a fundamental cause of injustice in three broad domains: socioeconomic opportunity, public recognition, and democratic politics. It stands to reason that integration should help dismantle these injustices.[19]

As sociologist Rogers Brubaker notes:

> Racial inequality in the post-Jim Crow era has been profoundly shaped by two massive institutional complexes. . . . The first is segregation; the second (which in a sense is just an extreme form of the first)[20] is incarceration. Residential segregation has been the 'structural linchpin' of racial inequality. Segregated neighborhoods have entailed not just segregated schools, churches, associations, and networks but also segregated experiences. And since this segregation has been imposed rather than chosen . . . it has generated and perpetuated massive, cumulative, and mutually reinforcing inequalities in housing, education, amenities, public safety, municipal services, trust, social capital, job opportunities, and exposure to environmental hazards, crime, delinquency, and stress.[21]

Relational theories of group inequality, Anderson argues, demonstrate that systemic geographic, institutional, and interpersonal racial segregation is both a result of, and contributor to, ongoing racial discrimination and inequality in the United States.[22]

Anderson's definition of racial integration, "the participation as equals of all groups in all social domains,"[23] is not a matter of "assimilation" or mere physical proximity.[24] Like Alexander's argument for "multicultural incorporation" in the democratic civil sphere, racial integration—unlike mere assimilation—requires de-centering majoritarian identities, norms, and structural advantages of "whiteness" in favor of full equitable inclusion and multicultural recognition of marginalized ethnic and racial identities on their own terms.[25] Racial integration involves both spatial and social integration in both formal and informal institutional and interactional settings.[26] In this it incorporates and extends Gordon Allport's well-known and widely corroborated "contact hypothesis," which describes how intergroup interaction can reduce bias and prejudice under the right social conditions. Namely, for intergroup contact to be effective at reducing prejudice, stigma, and bias against racial or social "others," contact must:

(1) be frequent enough to lead to personal acquaintance, (2) be cooperative, in pursuit of shared goals, (3) be supported by institutional authorities [and/or "any situation in which norms of amicable cooperation apply"], (4) take place among participants of equal status (equal roles within an organization).[27]

The more conditions like these obtain in a given social context, the more likely intergroup contact is to reduce prejudice, stigma, and bias against outgroups. In other words, the efficacy of intergroup contact to effectively reduce racial discrimination and prejudice hinges on the extent to which racial justice and equality obtains in a given setting, while also increasing its likelihood of obtaining in other settings.

In making her argument for the "imperative of integration," Anderson focuses on the effects of racial segregation and integration in the context of neighborhoods, schools, workplaces, and representative political bodies. Missing from her analysis is any sustained discussion of the effects of racial integration and separation in religious contexts, despite its obvious political relevance and the large and growing literature on the subject.[28] Aside from reflecting a general tendency among pragmatist and critical social theorists to overlook religion as a significant site of social difference,[29] this oversight is likely the result of Anderson's dubious decision to relegate religion to the "private" realm of family and friendship rather than "public" realm of political economy and civil society.[30]

However, where Anderson largely ignores the interplay of religion and racial integration (or its absence) in the United States, sociologists of religion have not.[31] While religious organizations in general reflect entrenched patterns of racial segregation and inequality in the United States, evangelical churches are the most racially homogeneous religious congregations in the United States, notwithstanding the increasing number of multiracial evangelical congregations in recent decades.[32] Religious congregations are less racially diverse than the neighborhoods in which they reside, despite persistently high levels of residential racial segregation.[33] Evangelical churches are more racially segregated than even the most highly segregated cities in the United States.[34] White evangelical congregations are also far less likely than Catholic, Black Protestant, and mainline Protestant congregations to become involved in faith-based community organizing coalitions, which are among the most economically and racially diverse institutions in the United States.[35] The relative lack of racial diversity within evangelical churches and religious organizations reflects the relative lack of commitment to racial justice in white evangelical religious history in the United States, particularly since the early 1900s.[36]

Among those social contexts she does attend to, Anderson argues that the imperative of integration is most difficult to achieve at the neighborhood level, where—unlike workplaces, schools, or government offices—the lack of formal rules of accountability, authority, and incentive regulation increases the likelihood of hostile, prejudicial, anxious, or inequitable relations across racial difference than in more formal contexts.[37] In the United States, the challenge of neighborhood-level racial integration is exacerbated by durable patterns of residential racial segregation that have persisted well beyond civil rights era legislation that made Jim Crow segregation and racial discrimination illegal.[38] While Black Americans of all socioeconomic status and income levels experience a high degree of racial isolation, low-income Black neighborhoods are even more isolated.[39] This is not primarily a matter of choice on the part of Black Americans, who consistently express preferences for living in neighborhoods that are more racially integrated than their own.[40] Rather, residential racial segregation in the United States "rests on a foundation of long-standing white racial prejudice."[41]

Moreover, as urban gentrification processes have marginally reduced residential racial segregation and increased the presence of middle- and upper-income residents in previously low-income neighborhoods of color, they have typically resulted in neighborhood turnover and displacement rather than equitable mixed-income racial integration, with less affluent residents of color being forced or nudged out to make room for more affluent renters and homeowners whose interests and preferences quickly come to dominate neighborhood politics and culture.[42] As such, like the racial integration of religious organizations, neighborhood-level racial integration often reproduces, rather than challenges, existing patterns of racial inequity.[43]

The steep challenges of just and equitable racial integration in general—and in neighborhoods and religious groups in particular—is part of what make the progressive dinner, neighborhood association, and religious nonprofit directors' meetings described at the beginning of this chapter so significant and unusual. They involved Black and white neighbors, coworkers, and people of faith pursuing shared projects, interacting freely and flexibly, in racially integrated, Black-led, majority-Black contexts under conditions of relative equality.[44] At the neighborhood level, such interactions would not have been possible except for the practice of strategic relocation by Black, white, and Hispanic PCDA leaders, staff, and volunteers.

Strategic Relocation

Strategic relocation (or simply "neighboring" or "re-neighboring," as Leonard and other PCDA-affiliated persons called it), involves the intentional practice of moving into disadvantaged contexts in order to learn from and participate with residents in projects of social empowerment and transformation.[45] Strategic relocation is a core practice of PCDA and other faith-based nonprofits connected to the Christian community development movement built by Black evangelical civil rights leader John M. Perkins and others since the 1960s.[46] As Leonard told me during a frequently interrupted conversation at PCDA's neighborhood café, "we continue to be an organization of a family moving into a neighborhood. That's where it starts. That's where it begins, that's the basis. Everything else that comes out of that. If you don't start there, it's not going to work out."

Leonard's journey to PCDA and the practice of strategic relocation was different than many of his white coworkers. He grew up in "one of the poorest places" in Black Philadelphia, with "plans to move, you know, out into suburbia. And have the house and the dog. That was what you do. My wife and I were definitely thinking that way." By his early twenties he was an associate minister in the Black Baptist church in which he grew up:

> No complaints about it. I enjoyed my church and my people. But theologically, it just kind of one day fell apart: The church is doing great, but my neighborhood is in shambles. Those two don't seem to be consistent.

Leonard's "understanding of church" and plans to move to the suburbs were further disrupted by a memorable and meaningful spiritual experience:

> I think that came to a head for me one night in a call: I clearly heard God say, "I want you doing something with the poor." I was like, "What are you talking about?" I had no idea what that meant. I was watching TV! That moment really changed my life. And it's funny: I remember that night much clearer than when I said 'the prayer' [the "sinner's prayer" or traditional evangelical prayer of conversion]. . . . That moment has really fueled me the last twenty-three, twenty-four years. How is my faith going to make sense in community, with people, among the poor?

Leonard's family soon moved back into their old neighborhood in Philly to, "live in a community of people. Where people can see your life:"

> That was kind of all I knew at the time. I need to live in this place and people need to see my life publicly where I live. It was pretty basic. I didn't know anything about CCDA [Christian Community Development Association] and all those things. I just kind of had this call. This intuition or this drive, this pull, that I felt was of God. So we started our first 501(c)(3). We wrote all the paperwork ourselves. We started a board. And we did this collaborative kind of ministry plan, working with the homeless, and did that for a number of years and learned a ton from that.

It wasn't until the early 1990s that Leonard "came across CCDA for the first time. It was new then too, a couple years, three years old:"

> I began with John Perkins's story and who he was and what he was writing about, which informed a lot. Read Ron Sider's *Rich Christians in the Age of Hunger*. Yeah. Just started diving into all of that stuff. Went back and reread

the Beatitudes '(Matthew 5:1–12), and that just came alive in a different way. Went back and read King's [Martin Luther King Jr.] stuff again. And so yeah, five years of learning for me. And it was good. It informed a lot of what I kind of live out now, and preach and teach myself now.

Over time, Leonard and his wife Deanna started and led several businesses, ministries, and youth programs, including a new school that brought them to Atlanta as the first strategic relocators to live in the neighborhood where PCDA was currently working.

In addition to running the school and settling in as neighbors, Leonard was asked to become involved in the neighborhood association:

In this neighborhood, when PCDA started almost eleven years ago now, the neighborhood association leadership was older. They were saying, "Hey, we need some younger people. Some new energy to come in." So Deanna and I moved here. Kind of as the first neighbors in this process, with the blessing of the neighborhood association. So we joined and dove deeply into that our first couple years here. I became VP, and served under one of the older community leaders. Learned a ton from her. Then I found myself in this process of bringing in younger people, introducing diversity to a community association that hasn't had it. And so that process has been, it's been enjoyable. Because I really also believe our work should be done in the background, from the backseat, introducing people and things, that sort of process. So now it's really cool to see this neighborhood association that's biracial. That has women and men, and Black and white, gay and straight. It's what you would dream of. And it's real. Different income levels. And if you go to your neighborhood association meetings, it looks like that. That's pretty fun to see.

Being involved in the neighborhood association has helped Leonard and others limit the extent to which white volunteers and outsiders have access to the neighborhood, while also establishing processes for neighborhood-owned partnership with outsiders under certain conditions:

We've been real resistant to inviting people to come in to start stuff. You just can't say, "Hey, I'm bringing A, B, C, D." Nah. And especially can't have, you just can't have white folks doing that. That's been pretty key. And now we have people that understand that. . . . You just can't do it. And that's hard for people. That's hard for evangelical Christian types, who are used to getting a project in their head and just jumping in and doing it. Resisting that has been important. Resisting the big groups of volunteers coming in and all those kinds of things. You can come and volunteer but here's how you need to do it. When we started doing the "Green My Hood" [a neighborhood-level environmental action initiative] stuff, I went to the neighborhood association and asked, "Hey, what do you think about how to do this?" And they were open [to working with some volunteers from outside the neighborhood] because they were like, "Well, the problem's kind of over-whelming. We can't do it all by ourselves." So this is a spot where we could do that [work with some outside volunteers]. That's dialogue. That's honoring. That's giving power to the people who: this is their community. And it's not perfect by any stretch of the imagination. But there is at least a process in place.

We will revisit neighborhood association dynamics and debates about the appropriate place of outside resources in combating racial and economic disadvantage and inequity at length in the next chapter.

In addition to serving as executive director of PCDA and another faith-based nonprofit that recruited, trained, and supported recent college graduates to practice strategic relocation in intentional spiritual service-learning communities for twelve months in disadvantaged urban neighborhoods across the United States, Leonard also served as co-lead pastor of a small multiracial, majority-Black church involving both long-time residents and strategic relocators connected to PCDA that grew organically out of a weekly neighborhood dinner he hosted with his wife Deanna:

We were doing a Wednesday night dinner in our home every night. Anybody from the neighborhood came. And we wound up every Wednesday having fifty, sixty people at our house. Big pot of beans or whatever. Out of that, this prayer time started afterwards. That eventually turned into Sundays. Deanna has a music background, so she started doing choir with some of the kids in the neighborhood. So we started a church in 2000 . . . I had actually developed an aversion to church. Not an aversion to church: a critique. I wanted more of my time to be spent in the community than thinking about Sunday.

As an outgrowth of Leonard's desire to focus more on the community than a Sunday event, the church invited another Black pastor, Pastor Martin, to take on a primary leadership role, with Leonard serving as co-pastor and other Black and white PCDA-affiliated (and nonaffiliated) people serving the church in various capacities. All church leaders and attendees live in the neighborhood or those immediately adjacent.

Leonard was a strong believer in strategic relocation, but he had an ironic view of the "buzzwords" and "justice hype" among many white evangelicals around "this whole thing of moving into neighborhoods now." In addition to his racial experience, Leonard brought a more ecumenical and historical perspective to the practice of strategic relocation as practiced in Christian community development,[47] intentional community,[48] new monastic,[49] and new parish[50] movements:

> I remember—in the "worst" neighborhoods, if you want to call them that—
> in Philly, there was always a parish. There was always a Catholic church. So
> that idea is not new. And Catholics have done it the best and the longest.
> The Catholics. Nuns. These white nuns walking around the toughest neigh-
> borhood you can name. I always kind of try to point that out.

For Leonard and other PCDA leaders, collaborative community development rooted in long-term strategic relocation was seen as a natural expression of Christian faith and a tool—one among many—through which to pursue racial and economic justice, rather than a "radical" innovation in religious practice emerging out of the churn of white evangelical entrepreneurship and distinction-making.[51]

For PCDA leaders and affiliated neighbors, strategic relocation was a foundational practice through which to pursue racial and economic justice, opportunity, and integration in keeping with their understanding of the gospel. After more than a decade of living and working as neighbors in its current neighborhood, evidence of spatial and social integration was abundant across multiple public and private settings.[52] PCDA's neighborhood café and thrift store employ Black and white individuals and are frequently attended by both Black and white neighborhood residents. Black and white volunteers work with neighborhood children in the neighborhood bike shop. Under the guidance of Black neighborhood association presidents, Black and white individuals serve the community as neighborhood association officials and volunteer committee members. Neighborhood governance meetings and community events bring Black and white individuals together to discuss issues, tell stories, make decisions, and have fun on a regular basis. A small multiracial church led by Black pastors serves as the spiritual home for Black and white longtime neighborhood residents and strategic relocators alike. Across each of these contexts, I witnessed thousands of routine interactions among Black and white individuals on terms of equality that provide strong evidence of social integration and the presence of bridging social capital across racial difference.[53] Increased spatial and social integration, in turn, facilitated a wide range of efforts to combat racial and economic inequity through new local investments in housing, employment and economic development, education and youth development, and public services, many of which are discussed below.

Strategic Relocation and Community-Economic Development

The PCDA café and marketplace anchors a low-profile, two-story, grey concrete and brick multiuse building that welcomes residents and visitors to this south Atlanta neighborhood with a colorful art mural proudly heralding its namesake. In addition to the café, the building hosts a neighborhood thrift store, bike shop, fair-trade jewelry business, co-working and community center spaces, and small storefront church. Opened in 2009, the café has become a lively community hub in which groups of Black youth from the neighborhood and local high school next door hang out alongside middle-aged, young professional, and older Black, white and (less frequent) Hispanic residents catching up over coffee, taking meetings, or working quietly on laptops amidst buzzing conversation and eclectic beats ranging from hot Atlanta hip hop to Michael Jackson and Johnny Cash. Neighborhood association meetings and events are often held here or in the adjacent community center space, along with poetry and art shows and other community and PCDA events. Alicia, Sheri, and Latoya—all Black women from the neighborhood—work and manage the café most hours, with occasional assistance from "White Dave," PCDA's head of economic development and longtime neighborhood resident.

With no other competitors in the neighborhood, the café draws a racially diverse, majority Black, intergenerational mix of neighborhood residents and routine customers of widely varying interests and conversation topics.

Along with scenes from the Introduction, a representative selection of fieldnote observations provides a sense of the people and setting:

April 30 fieldnotes
Laptops, conversation, middle-aged adults, Black and white, lively, sort of a 'typical' café scene. But there seems to be more talk about issues: voter registration, social problems, etc. . . . .

May 3 fieldnotes
Party atmosphere in here today. Alicia, Latoya, and about six other café visitors, all African American, dancing, laughing, singing, messing around. . . . A different group of younger African American men and one woman are having a discussion about killing, self-defense, and being a "gangster." Someone says something about "church buddies." "Church buddies!", one responds in a mocking voice, "*Khris* goes to church! I was like 'Khris, you go to *church*? What the fuck?!'" "If you see me at church [trailing off], never mind, you'll *never* see me at church."

June 12 (morning) fieldnotes
Three Black youth—I'd guess 4th or 5th grade—are hanging out with two high school or college-aged African American men from the neighborhood. I think they are PCDA summer camp counselors, though I'm not sure yet. The young men are answering questions and sharing advice with the younger kids. I hear one saying, "7th grade is when you have to decide who you're gonna be. Are you going to fit in with the crowd? Or are you gonna be yourself?" . . . "I got into all sorts of stuff I shouldn't have, that I regret." The kids start making fun of his "formal" way of talking, which they called "debating." He responds to them, "You think I'm bad?! Wait 'til you get to college!"

June 12 (late afternoon) fieldnotes
I come in at 4pm, there is no barista for a long time. Two men: one ~30s, one ~60s, one Black, one Hispanic . . . discuss the importance of knowing how to fight for street culture, but how that doesn't translate to mainstream work culture, and how a lot of urban youth bring a street approach into work. It seems like they are talking about a specific workplace assault incident? "Kids need to know how to fight in an urban environment, but they're only learning that style of communication. Instead, you need to control

your emotions, otherwise you give people power over you. But the kids just laugh at that." . . . After a short while, Hispanic conversation partner starts talking to a younger African American male, probably 8–9 years old, showing him things on his computer, teaching him life lessons. These two guys seem like village elders or something, fathers, old heads. "Watch who you hang out with. Who we hang out with influences us. Hang out with good people."

June 15 fieldnotes

Alicia gives me a side hug as I walk in; Sheri is having an extended, hushed conversation with a customer about a confrontation with neighborhood youth just outside the building 30 minutes ago in which she had to bluff about building having a security camera on roof. An ambulance is pulled off to side of road half-block away. Johnny Cash is playing. I ask whose music it is, Latoya laughs and says, "*Alicia's!*" Alicia says not to make fun of her music before showing me the album photograph of Johnny flipping the bird to the camera. I shake the hand of my developmentally disabled friend Ron, a young white man who for some reason has taken a liking to me and never lets me walk by his table without giving me a warm, vigorous handshake. He and his 20- or 30- something male caregiver are in the café most days for several hours. Ron occasionally calls out, or sings, random things. "Hi, hi, hi, hi, hi," "there you go, see you later," "Where's shoeless? Where's Ted?" Alicia answers: "He's on the way." Ron keeps asking. Later [Alicia] tells a neighborhood friend and customer: "You should look into PCDA housing! You're paying rent anyway, right? $550? They have a 20-year mortgage, no interest, and they can help you out. Your credit score is good I bet? I would do it, but my credit score isn't good. Latisha pays 3-[hundred]-something for her mortgage!"

Alicia comes to my table several minutes later, and speaks to me in a serious, distressed, lowered voice: "Wes, I want to tell you this for your [research]: I don't think it's fair that people help people that they want to help. [They] don't just help everybody; [they] help people that they want to help. I mean they're helping me, which I appreciate, but I don't think it's fair that they don't help everybody. I just wanted to tell you that."

Before leaving I ask Alicia: "Why did you tell me that thing about 'it's not fair'"? She gives a detailed response [paraphrase]: "Tried to get food stamps, can't, my income is too high. But my lights are probably getting turned off as we speak, because I couldn't afford to pay the utility bill. It's just not enough money. But then I watch these girls in the apartments across the street; they're drinking and getting high all day, don't do nothin', their hair and nails are done up, they have nice cars, and they don't work. We had a position open at the café awhile back and I asked if they wanted to apply for it, and they said, 'Oh no, I can't work, I'd lose my Section 8 and stuff.'" So here I am, working, trying to be productive and do things the right way, but they [government] won't help with my food, while these other girls don't work at all and get help. It's not fair! It just doesn't make sense. It can be real discouraging." She was muted, downcast, sad, not her usual exuberant/expressive self. "It's a Johnny Cash day," she said, "the man in Black."

"I been asking around all over and couldn't get any help anywhere, and then I talked to Aimee [a PCDA-affiliated neighbor] and she just told me that she'd put a word in for me and get some help. [Unclear how or what kind of help.] But now I'm wondering: why can only certain people get help? I'm only getting help because I happen to work here so I got to meet Aimee and all these people who can help. But why do you have to know someone to get help? And I probably need less help than a lot of other people, but they can't get it. Sheri just found out she needs to work two more hours per week to get into the CAPS program for childcare. Otherwise, she'll have to pay $180/week for childcare. That's a lot! Over two hours! So she needs to talk to Dave and try to get two more hours. And Dave's not going to lie about it. I could lie about my income; but I don't. I don't do it that way. But I get punished for that, and for working! But I don't think we can afford two more hours a week for Sheri. It's just wrong. It's not right."

Alicia's lament highlights the challenges facing race and class disadvantaged residents of low-income neighborhoods straddling the benefits cliff,[54] even those fortunate enough to land a rare job close to home with above-average compensation and network connections to individuals and institutions with middle-class resources. It also highlights the financial challenges of running a non-profit café, and of PCDA's community-economic development work more generally. As Dave discussed in the PCDA director's meeting described above, the café was raising money to increase Alicia and Sheri's hours and pay them as full-time managers. They did not yet have the money. Sales and revenue only covered 65 percent of the cost of running the café; the rest came through grants and private donations. The community-economic development arm of PCDA employed fifteen people in total, but only two full time. In a neighborhood with few job opportunities and an unemployment rate above 40 percent, PCDA's employment initiatives could only scratch the surface of need, as valuable and hard-won as it was.

Still, for those neighborhood residents who gained employment through PCDA community-economic development initiatives, the benefits were significant. Sheri—a thirty-four-year-old Black woman, life-long neighborhood resident, and mother of two whose developmentally disabled one-year-old son had undergone four major surgeries in his short life—called her PCDA café job a "life-saver." "I got laid off [from another job], and they just gave me a cheesy package, and I was pregnant with my second child," Sheri recounted, "when Dave said [PCDA] could hire me, I was so happy." Betsy—a forty-four-year-old African American woman, PCDA accountant's assistant, and single mother of six adult children—first encountered PCDA as a teenage high school student living in an extremely disadvantaged and sometimes dangerous east Atlanta housing project run by the Atlanta Housing Authority several decades prior.[55] Betsy attended a PCDA-affiliated youth group, got her sister into a PCDA summer program, and began helping a recently retired female PCDA executive leader with her newsletter before being hired to work part-time in the PCDA thrift store. From there, she transitioned to PCDA's administrative offices, first as a receptionist and then as assistant to the accountant, her current job.

Betsy's first and primary attraction to PCDA was practical, "being a young person and seeing the opportunity to have a job and steady income,"

> Not too many people that have the level of education that I have got the opportunity to have a job and steady income. Back in the day, $16,000 was a lot of money for a 20-year-old with three kids. . . . I think I've been a big positive support for PCDA for all these years. And I mean of course they've been very supportive and positive of me, for allowing me to learn as I go and continue to come in and do what I do. All of this has been on the job training for me. I've sent all my kids to college. I haven't [gone to college], but I've obtained my high school [GED] degree, and hopefully that will change in the next few years.

Betsy had three sons and three daughters, all in their twenties, each of whom attended college after being heavily involved in PCDA-affiliated youth development programs in academics, dance and theatre production. Several were still in school, one had a master's degree in sociology and was considering more schooling, one received a track scholarship to North Carolina, one was a dean of students at a local middle school charter, and one had dropped out. In this, Betsy's children had exceeded her best hopes for them:

> I used to share a lot of things with Jenny, one of PCDA's former accountants.... At the time I told Jenny, "Jen, you know what, I just want all my kids to graduate high school." And she said, "Betsy, that's a good something to want, but they can go to college!" I said, "Well, Jenny, I know that they could probably go to college, but I'm looking at it from the point of view of statistics. Statistically," I said, "for a single mother with six children, maybe two will graduate high school. I want all of them to graduate high school." I said, "That's my prayer, that's all I want, is for all my kids to graduate high school." And she gave me this look, and she said, "I think God will do that for you, Betsy, if you want that and you push your kids and you let them know what you want." And all of them have graduated high school and went to college.

Betsy proceeded to tell me about her own plans to attend college to study "sociology, anthropology, or African American religion" in the near future.

Betsy's story illustrates a core conviction of PCDA's community-economic development work. "We need to *create jobs*" (emphasis original), Dave told a group of fifty visiting nonprofit and religious leaders from across the country at an on-site PCDA training weekend, highlighting the severe lack of "jobs, job training, and transportation" available to his south Atlanta neighbors. "We prioritize two elements" or groups when we can, Dave told the group, "First, single moms without transportation. The bus makes an 8-hour workday into an 11-hour workday, which takes them completely out of the family-school loop." He continued,

> A lot of folks we work with are one problem away from disaster. Sickness, doctor visit, lack of transportation, etc. can make it very difficult to hold down a job. So jobs *in the neighborhood* are *huge* (emphasis original). And we hope, and work with people, to get people graduating to better and better jobs.

"Second," Dave said, "we focus on high school kids. I got my first job at age 14, which felt 'normal' to me. But it's not normal for many kids of unemployed or underemployed families in our neighborhood. There are not many businesses in the area compared to a middle-class suburb." Dave spoke of the virtuous "ripple effect" he has observed from making jobs available to high school youth in the neighborhood. It "changes the culture of a few high school kids," from, "Why would I get a job?" and "I can't get a job," to "*She* got a job, maybe I could too!" "You can watch it, the ripple effect. 'Soft' and small changes are key. But they're only visible up close." Dave's status as a neighbor, friend, and local business leader—aided by strategic relocation—gave him a different lens through which to "see" and engage racial and economic inequity than most white Americans. Much more will be said about the relationship between strategic relocation and the practice of social reflexivity in Chapters 5 and 6.

Beyond the "hard" economic work of job creation, support, and advancement served by the PCDA café, thrift store, housing arm, and other entities, the café also advanced the "soft" community and cultural work of "providing a positive public space in the neighborhood" for "misperceived teens," old-timers, parents, young professionals, and other Black, white, and Hispanic neighborhood residents to "build some trust and relationship" through the café and store as "neighborhood people come here each day to visit and work. How do you measure *that* for donors and foundations (emphasis original)? You can't. But it's real, and key."

> And just personally, from the perspective of a neighborhood resident, I love the idea of local small businesses. It's just nice to have a place to walk to. We know that there's a community element to the coffee shop and marketplace that really, I think, builds a lot of community for the neighborhood. And I realize there's a lot of people who use the coffee shop to get information. Not everyone in the neighborhood has email or access to internet. And so, your neighborhood listservs or Facebook groups or what not, that a lot of other neighborhoods use, doesn't include everyone in our neighborhood. So I really enjoy seeing this be a place that folks can come get the neighborhood gossip. It increases gender equity in neighborhood information.

When I reported my impressions of the café as a "lively social space" with a lot of people coming in, Dave nodded his head affirmatively and laughed, "Not always people buying stuff! But that's not always the point":

> At the end of the day, evaluating whether it has been a successful day or not isn't all about the bottom line. Part of it is about just creating a good

community space. I think there's some challenges in creating a space that people feel welcome and want to come to across a broad demographic spectrum. I think when you have folks that move into a neighborhood intentionally that aren't necessarily from the host culture, you know, there's just some natural things that divide us economically with no real reason for it other than that's just the way we were brought up. . . . So having the store be a place that a high school kid feels comfortable coming to and sitting there and hanging out all day, and a senior feels comfortable coming to, and a middle-class person feels comfortable coming to, and they can all be in there and enjoy it and feel welcome and want to come has been not an easy task.

When I responded, "I see Alicia and the staff trying to negotiate that often. They're really lively, they connect with the neighborhood, they connect with kids, it's great. Then also when there's somebody in there with a laptop, they do a nice job of trying to keep it a workspace as well," Dave nodded appreciatively, recognizing Alicia's central role in the café's success—who in two years had gone from a part-time employee working ten hours a week to nearly full-time employment with increasing managerial responsibilities:

> We're trying to give over some more of the managerial stuff of the store to her. And she serves as a mentor to our high school staff. A lot of what PCDA does it to ultimately have folks indigenous to the neighborhood end up being the leaders and the ones that are running things. Seeing that progression take place has been really neat. I've enjoyed that.

As recognized through advancing pay, promotion, and managerial responsibilities, Alicia was clearly instrumental in making the café a place in which race, class, age, ability, and occupation-diverse neighborhood residents all felt welcome and able to utilize the space for diverse purposes.

While Alicia—with Sheri and Latoya—bore large responsibility for the café's success as a bridge-building community space, an unsolicited comment from Leonard—PCDA's Black executive director—highlighted Dave's contributions as well. Leonard and I were talking about race and relocation over drinks at the café, concerning which he said:

> You just can't have white folks coming and saying, "Hey, I'm going to do this or that." And now we have people that understand that. [White] Dave,

who runs the [café], you know, understands that how people come in is really important; what you do is really important. He has a filter for that. Right? So that's been powerful. That's part of why this place has become a nice place to be in. And it gets youth and older folks and people who normally would go somewhere else and pay $4 for a cup of coffee to come in here. Both sets of people are using this place as a connection point, and making connections across [difference]. So being able to create some of those points has been good.

Deb, another neighborhood resident and PCDA leader, added:

Having these common places now since the café opened, where the community comes together, has been huge. There's a new energy. It helps especially, I think, that it's a business, where everybody has something to bring, and there's this exchange. It's not like a community center that some people would never come into, because, "Why do I need a community center?" But a lot of people want a cup of coffee. So yeah. It's definitely more diverse economically and racially.

Through the work and presence of Alicia, Sheri, Latoya, Dave, and others, the café had become a successful community space and employment generator across racial and economic divides.

By all accounts, strategic relocation was an important element of the café's race- and class-bridging successes. Dave's presence as a neighbor helped build trust and relationship beyond initial suspicion and skepticism, of which there was plenty. "When I first met Dave, I was like, 'He's mean,'" Sheri, Dave's thirty-four-year-old Black coworker and neighborhood resident told me. "But then as I got to know him—we went to a barbecue thing together, I got to know him and his wife—as I got to know him, he's a cool dude. It's just the way he looks [laughing]."

Dave, for his part, recognized the challenge. "I'm aware of the perceptions," he told me during an interview. After relocating to Atlanta and "not doing anything for the first four or five years in terms of leadership stuff," he said, "I think personally I've gotten to the point where I'm fairly comfortable with who I am:"

I was really fortunate to have some good people, good African American folks, that were like, "Hey, I'm gonna mentor you." Just being able to hang

out and hear stories and learn things by watching and being present; that
really helped.

Over time, within limits, as an established neighborhood resident, Dave became widely known and trusted in the neighborhood as "the crazy white guy
who runs the store."

After two years of working with him, in addition to giving "White Dave"
his nickname, Alicia had developed her own "up close" experience and evaluation of Dave and his work. "I see him more than I see my family!" Alicia
told me while taking a break outside the café one sunny afternoon:

> Dave is the type of person that you can talk to. You can talk to him. Dave
> and I have had arguments where I have totally lost my mind. Like, "I am
> yelling at the top of my lungs at you right now!" And the next day it's like,
> "Okay, alright I'm sorry, we're good," you know? I'm like that too. Once
> I have a chance to express it, I'm like, okay, now I understand what you are
> saying, now let's make adjustments. And that's how he is too.

As will be discussed further in Chapters 5 and 6, the experience of strategic
relocation, alongside scripture and spiritual reflection, aided the practice of
bridge-building and social reflexivity across different types of difference and
inequity among my multicultural evangelical research participants.

Strategic Relocation and Housing

A substantial body of social science research points to racial residential segregation and racial disparities in homeownership as major drivers
of Black–white wealth inequality in the United States.[56] Majority Black
neighborhoods have been subject to systematic disinvestment and anti-
Black discrimination from federal, state, and local governments, banks,
realtors, law enforcement, white homeowners, and other public and private institutions, thereby producing and reproducing social conditions
supporting white advancement and Black disadvantage.[57] Alternatively,
when majority Black neighborhoods become targets of gentrification, disadvantaged residents are often disproportionately marginalized and pushed
out of their neighborhoods by rising home prices, exogenous economic
interests, new local leadership, and inhospitable cultural norms.[58] PCDA's

housing division sought to reverse patterns of systemic disinvestment in historically Black neighborhoods by supporting neighborhood housing stability, Black homeownership, affordable subsidized and market-rate housing for existing residents, and wrap-around support services for new homeowners and renters, without thereby promoting the marginalization or displacement of long-time Black residents and economically disadvantaged neighbors that is so often associated with market-based gentrification processes.[59] In these efforts, PCDA had experienced significant successes and failures alike throughout its history, along with the inevitable tensions and conflicts that arise from engaging in the fraught politics of race and class in the United States.

Since being invited into the neighborhood ten years ago, PCDA-Housing had built or renovated eighty-three neighborhood homes under various federal and nonprofit affordable home programs, opening new pathways to homeownership and cutting into the neighborhood's 25 percent stock of vacant properties. Overall, the housing division of PCDA has been involved in purchasing, remodeling, managing, and selling 113 properties worth over $8 million—accounting for 17 percent of total neighborhood property value—since 2001. An impact study reported that PCDA-Housing "has increased the average value of all [neighborhood] properties by about $12,000, and has increased the total property value of the neighborhood by over $1,100,000 from what it would have been had PCDA-Housing not moved into the neighborhood."[60] The impact study further found that the value of PCDA-Housing properties averaged $15,000 higher per property and $110,000 higher per acre than the neighborhood mean. Excluding the large number of vacant or abandoned properties, the neighborhood's mean home value in 2011 was $74,951.

PCDA-Housing's (PCDA-H) core housing program, "PCDA-Housing Affordable," offered twenty-year mortgages at 0 percent interest on PCDA-H-acquired and renovated single-family homes to low-income homebuyers in the neighborhood. To be eligible, the household incomes of prospective homebuyers could not exceed 50–80 percent of the AMI (average mean income) for the zip code, compared to 30 percent AMI for Section 8 housing and 30–50 percent for Habitat for Humanity homes.[61] As such, prospective buyers' whose household incomes exceeded $35,000 annually were ineligible. PCDA-H prioritized first-time homebuyers who had a checking and savings account; $2,000 down payment; income, credit, and background checks; and at least one child.

The modal PCDA-H Affordable home program house was purchased by PCDA-H for $40,000, renovated for $35,000 (with significant assistance from general volunteers and skilled trade workers from local churches, faith communities, and business who donated time and labor to each home), and sold to program homebuyers for $90,000 after a twelve-month lease/purchase arrangement averaging ~$650/month, with PCDA-H retaining a $15,000 development fee to cover operational costs, homeowner services, and future property purchases. The affordable housing program was PCDA-H's largest by cost and number of homes.

A second program, "NSP Affordable," utilized Neighborhood Stabilization Program (NSP) funding from HUD, the US Department of Housing and Urban Development, to purchase, rehabilitate, and sell a smaller number of affordable homes in the neighborhood. The modal NSP home was purchased by PCDA-H for $70,000, renovated for $45,000, and sold at cost with down-payment assistance for eligible homebuyers, with PCDA-H retaining a $13,000 development fee.

A third program, "PCDA-H Workforce Housing," served the neighborhood's mixed-income aspirations by purchasing, renovating, and selling market-rate homes to traditional bank-qualified buyers. These homes were marketed to what PCDA-H called "workforce" professionals—teachers, nurses, firefighters, nonprofit workers, etc.—who sought to become homeowners but were priced out of more expensive and gentrified intown neighborhoods. The modal workforce home was purchased by PCDA-H for $70,000, renovated for $30,000, and sold for $125,000, with PCDA-H retaining a $15,000 development fee. The remaining $10,000 were either donated to PCDA-H for future purchases or returned to donor-investors at a profit rate capped at 4.5 percent.

Finally, in addition to PCDA-H's core homeownership programs, the organization also owned and managed a number of rental properties in the neighborhood, some affordable and some market-rate, the former of which served as a "feeder program" to PCDA-H's core "PCDA-H Affordable" homeownership program for low-income households. It also managed a legacy property from PCDA's work in a prior Atlanta neighborhood, a transitional housing property with over 65 units and 100 residents—40 percent of whom are women with children, many single retirement-age individuals, and others who had "fallen through the cracks" of affordable rental programs—whose apartments cost $350–$450/month. As such, the property was "the most affordable unsubsidized housing in the city. And folks live there typically a couple of years. It's kind of an entry point back into stable community living."[62] The property was acquired and renovated in the 1980s to provide transitional housing at a time "when homelessness was a big issue in Atlanta."[63] The nation's ongoing crisis in the lack of affordable housing, particularly in major cities, has kept the property in high demand, with a three-year wait-list for apartments. Along with managing the property, PCDA-H offered a variety of support services to residents, from job training and community chaplaincy to health and wellness programs. More broadly, PCDA-H offered a variety of grant- and donor-funded human services to the home buyers and renters with whom it works, including financial literacy training, job training, mortgage assistance and homebuyer training, community chaplaincy, and elderly assistance programs among others. PCDA-H's total annual budget was approximately $650,000, 25–30 percent of which came from grants and donations which, on a tight budget with "every dollar accounted for," allowed the organization to work on three to six new properties per year while funding support service programs and operational costs.[64]

Like many lower income Black communities, the neighborhood was hit hard by the Great Recession's foreclosure crisis and subsequent collapse of the housing market in 2008–2010.[65] In 2006–2007—at the height of the speculative real estate bubble—the neighborhood began to be "heavily speculated upon by investors."

> That was a whole different economic market. Prices were getting so high you couldn't get good rentals if you weren't Section 8. It felt a little out of control. A lot of house-flipping and bad renovations. It was like, 'What is this? This is not Grant Park, people!' "[66]

This despite the fact that the neighborhood at the time was replete with concentrated disadvantage, residential instability, and high levels of vacant lots and abandoned homes which attracted commensurable levels of drug dealing, prostitution, theft, and petty crime.

That all changed beginning in 2008. Amidst widespread foreclosures across the city and nation, which hit many low-income neighborhoods of color particularly hard, PCDA-H affiliated renters and homeowners "were able to stay. It really stabilized the neighborhood. I feel really in the last twelve months things have just got a lot more stable" (Deb). According to Jack, PCDA-H's director of housing, only "one or two" PCDA-H homeowners went into foreclosure. Speculators were driven out, rents stabilized, residents kept their homes, and the neighborhood weathered the storm.

At a PCDA training event attended by a group of visiting pastors and nonprofit leaders, Jack—the forty-six-year-old white evangelical former pastor and director of PCDA's housing division—laid out PCDA-H's vision of a "wholesome, viable, self-sustaining, mixed-income community" that "protect[s] affordable housing in the neighborhood." At the same time, Jack told us, the neighborhood and PCDA were not interested in developing and protecting *only* subsidized housing, because such neighborhoods were not viable or sustainable over the long-term. "What percentage of [subsidized] affordable housing can a neighborhood sustain to be healthy and thrive?" Jack asked the group, drawing on community economic development research. After fielding a few guesses from his audience, he answered, "35 percent. Currently we have 80 percent affordable housing," along with "140 vacant properties out of 530 total." The large percentage of vacant or abandoned properties "adds vulnerability to the neighborhood by attracting drugs, prostitution, theft, and safety issues" that "start on the main drag and move into other areas" which still lacked basic amenities like functioning street lights and sidewalks. "We don't want only affordable housing. Our aim is to be a mixed-income community," Jack continued, not one with "*only* [subsidized] affordable housing. Every neighborhood needs a mixed-income tax base," including "at least some commercial redevelopment." "This is a whole other side of *economic* development than the typical relocation focus of PCDA or CCDA," Jack added for effect. "Our goal is to protect affordable housing" while becoming a "workforce neighborhood" in which low-income, working class, and middle-class residents lived together as neighbors. In a separate interview, Deb echoed Jack's vision while speaking from her own perspective as a neighborhood resident, telling me, "My hope is that this neighborhood will always be a really healthy working class neighborhood. Because those kinds of places are needed in this city, and they're few and far between. A real affordable working class community."

Gentrification with Justice

Due to the nature of its work, PCDA-H could not avoid the explosive topic of gentrification.[67] Any disadvantaged neighborhood desiring economic justice and opportunity marked by a 25 percent vacant property and 80 percent subsidized housing rate requires new residents to move into the neighborhood. The PCDA-H strategy of buying and renovating distressed properties to sell (majority) or rent (minority) as subsidized affordable (majority) and affordable workforce (minority) homes aimed to reduce the number vacant properties in the neighborhood, thereby increasing the number of stakeholders personally invested in neighborhood stability, safety, schools, trust, and overall well-being.[68] PCDA-H prioritized selling and renting to existing neighborhood residents, often working with them to move from rentals into its subsidized affordable homeownership programs. However, with too few residents and too many vacant properties, there were simply not enough local indigenous human and economic resources in the neighborhood to achieve its own goals without increased access to external resources and support.[69]

But which resources, and whose support? Market-fueled gentrification brings external people and resources into race and class disadvantaged neighborhoods without concern for preserving affordable housing or enabling existing residents to benefit from neighborhood socioeconomic gains. Nor does market-fueled gentrification pause to consider neighborhood residents' own goals or wishes regarding neighborhood changes, amenities, racial composition, governance, or identity, particularly when those residents are economically disadvantaged people of color. Too often, gentrification means forcing disadvantaged people of color out of their homes and preferred communities into other—often more dangerous or disadvantaged—neighborhoods.[70] As Deb noted, even PCDA-H's current neighborhood—severely underpopulated and disadvantaged as it was—had started attracting outside real estate speculators and profiteers before the 2008 recession and housing crisis. The question was not so much whether the neighborhood needed or was likely to draw new residents at some point, but who and with what purpose they would enter. Would they be self-interested real estate speculators and profiteers who would remake the neighborhood in their own image with no concern for existing residents' prospects or wishes?[71] Would they displace disadvantaged Black with privileged white residents? Or, rather than typical market-fueled (and often, government-subsidized) gentrification processes, would new residents be community-minded workforce and strategic relocators interested in joining—rather than displacing—existing residents in seeking the long-term health and well-being of their neighbors and neighborhood?[72]

PCDA-H sought to promote the latter in order to block the former. In this, it was serving the interests and will of the long-time residents and community leaders who invited PCDA's presence into the neighborhood in the first place. Still, given the fraught history of gentrification and anti-Black racism in Atlanta and beyond, PCDA-H's work in the neighborhood was not without controversy. PCDA-H leaders and staff frequently, transparently, and directly discussed the "thorny" and "complicated" (Jack) racial dynamics involved in its position as a multiracial community development nonprofit working in a disadvantaged historically Black neighborhood. During one open house training event for Christian community development organizations across the region, Jack—PCDA-H's white evangelical director—began his presentation by foregrounding the "controversial" nature of PCDA-H for some neighborhood residents. While discussing PCDA's intentionally disorienting idea of "gentrification with justice"—an attempt to restrict and harness inexorable market-based gentrification processes in ways that benefit, rather than drive out, disadvantaged people of color in urban neighborhoods—Jack was candid about the neighborhood's at-times mixed response to PCDA-H's presence. "Part of the African American community in this neighborhood *hates* gentrification," Jack told us. "There is resistance." He proceeded to give an example of what he was talking about. "I was showing a neighborhood house to a buyer one afternoon," Jack recalled, "and I was approached by a single mom in the neighborhood, an African American woman. She came up and just lit into me verbally about the lack of affordable rentals in the neighborhood. 'So why are you selling houses [instead of renting them]? This is an *African American* community (emphasis original), historically, and you keep bringing in more white people!'" After listening to the woman's complaints, Jack responded that he shared her passion for affordable rental housing while pointing out that nearly all PCDA-H homes were sold to Black residents.[73]

In fact, according to PCDA-H staff and records, all but one of over twenty PCDA-H properties sold or rented in the neighborhood over the two-plus years prior to my fieldwork were occupied by Black residents, as were all but one of PCDA-H's total stock of rental properties in the neighborhood. Approximately 95 percent of new residents in the neighborhood were African American, "which we are excited about but we don't [completely] control," Jack told me during an interview, "There is intentionality around race." Approximately 85 percent of homeowners in PCDA-H's affordable home programs are African American. In terms of white residents, of the approximately twenty-five homes in the neighborhood owned or rented by white families, "probably 20 of them" (Jack) are strategic relocators affiliated in some way with PCDA.[74] In other words, the large majority of PCDA-H homes are sold or rented to new or existing Black residents, and the overwhelming majority of neighborhood newcomers during PCDA's ten-plus year presence in the neighborhood were African American. "We do talk about mixed income and mixed race, and we are intentional with some of our invitations. But the majority of the work that we do, in terms of who's buying in the neighborhood with the houses we're selling [or renting], is African American." Nevertheless, there was a perception among some in the neighborhood that PCDA was bringing a bunch of middle-class white people into a proud historically Black neighborhood that didn't need or want them.

Others recognized the tension but saw things differently. "I've never heard anyone say that to me," Sheri—a thirty-four-year-old Black female lifelong neighborhood resident—told me when I asked during an interview, "It doesn't seem like there's too many white folks that move into the neighborhood, but some. More than there used to be. Is that, I don't know, do people have a problem with that?" Pausing for effect, she continued, "No. I'm being honest," she insisted without prompting, immediately recognizing the possibility I might be skeptical of her willingness to tell a white sociologist the truth about how she and her neighbors perceived whites in the neighborhood. Sheri confirmed and restated her position when I reasked a similar question differently later in the interview as a sort of internal robustness check: "You hear stories of gentrification or whatever, like white folks moving in and trying to take over . . .," to which she responded, "I think change is for the better, no matter what race. If someone comes to a neighborhood and takes effort in making it better, I'm all for it. Everybody moving in, some white people: everything's getting better. It's gotten better."

Residents' Perspectives

As a lifelong neighborhood resident, Sheri had a more longitudinal perspective than most when it came to how the neighborhood had changed in recent decades. Her perspective was simultaneously affectionate and somewhat critical:

I've seen it at its worse up until now. It's come a long way.
I: Really?

Sheri: Yes.

I: Tell me about back in the day.

Sheri: Back in the day. You couldn't—I'll give you an example. You couldn't even—I had a plastic plant sitting out on the porch that someone took. I mean, as far as theft, it was very high. The houses, there were a lot of rundown houses, people not taking care of them. The neighborhood to me felt one of those abandoned towns you see in the movies. Just so few people. To me, that's how it used to be. . . . Over the years, people started moving in, developing some of the houses. And they kind of ran away all the drug dealers. There's still a few. And prostitution was terrible. All that's going away. You feel more comfortable sitting outside. When school is in, you have the students who don't want to go to school walking up and down the streets smoking marijuana. Other than that, you feel a little safer. Of course, the cops still don't do what they're supposed to do. You call the cops, they come an hour, hour and a half later. That hasn't changed at all. It's like, they already know, "Oh, *that* neighborhood." . . . There's still a few houses in the area that could use some work, and we don't have anything in the neighborhood for the kids per se. I always thought maybe someone would invest in a house. Taxes could be paid for it; just a house that could, you know, get volunteers or groups to come in and just make it a rec center, where kids have somewhere to hang out. . . . you know, volunteers, tutors. I just feel like the neighborhood needs that house to interest the kids. But it's come a long way.

I: Are there a lot of kids in the neighborhood?

Sheri: Yes. Yeah. [laughs] It's kinda limited what they can do, because there's not really much to do.

I: Did you like growing up here?

Sheri: Yeah. Mm-hm. I did. I had three best friends. One of my best friends stayed on my street. Two doors down. My other best friend, on the next street down. She still stays there at the bottom. And I had another best friend on the next street. Back then, kids were bad. When I was coming along, it was so bad. My great grandparents were raising me. And walking from my house to the high school, you would get mugged. They would take your coat, your shoes. It was just that bad. The high school has come a long way. When I went there, we had no band uniforms. Teaching materials: they sucked. There was always someone getting shot or stabbed. I've seen some crazy stuff. I graduated in '96 and they renovated the school. It's so much better.

I: It looks nice. The building's gorgeous.

Sheri: Mm-hm. And of course, this used to be a liquor store. Next door was an auto place. It was a spot for winos and stuff. And actually the bike shop used to be a store owned by a Cuban guy who got robbed and killed.

I: So kind of hard living.

Sheri: Yeah. It was hard. And it was lower class; poor. And there were a lot of senior citizens. A lot of them have passed away, but there's still some hanging on. . . . They would actually have like a Neighborhood Day and just invite everybody to come up to the park, barbecue and just sit back and talk. They don't do that anymore. I wish we would do that. But I can't speak on that because I don't go into the city meetings, so I have to start going before I can give my—start complaining! [laughs]

Sheri's recollections were consistent with those of Ms. Deborah, Latoya, Leonard, and other life-long and long-time neighborhood residents.

For example, Nathan—a thirty-three-year-old Black neighborhood association treasurer and director of a PCDA-affiliated modern dance program for young Black males—shared much of Sheri's perspective on the neighborhood after having purchased his house in foreclosure six years earlier as a PCDA strategic relocator:

> In my opinion, this neighborhood is like a village in the inner city. It wasn't always like that. Especially not when I first moved in about six years ago. Before [PCDA-H] built the new building over there, there was a liquor store with a crowd of guys that would go out there every day, light a fire in the barrel, and sit there and be dependent on alcohol every day. Prostitution was big deal: a lot of truckers come up and down this main road, pick up a lady, drop her off further down. There were five or six crack houses at the top end of the neighborhood. Vacant properties everywhere. And the neighborhood was riddled with litter. Tires, specifically. We have five or six tire shops in this neighborhood. It was about ten, now it's down to about six. I'm a treasurer for the executive board of the neighborhood association, and one of the big things we've done is to dispose of 3,800 tires out of this neighborhood in the last four years. That's not an exaggeration; it really is about 3,800 tires. We do three or four cleanups a year.

While the neighborhood remains challenged by the sort of environmental racism and zoning issues commonly experienced in low-income communities of color—"pocketed in by large factories and recycling plants and tow truck companies"[75]—most residents seemed to agree on the overall positive direction of neighborhood changes.

Sheri and Nathan's perspective on PCDA-H's work was consistent with the overwhelming majority of African American individuals I interviewed, observed, or spoke informally with while conducting my research. Betsy—whose experience with PCDA spanned thirty years across multiple neighborhoods as both long-time neighborhood resident and later PCDA employee—summarized her own view succinctly as such:

> PCDA—What I know is that these [PCDA-H staff and strategic relocators] are people who come into the neighborhood and try and make the neighborhood better, be Christlike, try and bring what they can to the neighborhood without overwhelming it. Being a positive force, not a negative.

When I pressed and asked her, "What do you think about the perspective of a person saying, "Hey, this kinda just looks like a bunch of white people going to take over the neighborhood?" she responded:

> I can see how someone can say that, because if people have been living a certain way in a neighborhood where there is no change—the neighborhood is not being revitalized . . . or there's a lot of crime in the neighborhood, or [people are afraid] of talking to the police, and then they see three or four white families move in and all of a sudden changes come—I think they can think, "Oh, so that's what has happened." . . . If someone comes in who cares about the neighborhood, if they are of a different race—white, Asian, Hispanic—and they help things begin to move, then the people who have been there all those years kind of get a chip on their shoulder.

While Betsy recognized the inevitably of conflict in the context of change, she had also witnessed such tensions stir existing residents to take more active leadership roles in the neighborhood, "to go to city council, or to the police chief and say, 'Hey, this is what we need. These are *our* concerns, could you help us with this.' From my experience, no matter much you try to keep things the same, change comes, regardless of whether you want it to come or not."

The question, from Betsy's perspective, was whether such changes increase racial and economic justice, opportunity, and ownership for existing

[Black] residents. Her answer with respect to PCDA's presence was unequivocally affirmative.

Past Neighborhoods and Organizational Dynamics

Pamela, a thirty-three-year-old African American woman, experienced the tensions of strategic relocation across race and class divisions from multiple perspectives: as a new resident in each of the two most recent majority-Black neighborhoods in which PCDA-H had been invited to work, and as a former PCDA employee who had worked her way up from administrative assistant to management positions in family services, community affairs director, and assistant director of PCDA-H. During an interview, Pamela recalled her experience living in an east Atlanta neighborhood before, during, and after PCDA-H's arrival:

> I enjoyed it. It was more concentrated. Apartment living. People yelling out their window to you. I think people trusted you more because they saw you go in your home. Everybody was in the same place. Market rate and low income . . . and you didn't know who was who. So I loved that. Our mailboxes were all in the same place, so we were all, "Hey! Hey!" There was a pool in the same place, so were always saying "Hi!" The community center was right there too, so we were always in there to pay rent and stuff . . . and then we built the day care in there too, and the grocery store, because we kept thinking everything needs to be self-sustaining. We had the senior high rise from when it was the housing project that we left there. So there were places that everybody had to go to: market-rate and low-income. It was really cool.

PCDA, in partnership with the city and several larger mission-driven developers, had just begun work in the neighborhood when Pamela moved into this first new mixed-income apartment building amid a cluster of high-density low-income apartment complexes in the process of being renovated and restructured for mixed-income residence. The project was designed to enable existing residents to remain in the neighborhood if they chose and gain access to high-quality affordable housing while benefiting from new neighborhood infrastructure, security, resources, and amenities wrought by new investment long overdue.

As much as Pamela enjoyed the neighborhood and built strong connections, she frequently felt caught between old and new, Black and white, middle-class and low-income communities and neighborhood cultures. Some of her neighbors were suspicious of her presence:

> One of the things they used to say a lot is, "you hang out with them white folks. They're trying to come take over. We don't trust them." Because they couldn't understand why anyone would want to move in here. Like, "What's their angle?" And then after a while, they stopped wanting to connect with [new residents]. Because they would notice that they would come in for a little while, do life, build relationships, fall in love with the neighborhood—and then move. Because a lot of young people would come. . . . And I started hearing from neighbors that they felt used. That they kind of felt, "I don't know if I want to put my heart out there because you may not be around very long." And I was doing the same thing they were doing, but I was I Black, and that made them open up to me. So I could hear different angles, and I was able to go back and tell [PCDA-affiliated residents and staff], "Hey, this what people are thinking." Sometimes they would even refer to *me* as, "You white folks." I was like, "Hey, I'm not white!"

Pamela was not white, but her new resident status and association with multiracial PCDA made her something of an outsider, despite enjoying a greater degree of trust with long-time residents through common racial and spatial identification and goodwill. Still, Pamela appreciated her position in the neighborhood:

> I feel honored, now, just looking back on the viewpoint that I had. Pretty cool. Some of the [long-time residents] felt excited. To be honest, some people nicknamed that neighborhood after a war zone. It was a place that even the postman wouldn't deliver mail. It was really bad. Some of them grew up in the roughest parts. And now to have a place where people were outside throwing a football and there wasn't broken glass everywhere, and there was landscaping, and we had community activities with a stage, they were like, in awe.

Pamela's experiences as a resident in both neighborhoods are explored further in Chapter 3's additional section on "gentrification with justice."

As a Black PCDA-H employee who worked directly with homeowners and renters of PCDA-H properties, Pamela also had an inside view on the sometimes fraught internal and external relations and perceptions of the organization's work. As a devout (Baptist) Christian, she also brought a vocally spiritual orientation to her work. Pamela did not withhold discussing the more negative aspects of her experiences with what she called the "old" PCDA-H which "before I came, had a pretty challenged reputation," despite her overall pride and satisfaction with PCDA-H's work. When I asked, "Did you hear things about the 'old' PCDA-H, either internally or externally?" she answered:

> Oh yeah. I would just say generally, some of the perception was that [PCDA-H] people don't care. "They will put you out, they will be mean when they talk to you, they're harsh. They don't even think about it, they just have this policy." Say for instance, a policy about a payment that's 30 days past due, [they would enforce it] with no thinking, just, "It's 30 days past due, sorry." People felt like it was harsh. But from my angle—because I knew some of the people that were there before I came—they just got involved with PCDA-H because they wanted to love people. But the hard parts of the job weren't part of their personality. So they just did it real quick, because it was part of their jobs that they hated to do. And they came off as unnatural and harsh. And it was. Because this was part of their job that they hated to do. But that was never communicated.

Because Pamela worked closely with tenants and homeowners who were often also her neighbors, residents' problems and perceptions of PCDA-H were always close at hand:

> Whenever people had issues . . . they would call me and I would go. I think just being available is important. . . . That almost led to some burnout. I was always on the go. Even in the neighborhood when I'm off work and I go to a party, it's like, "Oh, Pamela could help you with housing, come over here!" So I was still working.
>
> I: That's tough.
> Pamela: It was, yeah. But it's hard because this is what I love to do. You do
>   need to kind of figure out how to create some boundaries. 'Cause you
>   can get lost in it.

As a Black strategic relocator and PCDA-H manager whose racial identity matched the majority of her neighbors and clients, Pamela was deeply immersed in the lives and communicative networks of the neighborhood.

Because of her experiences as a resident and PCDA-H employee across multiple neighborhoods, Pamela also had special insight into perceptions of the organization in neighborhoods where its work had been largely completed:

> When I came to PCDA-H—because we were the mortgage company for [affordable] homeowners—we had interaction with people from all the old neighborhoods [that PCDA-H had worked in]. And because of those interactions I got to hear the voice of their heart. And some of them felt abandoned. We would persuade them—we're really good storytellers—like, "Come stay or move to this neighborhood God called you to, and we can do life together and you can have children here and grow!" And then when it's time for us to go to the next neighborhood, we leave them and focus our resources in the next neighborhood and the new programs and people we're courting. And they would barely hear from us. After a while, they were like, "What happened? We don't hear from PCDA-H unless we're late on our mortgage. You used to pray with us, you used to talk to us. You convinced us to live here and now we don't get the assistance that we need because you're focused on a new place."

> And the reality is we can't really do that all the time. Our staff is small. But we were like, "Wow, that wasn't our intention." So we began to think of ways to keep everyone included. How do we stay fully committed in our current neighborhood while keeping strong connections with people in those neighborhoods? I created a newsletter as a way of ministering to them and keeping them involved and committed. And we'd do a volunteer project where we reach out to some of the old families as well. Just little ways to do what we could, while accepting the reality that we couldn't be there all the time, because we need to focus resources on the current neighborhood. But there were ways we could still keep them connected and involved. I would have them come to the current neighborhood and help do volunteer projects. Just stuff so they can pay it forward, feel like they're invested. We created a place where they can donate five dollars so they can help another family go into a home . . . something small that they can feel like, "I helped another family."

That was one of the things I saw with PCDA-H. And we grew to be better at it. It's just always a learning process. We had to come to the understanding we're not the savior. We're not going to do everything perfect. But we've always got to have a posture of learning and healing in the community. And the only way you really do that is you live in the community as well. It's easy to care—because they're your neighbors, and you need to—that your neighbors are feeling hurt.

Like other research participants, becoming friends and neighbors—rather than distant allies—through strategic relocation appeared to accelerate and amplify Pamela's emotional investment, social reflexivity, and relational connection with people whom she lived and worked alongside.

In addition to her experiences as a strategic relocator, Pamela experienced the "ordeal of integration" as part of PCDA's multiracial management team.[76] She had much to say on the subject:

> Okay. Let's say we're [PCDA-H's multiracial staff] in the community and we're wanting to serve. The good part about that is we all have a heart to serve, and we all bring different aspects or gifts to it because of our [different] upbringing. So that's really good. But one of the negative things I find is that it's easy for me to be offended as an African American when I hear some of the "let's help those people" mentality. And I'm like, "Wait a minute. You can't—you need to check the way you're thinking. The way you're talking." I fight that type of thing. So I think some of that can be bad. I remember one time during the Obama presidential election, it was the first time I'd ever seen PCDA-H kind of divided. And it was odd for me. People I used to laugh and crack jokes with about race, like, "Girl, you think you Black," or "You think you're white."

> I: It got too loaded to do that type of thing?
> Pamela: Yeah. And it was the first time in all the years I'd been there that I ever noticed, hey, race makes a big difference here. I hadn't really realized that. I thought we all thought the same way. But I think the way that we work together is we don't talk about the details of our faith. We talk about our faith as far as we love God, we believe in his Word, Jesus Christ. We don't talk about theology, like do you believe in baptism? I think if we did, we would all start being on different pages. We just believe in Jesus Christ and we believe it's our responsibility to do good and seek justice on the earth.

I: So that's the kind of theological side. And the Obama election is the more political side. And there were divides there as well?

Pamela: Yeah. Until this presidency of a Black president coming in, nobody really talked about their political views. All the Black people were like, "Are we going to set up a viewing?! Are we going to watch this?" And a couple people were like, "We're not voting for him." And I'm, like, "What?!" Not everybody, obviously.

I: But there were some and it was shocking?

Pamela: It was shocking. I was like, "I didn't know you felt that way." They'd say, "I grew up in a strong Republican family and my core belief are still this and this." I'm like, "How can you live in this community and [not vote for Obama]? Is it just a project for you? Or a lifestyle?" You start having those kinds of questions. And it could be wrong to even question that. But I was like, "Whoa. Wow." Just that whole rift happening: we never had those kinds of conversations before. It was interesting.

I: Were there a lot of those kind of conversations?

Pamela: No, because we shut them down. You could feel the tension. Somebody would make a comment, and you would feel this tension. Or somebody would come in with a t-shirt, and you're like, "What?!" And you would realize, "I love this person, but this is definitely going to divide me from them. Let's just not talk about it."

I: Interesting. So it wasn't like, "Let's not talk about it at work but we'll talk about it in other contexts?" It was like, "No, we're just going to let this be and focus on what we have in common?"

Pamela: Yes. And it was never said. It was never an explicit thing. It was more like: the reason why we do what we do is because of relationship. And so, at the end of the day, I've spent life with you. And I know that we won't agree on everything. But if I spend time dwelling on these things, I would be so hurt and offended that I won't be able to move past that and see the person I've loved all these years. And it's challenging. But you know, you've got to ask yourself: Is this relationship worth it? Is what I'm doing all these years really what I believe in? Or am I just saying that? Because if it's really what you believe in, and you're asking the people in the community to forgive [white] people who have made them feel oppressed. Who have not fixed the potholes in their community; who have not come to answer the 911 calls right away. You're wanting them to forgive them, and start voting again, and coming to the neighborhood association meetings. But you're not willing to move past this person whose views politically are different than yours? That hypocritical. It's another way that God tests your heart.

Another thing I would see sometimes at PCDA-H—I don't know about the rest of PCDA—but you would hear an employee get upset about a homeowner not trusting us, like in a situation where we were trying to do something for them but they were asking for something else . . . and someone says, "Those people should be grateful that we're doing anything for them." No! They shouldn't be grateful and just take the crumb off the table. This is what we said we would do. But you'd hear some of that mindset. And you'll hear some of them say, "I'm so sorry, I don't know where that came from." Well, we have a lot of staff members who didn't come from the 'hood. They come from a suburban family with two parents in their household. And they had their own drama, but it was just so different. You know. It makes them check their heart too on a regular basis, because their heart is to serve God.

I: In the example you gave, they would verbalize apology?
Pamela: Oh yeah.
I: Was that common, that kind of reaction? To apologize and talk it out?
Pamela: On our team it was.
I: Would you call each other out too? Or say, "Hey, that made me feel this way."
Pamela: Oh yeah, definitely. It brought a lot of tension on our team, but we also had the most growth and closer relationships.
I: Because you were talking about it?
Pamela: Yeah. Let's talk about it. And you'd see people turn beet red, like, "You called me out." You got your little ghetto sister girl going on. Or if you're somebody like me, you'd get an attitude and not talk to anybody. But then I'd go out and come back in, and someone would say, "I noticed during the meeting, you checked out during the meeting because somebody said such and such. You ok?" And I'd say I did check out. But it made you better. It made you bigger. I think so anyway.

Pamela's comments on internal organizational conflict across racialized political lines complicate prior research on social reflexivity suggesting that the avoidance of controversial topics hinders the ability of groups to bridge social differences.[77] In some cases, Pamela and her PCDA-H coworkers practiced strategic *avoidance* of divisive conversations as a bridging strategy, while practicing direct communication and confrontation in others. In both cases, social reflexivity was required of all parties to maintain solidarity and cohesion in a racially, religiously, and politically diverse organizational setting.[78]

With respect to the culture of social reflexivity, correction, and engagement of racial issues within PCDA-H and PCDA more broadly, Pamela's comments were corroborated by participant observation and by other Black and white PCDA-H coworkers. Jack, Pamela's white evangelical former supervisor, spoke of being corrected often Black and white senior PCDA leaders:

> Richard will get on you, when he's sees you struggling with some issue. I would say he's not always gentle, but he's always gracious. And so I've learnt to sort of trust when he asks questions, "Why are you doing this?" . . . He'll make you think about what's happening . . . with race and privilege and things like that. Leonard and Nick both do that as well as. So you get that sort of education in PCDA.

Richard, for his part, receives the same sort of correction and challenge from coworkers such as Betsy (the forty-four-year-old Black woman and long-time PCDA employee introduced above):

> I can't truly say that I have a lot of negative experiences [working with white people in PCDA]. You know, like with any family, you'll have communication issues or see things you disagree with. And I've gone to Richard and asked, "Why did you do it that way? That didn't look right to me. That looked a little bit like you were just kicking out all the Black people." And he would try to explain. You do tend to look at things from the point of view of your race or your experience. But sometimes it's not really about that, and you have to realize that too sometimes.

Like Betsy, Nathan—a Black PCDA program director—reported that he had, "never really had or heard about any major conflicts" between Black and white PCDA staff and leaders, which he attributed to the fact that

PCDA's leadership is "very open to diversity"—in part because "the environment they're in every day is very diverse in the first place"—along with the fact that "we're all sharing the same resources." Nor did I witness any such conflicts.[79] We will learn more about Jack and other white evangelicals' experience of learning to see and "feel" (Alexei) racial difference and inequity in new ways—that is, to practice the social and racial reflexivity required of ethical democracy—while living and working in multiracial, majority Black contexts in Chapters 5 and 6.[80]

Strategic Relocation and Youth Development

Summer Program

When Deanna—a forty-eight-year-old African American woman, mother of five, and PCDA director of youth development—asked me to meet her at her house to complete our scheduled in-depth interview, I did not know it was the birthplace of PCDA's award-winning summer youth program of which Deanna was the founding director. It was a busy week and she was running late finalizing summer program payments and details while juggling the rush of early summer parenting responsibilities. We started the interview in her kitchen, with me at the kitchen table and Deanna directing children and organizing schedules and clean-up in anticipation of a busy afternoon. "The first thing that struck me when I moved here was the number of children who were just kind of hanging around with nothing to do," she said, "unlike in suburban areas where there are way fewer children and so much more for them." Deanna called out one last instruction to someone upstairs before asking if we could continue our interview in the car as she ran some summer program-related errands. I assented.

A week-and-a-half later, I drove to the neighborhood public elementary school into which PCDA's summer program had expanded. It was a grim drive to a bright destination, past old tire piles and over-abundant railroad crossings, factories and recycling centers, abandoned houses and weedy lots, culminating in a striking split-view image. On one side of the road sat the handsome elementary school building with well-kept grounds and a colorful "Reach for the Stars" sign welcoming visitors. Directly across the street sat a massive industrial container facility, surrounded by barbed-wire fences with a steady stream of large diesel semitrucks spewing smoke and kicking up dust as they entered and exited the facility's driveway, situated directly in front of the school. "There is no way this would be okay in a middle or upper middle-class neighborhood," I recorded thinking in my field notes later as I pulled into the elementary school parking lot, shooting into a small gap between large semitruck trailers exiting and entering the industrial facility.

Inside, the school was clean and new. Forty-five neighborhood youth, almost all African American, were enrolled in the PCDA summer program, with one high-school-aged counselor (all former PCDA summer program participants themselves) per every five students, plus a few extra volunteer teens and teachers. The summer program runs for six to seven hours a day, Monday through Thursday—about thirty-five hours a week for seven weeks each year. "It's a lot of planning," Ada, a thirty-year-old white female neighborhood resident, PCDA-affiliated strategic relocator, and assistant summer program director, says while showing me around. "There's academics, art, team building, recreation, and trips. We have a community service project, which is one full week over the summer. And overnight camp." I asked about the community service project. "The teens actually plan it," Ada responded:

One year we painted the swing sets and other things up at the park. One year the middle schoolers got a grant from DeVos Urban Leaders Initiative and they painted two different houses for a couple of elderly neighbors. That was a huge project. The counselors help them budget and make a shopping list and actually go to places to purchase what's needed. They've gone to the grocery store and gotten food for some of the seniors in the neighborhood, or they've gone to Lowe's and gotten flowers and pots to paint and hand-deliver them to neighbors. Some clean up and yard work stuff. Various things like that.

Themes of empowerment, support, and stepping aside for Black youth leaders saturated the summer program at every level, reflecting Deanna's conviction that, "The leaders of this community, to change a neighborhood, weren't going to come from the outside, but from *kids in the neighborhood* (emphasis original)."[81] Ada continued, "We're considered staff coaches. So instead of high interactions with campers, we're dealing with the teens who are in the leadership program" and who run most of the day-to-day operations of the camp.

The leadership program, for camp counselors in their teens to early twenties, "covers a lot of job skills, college applications, practicalities of making a five-year plan, ten-year plan . . . along with emotional, spiritual health kinds of things." Ada proceeded to describe a newly minted employment and entrepreneurship initiative linking leadership program participants to local businesses, entrepreneurs, and grantees:

> That's the next level . . . where we can train them at summer camp and get more permanent jobs elsewhere. That's the goal. This year we've added a partnership with Urban Launch [a PCDA-affiliated coworking space and business incubator], which is bringing in business entrepreneur partners and mentors to mentor some of the youth. We have a few who really want to start their own businesses. So Urban Launch is actually doing a $1,000 grant to kickstart a business. So they'll have a mentor, and by the end of the summer, they will have written a business plan and can possibly get this grant.

Ada gave some examples of success stories of neighborhood youth who had attended summer program, become counselors as teens, went through the leadership program, and were now working management jobs, some married with kids of their own.

"So they're doing all that," I asked, "but then they're also counselors for the kids?" Ada affirmed, "They run the camp essentially." "Is that paid?" I asked:

> Yes, they get paid. It's all fundraised through PCDA. Deanna's recently added a manager position. The manager will run the staff meetings. Mitch [Ada's co-assistant director] and I are hands-off as much as possible and they kind of run the show.

> I: And the manager is?
> Ada: It's one of the veteran counselors. So it's usually a counselor who has been in the leadership program two or three years.
> I: And gone through it themselves as kids?
> Ada: Yeah. So they have to apply and they go through a whole different interview process. They run the whole show. They're in charge of the kids. They look at me and ask me what to do, and I'm like, "They're your kids." They do really well.

Ada wasn't lying: they did do really well. Not only did these neighborhood teens and young adults offer impressive leadership at the summer program, but I frequently observed them out in the neighborhood or at the café chatting, answering questions, and giving life tips to other neighborhood youth who clearly looked up to them.

None of this was by accident. Months earlier at a PCDA weekend training event, I had listened with others as Deanna, PCDA's Black director of youth development under whom Ada worked, described the history and philosophy of the now fourteen-year-old summer program. A dynamic communicator, Deanna opened with a sharp criticism of typical "program-centered" nonprofit community development work. Such programs, Deanna argued:

> Identify a problem, then start a program to fix the problem. One "problem" with this approach is that the program *needs* the problem to keep going. We keep the problem alive: for recruitment, for donors, and so on. We exaggerate the problem. The program serves the problem. Then over time, the people, the community, the children, become seen *as* "the problem" or "a problem." Then *we* become part of the problem. We perpetuate stereotypes of division, inequality, race, and so on. We think, "We have to make things look and sound really bad in order to keep donors giving." In this model, you need kids to be in crisis in order to help them. That is a problem. Problem-centered programs *objectify people*. The work isn't about the person as they are. It's about the *hype*, the *idea*, the *radicality* of the work. This is in contrast to an "investor" mentality, which looks for promise and potential rather than problems.

Deanna then contrasted the typical program-centered nonprofit model with a person or "child-centered development" model rooted in "what do *they* need?":

> Good teachers know that if a kid is engaged and inspired, they will regulate *themselves*.
>
> They will discipline themselves, to buy in, to want to be present, to learn. So our question must be, "How do we engage and inspire?", not "How do we control and contain?" The goal is positive change *in and for the kids*, not "running the program." Not in increasing our money or numbers or the size of our buildings or budgets.
>
> This means we need to always be adaptive and evolving, to be open to new people, new ideas, new ways of doing things, instead of holding to routine and the way we've always done things.[82]

The existence of the summer program itself, as described by Deanna at the beginning of this section, emerged from the child-centered question, "what do *they* need?" rather than "what do I want to give them":

> In summer, kids lose about two months of [academic] retention, so one of our summer program goals is to maintain or improve end-of-year reading and math levels. 85 percent of our students met this goal in math last year.... In addition to our own programming, we send kids to other leadership development programs. We buy tickets for the theatre. We help them find their "gift" and build up confidence to use it, and translate their gifts to areas of struggle. We sometimes partner with the Atlanta Public Schools, with the city, with dance and theatre programs, with different neighborhood churches. We help our kids learn to talk to people in authority. The kids in my community don't have connections, networks, and such to access jobs, schools, and so on—things that are taken for granted in a lot of middle-class or higher [income] communities.

"So don't just write checks," Deanna admonished the group, "open up your networks to people. Write a recommendation letter. Make a call. Make an interview contact. *That* is of great value."

Knowing her majority-white evangelical audience, Deanna also used the opportunity to encourage evangelical Christians to expand their vision of what faithful public witness looks like in a nation built and torn apart by racial injustice:

> I want my kids to know Jesus. I want them to have eternal life. But I also know that Jesus wants them to have *abundant* life. So I see injustice, I see the inattention of government, of not getting city services, of kids in my neighborhood struggling in school, struggling to get a job, struggling to find safety in their neighborhoods, and it upsets me. I care about *justice*, because I care about them, about these kids, about this neighborhood, and because I care about *me* and *my* kids, because I live in this neighborhood.[83]

Here once again, strategic relocation—and outsiders' exposure to its lessons—played an important role in the flexible philosophy and form of PCDA's presence and work in the neighborhood, exemplifying the social reflexivity discussed further in Chapters 5 and 6.

Bike Shop

In addition to the summer program, one other youth development initiative merits attention here: PCDA's award-winning bike repair shop, where neighborhood youth are mentored in the art of fixing bikes, learning soft job skills and earning work credits they use to purchase bikes for themselves. Alexei, the bike shop's founder and director, is a white, thirty-year-old father of four who had relocated to Atlanta from the Upper Midwest several years earlier:

> Richard [PCDA's founding director] gave us some advice when we moved here. He said, "In the first six to nine months, try everything, commit to nothing." Which is very good advice, because you get to taste different things and see how different programs interact with individuals. . . . When you're present at different ministries, you can see how they engage their quote-on-quote "constituents." You can kind of feel if there's a lot of mutual respect. Or you can feel like, "This is kind of demeaning. That guy is wearing a shirt that says, 'For the least of these.' "[84]

After about a year in the neighborhood, the idea for the bike shop was born during a sixty-five-mile bike trip Alexei took with a Black PCDA colleague and friend:

> So I did the things I knew how to do. I put together a plan of what the vision was, what I wanted the kids to experience. I invited some of the community development veterans to speak into it, asking, "Hey, this is my idea, what do you think? Is this going to make a difference? Is this viable?" I got a lot of good feedback from that I incorporated. I opened it up and asked, "What do you think?" to veterans in the neighborhood, to local church leaders, to the neighborhood association, to my neighbors, to some of the youth. I basically asked all around, every stakeholder, "What do you think?" When I asked for input and questions from people at the neighborhood association, the first input was: "Hey, I have some tools you can have!" Just about everybody had immediate buy-in and encouragement. "You should do it."

Alexei built a website, four bikes were donated, and he was granted permission to use a concrete slab behind the PCDA building. "So that was the first bike shop: outside, on the concrete. I brought a handful of wrenches, a hammer, and WD-40. We had no replacement parts. But kids started coming in." Today, bikes are donated from Atlanta-area civic organizations, churches, businesses, individuals, and other word-of-mouth sources, repaired and improved by neighborhood youth working with Alexei or another adult mentor, and purchased without cash by participants when they have accumulated sufficient work credits to take home a bike. Now resourced with a robust supply of bike stands, tools, and parts, Alexei was also able to move the bike shop indoors: "We've been blessed with a lot of partnerships that you can't manufacture. There are two businessmen that pay the rent every month. They told me verbatim, 'You worry about the kids and we'll worry about the rent.' That was it. That's how I moved into this space."

The space was small and no-nonsense: well-organized, if a bit crowded. In it, over 100 bikes had been repaired and bought or sold by neighborhood youth—most of whom were Black male teens and youth from low-income backgrounds. After describing the bike shop process from the perspective of youth participants, Alexei proceeded to discuss connections made through the shop with neighborhood parents, including one challenging experience involving a young man, his family, and the police:

One of the older teens got involved in an altercation and was arrested. I ended up having to go and pick up his dad and tell his mom; to bring his dad to the scene and have his dad talk to the officers. Witnessing the conversation of a father and son across bars in the police cruiser: it was intense. I didn't go to school for this stuff. I can't pull up a manual. What do you do? But that situation, it turned out good for the parents. They were originally apprehensive. They're Muslim, so there's a level of distrust knowing [I'm] a Christian. [The bike shop] is not openly Christian, but we are associated with PCDA. I mean, the church is in the same building as the bike shop, and I go to the church. Some of the kids come to the youth group. But the fact that I was present: I didn't change the officer's mind. I didn't yell at the youth. I did what for me was the hardest thing there was to do in the situation: go and talk to his parents, and bring them to the scene. I didn't know what the parents would do. All the neighbors were out at the scene. And here I am bringing the parents; that may end up causing a scene. But I just looked at it as a father. My child—if he's in a situation, I want to be there. So I went and talked to both of the parents and then we went back to their house and we talked. And the young man learned a lot from the experience. He knew that he made a mistake. But he learned a lot more from the experience than just, "don't make a mistake." He's still learning. He stuck around.

And what I wanted him to understand was that I recognized that what he did was wrong but I wasn't turning my back on him. That I still want him involved in the bike shop: even as a mentor. He has that kind of maturity growing in him. I wanted him to know that, yes, he'll pay for what he did. But as far as I'm concerned—I'm careful, I'm not going to put youth at the shop in danger—but I know him better than that. And I want him around.

Alexei's approach at the bike shop mirrored Deanna's summer program and PCDA youth development initiatives more generally: when youth are provided opportunities to be inspired, engaged, supported, and believed in, they learn to regulate themselves and mature through mistakes, as opposed to adopting more harsh and punitive control-oriented approaches to policing the lives of race and class disadvantaged youth.[85]

The bike shop also unexpectedly involved Alexei in the fraught relations between law enforcement and disadvantaged Black neighborhoods in other ways. Alexei mentioned a Black female police officer who had become a mentor at the bike shop, and I asked how she had become a bike repair mentor. Alexei responded:

[The bike shop] was somehow discovered by the COPS unit. COPS stands for Community Oriented Policing. It's covered by federal funding that expires next year. Fears are that it's not going to get renewed. It's a proactive branch of the force where experienced uniformed officers, who were all on the street for plenty of years, are allocated to the unit. They have different kinds of youth and other programs in different neighborhoods and they try to build proactive relationships and trust. . . . They discovered what was going on here. Long story short, I was riding my adult tricycle with my 3-year-old standing in the basket behind me holding onto my shirt. An officer pulled us over. I tried to get away [laughing, clearly joking]. He asked me if I'm the guy running the bike shop. I said yeah. Turns out he wanted to bring some kids over with him from a neighborhood that's really close by. He said he always sees them on the corner. They have bikes but none of them are ridable. They keep working on them but they can never fix them. He asked if he could bring them. I said, "Well, you can bring them, but I'll need to first find some volunteer mentors. He says, "I'll volunteer." All right. Next time we open the shop, two cops come barging in through the back door. They ask, "Hey, we just want to make sure you're still planning on doing this. Both of us will volunteer." "All right," I tell them, "bring them on

Wednesday." On Wednesday, six cops showed up. They brought seven kids with them. And you know, neighbors came out like, "Who got killed?" And neighbors across the street saw it and they realized it's a good thing. So they ordered pizza for the officers to show their appreciation. I did not plan it, nobody planned it. Cops, kids, neighbors, pizza. A senior came out, she's like, "I have never in my life seen this many cop cars for a good thing." That was a quote, on record, from a senior that spent her whole life here.

Alexei paused before shifting gears,

One thing though: there are 50 officers in the COPS unit. And they came in here very strong. They had backing from the mayor. It was very gung-ho. "We need to do this and this and this. We're bringing Channel 26, we're bringing Channel 2, Channel 11," you know, all these folks. They came very strong. And the first guy that pulled me over: I warned him. I said, "If you're going to start out this strong, you're going to burn out pretty quick." 'Cause they basically started bussing kids to the bike shop from other neighborhoods in shifts. Multiple shifts a day. I said, "You're going to burn out." And not all the officers were so excited about it. Some of them were excited, some of them were just kind of bored, like, "Doing this is much better than serving on boards," or whatever they were doing before. But they were not engaged. So I said, "Don't start if you're going to stop in three months. Stop now. It's going to hurt the trust you're trying to build with the kids, with the neighbors. You're going to tear it down. Don't do this for two or three months and then stop." Guess what?

I: What happened?

Alexei: He convinced me, "No, no, we're here to stay." Three months later, they were gone. All but one. And her friends sometimes came. But that one officer, she kept coming. It's been over a year and she's still coming.

Alexei continued,

She had quite the learning moment one of the first times she was here. There was a kid that wouldn't talk to her. And, you know, police officers, they can very quickly turn into A-holes, as they say. Flip of a switch: say the wrong thing to them and you are treated like the worst person in the world. So that was about to unleash, and I saw it coming. I tried to intervene: "Let me tell you about this particular child. Let me tell you briefly what he's been through." And so instead of unleashing all that "you're not going to disrespect me" fury, she gave him another chance, and they actually became pretty good friends. She earned his trust. Just a bit later that day, he was standing on the pegs of a bike she was riding, the two of them. She's riding the bike in uniform, bullet proof vest, gun, everything. And behind her, standing on the pegs of a little kid bike, is this little boy. And he's all smiles. I got a picture. So that happened that day. And two weeks ago, she was in the coffee shop. The same kid was there with a friend, and the friend yelled out across the room, "Hey, Officer X, is it true that you are Jamal's best friend?" He told his friend that his best friend was an officer! That was huge, given the mistrust and downright hatred of police. I think she has been successful in building some trust. Some of the officers are seen in a different light. She has conversations in the shop, "What happens if my friend is arrested? What happens in these different situations?" And she gives the police perspective. So they are learning a ton from just that perspective.

The bike shop, like other PCDA projects and the practice of strategic relocation in general, generated different sorts of social relations across different types of difference and structural inequality, along with additional resources of varying kinds, than were previously typical in the neighborhood. These relations and resources did not magically erase the effects of centuries of racial oppression, disinvestment, and hostility. But they did move in the opposite direction of those forces rather than actively or passively reproducing them.

As witness to the harsh effects of racism, broken trust, abandonment, and animus in interpersonal and institutional relations among his friends and neighbors, Alexei continued expanding his commitment to the bike shop despite weathering "some rough financial times" of the sort many of his neighbors were familiar with, "Like, all right, paying the electric bill can wait. The water company's only going to get some of what I owe them this week." In this limited way, his low-income status mirrored many of his PCDA colleagues, neighbors, and friends, although unlike many of them, his financial position was a matter of mission-driven choice amidst multiple options rather than an involuntary necessity born of racially and economically proscribed pathways to flourishing.

Overall, PCDA's combination of multiracial strategic relocation, multiracial civic and religious organizations with strong Black leadership, youth-centered development focused on empowering and supporting young Black leaders in a neighborhood, and access to mixed-income, multiracial personal networks and institutional partners brought significant resources to bear on the lives of race and class disadvantaged neighborhood youth.

Race and Relocation in Los Angeles and Boston

A pillar of PCDA and CCDA-affiliates across the country, strategic relocation for racial and economic justice was practiced by other multicultural evangelical groups in Los Angeles, Boston, and Portland. In LA's inland empire, strategic relocation was central to Sunrise Community Church, Justice in the City, and related initiatives. The oldest of these initiatives dated back to the 1992 Los Angeles uprising in response to the acquittal of officers charged in the beating of Rodney King, after which a small group of recent college graduates connected to an evangelical campus ministry relocated to a low-income Black and Hispanic neighborhood in south central LA. In the ensuing two decades, over seventy-five additional Asian, white, Black, and Hispanic individuals joined the original group in adjacent blocks and neighborhoods, starting a new multiracial church and nonprofit organization in conjunction with neighborhood residents. "It's a neighbor-driven effort," Will—a forty-something white evangelical man who was part of the original group—told me while having coffee across the street from the underperforming public elementary school his children attended, "a community transformation effort around education and community building and building social capital through community organizing."

The group's first major community organizing effort involved working with neighbors to petition and pressure the city to close a neighborhood liquor store connected to multiple murders, assaults, robberies, and gang-related violence. After a high-profile three-year fight with the city of Los Angeles, neighbors were ultimately successful in getting the liquor store shut down and replaced with a Hispanic grocery store with fresh food, a meat counter, and popular takeout service:

> For our neighbors who participated in that process, that grocery
> store has really become a monument. Both of God's love for our

neighborhood—because he answered a prayer—and of what could happen when we work together. It was all just people from the community. And their sense of ownership of what had happened was very palpable. That was a huge deal . . . because the racial tension [after the riots] was just enormous.

In subsequent years residents tackled a variety of community organizing efforts around public school performance and equity, tutoring and after-school programs, handicap-accessible sidewalk repair and neighborhood beautification projects, and local environmental action initiatives. Like most PCDA-affiliated relocators in Atlanta, Will and his wife—along with their relocating friends and neighbors—send their children to the local public school in solidarity with their neighbors, working together to address racial and economic disparities in educational equity.[86] "It's slow, it's harder than it should be," Will sighed, "that's just the way it is. But we're working together to try and create opportunities for our kids, *all* of our kids, to really reach their full potential."

In a predominantly immigrant Hispanic neighborhood in east Los Angeles, another group of white, Asian, and Hispanic evangelical relocators experienced breakthrough in their community organizing efforts when an accidental game of pick-up football with neighborhood youth in a back alleyway turned into a rallying point for parents to take back their street and apartment complex from violent drug dealers. After struggling for years to find ways to better connect with their neighbors, Cooper—a thirty-seven-year-old white evangelical pastor and church planter—and his team soon found themselves coaching high school football, organizing tutoring programs for second-language neighborhood teens, hiring a bilingual Latina community organizer from the neighborhood to lead a new local nonprofit, and consulting with the local high school on ways to build community and support for struggling Latino immigrant students from disadvantaged backgrounds.

Like Will's group and many Justice in the City initiatives, Cooper's team combined traditional evangelical practices of evangelism and church planting with community organizing for racial and economic equity—the spiritual and social gospel united.[87] However, while sharing an underlying theological motivation, it is common for these groups to bifurcate their efforts institutionally, creating secular nonprofit organizations distinct from their more particularist religious work. Cooper noted the widespread "mistrust" of religion and religious institutions in the community, leading them to form a separate nonprofit. "We have had so much more access into meetings and decision-making," Cooper noted, because, "it's a non-religious nonprofit":

> Our focus right now is organizing the community to really help teenagers do better in school, develop character and actually dream about the future. [Dropping out] is an epidemic around here. 17 percent of parents graduated from high school. Only 50 percent of our kids are graduating from high school. Only 8 percent are going to college. When they leave high school, so many just fall into the pit of the cycle of poverty. So that's what everybody in the community is fired up for—that's the focus of our organizing effort right now. We've got a long way to go. But we're working with 140 students right now and their families, and with the school. We've been able to build real relationships. . . . Our [Latina] lead organizer was a teen mom from the neighborhood. When I step out [Cooper was preparing for a sabbatical year of study], they're [the mom and her partner] going to lead the whole nonprofit. They're diplomats, they can talk to anybody. They're really good at building relationship. Bilingual. They're awesome.

Eight years after a "very messy start" and some "very, very hard years" with "probably three good waves of thinking we had something going before it fell apart," both the church planting and community organizing aspects of the work had finally taken hold—with indigenous neighborhood leadership for both. Chapters 4 and 5 explore in greater detail how Cooper and other multicultural evangelicals navigate commitments to pluralism, evangelism, and religious difference.

In the opposite corner of the country, Kaito—a forty-year-old evangelical Japanese American campus minister and former tech worker—moved with his family into a low-income immigrant African, Black, and Hispanic community in South Boston to establish a multiracial, multigenerational intentional Christian community. At the time of my visit, it was home to over twenty Asian American (Korean, Japanese, Chinese), white, Black, and Hispanic (Colombian, other) individuals and families, most of whom lived together in a multiplex house purchased by Kaito's family around the year 2000. House residents included strategic relocators and a couple of single Black mothers and their children from the neighborhood. Another intentional community member purchased a tri-level house down the street in which she lived with three young single moms in a "co-op living situation," along with a small group of college-aged individuals participating in a Christian discipleship program hosted by the community.

"I wouldn't say we have broad impact" in the neighborhood, Kaito told me during a lengthy interview in a community living area while his son worked on summer homework in an adjacent room. "One of the challenges is there are four languages spoken among our neighbors. So it's always been hard to bring people together. . . . I'm trying to learn songs in French so that our Haitian neighbors"—several of whom participated in one of the community's house churches, for which Kaito often taught and led worship—"can sing in their heart language. My gosh, that is so hard." "The garden has been helpful in that," Kaito continued, gesturing to a recently cultivated community garden plot occupying a formerly vacant lot next door. "It was just a field that people left their trash in. Really ugly. Now it's beautiful. And that helped start a neighborhood monthly meeting. We filled out some grants and receive money from the mayor's office and other places with a few others in the neighborhood. We've done things like outdoor movies, or family game nights, barbecues in the garden. That was fun."

In addition to three house church meetings on Sunday and a weekly Tuesday meal for house residents, community members also attend the monthly neighborhood meetings in the community center across the street, which has developed to the point of having three elected officers along with "some random food committee people." In addition to the community garden, the neighborhood group has initiated voter registration drives and participated in city-level advocacy for expanded pedestrian and bike lanes in the community. "I'd say we'd still love to see more," Kaito noted, nodding to the significant but limited impact of the community's decidedly grassroots character. "It's hard to really make it work. I'm not sure how we're doing. Just to be on record. It's not perfect."

The immense challenge of practicing strategic relocation well, along with inherent limitations of scale, led Kaito and other strategic relocators to emphasize repeatedly the importance of pursuing racial and economic justice through voting, political advocacy, professional institutions, and other means as well:

I think [my campus ministry organization] does decently at incarnational stuff.[88] But I think 95 percent of our students won't [practice strategic relocation]. And they probably shouldn't. At least right out of school. They're not ready. So then the question for them is: How do they influence corporations as employees? As shareholders? How do they vote? How do they talk to people? How does this translate into institutional life—our life in institutions? Have they integrated economic discipleship about poverty and wealth, human dignity, political advocacy on behalf of the poor, into their mind, heart, life? And I think for whatever reason, we haven't. So that is what I'm hoping for: a Christian reengagement with politics and political discipleship. Because sometimes we don't recognize when we're causing distortions or injustices to happen, through policies that we may or may not know about.

The strengths and limits of strategic relocation as a means of pursuing racial justice and democracy, the spiritual and secular meanings and motivations behind the practice of strategic relocation, and the learning experiences and impact of strategic relocation on evangelical practitioners' understanding of and engagement with racial difference and inequality are all themes we will return to below and in later chapters.

Strategic Relocation and Racial Democracy

When practiced with care and social reflexivity, strategic relocation combats neighborhood-based racial segregation and economic inequity while contributing to the racial integration of neighborhoods, civic and religious organizations, institutional leadership and interpersonal social networks. If Anderson and others are right about the imperative of integration as an indispensable means of attaining racial justice and an irreplaceable end of racial democracy, there is reason for advocates of ethical democracy to consider strategic relocation one of many modes of social engagement with potential to challenge interpersonal and systemic racism and inequality in the United States.

Strategic relocation is, however, clearly insufficient in itself as a strategy of individual and collective action in pursuit of racial justice and democracy. Even when strategic relocation is combined with robust social, political, and economic resource mobilization and redistribution—as it is to varying degrees in the cases described above—it remains, as Kaito and others recognized, a relatively rare, difficult, time-intensive, and small-scale intervention when viewed from the perspective of the historically sedimented and multi-scalar structures of racial domination and division that characterize life in the contemporary United States. To challenge and transform these structures, many tools are needed, of which increased residential, religious, institutional, and interpersonal racial integration with justice is just one.

These include, but are not limited to (in no particular order): voting to increase the racial and multicultural representativeness of our elected officials, opposing tacitly or overtly racist public and political leaders, funding and participating in equitable housing and education initiatives, channeling money and resources to institutions owned and led by people of color, increasing leadership and equitable representation of people of color in predominantly-white institutions, advocating for criminal justice reform and increased public investment in race and class disadvantaged neighborhoods, participating in constructive protest and social movement activism alongside leaders and people of color, actively learning and working to combat racial bias in one's self and interpersonal relationships, and seeking out racially integrated settings and situations in which to learn and participate with humility in reciprocal relations across difference, among many others.

Strategic relocation accomplishes or facilitates some of these practices; it is not required for all of them. Nor is strategic relocation (or racial integration more generally) a viable, desirable, or achievable practice in all cases.[89] For example, there is legitimate warrant for preserving Black- or people of color–only spaces and institutions in light of pervasive ongoing white racial privilege and prejudice in many settings across the United States.[90] The imperative of integration—derived as it is from pragmatist and contextual, rather than deontological and universalist, principles—is limited and conditional, requiring flexible negotiation and adjustment to different social, historical, and institutional settings.[91] Strategic relocation requires certain constraints and conditions to be justifiable and effective as an ethical democratic practice.

Some of these conditions and best practices emerge through examination of the cases under investigation in the pages above; others emerge from examination of cases and data presented in subsequent chapters. First, strategic relocation works best when groups are invited into the neighborhood by existing residents and remain accountable to existing or emergent structures of neighborhood authority. Second, in historically Black or other neighborhoods of color, the number of new white residents must be limited. Third, in light of historic and ongoing patterns racial segregation, oppression, and disinvestment, the practice of strategic relocation must be intentional and long-term in order to promote investment of time and resources necessary to listen and learn from existing residents; build trust, solidarity, and reciprocal relations across difference; discover effective and honoring ways to invest resources and gifts; and begin to see, think, and feel racial identity, difference, and injustice in new ways. Fourth, new strategic relocators must be committed to an initial extended period of quiescence and learning through informal and/or formal training in strategic relocation, community assets and challenges, and their relation to larger structures of racial, economic, and social inequality. Fifth, strategic relocators must exhibit and/or develop capacities for humility, conviction, and transposable and deep social reflexivity.[92] Sixth and finally, in light of these conditions (and as Kaito and others noted above), not everyone should be expected, allowed, or encouraged to practice strategic relocation.

When these conditions are met, however, evidence suggests that strategic relocation can achieve many goods. It establishes new multiracial institutional and interpersonal networks through which economic redistribution and exchange can occur. It increases bridging social capital and solidarity across difference that increase neighborhood collective efficacy and more equitable access to resources.[93] It facilitates the formation of new psychological and social skills and habits more conducive to racial justice and democracy.[94] It generates new habits of thinking and feeling race among structurally privileged white Americans, which—as we will explore more fully in Chapter 5—can lead to real changes in personal and political belief and practice. It increases resources and opportunities in race and class disadvantaged neighborhoods. As John Perkins's classic formulation suggests, it affords opportunities for reconciliation and redistribution across racial lines.[95] And for many strategic relocators and their neighbors and partners, it is a way to participate in efforts to advance racial and economic justice in a deeply committed, personal, meaningful, and sometimes costly way, while also—in the words of many of my research participants—being a source of transformation, redemption, healing, and joy.

3

Engaging Poverty and Inequality

Ethical democracy calls for people to have broadly equal access to the material and social means necessary to participate as equals in democratic public and political life.[1] Such means include but go beyond subsistence-level requirements for food, housing, jobs, security, health care, and fair treatment under the law to include more advanced human capabilities and opportunities for flourishing and self-government.[2] Individuals and groups cannot participate as equals in democratic life if they lack standing or access to the social and material goods necessary for the development of empowered individual and collective self-government and well-being.[3] As such, poverty and economic inequity are grave threats to ethical democracy. This chapter investigates multicultural evangelical approaches to combating poverty and economic inequality across the country through grassroots community development, community organizing, public service, and political advocacy work—work that is relatively uncommon and underreported among evangelical practitioners and observers. The first two sections focus on grassroots food security and community development efforts in Atlanta (The Food Co-op) and Portland (Neighborhood Partners), exploring how multicultural evangelical individuals and groups in these settings enact ethical democratic principles of empowerment, participatory governance, pluralism, redistribution, and reciprocal learning and solidarity across difference while remaining rooted in particularistic religious convictions. The next section builds on Chapter 2's investigation of "gentrification with justice" as a strategy of economic empowerment in disadvantaged neighborhoods, tracing its limits and potentials through empirical examples and comparisons to other influential approaches to grassroots social transformation, such as asset-based community development and the "iron rule" of democratic community organizing.[4] After briefly describing other public service, financial giving, and advocacy-based approaches to combating poverty and economic inequality—one of which (Christians for the Common Good) will be expanded upon at length in Chapter 4—I describe how multicultural evangelical research participants answered questions about the biblical view of poverty, economic inequality,

Good News for Common Goods. Wes Markofski, Oxford University Press. © Oxford University Press 2023.
DOI: 10.1093/oso/9780197659694.003.0004

the role of government, and the role of individual Christians or the church in addressing them. The chapter concludes with a summary and assessment, from the perspective of ethical democracy, of the strengths and weaknesses of different approaches to combating poverty and economic inequality that were observed in my research and are popular among multicultural evangelicals and non-evangelicals alike.

The Food Co-op

I pull up to a small, historic red brick church tucked away in a residential neighborhood in southeast Atlanta on a sunny morning in April. I am struck once again by the immaculately preserved Victorian homes—resplendent with vibrant color, meticulous landscaping, and bubbling fountains—that populate part of this block. The neighborhoods I passed through to get here alternate between blocks like this one—with beautiful white and Black-owned historic homes from which middle-class residents often used to walk to Turner Field to catch a baseball game—to blocks dominated by vacant lots and run-down buildings with barred windows and doors, abundant barbed wire fencing, pawn shops and corner stores, and seemingly non-stop police surveillance. In this partially gentrified section of Atlanta, poor and privileged Black and white residents live blocks away but worlds apart. As I depart my vehicle and make my way towards the church, I am greeted by two Black men sitting on the front steps, and again by several Black women making their way to a side alley that will soon be bustling with food co-op members unloading this week's delivery from the old adapted pick-up truck with homemade wooden side- and back-boards that co-op members use to transport food from the Atlanta Food Bank.

Every other week, representatives from fifty low-income households converge on this little church and proceed downstairs to the basement, where they gather with fellow co-op members to unload the truck, organize food into boxes based on family size, collect membership dues, take care of co-op business, catch up with friends and acquaintances, and share in a devotional or reflection time guided loosely by fellow co-op members. At times, the co-ops welcome visitors to share information about public health, education, or economic opportunities available to co-op members and their neighbors. Because of the demographics of southeast Atlanta, nearly all the members of this food co-op are Black, as are members of the five other co-ops that together provide food security, jobs, leadership opportunities, support, and social connections for 300 low-income families. The co-ops are member-run, with an elected leadership and one paid coordinator per co-op, along with other paid part-time administrators who help oversee the entire co-op program while also being members themselves. These positions are filled by middle-aged Black women—often mothers or grandmothers—who constitute the majority of active co-op participants. As such, "the members themselves are in charge of the success of the co-op."[5] There also younger women and men of varying ages—mostly in their thirties to fifties—who are regular participants.

Neighborhood opinion concerning the co-op is mixed. In the early 1990s, before gentrification hit, nobody noticed or cared about the low-income persons who were drawn to this little church and its food program. They blended right into the neighborhood. After gentrification, the story changed. Some neighbors have tried to shut down the co-ops, complaining of loitering and noise violations and worries about attracting the "wrong sort of people" (that is, Black and poor) at neighborhood association meetings of this increasingly affluent block.[6] There are murmurs of crime, theft, disorder, fear, unease. Other neighbors, however, defend the co-ops. "They were here before we were!" they argue, "We want to be this kind of neighborhood. They do good work!" After spending many months here among co-op participants, I cannot imagine a single neighborhood or community in the world that would not benefit from the presence, knowledge, and work of the people I have met here.

On this morning, the food truck is running late, so I refresh acquaintances and make new connections with co-op members as we wait together for the truck to arrive. The room buzzes with conversation, laughter, and encouragement as members catch up on each other's lives and families. There is a strong sense of community and connection. When the truck arrives, members snap into action. Many members move with the quickness and ease born of routinized coordinated action made efficient through habit and spontaneous divisions of labor, while others mill about asking for instructions and looking for ways to pitch in. Some members form a human chain to unload boxes of food off the truck, some prepare empty cardboard boxes into which food allocations will be distributed to each co-op member according to family size—single, double, and triple boxes for different size households—while others begin to distribute food into boxes equitably by food type: meat, vegetables, soup, cereal, canned goods, snacks, and so on. A few elderly and disabled persons remain seated, carrying on conversations—some lively and boisterous, others intense and personal—with each other and other co-op members as they work.

A little more than an hour later, the boxes are filled and an elected leader fights to gain the room's attention above the energetic buzz of conversation and laughter bouncing off cinder block basement walls painted colorfully with cityscape and neighborhood murals. We begin with a "devotion"—a mix of prayer, song, and scripture reading that varies from co-op to co-op, depending on the composition of its membership and chosen leaders. Like many other African American communities across the United States, the co-ops frequently enact familiar styles of communication and interaction from Black church practices in nonchurch contexts,[7] despite the fact that the co-ops are open to all and include members that do not identify as Christian. As long-time pastor, neighborhood resident, and founding director of the co-op program Pastor James insists,

> We cannot use food to proselytize. We make it clear that we serve people in the name of Jesus, but we also make it very clear that we serve everyone with respect and care—regardless of who they are or what they believe. Still, a lot of people will call [this] their church—even if they never come through the door on Sunday.[8]

Today's meeting hews to the familiar script. The Black female co-op leader fighting for our attention begins devotional time with an invitation, "If you want to join in you can, but you don't have to." She then asks, "Anyone here that wants to bless us with a song?"

A woman across the room stands up: "Everybody knows this song. Y'all can stand again. Jesus, help me out!" She then begins singing acapella, her voice quickly rising in resonance with the syncopated clapping and voices of fellow co-op members who join her in reprising a centuries-old Black spiritual turned familiar campfire song:

> Come by here, my Lord, come by here.
> Come by here, my Lord, come by here.
> Come by here, my Lord, come by here.
> Oh Lord, come by here.
>
> Somebody needs you, Lord, come by here.
> Somebody needs you, Lord, come by here.
> Somebody needs you, Lord, come by here.
> Oh Lord, come by here. . . .

The song crescendos into loud clapping and exclamations of praise—
"Hallelujah! Amen! Yes, Lord! Thank you, Lord!"—before another leader
channels the group's energy into call-and-response prayer. "I'm gonna pray,"
she begins, "and if I say anything you're in agreement with, say Amen":

> Let us just continue to be one in love [*"Yes, Yes, All right!"*]. We must love
> one another. Love! We can see how we were hugging Lord: many of us had
> not *had* a hug today! [*emphasis original, with cheers, clapping, "Yes!"*].... We
> thank you for the pastor here, Lord God, all the members of this congre-
> gation, continue to bless them, because they're doing a great thing for the
> community Lord God.... Bless our families and our communities. In Jesus'
> Name! Amen. [*Clapping, cheers, "Amen, Amen. Hallelujah."*]

The devotional leader proceeds to pray for co-op leaders and specific
individuals who are hospitalized, sick, in trouble, or needing help. Several
women start praying in tongues. Another begins a spontaneous hymn,
beautifully sung with remarkable range, with more clapping, singing, and
exclamations of "Hallelujah!" interjected at opportune moments.

As the song reaches its conclusion, the devotional leader transitions the
group out of prayer and song: "Good morning! Thank you for your participation." She then invites another female leader to read a Bible passage, Psalm
24, before turning things over to the co-op coordinator for announcements
and co-op business. Several lost and found items are discussed. Members are
invited to attend and spread the word about the annual co-op fundraiser, a
gospel music extravaganza with a $5 suggested donation. If members could
afford to set 50 cents aside at each co-op meeting, the co-op coordinator tells
us, it would add up to $5 by the day of the event. This can be done on your
own, or by giving 50 cents to the coordinator who will keep a record of individual contributions alongside the usual food distribution and members fee
record keeping. We are also told the next meeting will be the last chance to
sign someone up for the co-op wait list, after which the list will be closed due
to high demand. It often takes a year or more for new members to be able to
join a co-op, either through spaces opening up in existing co-ops or, more
commonly, a new fifty-household co-op group being formed.

The expansion of the co-op program from one fifty-household co-op to
the current six, not counting other groups that have been trained to run
similar co-ops around greater Atlanta and beyond, was driven by co-op
members themselves. Three years after the launch of the first co-op, it had a

waiting list of 112 families desiring to join. Two female members of the first co-op approached Pastor James with an idea to apply for a denominational "self-development grant" available to "poor women and women of color" to help start a second food co-op. "These two women said they wanted to see these folks begin to obtain food."[9] They wrote and submitted a two-page handwritten grant application and were awarded funds to help cover food costs and miscellaneous expenses for one year, along with a "modest stipend" for the two women who would organize and lead the new co-op. "The idea to start a 2nd co-op was entirely their idea, and it grew out of their concern for others who do not have enough food."

After answering some questions about the closing of the waiting list, a food co-op administrator—a small, slender, no-nonsense African refugee in her fifties with tight black curls and distinctive accent—moves on to a pressing matter, theft, which is an infrequent but semiregular occurrence at co-op gatherings. This particular theft involved the loss of one member's allotted portion of food at the previous co-op meeting:

> Somebody at last co-op decided to take X's box; to take it home. It's the second time. [*Murmurs of concern and disapproval.*] We need to pray. Can't let the devil come in here. . . . If that person is a member of this co-op, stop it. Cause if you got your box and you got somebody else's box [*Pause, members jump in, "That's wrong, that's wrong."*].

The coordinator moves on:

> Please let's keep each other in prayer. Let's keep all the co-ops in prayer. We've had a lot of sickness in our co-ops. We've had death in our co-ops. Let's hold each other up. Let's pray for each other. Now starting next week, this person over there is going to be doing what I'm doing. [*Clapping, "Hallelujah!", as a new co-op coordinator is introduced*]. She's going to be the one telling you how many to put in a box, what to put in a box. . . . Any questions? Any comments?

One member asks about the availability of a specific food item that isn't in this week's box. Another mentions a neighbor's complaint that someone was blocking the driveway. The coordinator reminds the group that an extra allotment of corn and peaches are available for $2. A baby starts crying, and the meeting ends.

The Food Co-op: Operations and Impact

Taken together, the Food Co-op has made it possible for 300 low-income households in southeast Atlanta to move from food scarcity to food security, while also providing access to jobs and skill development, social connections and community resources, and fighting social isolation and homelessness by providing enough low-cost food to free up money for co-op members to pay rent, mortgage, and utility bills to keep them and their families in their homes.[10] Through its partnership with the Atlanta Food Bank and other small grants and charitable donations, the Food Co-op is able to provide over $500,000 worth of food to co-op member households each year while operating with food budget of just over $40,000. Members pay a $4 program fee every other week and receive over $100 worth of food for a household of four to seven people (larger households receive more), or between $3,500 and $6,000 worth of food per year.[11] All members have household incomes that fall below the federal government poverty guideline, with typical incomes ranging from $600–$1200 per month.[12] Sixty-eight percent of members have annual incomes of less than $11,000. As a Food Co-op document notes:

> At this level of income, many food choices are either not within budget, or of a less healthy source. Individuals must place reliance on food pantries or other giveaway sources from which they often do not have a choice over the types or amount of food received to meet their needs. With our first six co-ops, we have already seen the difference in changing these causes of hunger.[13]

Every other week, over 3,000 lbs. of food are ordered, picked up, unloaded, sorted into boxes, and distributed by and to representatives of each fifty-member co-op household in the manner described above.

Co-op members report enormous benefits from their involvement. 89 percent of members say they "always" or "usually" have enough food in their homes, compared to 39 percent before joining the co-op.[14] One member reported, "Before I got here, we had to space our food out little by little. We had to eat twice a day. But since I got here, my kids eat three times a day." Another told me:

> It really helps. . . . From medical bills, household bills, other bills, it's hard to budget all of that when you've got only this little amount. It's a lot better

[with the co-op]. I'm a diabetic, so sure, there's a lot of the food that I cannot eat, that I cannot use, but I always give it to someone in my neighborhood. Or I'll call [my partner's] daughter and tell her to come pick it up, because she has little kids. So I share. And if you pay an extra $2, then you can get extra fruits and vegetables. So that's my big thing, because I love fruit, and I love vegetables.

Sixty-two percent of co-op members report sharing food each month with people outside their own household, compared to 29 percent before becoming co-op members.[15] The food security benefits of co-op membership spill over from member households to others in the community.

These benefits are not limited to dramatic increases in food security. Co-op members also report significant improvements in mental health, wellness, human and social capital as a result of their involvement. Eighty-five percent of co-op members report feeling strong connections with others, compared to 55 percent before joining the co-op.[16] Seventy-four percent of co-op members report it being "very true" that they "feel important to others" compared to 52 percent before joining. When I asked one member, "Do you enjoy coming to the co-op?" she responded:

Oh yeah. Even if you're not a Christian, you will get spiritually uplifted. . . . A lot of times I've come and been depressed, or going through something bad, you know, but I would always be uplifted by the prayers and singing and things. I've gotten to know a lot of people.

Another co-op member recalled:

I was raising my baby sister's five kids at the time, I had my grandkids in the house, it was about 11 or 12 of us in the house. My husband had had a bad accident and was not working. Our finances went from kind of up here [holding hand high], to down here [lowering hand down]. Needed some help. If I didn't have the co-op, I probably would be in a hospital somewhere because it's stressful. . . . It's not the kind of place like a pantry where you just go and get food. Take this morning. I had a sad place in my heart. But when I got to the co-op, I had a little joy, you know, just a hug. Sometimes that's all you need, just a, "Oh, I'm so glad to see you! How you doing?!" Everything is real personal there. It's like having an extended family. If someone is not there, you notice it immediately and you wonder, "Where's so-and-so?", and you love 'em, and you want to be there because you're a part of this extended family. Some of them are closer than family. When you're sitting there and waiting on the truck to arrive, you get sit back and you get to laugh together, catch up on what's going on with a person, and what's comin' up in their life. You also get to cry a little, sometime. It's like, when one hurt, all hurt.

Yet another reported that The Food Co-op "saved my life. It made me feel like I'm worthy. It gave me my *me* back."[17]

Co-op leaders are well aware of the material and social psychological benefits that accrue to members beyond the primary goal of food security, benefits that standard benevolence-based food pantry approaches are hard-pressed to provide:

Pastor James: The first goal is to create food security. Our sense is that if people have enough food, it frees them in many other areas. They are not worried at the end of the month if they're going to have enough food for their children or grandchildren. Another piece is . . . charging a member-ship fee and contributing energy to help one another. There is no sense of "I'm getting a handout here." It's more "I am making a contribution."[18]

Sybil (Co-op member and coordinator): We have what we call a steering committee. The steering committee is the link between the staff and the people. Some steering committee members take care of the money, some help with food, and things like that. Others are more like, "I want to sing, I want to read the scripture, I want to pray." . . . One of the differences be-tween a co-op and a food pantry is ownership. People in the co-ops feel like they *own* this, it's theirs, so they decide what happens. If we just want to come in, put the food in the boxes and grab the boxes and go, we can do that. . . . But for some people, the devotional time that we have downstairs is the only church they have. And for some people, it's their gift, so they want to share their gift. That's another thing we focus on in the co-ops, you know: let's share gifts. What gift do you have? And, for some people, their gifts have never been acknowledged or appreciated.[19] . . . Even though we are not saying if you are not a Christian you cannot be a member.

The Food Co-op began as a standard food pantry, in which people of means donated time and goods for people in need to receive as charity. This arrange-ment quickly soured:

With food pantries, our members report that they often feel humiliated, have to wait in long lines, have no choice of food, and usually receive enough for only three days or less. However, when you create community, it makes a huge difference. When people are working together, there is a sense of ownership and dignity. And you can do programing that you wouldn't be able to do if you just had people walking in and out. We've had demonstrations on how to do healthy cooking; we've had the Morehouse School of Medicine come and make presentations about how to deal with diabetic issues, basic nutrition, and so forth.[20]

During my time at the co-ops, I witnessed several health, education, and economic assistance announcements and short presentations by local community partners and allies, all of which were respectfully conducted and well-received by co-op members. One as-yet-unrealized programming idea in the works was an "Urban People's Academy" that would use The Food Co-op as a vehicle enabling disadvantaged persons to educate political, educational, religious, and nonprofit leaders and others with the experience-based knowledge and perspectives of co-op members on issues relating to poverty and economic inequality, thereby creating reciprocal two-way—rather than one-way—channels of communication, learning, and power. "Our people have a *lot* to say," Pastor James told me, "A lot to teach. That people at the seminaries and universities need to hear." He mentioned a particular co-op member as an example, "She's uneducated, her health is poor, but she is *so* intelligent. I would not be surprised if she had a genius IQ. She's brilliant." My thirteen in-depth interviews and countless conversations, advice, and prayer received from co-op members certainly corroborated Pastor James's experience.

In addition to increased food security, the co-ops provided drivers and co-op coordinators a small income stream and meaningful work along with food security and social connection. These were precious commodities, as Brandon—a Black co-op member in his forties whose history with The Food Co-op and Peachtree Community Development Association (PCDA) spanned two decades—relayed to me. Brandon was The Food Co-op's primary truck driver, picking up and delivering food from the Atlanta Food Bank several times a week. He worked sixteen hours a week on average, some paid and some volunteer. When I asked Brandon why he spent so much time at the co-op beyond his paid hours driving the truck, he said, "I tell you what, I'm welcome here. I know I'm not gonna get myself in any trouble. Putting back in the community. . . . The co-op, they've helped me a lot." "How so?" He responded, "Well for food. Spiritual things sometimes. When I need to talk to somebody, I know I can come talk to [Pastor] James about it. He won't let it get any further than I want it to go." I asked, "You trust him?" "Yeah," Brandon answered, "You have to be very careful who you give your personal information to."

Trust for Brandon was a rare and valued commodity.[21] At the time of my interview, Brandon was an ex-felon with an outstanding warrant for a minor parole violation. "I haven't been reporting because of my finances," he told me, by which he meant he didn't have the money to pay for transportation to meet his parole officer and search for jobs as mandated by his program. He was searching for additional work and soon to report to his parole officer, but he was not sanguine about his prospects:

> How am I gonna be able to survive when, three times a week, you're sending me on job leads knowing that I'm not bonded? So basically I feel like they should go ahead and bond convicted felons before they release them.[22] Jobs are hard to find out here. You can't get out of prison and get a job today or tomorrow. They want everything to happen so quickly. They want to send you out looking for jobs with no transportation. I'm like, how can I get out there with no transportation? And the government don't have funding for parolees or convicts. They're like, "Taxpayers do not want to put their money towards transportation for a convict."

Brandon's trouble with the law was drug related. "They gave me ten years. Gave me too much time for the type of drugs." When I noted the prevalence of racial disparities in sentencing for drug crimes, he retorted, "I don't wanna say that. I would just say my record—I hold total responsibility with the way this went." He recounted his experience of judges "giving me breaks, giving me breaks, giving me breaks," before finally deciding, "Okay, time's up . . . we have been giving you a break, but this time, we're gonna put you on recidivist. My record speaks for itself."

Brandon was a universally known, trusted, and well-liked presence at all the food co-ops where he participated, worked, and volunteered. He helped many elderly women and disabled persons get their boxes home from the co-op on a regular basis. He often volunteered to help unloading the food truck when he wasn't driving. He helped co-op members move on his days off. He sorted boxes and cleaned up after co-op meetings. He kept in touch with coordinators about problems, needs, and upcoming events. He mediated disputes among co-op members and kept a watchful eye on the building. People would go to him with problems and concerns related to co-op and other business. The co-op relied on Brandon as much as Brandon relied on the co-op. Mutual help and benefit flowed freely both ways. Participatory governance, member empowerment, and "asset-based community development" were more than just philosophies espoused by co-op leaders and members, they were consistently practiced on-the-ground realities.

The Food Co-op: Cooperation and Conflict

Like Brandon, Sybil's relationship with The Food Co-op spans decades, with periods of connection and periods of absence. Sybil's absences were due to her refugee status, which involved a short-term stay in the United States, followed by a stint in Ghana after the denial of her application for political asylum, and back to the United States after she was eventually granted status as a legal resident. Sybil is a fifty-five-year-old Black woman and mother of four adult children. In addition to being a co-op member herself, Sybil coordinates one fifty-member-household co-op and is one of two primary administrators—both Black women—who have part-time jobs overseeing all six of the program's fifty-member-household co-ops. These two women work with the elected leaders of individual co-ops, resolve conflicts and problems among co-op leaders and members, fill out monthly reports on food distribution for the food bank, and oversee record keeping and administration in partnership with Pastor James. Sybil is looked up to by her fellow co-op members and coordinators as a tough, smart, open, no-nonsense leader, colleague, and friend.

As she shared with me during an in-depth interview, Sybil's relationship with The Food Co-op and Pastor James has been dramatic and transformative:

> I'm from South Africa originally. You know refugee life: it takes you everywhere . . . Tanzania, Ghana . . . I had to move the kids to Ghana because I couldn't get asylum. I became sick there, but [Pastor James's] church communicated with me while I was in Ghana. They sent me packages and some money. I came back to the U.S. and I've been a member since then. My kids grew up in this church . . . my children still consider this their church,

and consider James their pastor. My daughter said when she gets married, she wants James to perform the ceremony.

A refugee family finding support and community in a church that becomes family is not particularly unusual. Because of Sybil's experience with racial oppression in South Africa, however, her experience with Pastor James and the multiracial church out of which The Food Co-op was born was wildly unexpected:

> I come from a background of oppression. And when I first came to the United States, I *really* didn't [long pause]: I hated white people. I just hated them. But you know, God took that hate away from me because I ended up right in the middle of all these white people. And they embraced me. I mean Bill and Jan, [*two white former church members and co-op workers*], when I came back to the United States sick, and I was going for surgery and I didn't have a place to live—because my step-mother had died and my father had messed up stuff so we didn't have a place to live—when I went to the hospital, Jan and Bill took in my eight-month-old daughter. And I didn't know them from nothing. . . . And another couple took my two older daughters. And they were not racist people. They are the most caring and loving and open-minded people, people that just wanted the right thing to be done. They wanted everybody to be treated like God's people regardless of color or whatever. . . . My mom and the people back home were like, "Huh? White people? They do that?" . . . They were the most progressive people, just phenomenal people you know, who want everybody to have their rights.

Through relationships developed at the church and The Food Co-op, Sybil experienced antiracist white people for the first time, relationships that have proven themselves over decades of mutual friendship, challenge, and trust. Sybil characterized her work with Pastor James and other food co-op leaders in similar terms:

> The thing about James is, I don't have to bite my tongue. You know, whatever's on my mind, I say it. If he's wrong, he's wrong, and it has been like that with the church and co-ops. . . . We talk, we have political discussions, and we agree or disagree, and it's okay. So that has been very, very good for

me. I don't feel like I'm in a place where white people want to tell me what to do or how to feel and all that. I'm treated like a human being who has a mind of their own.

As in any authentic human community—not least those involving the distribution of resources and responsibilities across race and class lines—disagreement and conflict was not uncommon among co-op members and leaders. These took myriad forms—from complaints about unfair distribution of food box allotments, to accusations of theft and shirking payments or co-op member responsibilities, to disagreements over co-op policies and procedures, to co-op members challenging the authority of newly elected co-op coordinators, to various personal disagreements and grievances—all of which I witnessed during my months at the co-op, along with the co-ops' impressive capacity for effective, accountable, responsible, collective problem-solving and conflict resolution across all levels of participation. As described in the opening vignette, co-op members took collective responsibility to uphold co-op rules while prioritizing restorative rather than punitive responses to violations. Co-op leaders listened to members and made changes to individual and collective practices.

I directly observed roughly a dozen conflicts of note during my time working with the co-ops, all of which were resolved through sometimes heated and extended, sometimes brief and apologetic, conversations among co-op members and leaders. Co-op members typically resolved conflicts amongst themselves without any appeals for assistance from leadership. A small number of conflicts required the involvement of one or two co-op managers—primarily involving theft or complaints of unfair food distribution. One of these conflicts took several conversations to address, and was the only conflict in which co-op member-managers considered appealing to Pastor James for assistance. After a brief query, Pastor James expressed confidence that the member-managers could resolve the issue themselves, which they did. By all accounts, co-op members and their self-selected leaders effectively ran the co-ops themselves, working through conflict through well-established practices and norms of mutual accountability, affection, trust, and openness to critique. In this and other ways, co-op members and leaders practiced the sort of resource redistribution, participatory governance, social reflexivity and bridge-building across differences that are essential components of reflexive evangelicalism and ethical democracy.[23]

Scaling Up: Food Co-op America

Due to its long-term success across multiple economic, social, and spiritual dimensions, other groups and organizations have been increasingly drawn to the food co-op model as a source of inspiration and training for similar initiatives in greater Atlanta and beyond. One organization, Food Co-op America, grew directly out of increased demands for training and access to food co-ops beyond The Food Co-op's origins in southeast Atlanta. The organization's director, Reverend Cindy, "fell in love with the program" and left her job in faith-based social services after attending a co-op training event led by Pastor James. "He needed help!" she added, laughing, "I mean he was having so many people come and call about this. And I said, well, I'll do some consulting with you for a little while." After spending two years working with Pastor James to run training events and co-op expansions under The Food Co-op umbrella, Reverend Cindy was authorized to start a new nonprofit, Food Co-op America, to expand the geographic reach of the model through training and new co-op launches. "My part of the work is growth," Cindy told me over lunch with her adult daughter—who also assisted with Food Co-op America—on the eve of the organization's launch:

> There is such an incredible opportunity to spread the co-op movement. Because it is so simple. Believe it or not, there are probably 10,000+ food pantries in this country, but nobody that we could find is doing this. . . . So there seems to be a need for someone to focus on growth. We're doing that in two ways. One is to go out and run them ourselves and take the co-ops to the people where they live [around the city of Atlanta]. And the other one is training people how to run it themselves.

Pastor James, Reverend Cindy, Sybil, Etta, and other co-op member-leaders have since trained hundreds of individuals and organizations from Georgia, Colorado, Indiana, Connecticut, North Carolina, Wisconsin, Tokyo, Hong Kong, and elsewhere.

I visited several newer Atlanta-area food co-ops run by Food Co-op America [FCA] to see how they compared to the original co-ops that have been running in southeast Atlanta for decades. For the most part, they looked quite similar in format and spirit, if somewhat less established in culture and member-ownership. FCA food co-ops mirrored the original Food

Co-op co-ops across multiple dimensions: they provided meaningful part-time work and income to co-op members, offered voluntary devotional times that some members participated in and others never attended, were religiously based but respectful of nonreligious members, were predominantly led and utilized by women, became sites of broader health and education initiatives, and were significant sources of social connection and capital for many participants. They also focused their programming elements more specifically on health. "Since the co-ops are based around food," Reverend Cindy noted, "and there is such an incredible national emergency around food and health, I like to focus a lot of the educational efforts around that."

Food Co-op America was involved in running twenty food co-ops in the greater Atlanta area, six of them directly overseen by Reverend Cindy. Many FCA co-ops are hosted in low-income apartment complexes across the Atlanta metro region:

> We started off with the idea that if we go into apartments, if people are members of a food co-op, they should be able stay in the apartments longer, which is good for the landlord, which is good for everybody. We should actually be able to show retention rates. Which we have been able to do.

Because of the win-win nature of the arrangement, Reverend Cindy anticipated that "key landlords would hear about this and they would be falling all over themselves to sponsor a co-op" in their apartment complexes. "But it has not turned out that way," Cindy sighed. Apart from a few mission-driven apartment owners from Christian backgrounds, "when I've talked to other apartment owners, they can't get past the bottom line." Launching a new fifty-household food co-op requires modest start-up costs that FCA asks apartment complex landlords to cover, since, Reverend Cindy tells them, "You know what, at the end of the day, I know you're making money off of this." However, relatively few landlords have been interested. "If I really talk to them, they would let me go and raise money" to cover start-up costs, Reverend Cindy said, but she expressed disappointment that so few landlords were willing to enter into a partnership with their tenants and FCA to produce an outcome—increased food security, health, and residential stability—that would benefit tenant and landlord alike.[24]

Charlie, father of four adult children and son of an African American man and American Indian woman who had recently relocated to Atlanta from Boston, was one of the apartment tenants who joined a food co-op immediately upon its launch a year prior to our meeting. In addition to helping him get through the month with adequate food and money for bills, Charlie appreciated the sense of respect and positive social connections he experienced at the co-op. He quickly became a backbone volunteer at his own co-op, then at another co-op, and after a few months he was offered a job as the primary food truck driver for the six co-ops directly overseen by Reverend Cindy. He typically worked between sixteen to twenty-four hours a week with the co-ops, which helped supplement his modest income from social security. "It has been fun," Charlie told me during a cigarette break between food truck unloading, "I'm learning a lot. Meeting a lot of great people."

When I asked him what he thought of the work, Charlie launched into an unexpectedly personal account of how the co-ops had influenced him:

> This work is great. You know Miss Cindy and Miss Cassie [program assistant]? It's enhanced my life. Because you know, I'm a single man and sometimes when you're a single man, you become lonely and you act kinda doggish. Mannish. But being around them has changed me, because they're religious-based people. . . . That's how this job has helped me. Plus, when you get around some people, you see they miss the whole purpose. Whatever you give them, they're never satisfied. . . . That kind of stuff can turn you off a little bit, when you see people who are just ungrateful. Then you got the other people, you give them a basket of food and they start crying because they're so grateful. So that can fill your heart. With the unappreciative people, I'm like, "You're missing it! You're missing it!" Because Cindy is too nice. She's like the real McCoy, a real Christian, not just putting on airs. So, all in all, just being around them two ladies, it changed my attitude on life. They've been a blessing in my life. I've enjoyed this. I've got to the point now where if they couldn't afford me, I'd do it for free.

Charlie proceeded to discuss his disenchantment with the "million-dollar" Christianity of the Bible Belt: "Jesus wasn't no millionaire. But they got these millionaire preachers living in these million-dollar houses down here in the Bible Belt. You know what I'm saying? Or it's football: the church of football [*laughing and shaking head ruefully*]."

The Food Co-op: Deserving and Undeserving

While a co-op member himself, Charlie's comments on what he perceived to be "grateful" versus "ungrateful" co-op members reflects long-standing debates and distinctions concerning the "deserving" and "undeserving" poor.[25] The food co-ops were not immune from such controversies, whether internally among rule-breaking and rule-following co-op members or externally between The Food Co-op and its neighbors. Pastor James reflected on these distinctions during a season of heightened conflict and tension with residential neighbors surrounding The Food Co-op building:

> Some of the neighbors around the church building are not too happy with us. They think that reaching out to people in need creates trouble. The neighbors on the west are angry, saying we trash the place and invite thieves into our building. Their home and cars have been broken into several times. They have moved and rent the house out now. They've really been on the warpath this past week, coming in and yelling at Bill and me. "Why don't you only invite in the deserving ones? The undeserving don't merit one bit of your attention!" Our neighbor across the street on the east is questioning whether we should have our meal [a weekly meal followed by optional Bible study frequented largely by homeless Black men] and our co-ops. She, too, has experienced theft and break-ins of her car. I find it hard to believe that this woman, who is Black and who not that long ago couldn't have bought into this neighborhood because of her race, is so ready to ban others—and she is vocal about being a Christian. Our neighbor on the north is one of the officers of the neighborhood association. I think it would be fair to say that he and most of the association place high priority on raising property values and fighting crime. They don't seem too concerned about diversity and those in need; these are not neighbors they want to have anything to do with. We (our co-op members) invited him and the other officers of that association to a dinner so we could get acquainted and let them know what we are doing. He said no . . .

> Of course, we didn't invent crime or bring it into our neighborhood; conditions that breed poverty and crime are some of the reasons I came here. . . . Poor neighborhoods increasingly surround [our neighborhood]. Whether I do anything or not, the "undeserving" are going to keep making

forays into the area. And I'll be honest with you—for the most part, I can't tell the "deserving" from the "undeserving"; all of them are people, my neighbors, who live in this area. So, do we quit caring for everyone so we can keep the "undeserving" away? We have redoubled our efforts to make sure our people are not throwing down trash after our Wednesday meal. The crime is not OK, for sure, but we're not responsible for it; in fact, I would like to think we are working in our own way to stop it. Several alcoholics and drug dealers have been converted; some who were thieves are no longer; and we provide for people so they don't need to steal. I admit the problems get to me sometime, too; I have no magical immunity from them. My wheelbarrow was stolen last week, the hubcaps from the car two nights ago, our trash herbie's been stolen twice, our home was broken into, our cars have been too. And there are other concerns. . . .

I have to say, though, sometimes it seems at least an aspect of "the problem" is not the people who are poor, but the people who think they know who are the "deserving" and the "undeserving." Who of us is "deserving?" What does that mean? Do the scriptures say, "Love your *deserving* neighbor as yourself?" I see little movement among the more advantaged residents to get to know neighbors of poverty and color and their concerns and needs and to be neighbors to them. What's more, there is a readiness to see those of us who do as some sort of "enemy." None of this exempts me from the command to love these neighbors, too, but it's a bit of a test at times.[26]

This excerpt from a newsletter to co-op supporters gives a window into the messy, real-world tensions raised by neighborhood-level race- and class-integration explored in Chapter 2 and below, along with some of Pastor James's own reflective processing of these tensions in the context of the food co-op.

The Food Co-op's socially reflexive journey from a charity-based food pantry to a relationally-based collaborative food co-op also called into question participants' views of how best to think about relations between privileged and poor persons in the deeply separate and unequal U.S. church and society. Decades of living as neighbor and working closely as colleagues with economically disadvantaged people had given Pastor James's significant opportunity to reflect on the matter:

Our food cooperative grew as an opportunity to work with people in a way that had dignity and created community as opposed to being a handout where the "person in charge" feels good about himself. I think a lot of church charity seems to be about salving our consciences without really having to know people or to create risks. . . . I didn't really want to do something "for" people—I really wanted to do something "with" people.[27]

A longtime practitioner of strategic relocation, Pastor James had come to bear witness to the urgent need for religious leaders to teach and embody new ways of thinking about and relating to one another:

In our society poor people are forever being battered, treated as though they are worth less because they have less, and I thought it important to clarify to my church brothers and sisters that such a stance isn't one we Christians can adopt, that people who are poor are important to [Jesus], who was himself poor and identifies with those who are. . . .

I do not believe the importance of the subject of poverty in the scriptures can be overstated; it is essential to study and hear at all times, but it seems especially important in our present atmosphere in the U.S., even though it's an inconvenient theme that raises uncomfortable questions, and runs counter to the secular American dream and values.

It is not the primary stance of scriptures, as I understand them, that people who "have" should be *helping* poor people; it is that in the church we are to be a new family of every class and race loving one another. . . . We are to learn from each other and look out for each other as members together in the new family of God. . . .

The picture reflected in the scriptures is one of economic diversity in the new church, of Lazarus and the rich man being together, of walls being broken down. . . . And that made for struggles, just as it does for us in the twenty-first century. . . . We're to be a new community, a beloved community, shaped by the values of Jesus.

Even now it is widespread in the church that we are stratified and isolated in our homogeneous groups; therefore, it is our work to pray and put in the effort to create the conditions where we have to engage the struggle instead of disregarding Jesus and only worshipping with and relating to those with whom we are comfortable. How can we share in the Eucharist, communion, the Lord's Supper, "in remembrance" of Christ (1 Cor. 11:24) if we are not embracing the poor but subtly or otherwise making sure they are not at the table? (Matt. 25:31–40, Luke 14:12–14).

Remembering Jesus is not just a mental exercise about how we think, it is a social exercise about how we relate to one another and whom we include. We're in a moment where to "remember," means, to some degree, to "re-member"—intentionally embrace new and *different* people.[28]

For Pastor James, the food co-ops were a way to embody beloved community across race and class lines in keeping with the life and teaching of Jesus and Christian scripture, and to participate as equals across difference in the struggle against poverty, economic inequity, and social division by living and working "with" class disadvantaged people and communities rather than avoiding, exploiting,[29] or trying to do things "for" them.

"Stories of With"

Training evangelical and other religious and secular nonprofit community organizations to move from charity-based "for" models of engaging poverty and inequality toward more participatory and collaborative models or "stories of with" was also a central pillar of Neighborhood Partners' work in Portland. Whereas Pastor James and The Food Co-op embodied asset-based community development (ABCD) principles while only rarely referring to the model explicitly, ABCD lay at the heart, and on the tip of the tongue, of Neighborhood Partners' approach to public engagement as the organization's "recommended common space modality for building inclusive relationships and partnerships where positive neighborhood impact can be accomplished."[30] In all its education and community work—whether mobilizing and training churches to partner with "housing first" nonprofits focused on homelessness, organizing weekly "community listening sessions" in southeast Portland neighborhoods, leading week-long immersion experiences for out-of-town church groups interested in learning how to better engage religious difference and social disadvantage in urban contexts, teaching community-based classes and internships for local college students, coordinating free one-day medical and dental clinics for uninsured or underinsured southeast Portland residents, mentoring AmeriCorps workers and projects arising from Neighborhood Partners affiliated staff and volunteers, working with low-income apartment complex residents to improve access to economic and educational opportunities of interest to them, coaching churches and secular nonprofit agencies in the art of asset-based community development work, or running ABCD training events for neighborhood leaders and city officials—I did not witness a single setting that did not explicitly highlight the difference between doing things "for" people in one-way service oriented relationships versus doing things "with" disadvantaged people in reciprocal relationships of mutual benefit. In this, Neighborhood Partners is an example of multicultural evangelical public engagement focused on common goods and ethical democratic grassroots decision-making and empowerment in economically disadvantaged contexts. Two examples will suffice.

Asset-Based Community Development Training

At a day-long ABCD training event attended by a mix of religious and non-religious nonprofit and neighborhood association leaders, church members, university students, and low-income neighborhood residents, Neighborhood Partners white, male evangelical staff trainers criticized top-down, programmatic, expert-driven, outsider-led approaches to social transformation based on "affluent middle-class" assumptions and values (such as "efficiency," "fast progress," "quick quantifiability," "relief-focused," "money-based," and "consumer-orientation") in favor of a "community-centered," "relationship-driven," "assets and gifts-focused" approach in which all members of a community "struggle together" to "identify common interests" and achieve common goals. Rather than searching for people to "fill a role" in order to accomplish objectives set by outside experts or program managers, asset-based community development requires us to "start with a question, not an answer" while seeking to "uncover the community concerns" that people are actually motivated to act on, searching for the "gifts of head, heart, and hands" (i.e., cognitive, emotional, and practical/physical strengths of individuals) through which to collaboratively identify and pursue common aims. Echoing long-standing broad-based community organizing principles,[31] Neighborhood Partners staff emphasized the "slow" but irreplaceable work of "one-on-one listening," asserting that, "the only way to find out what people care about is through one-on-one conversations." In addition to building relationships and an "internal empowerment culture" that develops indigenous citizen leaders, a disciplined ongoing commitment to one-on-one conversations constantly forces leaders to face the question, "Do people *want* X, or do *I* think they need it?" They also echoed the familiar "iron rule of organizing," paraphrased, "don't do for others what they can do for themselves."

Adopting a widely used metaphor, Neighborhood Partners staff metaphorically distinguished between "relief" and "development" oriented approaches to social change in favor of the latter. Rather than "giving" or "teaching people how to fish," asset-based community development empowers people to "own the pond." They also distinguished between "People-Oriented Citizens Associations"—represented as an egalitarian circle—and "Program-Oriented Government, Non-profit, and Business" institutions—represented as a hierarchical pyramid—favoring the former while acknowledging the necessity of the latter so long as they incorporate ABCD principles of inclusion, listening, relationship-building, power-sharing, and collaboration into their operations. Whereas People-Oriented Citizens Associations "get things done" through "consensus-building, care (motivation), and citizens," Program-Oriented institutions get things done through "control, production, and staff." Citizens Associations "focus on assets (what is there)" and work through "connections and contributions" of invested people, while Program-Oriented institutions "focus on needs (what is not there)" and produce "services to meet needs." The "impact" of People-Oriented Citizens Associations is to generate "citizens" who understand that "people are the answer" to effective social change, while the impact of Program-Oriented Government, Non-profit, and Business institutions is to produce "consumers" who believe that "programs are the answer" to accomplish effective social change. Neighborhood Partners' staff also distinguished between elite-outsider versus indigenous-community-controlled approaches to "development," trashing the former while valorizing the latter.

As the day advanced, our three Neighborhood Partners staff trainers proceeded to address challenges of inclusivity, participation, and language. "Labeled people are marginalized," one trainer remarked, "we label, and by default, we exclude." ABCD's insistence on "listening" and "discovering assets and gifts" in all members of a community, another chimed in, addresses the "need to bring everyone in from the margins to participate" in inclusive, indigenous ownership of shared places and projects. "Language can exclude," he added, describing ways that dominant discourses in the United States can disparage and distance poor and marginalized persons and communities, "We need language that motivates *all*, connects with *all*." Responding to a prompt—"Who are the under-represented, or under-heard people in your community? Who doesn't get heard?"—trainees generated a list of eight groups, (1) "the elderly," (2) "children," (3) "immigrants," (4) "the poor," (5) "people of color," ("poor people of color in particular," one woman added), (6) "disabled people," (7) "the long-term unemployed," and (8) "people of certain religious beliefs." In light of affluent and middle-class Americans' "default" bent towards efficiency and in-group bias, "We always have to work *hard* to think about who is not being heard," a trainer summarized, concluding the segment.

The Greenbush Initiative

Neighborhood Partners work with the Greenbush Initiative offers a second example.

Out of many legitimate success stories, the Greenbush Initiative—described briefly in the Introduction—was a Neighborhood Partners exemplar for effectively embodying ABCD principles of working "with" rather than "for" disadvantaged persons and communities. Kent, Neighborhood Partners founding director and lead ABCD trainer at events such as the one described above, was responsible for placing Angel—the extremely effective lead organizer of the Greenbush Initiative—to work in an east Portland neighborhood office as an AmeriCorps volunteer, providing supervision and training in the asset-based community development principles she effectively mobilized to help turn the Greenbush Initiative into a dynamic grassroots coalition of Hispanic, white, Black, and Asian low-income neighborhood residents in southeast Portland. Initially imagined as a community policing initiative that emerged in response to increases in violent crime and gang activity in the Greenbush neighborhood—including a troubling murder that shocked neighborhood residents into organizing—Kent gave Angel credit for "steering the policing work of the Greenbush Initiative to where now it's actually more about, 'How can we create a community space that helps us build a neighborhood identity that is positive? That creates relational connectivity? That's going to strengthen the neighborhood more than just having people out with flashlights and badges?' . . . That's much more effective for the long run." Peter, another Neighborhood Partners staff volunteer and ABCD trainer, was also deeply involved in the initiative.

While participating in a wide variety of Greenbush Initiative events and gatherings—from pop-up craft markets and slam poetry readings to planning meetings and local business canvassing—neighborhood resident reports and observations repeatedly confirmed multiracial grassroots power and ownership of the initiative. "The difference between this and the stuff that usually happens in neighborhoods like ours," a working class Latino resident and grassroots leader told me after a planning meeting, "is that we're usually fighting for scraps or a place at the table." "Here," he said, pausing for effect before pounding his fist firmly on the table in front of us, "we own the table." The entire enterprise was permeated with the practice and discourse of grassroots leadership, community ownership, and inclusive empowerment. Hispanic mothers and business owners, Black teenagers, immigrant workers, elderly white working class residents, members of small Black Pentecostal and white evangelical neighborhood churches, and other ethnically diverse neighborhood residents had taken leadership in establishing a dizzying array of creative initiatives to tap assets, meet needs, and fulfill dreams for themselves and others in the neighborhood.

Greenbush Initiative participants were not naïve to the challenges they faced. A promotional flyer described some of these challenges in a section, "What problems do we need to address?" The answer:

Greenbush is a struggling community. Public safety is a major concern for residents and businesses. Traditional policing methods have not been effective against drugs, theft, gang violence, and human trafficking.

A bullet point list of issues followed:

- High crime rate: drugs, gangs, violence, human trafficking
- Overall resident safety
- Negative public perception
- Few activities and mentorship opportunities for youth
- Graffiti and litter
- Lack of coordination and community-based problem solving

While acknowledging challenges, the flyer simultaneously highlighted successes, "How is the Greenbush Initiative making a difference?" with invitations to residents to get involved in various ways. "It's already working!" the colorful flyer exclaimed, "You can help!"[32]

The Greenbush Initiative was a decidedly barebones, grassroots affair throughout my time in the neighborhood. The group's recurring Good Neighbor Meeting was held in a vacant, unfinished, unheated, cement-floored room in a strip-mall, where residents shuffled in every few weeks to plan and dream of what might become of this rugged adopted "community center" space and its many activities. It was February, and we kept our winter coats on as we lowered ourselves onto the cold hard seats of metal folding chairs spread haphazardly across the otherwise empty room, greeting each other over the echoing shrill of metal scraped across concrete. Approximately thirty adults and ten youth were in attendance—Hispanic, white, and Black—present to discuss news of the neighborhood. A Latino construction worker discussed the costs and labor involved in ongoing renovations to the community center, much of which relied on the volunteer labor of local residents. A white police officer and neighborhood resident discussed the results of a year-long "innovations in policing" initiative, one of several ongoing community policing efforts to "reduce crime and rebuild community" in Greenbush. Angel discussed impending deadlines for the city's new TIF-supported funding for grassroots community groups in "communities of color and priority neighborhoods" described in the Introduction.[33] After updating everyone on the status of application materials, she announced a "community visioning" session to be held the following week to continue working on materials for the proposal.

A brainstorming session ensued, focusing largely on income-generating ideas, given that, "money is an issue the next few months. We have to find a way to get to July." Recent income-generating events had included a scrap metal collection, summer car wash, rummage sale, and sidewalk craft-and-bake sale. These events did not generate a great deal of income, but they were enthusiastically organized and attended by a growing and diverse network of engaged neighborhood residents. Those present clearly felt a well-earned sense of pride and forward momentum that matched the cheerful Greenbush Initiative graphic and sign projected outside—"Wi-fi! Ping-pong! Hula hoops!"—notwithstanding the cold and the hardscrabble reality reflected inside. "Now is the time to ask and celebrate all we've done with so few resources," a resident asserted, to wide assent.

The community visioning events held in the same space the following week—repeated over a free lunch and dinner to give residents multiple chances of attending—was even more upbeat. Five men and fifteen women were at the session I attended—white, Black, and Hispanic, including a volunteer Spanish translator—to participate in a "blue sky" visioning session intended to set priorities for the Greenbush Initiative's grant application and work in the neighborhood. After brief introductions, attendees began sharing what they hoped to see Greenbush become. One attendee stood with a marker next to a large easel pad to record everyone's suggestions and priorities: "Diversity honored," "respect," "people are important," "nonviolence," "listening," "kindness," "fairness," "sustainability," "willingness to share," "reciprocity," "support existing local businesses," "accept *progress* not just perfection," "commitment," "safety," "non-judgmental," "acceptance," "embrace change," "empower kids," "education," "inclusion," "model healthy living," and "moving from tolerance to seeing gifts, from accepting to celebrating each other." "We want to the community to feel safe any time, day or night," a female resident said. Others added: "A community that looks nice! A beautiful clean place." "A place where people *want* to live, that they're proud of." "Where people know each other." "If one person hurts, we all hurt." "Walk to health and food." "Mentoring/internship programs for kids of all races, with job training for new skills." Someone mentioned the need for digital literacy, internships, and job training for high-paying tech jobs and skills, rather than agreeing with the outside world's low expectations for neighborhood youth. "We need to give kids the benefit of the doubt!", a Latina woman insisted. "We can't be healthy without being economically viable," another added, "we have to be able to *create* things of value that people want." "We have renters who are really good people who can't pay the rent." Someone spoke of "economic gardening" as a metaphor for using potential grant funds to develop community-controlled economic resources and opportunities for all residents. "Whatever we do," Angel said, repeating the ABCD language she used consistently throughout the session, "it must be *community-driven* (emphasis original), not organization-driven or 'public sector' or 'private sector'-driven. The *community* is the best articulator of the common good."

In the end, participants agreed on "reciprocity," "commitment," "respect," and "community/solidarity," as core values to build their work around, with no tension or dissension in the room. As they attempted to form a vision statement, a male Hispanic resident noted soberly, "We don't *have* community yet, but *we are building a community that*" is marked by certain values. "I used to know everybody two blocks either way," he told me later as we ate together after the meeting, "now I don't know anybody." His remarks became the backbone of the new Greenbush Initiative vision statement: "Building our [Safe, Healthy, Respectful, Vibrant, Inclusive] community together," with the bracketed words stacked vertically on top of one another in different fonts and script styles.

In the Neighborhood Partners and Greenbush Initiative orbit, perhaps no one was more committed to ABCD principles of reciprocal relations and inclusive, community-controlled decision-making than Peter, Angel's former AmeriCorps supervisor and a Neighborhood Partners volunteer staff member:

> What I *love* about asset-based community development is that it's not a "handout" approach and it's not a "go pull yourself up by your bootstraps" approach. It's a "let's live responsibly together, let's develop and understand those patterns of cooperation that are sustainable" approach. Finding common ground with people that don't share your same belief system, but still finding those touchpoints where you can coexist—because you have to coexist—and because we're called to be in relationship. We're not called to hunker down in a bunker somewhere and live out this existence and survive. We're called to thrive in this existence. And we're called to be with the people who God has placed us with, and to bloom where we're planted.

With Angel, Peter played a significant role in establishing the Greenbush Initiative's fiercely grassroots, reciprocal, collaborative, community-led praxis and ethos.

The Iron Rule and "Gentrification with Justice"

> *"Never do for others what they can do for themselves." – IAF Iron Rule of Organizing*

> *"Ain't nothin' free at PCDA." – Oft-repeated PCDA mantra*

Peter and Neighborhood Partners' dogged adherence to asset-based community development principles and practices did much to prevent one-way, top-down, outsider-controlled "service for" or "ministry to" modes of engaging poverty and inequality from taking hold in the secular and religious settings in which they worked. Sybil, Pastor James, and The Food Co-op operated in similar fashion. On balance, these groups' focus on listening, collaboration, inclusive empowerment, and working "with" disadvantaged persons and communities to achieve objectives and goals set forth by disadvantaged persons and resident stakeholders themselves warrants positive evaluation from the perspective of ethical democracy. There is a danger, however, in romanticizing, idealizing, or otherwise overstating the extent to which asset-based community development and other grassroots approaches to combating poverty and economic inequality are capable of empowering disadvantaged individuals and communities to achieve ethical democratic ends on their own.

David—Naomi's white evangelical founding co-director of Justice in the City and an active citizen-leader in Together for Justice—noted one such danger as we talked in his office in the low-income majority Hispanic neighborhood in LA's inland empire where he and his family lived. As experienced practitioners of grassroots democratic organizing and community development work in the United States and around the world, Naomi and David were deeply committed to stakeholder principles of empowerment and equity embodied in the IAF's iron rule of organizing. David also recognized that broad-based community organizing can sometimes fail to live up to its own best principles of inclusive empowerment for all members of a community: "With institutional [broad-based] organizing, it's possible just to circulate leaders over time. Where just the leaders are organizing everything and you're not necessarily raising up leaders from your institutions and communities." David contrasted this with the "very grassroots organizing" Naomi, David, and others had done in their neighborhood with Justice in the City:

When we started doing work in the neighborhood, we'd draw people together and do these house meetings and ask, "So what are the things you're concerned about?" You're organizing a community. What's great about grassroots [neighborhood] organizing is you're engaged with the people at the very lowest [socioeconomic] level. So the strength of grassroots organizing is you're drawing people in the community into the process.

"On a larger scale," David noted, "it's really about democracy. It's about trying to get people in the community to influence the direction of their community." In the case of Naomi and David's neighborhood, a lack of street lights and public safety were top concerns of neighborhood residents, both of which were addressed by residents over a years-long organizing process.

I just started to realize this could be a very effective tool for systemic change that works particularly well in places where democracy is rooted and has value. . . . A lot of other stuff that I've seen doesn't deal with systemic change. Community organizing *is* about systemic change, and also about empowering people to take responsibility for their communities. It has that value of ours, which is we don't come in and tell people what to do. We come in and work with people and help them do what they want to do.

In its embodied commitment to indigenous leadership, inclusive empowerment, and local control, Justice in the City mirrored the asset-based community development practices of Neighborhood Partners and The Food Co-op, albeit with greater emphasis on the impossibility of dealing with poverty and inequality effectively without engaging democratically in political struggles for "systemic change."

However, despite deep-seated commitment and decades-long experience with grassroots democratic organizing in extremely disadvantaged communities in Los Angeles and around the world, David was skeptical of practical and rhetorical modes of engaging poverty and inequality that relied solely on the resources, ideas, people, and leadership available within disadvantaged communities themselves:

You have to walk that line where you don't just come as the outsider and say, "This is what you need to do." On the other hand, I think people sometimes go overboard and say, "Oh, people will somehow magically do everything by themselves." That somehow within them they have this innate ability [to create social change on their own, with no outside resources or relationships]. But in our experience people often don't have hope for what could happen. They don't have an imagination for it. You often have to walk with people for a time . . . so I think you have to have some idea of what is possible when you come in.

In other words, if humans are social creatures, shaped by social conditions, some of which are intensely inequitable, degrading, disempowering, and delegitimizing, it is unrealistic (and probably unethical or immoral) to expect oppressed people and communities to suddenly rise up on their own with full capability and power to transform durable structures of economic, political, cultural, and social psychological inequity spontaneously on their own, without support. "How is it serving to come into a community and hold back your gifts [and] insider resources?" David asked rhetorically. Nor, he added, was it right to just "take charge, make things happen . . . which works in some ways but doesn't build ownership. So once you're gone, the thing dies."

A white man who lived and worked closely alongside people of color at home and around the world, David recognized how race often complicated discussions of empowerment and indigenous leadership in grassroots community organizing and development:

> I think a lot of that discussion—some of it happens on the international level—but I think domestically, particularly in Black communities, there's been such defensiveness about white people coming in. There's some white guilt. This is true in a lot of parts of the world. And there's a right corrective in that.

As with the practice of strategic relocation in general, ongoing struggles with personal and systemic racism make it impossible to engage poverty and economic inequality in the United States without also directly dealing with issues of race and ethnicity, which required adaption and added complicated layers to relationships between "insiders" and "outsiders" across settings.

Gentrification with Justice?

Of the many ways that Peachtree Community Development Association in Atlanta practiced and preached the "three R's" (relocation, reconciliation, and redistribution) of Christian community development made famous in evangelical circles by Black evangelical leader John Perkins,[34] one formulation stands out as particularly freighted with race, class, and political baggage: the idea of "gentrification with justice." For PCDA, "gentrification with justice" meant strategic relocation and neighborhood investment that benefited rather than displaced existing low-income Black and brown residents.[35] It was not the primary way that PCDA leaders and affiliates described their work, but it was one way, and the concept accurately captured some aspects of it.

To be sure, PCDA leaders and participants were firmly opposed to "gentrification without justice," that is, to market-driven gentrification processes that serve the interests and pocketbooks of corporate developers, speculative

real estate interests, wealthy residents, middle-class property owners, and affluent outsiders—often but not always white—while making neighborhoods
unaffordable to lower-income residents and long-established communities
of color, whose economic, cultural, and political marginalization prevents
them from benefiting from neighborhood economic advancement. However,
PCDA leaders, staff, and strategic relocators—Black, white, and Hispanic
alike—considered economic development and job creation, mixed-income
housing and Black homeownership, public safety and collective efficacy,
good schools and youth programs, healthy food and environmental sustainability, attractive public spaces and cultural amenities, and some movement towards racial integration to be necessary and desirable elements of
thriving neighborhoods that most often required resources beyond those
already present in historically oppressed and economically disadvantaged
communities.[36] "Gentrification with justice" was one way PCDA spoke of
such resources.

When I asked Richard, the founding director of PCDA, if he was familiar
with the asset-based community development model and if so, what he
thought of it, he responded:

> I think asset-based community development should be credited with
> making the public aware that the poor have assets rather than debts, or not
> exclusively debts. So it's had a significant influence in changing a mindset.
> Lots of folks are doing ABCD and that in itself is very positive. I view it
> as a useful tool in the larger community transformation work. It's a very
> positive, affirming tool and technique. It emphasizes indigenous capacity,
> which is greatly important. What it does not do is admit to the need for
> external resources. No community is gonna to come back to health un-
> less it has disposable income coming in and remaining, and ABCD does
> not address that. It's an important tool that's changed the mind set, but it's
> one part of it. It affirms the capacities of local people and it challenges the
> typical "least, the last and the lost" kind of thinking. That needs to be chal-
> lenged, and in that sense it's very important. But John McKnight: he's an
> academic and he's a community organizer, but he's not a business person.
> When you ask the question, "How do you make the community economi-
> cally viable?", then it takes you down a different road, and you don't do that
> by helping folks pull themselves up by the bootstraps. Particularly after
> communities have been losing their leadership like a hemorrhage for fifty
> years.[37]

Richard was no friend of gentrification per se—in fact, he counted early PCDA work in one southeast Atlanta neighborhood in the 1980s a failure because "it gentrified before we knew what gentrification was, and so most of the poor got displaced." However, like David, Richard's forty-plus years of experience living and working in race and class disadvantaged neighborhoods made him skeptical of "pull yourselves up by the bootstraps" interpretations of asset-based community development and social transformation.

This applied to government support for low-income communities as well. Just as Richard and PCDA pursued economic empowerment by mobilizing people and resources from both inside and outside the neighborhoods into which they had been invited to live and work, they recognized that, "You have to have government involvement for community transformation":

> You've got to have a decent non-corrupt police force. You've got to have a relationship with the city planning department that says we'll stop certain bad zoning practices here, we'll do code enforcement on slum lords, we'll provide CDBG block grants to help you do some things. We'll fix the shot-out street lights and we'll give you some tools that will help you. We'll give you property tax abatement for the next ten years, so that when you develop new housing you won't have to pay property taxes for ten years as an incentive. We'll put in infrastructure, we'll put in the sidewalks. We'll do TADs, tax allocation districts: that if people are building big rise stuff here they have to put affordable or mixed-income housing in. We'll give you TIFs—tax incremental financing—so that, if your land isn't worth much now but in ten years it will be . . . we'll issue bonds based on the projected increase in value. That's all city stuff, government stuff, and very, very important for community transformation.

Richard and PCDA were vocal critics of one-way "service-based," "handout," or "charity-only" approaches to engaging poverty and economic inequality; they were also discerning supporters of extralocal government and nongovernment economic investment in race and class disadvantaged communities that would empower existing residents to better control their own fate.

Deb—PCDA's white, thirty-four-year-old Chief Operating Officer, neighborhood association executive committee member, mother of two, and neighborhood resident who strategically relocated to Atlanta eleven years prior—described her hopeful future for the neighborhood as "a really healthy, affordable working class neighborhood." This vision included welcoming new residents, predominantly Black but some white and Hispanic, to increase racial integration and economic diversity while maintaining the historically Black character of the neighborhood as desired by residents. As described in Chapter 2, PCDA's housing arm focused on recruiting "working class people buying their first home. Almost entirely Black. Kind of professional [teachers and firefighters, office workers and administrative assistants, nurses and health care workers were typical occupations]. . . . A lot of them are women. Tend to be a little younger. Some are having kids. When people start having babies in the neighborhood, that's huge. We've got to keep this a place where people want to raise their kids."[38]

In terms of community economic development, Richard emphasized housing and jobs as major drivers of neighborhood transformation, reflecting PCDA's nonprofit housing and business ventures in the neighborhood, all of which employed local residents. "Connecting low-income folks to good jobs is the optimal development strategy, along with affordable housing," he explained, "so you can afford a house, and you have stability, your kids aren't changing schools because you're getting evicted or have get out of the apartment."[39] Richard's highest aspirations in this arena were to locate and support emerging indigenous Black entrepreneurs and business start-ups to establish and grow successful enterprises that would employ local residents and contribute to neighborhood prosperity. Alternatively, when such enterprises were in limited supply, "the best thing we can do is provide training and a job experience which folks can then leverage to a better job experience." We have met some real-life exemplars of this process in earlier chapters. Alicia began working ten hours at PCDA's nonprofit café before more than doubling her hours and adding management responsibilities, with living wage increases along the way. Sheri—another café worker, neighborhood resident, and PCDA-supported affordable homeowner mentioned in the Introduction— was on her way to an assistant manager position. Brandon worked in a PCDA-run furniture store for several years before moving into management and then launching his own entrepreneurial PCDA-supported street-vending business. Other residents worked for PCDA's housing arm, ran PCDA youth programs and summer camps, taught at a nearby charter school started by a former PCDA staff team, worked in PCDA-run businesses, and so on.

PCDA staff's focus on work, employment, and economic advancement— combined with frequent rhetoric against "charity-only" or "handout" approaches to combating poverty and economic inequality—sometimes sounded, to me, uncomfortably similar to conservative anti-welfare arguments in national electoral politics, which seemed at odds with PCDA's mission and values.[40] I asked them about this. Leonard—PCDA's co-executive director, a Black man in his mid-forties—understood the question before it was halfway out of my mouth:

> My answer to that is, our work is so based in relationship—about "Who is my neighbor?"—that it really isn't saying, "Go work without me. You're on your own." It's saying, "How are we going to figure out together the common good for both of us?"

Like many (but not all) PCDA leaders and participants, Leonard was politically progressive: a Democratic party supporter who held firmly left-of-center positions on all the racial, gender and sexuality, environmental, and economic issues we discussed. Richard was a somewhat more conservative political centrist, while Deb fell in between. Leonard had an example for me ready at hand:

> I'm talking to a group of ladies from the community on Monday about a really good business idea. A nail salon. African American women use hair products to the tune of billions of dollars a year. But the industry is controlled by Koreans. So a local shop owned by Black women, with Black women hopefully becoming suppliers and buyers, is wide open if they're able to do it right. Because it's an industry entirely for women of color. . . . I'm going to tell them, I think you need to do this! For the next six months, I want you to save every dollar you can. Then I'm going to talk to the bank about a loan. You'll be able to launch this business in about six months. Now you gotta work on your plan, your marketing, all these things. It's not because I think they "need to work!" It's because our neighborhood needs this, this will be great for our neighborhood, and it will be great that *you* own it. Because the wealth generated from it is going to be yours. That's not coming from: "I think you need to work." That's coming from: "This would be a great business for our neighborhood." It's just a different, different dynamic.

Leonard's response captures much about PCDA's philosophy and how it operated in the neighborhood. Like Neighborhood Partners and other asset-based community development work, PCDA was highly invested in working "with" low-income residents in disadvantaged communities rather than trying to do things "for" them. However, unlike Neighborhood Partners' sometimes dogmatic rhetoric about relying *solely* on local indigenous neighborhood resources and initiative, PCDA was more willing to initiate ideas and draw on outside resources as well, so long as they reflected residents' wishes and PCDA's commitments to racial and economic equity and empowerment. In this, they resembled David and Justice in the City's position on the need to combine both local and translocal resources and people when working alongside residents of disadvantaged communities towards greater racial and economic justice.

As such, Richard's adoption of the term "gentrification with justice" reflected PCDA's belief in the need to bring both external and local resources to bear on the challenges facing race and class disadvantaged neighborhoods:

> You see that community development—if it's pure community development without outside [resources] . . . that is a very, very long process. That's over generations. Most of us don't have time for that. So the way to speed that process up is that you bring in partners who can make it happen a lot quicker.

Just as it often takes decades (or, in the case of anti-Black racism in the United States, centuries) to generate the sort of inequitable conditions that ensnare people and communities in intergenerational poverty, it can take just as long or longer to dismantle those conditions and their consequences apart from major resource investments, institutional partnerships, and systemic change.[41] And just as people and forces external to disadvantaged communities are often responsible for their creation and ongoing exploitation,[42] so external resources are often necessary to empower residents to move themselves and their communities towards greater justice and flourishing.

Race and Gentrification with Justice

In light of the fraught histories of race, class, gentrification, and displacement in cities and neighborhoods across the United States, PCDA leaders were also exceedingly wary of the racial dynamics and implications of typical gentrification processes in Atlanta and beyond. Deb, speaking of the neighborhood association composition and dynamics described in Chapter 2, acknowledged:

> Those can be some really horrible transitions. Really nasty. Yeah. I'm sure you know all about that. We've gotten feedback from the city and our city council person who say, "This is different. Your diversity, your unity. It's not how most intown neighborhoods make this transition." So that feels—of course, they're politicians, so they say a lot [laughing]. But that always feels affirming. . . . What I see a lot [in other gentrifying neighborhoods] is new whites start their own association. And they're connected to the city and they start getting everything. That happens all the time. There's a lot of that. I mean, it's all about power and resources. About who supposedly "knows what's best."

As Leonard described in Chapter 2, their own neighborhood association had undergone a transition from the long-standing leadership of a group of older Black residents to the current, younger, multiracial leadership group. "We're very mindful of some of the old leaders and try to include and support" them, Deb added, when they have something they want to lead—a claim I corroborated through participant observation and interviews with older Black leaders themselves.

As one of two PCDA-affiliated members (one white and one Black) on the neighborhood association's multiracial executive committee, Deb was reflexive about the race, class, and cultural power dynamics involved in neighborhood association leadership and representation:

> The president, since I've been here, the presidents have always been African American. . . . And the vice president is a white man. A white gay man. I think that's okay as vice president, I'm not sure that's going to fly as president. Though he would be good at it. Yeah. I think it still needs to be an African American.

She also vividly described new neighborhood resident constituents, some of whose voices neighborhood association leaders sought to amplify, and others they sought to quiet:

> I think there's a group of folks in the neighborhood—a little bit more white than Black, but not entirely—who found a good deal [on their house],

they're artists, and wanted to live: they were kind of on the gentrification train. And they could afford this neighborhood probably more than some of the up-and-coming areas and wanted to do their own thing. Risk takers. Not people of faith necessarily. More interested in kind of this neighborhood being a cool—a good intown neighborhood. Some of those voices, we try to tame a little. Not in a controlling way. But not let that be the dominant voice. Because those are the voices that sometimes start to dominate. There's those folks. Then there's some young African American professionals who have moved in. Got good deals on houses. I don't think the same need to live in the cool, trendy neighborhood. But definitely concerned with their property values. And then also, some are just civic minded people who think, yeah, we should care about our neighborhood and getting to know people that maybe they would normally not get to know. That's kind of cool. And then there's folks who've moved in because they're connected to PCDA.

Each of these constituencies were visible at the neighborhood association events I attended—such as the progressive dinner described at the beginning of Chapter 2—and had developed ways to interact effectively with conviviality across differences in age, race, class, gender, sexuality, and religion.

Gentrification with Justice? Challenges and Critics

Neighborhood gentrification does not always pit encroaching economically advantaged white newcomers against long-time Black or low-income residents of color. As brilliantly chronicled by Northwestern sociologist and ethnographer Mary Patillo, challenges and tensions frequently arise among new and old, economically advantaged and disadvantaged Black residents of mixed-income neighborhoods as well.[43] Pamela—the thirty-three-year-old Black evangelical woman and long-time PCDA associate recently hired by Fulton County to lead a new antipoverty initiative in Atlanta whom we met in Chapter 2—experienced the complexity of PCDA's work in the organization's two most recent neighborhood sites, both predominantly Black neighborhoods in Atlanta's urban core. As a PCDA-affiliated newcomer to each neighborhood, being Black herself did not shield Pamela from experiencing tension and conflict—as well as friendship and solidarity—with longer-tenured neighborhood residents. Her experiences and identity positioned her to be an informed and sensitive channel of existing residents' concerns:

> One of the negative things we have to be careful of is to not make the people that were here first feel like they're being forced out. Their culture, it is going to change. They were comfortable with their culture. Some of them didn't request change. They learned to adapt to where they were. But with new people coming in, they're going to make this neighborhood association more like the one that they used to have. Or they're used to this community event going this certain way, just because "that's the way we've always done it where I'm from. So now I'm here, I'm going to try to make it happen here." Then you have the people that have been here for a while that feel like, "You're changing everything. You're making it seem like what we had was horrible, and it wasn't."
>
> I think it's good to find a balance. Because everything that was here wasn't horrible. But there were some things that were really bad. And everything that we or others bring from their other life or culture or experience is not good, but there are some good things that come with it. We can meet in the middle and find a great balance. I think it's awesome. Which is one of the strong points of PCDA. We don't come to fix everything. I think we come to kind of draw everybody together that's here. We do community asset mapping. Who's in the community already, what are they already doing, what assets do you already have? And let us be that mechanism that draws everybody together.

In both neighborhoods, Pamela experienced personally the challenges and rewards of attempting to bridge old and new in increasingly mixed-income, majority Black neighborhoods.

As described in Chapter 2, while Pamela's experience in both neighborhoods mirrored the generally positive experiences of residents, a vocal minority of residents and advocates were more critical. PCDA listened to these voices as well, sometimes agreeing and adjusting plans and policies and sometimes defending itself against criticisms and proposals it deemed unhelpful or unrepresentative of the neighborhood as a whole. While describing the origins of PCDA's summer program, Deanna—PCDA's Black director of youth development—recalled the displacement of a number of families from the east Atlanta redevelopment project, along with her friend Max's vocal advocacy for lower-income residents of the neighborhood:

Several of the families who had lived in that neighborhood were being displaced as they were revitalizing the area. In redoing the housing over there, there were people who were displaced. Some of them were moved into this [PCDA's current] neighborhood and some went elsewhere. So you saw this great thing—something that looks to the world like this great thing happening—and it was a good thing. But there were also these other stories of peoples' lives being impacted in ways that maybe weren't so great. And we were able to see because we were living there. Whereas the other [non-PCDA] people who were doing the work weren't living there and couldn't see it in the same way. So Max was a very outspoken, very aggressive woman who was fighting, advocating for these families. We worked with her, and she worked with us to help when we started the summer camp.

I asked whether Max was opposed to PCDA's work in the previous neighborhood. Deanna responded:

> She wasn't opposing the development itself. She was just trying to be a voice for low-income families in the neighborhood. Often—at least at that time, I think people are a little better at it now—there is a tendency to cater to the dominant culture. And in this case, the dominant culture is not white suburban people necessarily, it was also Black people who were paying the most money. So when you have a mixed-income housing community and half of the people are at market rate and half of the people are low income, the people who are managing a place tend to listen more to the people who are paying more to live there. So if there's a disagreement, they get the benefit of the doubt, or they demand and get more concessions than the [lower income] group. So Max was seeing these things and really crying out for the low-income families. Some of it is just cultural preferences—not whether something is right or wrong. . . . In the city, backyard barbecues—or even front yard barbecues, wherever you do it—they're an important part of relationship with your neighbors. People come together and talk and play music on holidays and all that. And you weren't allowed to do that at the new development. So it appeared that they were taking a suburban housing or cul-de-sac mindset and culture and putting it into the middle of the city, and saying this is now how you have to live. Those were the things that Max would scream about [laughing]. She was like no, that's not fair, that's not right.

Deanna's depiction of events closely mirrors Mary Patillo's *Black on the Block: The Politics of Race and Class in the City* and other work on neighborhood conflict in mixed-income Black neighborhoods amidst the larger context white-dominated economic and political structures.

In PCDA's current neighborhood, one event stood out to Pamela as particularly painful: the community garden debacle. "We were just thinking, it would be so cool to have produce in the community. There's no place around where we can buy fresh fruits and vegetables," she recalled. The "we" Pamela is referring to consisted primarily of newer residents, neighborhood association participants, and people connected to PCDA. She continued:

So we picked a place in the neighborhood that looked like it would be cool, because it's right in the middle of everything, so any families or whoever wanted to use it, they'd feel welcome because it's right there on the street. We were excited. We were thought we were doing good. What we didn't know was there was a reason that spot was empty. Many years ago, there used to be a community center there. And some of the drug dealers in the neighborhood today used to be kids that played at that community center. When [the city] shut it down, they tried to get it turned into a park for the lady that used to run the community center before she died. But the city didn't listen. They were just a small group of Black people that didn't have the right channels politically to get this done. So they kept getting shut down.

Then here we come, and we knew the channels to go through to make [the community garden] happen. So we're just moving and going. And as soon as we got started, they were livid. Disrespected and everything. We were like, "Hey, this is a good thing, this is a community garden!" They were like, "We're going to go to the courthouse and tell them we are not for this, that you guys are just taking over." I was like, "Wow, they have really been hurt." I know that was one that really kind of hurt me. Some of the residents still don't talk to me. It's taken time for them to kind of come around. Because we got a vote passed. Even though they fought against it, [the garden] still went through, because the majority of us at the meetings thought it was a great idea. But those few people that live on that street and have been taking care of that area before we "decided to take it," they were livid. "Where were you all these years that we've been cutting the grass? When we've been going

over there and playing horseshoes?" We were like, "Well, you're also selling drugs over there; playing loud music." But in their defense, they loved
that area. It reminded them of when they were kids and of somebody who
believed in them and played with them. So they wanted to keep that space.

Pamela recognized the standpoint of her community garden opponents as
reasonable and legitimate, even though she disagreed with them as to the
best use of the space for the neighborhood. The episode was a reminder that
social change—no matter how equitable and collaborative it may aim to
be—inevitably involves proximate winners and losers, charged emotions and
strained relationships, contentious politics and forced compromises, and ac-
commodation to chosen and unchosen circumstances. It is also a reminder
that, in most cases, the outcomes of community and democratic struggles
favor those who have more resources than their opponents.

Advocacy, Giving, Service: Alternative Approaches to Combating Poverty and Inequality

If PCDA's talk of "gentrification with justice" signaled the organization's
efforts to mobilize outside resources, relationships, and ideas to combat
poverty and inequality in partnership with residents of race and class disadvantaged neighborhoods, other groups and organizations departed even
further from the ABCD ideal of seeking change exclusively through local
assets, people, and resources. In Portland, Healing Hands mobilized evangelical churches, individuals, and businesses to offer free one-day medical
and dental clinics in their neighborhoods for uninsured and underinsured
residents in their communities. The professional staff and volunteers of
Christians for the Common Good (or CCG) lobbied the Oregon state legislature on behalf of disadvantaged residents in pursuit of law and policies
supporting "economic justice." (We will explore CCG's work in detail in
Chapter 4.) Serving the City mobilized evangelical churches in Portland to
donate time and resources annually to support public schools, programs,
and initiatives in underfunded areas. The Christian Social Justice Network
(CSJN) in Boston organized events and curriculum aimed at educating privileged American Christians about global poverty and economic inequality
from a biblical perspective while mobilizing them to action. Each of these

groups and organizations tended to operate in more of a "for" rather than "with" mode of combating poverty and economic inequality.

The CSJN, for example, developed an "economic discipleship" Bible study curriculum and app suite that, in its first four years in existence, mobilized over 300 individuals in 40 Bible study groups—mostly middle-class evangelical and mainline Protestant churchgoers in their twenties and thirties—to donate $500,000 to "fight hunger, poverty and injustice at home and abroad in the name of Christ."[44] Using an open source curriculum originally written by two evangelical ministry leaders, one Asian American and one white—with additional early contributions from white female Lutheran and Episcopalian ministers—participants gather for eight to twelve weeks in groups of eight to twelve people in order to pursue "economic discipleship." Groups meet weekly to discuss the biblical view of poverty and economic justice; learn about global poverty and economic inequality; share their personal household budgets, giving, and spending habits with one another; commit to reduced consumption and lifestyle changes that enable increased giving to combat global poverty and inequality; and collectively donate money saved by these changes to one to four international nonprofit organizations involved in antipoverty work. The curriculum combines Bible study with sociological analysis, global statistics on poverty and economic inequality, studies of best and worst practices in global antipoverty work from the academic literature on international development, theological research on poverty and economic justice in the Christian and Hebrew scriptures, and personal stories and reflections from various authors and past participants.

CSJN's curriculum—like Pastor James's lament against race and class inequities in the U.S. church and society described above—is centered on the biblical parable of Lazarus as told by Jesus in Luke 16:19–31:

> There was a rich man who was dressed in purple and fine linen who feasted sumptuously every day. And at his gate lay a poor man named Lazarus, covered with sores, who longed to satisfy his hunger with what fell from the rich man's table; even the dogs would come and lick his sores.[45]

When Lazarus dies, he is "carried away by the angels to be with Abraham"; when the rich man dies, he is tormented in Hades. Upon seeing Lazarus comforted and restored at Abraham's side, the rich man begs for mercy but cannot receive it, his opportunity for salvation squandered by his

self-indulgent luxury, callous disregard for the suffering of others, and refusal to obey Hebrew law and prophets concerning economic justice and
mercy. In a bit of tragic irony, the Introduction to the 2008 version of the curriculum included a reference to Donald Trump as chief exemplar the sort of
materialistic excess that American Christians condemn in theory but resist
accountability for in practice.[46] This "blind spot" in American Christian discipleship, the authors argue, "makes it very difficult to hear any biblical challenge regarding money." Hence American Christians' need for "economic
discipleship," defined in the curriculum as "practicing Jesus' words as they
relate to money."[47]

CSJN's curriculum offers a window into multicultural evangelical
approaches to biblical interpretation and practice with respect to economic
issues. Along with a reflection on the story of Lazarus and global poverty and
inequality statistics, the introductory session urges participants to bring an
open and reflexive posture to the endeavor:

> When addressing issues of poverty and inequality, especially on a global
> scale, it can be very difficult to identify the "optimal" or "morally ideal"
> choice. Consider adopting an experiential learning approach: action is a way
> to learn, and action should be followed by reflection and re-evaluation.[48]

Subsequent sessions center on particular aspects of economic discipleship
and education intended to help participants contextualize their personal economic positions and practices in relation to global poverty, economic inequality, and international antipoverty and economic justice efforts.

Each weekly session combines practical exercises (such as examining
household budgets or researching international NGOs) with scriptural
reflections, prayer, and research on topics such as fair trade, ethical consumption, microfinance, debt and development, and the prevalence of negative unintended consequences of Euro-American international aid work
from sources such as Human Rights Watch, Millennium Development
Goals, Catholic Relief Services, and sociological research on globalization
and inequality. The introductory session is followed, in order, by sessions on:

- "Wealth as a Blessing" (with biblical reflections drawn from Genesis
  1:28–31, Proverbs 13:21, and Deuteronomy 28:1–11)
- "Wealth must be Justly Distributed" (Exodus 16:16–18, Leviticus 25:8–
  10 and 23–28, Deuteronomy 24:10, 14–15, and 17–18)

- "Wealth is a Potential Idol" (Mark 4:18–19, Matthew 6:19–24, Luke 12:16–21, and 1 Timothy 6:10)
- "Wealth is for Sharing with the Poor" (1 Timothy 5:9, Acts 6, Matthew 25, Luke 16:19–31, 1 Corinthians 9:3, and Romans 15:29)
- "Living Economic Discipleship" (II Corinthians 8–9)
- "The Giving Circle" (two sessions, with scriptural reflection from Psalm 140:12, Deuteronomy 26:5–9, Isaiah 41:17, Romans 12:4–5, 1 Corinthians 12:14–27, and Isaiah 65:17–25)
- "Microfinance and Fair Trade" (Luke 12:13–35, Acts 2:42–47)
- "Political Advocacy" (Luke 14:12–14 and 3:7–14)
- "Choosing where to Give" (Philippians 1:9–11), and
- "Giving Together" (with a spiritual reflection on living simply from the writings of St. John Chrysostom).

CSJN's economic discipleship curriculum provides a snapshot of the sort antipoverty and economic equity work it engaged in more broadly, which was clearly targeted towards educating and mobilizing relatively affluent middle-class American Christians to engage in more just and biblical approaches to personal, social, and political practices relating to wealth, poverty, and inequality. It also provides a window into the sort of biblically rooted theological work CSJN and other multicultural evangelical groups across the country engaged in to inspire, motivate, and justify their religious, social, and political standpoints and strategies of action.[49] As we will see in Chapter 4, Christians for the Common Good (CCG) never took a policy position without collectively constructing a biblically rooted "theological reflection" that aimed to justify its position on biblical grounds. A dense forty-five-page document outlining the "theological foundations" of CCG's organizational mission, policy platform, and approach to political advocacy drew on over 260 Bible quotations and references along with page-level citations and quotes from over thirty-five books and articles written by leading Christian theologians, scholars, activists, and movement leaders.[50]

In keeping with this recognizably evangelical emphasis on biblical and theological justification, the penultimate section of this chapter examines how multicultural evangelical research participants described their understanding of the biblical view of poverty and inequality, and with it, what role they believed individual Christians, churches, and the government should or should not play in addressing poverty and economic inequality in the United States and beyond.

Church and State: The Biblical View of
Poverty and Inequality

How do multicultural evangelicals engaged in community development, community organizing, progressive advocacy, and public service work in Portland, Atlanta, Los Angeles, and Boston understand the biblical view of poverty and economic inequality? What role (if any) do they think Christians or churches should play in addressing poverty and economic inequality? What role (if any) do they think government should play? I asked fifty white, Black, Asian, and Hispanic evangelicals across the United States to answer these questions in in-depth interviews while conducting research for this book (see Table 3.1).[51] They responded:

"The biblical view of poverty and inequality? That it exists but it shouldn't."
        —Heather, white evangelical CCG board member, Portland

"'Lazarus' can only come as far as the gate, you know. That's all they can do. Because we won't let them in our neighborhoods. I have the ability to move into this neighborhood. But they don't have the ability to move to Pasadena."
        —Cooper, white evangelical pastor and strategic relocator, Justice in the
                                                                    City, Los Angeles

Table 3.1 Biblical View of Economic Justice and Responsibility

	Economic justice: progressive	Economic justice: mixed	Church and Government Responsibility	Church, Limited Government Responsibility	Limited / No Church or Government Responsibility
White (n = 40)	37	3	29	8	3
Black (n = 4)	4	—	4	—	—
Hispanic (n = 3)	3	—	1	2	—
Asian (n = 3)	3	—	2	1	—
Total (n = 50)	47	3	36	11	3

"We live in a country where the history is—and we're living it still—lends itself to racism and profiling and broken communities, divided communities. So you wind up with a system that creates poverty influenced by racism. A lot of the poverty then gets connected to certain groups of people. So now we can't separate race and poverty. They go hand in hand. And the biblical view then becomes, what does God say about the poor and about poverty? And what does God say about people? My whole view is that I need to be deeply rooted in a theology that works against poverty and injustice, and I have to be deeply rooted in a theology that lifts all people."

—*Leonard, Black evangelical, PCDA co-executive director, Atlanta*

"We typically come to scripture with preconceived questions, like, 'How much should I be saving for retirement?' As opposed to, 'What does scripture say about money and people in general? Are we even asking the right questions?' For example, in Leviticus 25 you see God's heart that every Israelite family would have land. That God designed wealth to be a blessing to everyone in roughly equal proportions. . . . [the Bible] literally doesn't support the idea of a dominion where you carve out resources and claim them as your exclusive possession. It's all meant for unlimited generosity."

—*Kaito, Japanese American evangelical, CSJN, Boston*

"I just don't understand it. I know we can't all be millionaires, but there shouldn't be people that are homeless, there shouldn't be children that go without food, there shouldn't be mothers and fathers who can't look their kids in the eyes because the kids are asking, "What are we going to eat?" and they don't have anything. There shouldn't be kids living under bridges, there shouldn't be any of that in a country that is supposedly the richest country in the world. But when you think about capitalism, hey, that's the way it works. That's how capitalism works. My political background is closer to socialism: everybody gets what they need, you know, especially their basic needs. We can't all be rich, we cannot all have Mercedes Benz, but everybody has basic needs that should be met. It's a question that I struggle with all the time.

—*Sybil, Black evangelical co-op coordinator, The Food Co-op, Atlanta*

"Most evangelical Christians can tell you the dangers of socialism. But they can't always articulate the dangers of capitalism. I don't feel like it's our responsibility as Christians to ascribe to a certain economic system, but to hold economic systems accountable to the values that we hold. If capitalism is the system we want to go with, fine. But we have to protect workers, we have to protect the environment. We have to take heed of people's health and all that stuff along the way. That's our responsibility as Christians within an economic system."

—*Sandy, white evangelical, PCDA-affiliated strategic relocator, Atlanta*

"If God is generous and open-handed toward us, we are to be the same way toward others. And that's not just about individuals: it's also about [groups] of individuals who make up the different institutions, the different systems of the world, the religious systems, the political systems, the economic systems. That these communities of power seem to exist for the sake of perpetuating themselves at the expense of others, I think, is a reflection of the brokenness, the sin in the world. I think that's why—it seems to me anyway—if God can be said to have a bias, he has a bias towards the poor. Not because he loves the poor more than he loves those who are not, but because many, if not perhaps most, of those who are poor are poor because of those who retain their wealth at the expense of those who are poor. So God seems to have something to say about that. . . . There should be no poor among us.[52] That means that those of us that have a bit more ought to be able to be in community with those who have less. . . . All the different systems seem to want to separate us and make us adversarial, versus moving us more towards a deeper sense of partnership."

—*Brent, white reformed pastor, Together for Justice, Los Angeles*

Of the fifty individuals who were directly asked these questions, forty-seven expressed strong support for what might be called "progressive" economic perspectives regarding the biblical view of poverty and economic inequality: that pursuing economic justice and fairness is a central matter of Christian discipleship, that Christians must be personally and collectively involved in efforts to combat poverty and economic inequity, that poverty and economic inequality is most often caused by greed, misfortune, and economic injustice rather than by individual choices or failures, and that God's will is for all people to have enough. Three individuals expressed a mix of what might be called "progressive" and "conservative" perspectives on the biblical view of poverty and inequality, combining concern for the poor and God's call to economic justice and fairness with a stronger tendency to defend the fairness of existing socioeconomic arrangements and to accept poverty and inequality as a natural consequence of the better or worse choices of individuals and communities (Table 3.1).

David, Justice in the City's coexecutive director, drew on the work of Viv Grigg—an international evangelical missions leader, author, and professor at Fuller Theological Seminary—to offer an overview of biblical teaching on "God's concern about eliminating poverty":

> Viv Grigg looks at the Old Testament and says there are three categories that land people into poverty. First, things that happen beyond your control: natural disaster, famine, flood. So a lot of that first category is talked about in the earliest texts like Deuteronomy and Exodus, because there wasn't a massive disparity of wealth in the early days of Israel's history. Right? So most poverty comes from some horror that befalls you. The second is personal sin or foolishness. And the Proverbs speak to a great deal of that. And the third is oppression. People victimizing you. And you see a lot of that addressed in the prophets, in the later history of Israel, where there's a greater disparity of wealth and power. . . . So I think you have those different causes. And because of that, there are different ways that you respond to those different causes of poverty. I think by the time you get to Jesus—I think they're all in play—but it's mostly oppression. I think Jesus deals mostly with the prophetic, it's mostly about oppression. . . . People start using wealth to oppress, later in Israel's history. So there are a lot of calls to end oppression. And God continually sides with the poor from Deuteronomy and Leviticus and all the way to the prophets. He continually sides with the poor. The oppressed. And then I think by the time you get to Jesus, the teaching has shifted from, "It's okay to be rich as long as you're looking out for the poor," to "It's not okay to be rich." That your wealth is to be used to bless people who have less. So it's not like you have to become poor yourself, although many are called to that as well. But that your wealth is not for your enjoyment. Rather, it's to supply your needs and to care for people who have greater needs. Then we build on all that to the modern era that is no longer agrarian: how do we actually help that happen? How do you do that? I hold that, in Jesus's teaching, wealth is considered a negative thing. It borders on demonic.

David's response highlights a number of common themes and texts— Deuteronomy 15, Leviticus 25, the life and teachings of Jesus, the Hebrew (or Old Testament) prophets, the Jubilee laws (which called for debt forgiveness, prisoner release, and property redistribution at regular seven and fifty year intervals), systemic and personal sin, a relational analysis of poverty and economic inequality—raised by many interview respondents (Table 3.2).

In a separate interview, Naomi—Justice in the City's other coexecutive director—elaborated on David's analysis of the multiple systemic and individual causes and responses to poverty in scripture while applying it to contemporary issues: health care access, the exploitation of low wage workers,

Table 3.2 Biblical References Cited: Poverty and Economic Inequality

Scripture Reference	Number of Times Cited
Leviticus 25 / Jubilee laws	12
Mark 14:7 / Deuteronomy 15:11 ("poor always with you")	10
Life / Teachings of Jesus	7
Deuteronomy	5
Pentateuch & Hebrew (OT) Prophets	4
Matthew 19:16–22 (Jesus and rich young ruler)	4
Luke 4:18–19 / Isaiah 61:1–2 and 58:6	3
Acts 2:42–47	2
Pauline epistles	2
Genesis	1
Exodus	1
Deuteronomy 15:4 ("need be no poor among you")	1
Deuteronomy 15	1
Zechariah 8	1
Malachi 3	1
Isaiah 58	1
Proverbs	1
Gospels	1
Mark	1
Luke 15:11–31 (parable of the prodigal son)	1
Luke 16:19–31 (parable of Lazarus & rich man)	1
John 1 / Jesus' incarnation	1
John 13:34–35	1
Acts 3:6–7	1
Acts 16	1
1 Corinthians 12	1
James	1

addiction and homelessness, immigration status, American materialism and greed, evangelical individualism, theodicies of poverty and wealth, and making the poor "illegal":

I think, in Viv Grigg and Betty Sue Brewster's word studies related to the poor in scripture, it seems like the major cause of poverty is oppression. The most common is oppression: abuse of people by the powers. There are also people that are poor through sin or addiction ... or weakness: that would be people through sickness or old age, widows, where frailty brings you poverty. Actually, that one is multiplying in our culture, with people becoming poor through lack of health insurance, which is now a really big cause of people falling from the middle class into poverty. You became weak and then you became poor. And then the other is calamity: famine, disaster. My sense is there's something true to that paradigm: that there is a complexity to poverty. Because there are multiple roots it can come from, and they can overlap and intersect in people's lives. . . .

And then there are the different religious beliefs about why people are poor. In [the U.S.], I think it's often, "Oh, they're all lazy or they're not as gifted or smart." There are all those different myths around it. And you can find a few examples; there's a little bit of biblical truth in that. Then there's people on the street; maybe addiction is the issue. Then there's other situations, like with this warehouse stuff [speaking of undocumented immigrant warehouse workers in L.A.'s inland empire]: you can work as hard as can be and you're still going to be in poverty. And these are for some of the richest companies on the whole globe. Walmart's warehouse, is out there, Home Depot and Target and whoever else. And you see: "How does the wealth of the nation move through our area, pass through our backyard, and leave only poverty behind?" That's a systemic problem. . . .

I think poverty is a sign—one of the signs of the fall—not of poor peoples' individual or particular sin, but of our collective sin, like: "something's wrong." Nature is out of whack, our hearts are out of whack, there's disease in the world. We're not following God as a people. If we were, there would need be no poor among us. But because it's a fallen world, there will always be some of that I think. There are sin roots to poverty. Primarily, I think, systemic sin. And then also some individual sin that finds its way in that. There's a moral side to it. And Jesus makes our accountability for that very personal. In the parable of the sheep and the goats (Matthew 25), he's there at the final judgment taking personally what we have done or not done towards the poor. So somehow with God this is a personal issue: both the individual and collective responsibility. It seems like both dimensions are there in the scripture. And you see God taking it personally. You see the emotion of God, the anger of God. In my own reflection on anger I've come to see that a right kind of anger is an aspect of love, or it wouldn't be displayed in the character of God. Anger at injustice comes out of the violation of precious things. Like relationships, the law of God, the dignity of human beings, economic abuses. There's a right anger when that is violated. And you see that in God. . . .

If there's an American blindness, part is that we have trouble hearing Jesus's teaching on money: really understanding economic dynamics as being related to sin or evil connected with greed, or of our responsibility to the poor being as relevant to faith as they are. Maybe some of that is changing. Probably the danger for evangelicals is we hear everything individually and nothing through any corporate dimension. Or that we have so deeply ingested the American idea that making money is always right and it doesn't matter how it's done or if there is fairness in worker's wages.

Here, people instantly here think of the homeless when you talk about the poor. They don't think of the working poor. And the poor in most places are "illegal" in some way. You see that here with the homeless: "You can't sit there or stand there, you're loitering." Or with people who have come from Mexico. All the squatters that we work with, they're on land that isn't theirs. They're siphoning off electricity. They're eking out their living. They have whole informal economies. People here have a lot of self-righteousness and say, "You're illegal." But actually, it's being poor that makes people "illegal." That puts that label over them. Being outside the system in some way puts you in that territory. And yeah, it's uncomfortable and complex, but doesn't a person have a right to survive? When we think of "illegal" we think of robbing, killing, those kinds of things. But putting a shack up on a strip of someone's land, is that the same? "I crossed the border to help my family out of poverty." That kind of seems like a moral person.

Naomi, like the large majority of interview respondents, emphasized economic injustice and systemic or corporate sin as primary causes of poverty and economic inequality alongside other natural and individual factors, while adding an intersectional component born of her experience working with undocumented workers and families in LA's inland empire.

An intersectional view of poverty and economic inequality was a surprisingly common theme among interview respondents. In fact, it was one of the three most common themes raised by the multicultural evangelicals I spoke with, along with a relational view of poverty and a belief that scripture demonstrates God's "preferential option for the poor" (Erica, white evangelical, Los Angeles) in economic and political matters. Cooper, a thirty-seven-year-old white evangelical church planter, neighborhood resident, and pastor of a small low-income immigrant- and US-born majority-Hispanic church in Los Angeles, used the word "holistic" to describe his understanding of the Bible's intersectional view of poverty and inequality. For Cooper and the other one in five evangelical interview respondents who viewed the Bible's view of poverty and inequality through an intersectional lens—all but three of whom were white—race, gender, education, language, skin color, immigration status, religion, and belonging to a majority or minority cultural group were among the many intersecting forces that determined the economic well-being of individuals and families in the United States.

A roughly equal number of interview respondents discussed poverty and economic inequality in relational terms, as symptoms of a "poverty of relationships" (Kent, white evangelical, Portland) or "broken relationships" (Doug, white evangelical, Atlanta) in the material and spiritual world. Given the well-documented nature of white American evangelicals' tendency to view race, class, and social relations through the lens of interpersonal relationships, this is a less surprising finding.[53] The scope and implications of interview respondents' relational view of poverty, however, diverged from the narrowly individualist and anti-structuralist views of their conservative white evangelical co-religionists. Doug, a thirty-five-year-old white evangelical strategic relocator and nonprofit leader affiliated with PCDA, referred to a widely-cited book among interview respondents across the country, *When Helping Hurts: How to Alleviate Poverty Without Hurting the Poor . . . and Yourself*, to describe his views:

> That book describes [poverty and inequality] as coming from broken relationships with God, self, others, and creation. I think that's a good way of describing it. Broken relationships. What I like about that definition is, if we describe poverty that way, then we're all poor. But there is also material poverty that I would describe as not having enough. . . . But instead of the "American dream," let's tie this back to Christ. Not the spiritualized, "Well, you're poor, but if you have Jesus, you're fine!" No. Christ meant for us to

live well and have enough and not just scrape by day-by-day. I would say sustainability, having enough, is the goal.

For Doug, interpreting poverty relationally did not mean spiritualizing its solution or ignoring its very real material consequences.

Kent, the white evangelical founding director of Neighborhood Partners in Portland, was similarly drawn to relational analyses and solutions to poverty, though, like David above, he situated these relations in larger political and economic structures and in a multidimensional understanding of the causes and consequences of poverty. When asked about solutions to poverty, Kent responded:

> It really boils down to good and healthy relationships, in multiple arenas. Within the family unit. With my neighbor. With the poor. And the kind of relationship I mean is the kind that has reciprocity and mutuality built into it. To where I recognize I need that person who is experiencing economic poverty. I need that person. They have things to teach me, to enrich my life. Of course, I don't mean keep people in [poverty]. I'm just saying I need to recognize my need for mutual and reciprocal relationship with that person, rather than thinking that because I'm part of the top 5% of wealthiest people in the world that I don't need people that are in a lower economic standing. . . . It sounds kind of simplistic. But when I know William, my homeless friend, my life is enriched. I am enriched. But he is as well. Not because I buy him socks or whatever. But because we have this connection. And if we were able to foster that relationship to where we clocked more time or we lived in closer proximity, that would just become more and more true. And then I would be able to understand him well enough to advocate for him wisely on a policy level. As it is, we mostly advocate for the poor, the homeless, from a distance. And we have assumptions about what would be good for them.

Rather than pitting interpersonal and systemic approaches to poverty alleviation against each other, Kent's relational understanding of poverty combined them into a holistic asset-based interpersonal advocacy approach rooted in reciprocal relationships.

Kent also—like David, Naomi, Cooper, Leonard, and Sandy above— viewed poverty as a result of multiple diverse and intersecting forces, "greed" being first and foremost among them:

I don't have a well-developed political ideology. It's sort of fragmented. I'm sure I have a lot of inconsistencies. There are a lot of positive things about free market. But there are also some tremendous dangers with it. And a capitalistic culture creates or energizes greed and selfishness. And yeah, we could also say a Marxist or socialist culture drains motivations. Nothing's perfect. Nevertheless, I think a free market, an absolutely free market, in a society that is fallen, is going to, in some ways, manifest itself in policies and structures that actually generates poverty. That make it difficult for people. So that's one thing. . . . Mental illness can spin out and result in poverty. Tragedy. Trauma. Education. Generational poverty. Bad relationships. That's certainly not exhaustive. I think we're in a society that has championed, from our founding documents, an individualism that fosters relational poverty and manifests itself in a variety of ways, economic poverty being one. I said recently to a conservative friend—and I was scared saying it but I really believe it—I told him I think some of the elements of the founding documents of the U.S. are anti-Christ-like. Not anti-Christ. But they're contrary to the values of the kingdom of God and what the church is called to. That being one of them.

I: What did your conservative friend say?

Kent: I mean, he argued. He's a smart guy. He was offended and hurt by it. But I believe it. If we create policies that protect the individual, we will inadvertently, in the long run, harm the individual. If we created policies that have the community as the primary benefactor, then we create policies that actually also help the individual.

Kent's multidimensional view of the causes of poverty and economic inequality, along with his combination of interpersonal and policy-based approach to poverty reduction, were indicative of other interview respondents who shared a relational view of poverty.

Anders, a thirty-three-year-old white evangelical Scandinavian immigrant and colleague of Kent's at Neighborhood Partners, independently confirmed Kent's expansive interpretation of relational causes and consequences of poverty—while also pushing it farther in the policy or structural direction—during an amusing interview a few days after I spoke with Kent. After answering, "Oh, hell," in mock exasperation when I asked, "How would you describe the biblical view of poverty and inequality?" Anders proceeded:

That's been a struggle for me actually with Neighborhood Partners and ABCD and kind of the American mindset. Because the way—and I wouldn't say I disagree with Kent—but he talks a lot about poverty as something along the lines of lacking in relationship.

I: Right.

Anders: Did you did you meet with Kent already?

I: Yeah.

Anders: I'm sure that's where he went.

I: Yep.

Anders: Lacking in relationship. On the other hand, I think he's pretty in-clusive there. So I think he would fit structures within that framework as well. And lack of relationship ultimately leads to bad structures. Coming from Sweden, I can see how the structures really come into play. . . . I tend to gravitate more towards starting with structures and fitting relationship into it rather than the other way around. But I think it goes both ways. I wouldn't say I'm a conservative in that sense. At Multnomah [Seminary] you hear a lot about, "If you just preach the gospel, the structures will be slowly transformed."

I: Right.

Anders: That's a cop out for people who don't want to change their ways.

Anders endorsement of a positive role for government in the prevention and alleviation of poverty leads naturally into the second question I asked inter-view respondents, namely, "What role, if any, should Christians or churches play in addressing poverty and inequality, and what role, if any, do you think the government should play?"

If the overwhelming majority of interview respondents took more "pro-gressive" standpoints on the biblical view of poverty and inequality, what of their views on the role of churches and individual Christians—as op-posed to the role of government—in combating poverty and inequality? Of my fifty interview respondents, thirty-six expressed strong support for both churches and government institutions to be actively involved in combating poverty and economic inequality through policy and practice (see Table 3.1). Eleven individuals expressed strong support for individual Christians and churches to be active in combatting poverty and economic inequality while expressing limited or ambivalent support for government involvement. Three individuals expressed limited or no support for government or church involvement in efforts to combat poverty and economic inequality.

Doug (white evangelical, Atlanta), like Anders, described poverty in relational terms while also pointing to a robust governmental role in addressing poverty and inequality. When I asked, "What would you say are Christians' or the church's role in addressing poverty and inequality? And then, the other side of that, the state or government's role?" Doug responded:

> What is sin? Do we define sin as being personal or systemic? Well, it's both. So I believe the church has a vital role to play in dealing with all sin. Systemic and personal. And as far as the government, I definitely believe government has a role. What is that role? I think it's common good theology: to create as many just structures and opportunities for people as you can. That's the role of the government. I mean, you can't address racism and segregation in the culture without government interceding. Now, how much government should step in? It's a tough balance. Obviously, that deals with different conservative and liberal ideologies.

Doug then proceeded to describe how his own political views had "drastically" changed since strategically relocating to Atlanta after growing up in a deeply conservative—religiously and politically—white rural community.[54]

Kent, Neighborhood Partners founding director, voiced strong support for church involvement in addressing poverty and mixed support for government involvement:

> *I:* What role do you think Christians or the church should play in addressing poverty?
> *Kent:* Well. I think they need to be deeply involved and passionate about it. I love how [evangelical pastor and author] Tim Keller speaks to this. One of the profound things he says out of James chapter 2 is that Gospel empowers the poor, and that anybody who is in relationship with Christ will do the same. Then he follows that up and says, if you're not involved in that in any way, you should question whether you know Jesus. . . . So, what role? Well, I think we should be involved in every level. From grassroots relationship building and relief responses, to interacting with or developing programs for

empowerment and advocacy in policy development on the governmental level. The followers of Jesus should be engaged in every level.

I: What role should the government play in addressing poverty?
Kent: That's a muddy issue for me. I don't have a lot of clarity. I have
at times thought if the church was really hitting it out of the park, it
would reduce the need for the government to be involved and could
perhaps enable government to be smaller. And yet, you can't wait for
that to happen. We have a mechanism—i.e., the government—to deal
with broad-scale issues. So should we not utilize that? I can't land
there either. . . . I think at this point, one of the best things to do, at
least on a local level, is to collaborate. With the government. And say
that policies that push for a greater justice and equity, we would agree
in the principle of it, and so we want to join and we want to work
together.

In advocating for Christian collaboration with government to move towards
"greater justice and equity" with respect to poverty and economic inequality,
Kent spontaneously raised issues of religious and cultural pluralism that we'll
return to in Chapters 4 and 5:

We have to recognize we are in a multicultural context. We have to be able
to play well with others. We have to be able to partner. We have to be able to
work together across faith ideologies. The church's efforts for dealing with
poverty can be greatly enhanced by the participation of other voices and
perspectives.

Kent, Doug, Anders, and the other proponents of the relational view of poverty and economic inequality consistently affirmed a positive role for government while representing a continuum of how large and central governmental
action to address poverty and economic inequality ought to be.

As reported in Table 3.1, regardless of where exactly they fell on this continuum, one thing nearly all interview respondents agreed on was the ina-
bility of churches or Christians alone to adequately address the challenges of
poverty and economic inequality. Heather (white evangelical, Portland) gave
an apt summary of this generally agreed upon point, while also adding a critique of purely charity-based approaches—whether church or government-
based—to combating poverty and economic inequality:

When I hear people make the argument that it's the responsibility of churches to do the work of charity, I say well, that's great! That's great. Yes. Churches should do the work of charity. But churches cannot bear the full cost of charity. I mean, not even close. The nonprofit I work with is a great example: it's faith-based, it addresses poverty, but churches contribute less than one percent of our budget. That's not unusual. I hear a lot of this "either-or" discourse, you know, "The church should do it," or, "The state should do it." I feel like it's absolutely "both-and," and it can't just be about charity. I read this article by some sociologist about how charity actually undermines justice: that charity is often more a function of affluent people's need to feel good about themselves and to maintain the status quo. It doesn't actually change anything, and so therefore undermines justice. And when I think about that with the church, I certainly don't think anything in that is intentional. I think it more likely has to do with people's misunderstandings about the operation of structural and systemic oppression. But charity doesn't change systems. It perpetuates them, without coordinating work on the other end. I feel like that's where the church really has power and has the ability to be prophetic. . . . The church can and should contribute to charity, but more importantly, the church should be looking at the system and being prophetic about the structures that perpetuate [poverty and inequality].

Heather's argument for the church's "prophetic" or advocacy role in combating poverty and economic inequality is central to the identity and mission of Christians for the Common Good, an advocacy organization discussed in detail in Chapter 4.

Sandy (white evangelical, Atlanta) brought together Heather's critique of charity-only modes of church engagement with Naomi's focus on the intersection of poverty and immigration in her discussion of the church's advocacy role:

I'm really passionate about immigration, obviously, because of my family [Sandy is married to a Latino immigrant]. The church can't fix that without the state. The church absolutely has to stand in the gap between the poor and the state. Use your privilege as a citizen of the country to demand fair reform. It has to be political. Just being nice to immigrants who live here, while good—you know, it's great if you want to register their car in your name, it's great if you want to give food to their kids—but they have no power. And you're always going to be the helper and they're always going to be the helpee. And if that's your brother and sister in Christ and in the community, you want for them to be on an equal playing field. And that absolutely has to be political. The state or federal government has to deal with that. I also think one of the biggest barriers for the church is this element of always needing to be in the helping role. I come from an evangelical background, so I definitely want people to know Christ and all these things, but the dynamic of that within the helping framework is really tenuous to me—and the underlying assumption that "poor" equals "not a Christian"— is really disturbing.

Sandy was representative of other interview respondents in her disdain for American Christians' "prosperity gospel mindset" and its conflation of wealth with religious or moral standing.

Combating Poverty and Inequality: With, For, and Against

How are we to think about the multicultural evangelical approaches to engaging poverty and inequality described in this chapter from the perspective of ethical democracy? To begin, there is much to be said for pursuing social justice and equity "with" rather than "for" economically disadvantaged persons and communities. Charity programs frequently address the symptoms rather than causes of poverty and inequality; create feel-good experiences for economically advantaged persons that are not shared by intended beneficiaries;[55] reinforce religious, moral, or cultural superiority and pernicious paternalism among the privileged; individualize and pathologize—or criminalize and homogenize—the poor and their troubles;[56] do nothing to question or challenge long-term systemic inequality at the roots; and fail to build reciprocal relationships of respect, solidarity, and power-sharing among class advantaged and disadvantaged persons, thereby reinforcing rather than challenging symbolic and material divides between the privileged and the poor. As such, there is much to commend people and groups involved in efforts to move away from charity-based "ministry to" or "service for" paradigms of combatting poverty and economic inequality.

At the same time, however, there are reasons to be cautious about overstating the efficacy of simply moving from "for" to "with" paradigms of community development, community organizing, and social change—whether faith-based or secular—to address poverty and economic inequality. "With" is no panacea, and if interpreted narrowly, it can obscure how macro-level political, economic, and social structures, relations, and histories are responsible for contributing to the existence and experiences of economically disadvantaged people and our shared responsibility to change them. Local efforts, no matter how transformative and collaborative, are not sufficient to address the scale of change and action necessary to effectively combat poverty and economic inequality in the United States. This is one reason why advocacy organizations—such as Christian for the Common Good, which we will discuss at length in Chapter 4—can make essential contributions to the pursuit of economic equity and ethical democracy, despite sometimes operating in a "for" rather than "with" mode of social change.

Moreover, even among groups that are most firmly committed to asset-based community development practices of indigenous leadership and resource mobilization—such as Neighborhood Partners and the Greenbush Initiative—the "with" paradigm never relies solely on local assets. For all its grassroots bona fides, the Greenbush Initiative still sought and relied on significant investment from extralocal political, economic, religious, and social sources: including the city of Portland's neighborhood office, development commission, and law enforcement agencies; educational and businesses institutions outside the neighborhood; and voluntary donations of time, money, and expertise from nonresident community activists, church members, and nonprofit workers. These resources were generated and kept under local neighborhood control to a greater-than-usual degree, in line with ABCD and participatory democracy principles. But they were not purely local, indigenous, grassroots, or neighborhood-based. Nor could they be, in order to achieve the type and scale of change neighborhood residents were seeking for their community through the Greenbush Initiative.[57] The iron rule of organizing—"Never do for others what they can do for themselves"—may be a helpful heuristic to ward off disempowering, expert-led, paternalistic, charity-only, nonstakeholder modes of personal and social change, yet the fact remains there are many things we *cannot* do for ourselves without help from others. This is true of all people—rich and poor alike—though we are not all equally endowed with capacities and conditions necessary to achieve our highest aspirations, or even more modest aims, for ourselves and our communities. Put simply, we all need each other.

Too great a focus, or to narrow an interpretation, of ABCD principles and the iron rule of organizing can promote a sort of "bootstrap communitarianism" akin to the bootstrap individualism of those who believe that the plight of the economically disadvantaged is entirely of their own making, to be remedied only by their own redoubled efforts to advance. This is folly. Of the many causes of poverty and economic disadvantage, a lack of hard work or desire for economic advancement is not chief among them. No individual finds their way to economic flourishing without the aid of myriad interpersonal and institutional supports—notwithstanding the all-American myth of the "self-made man (sic)" and its host of trumpeters whose self-congratulatory admonitions echo incessantly from the commanding heights of privilege—nor does any community in isolation. Bootstrap communitarianism is no better a philosophy of human flourishing and social change than bootstrap individualism.

To be sure, my research participants did not on the whole intend to promote bootstrap communitarianism as such. They had complex views of the causes of poverty and economic inequality—and of their mitigation—that weaved together exploitation and ambition, advantage and ability, access and addiction, compulsion and choice, the social and the spiritual, or, in sociological terms, structure and agency. They believed government should—nay, must—be actively involved in the work of reducing poverty and inequality in disadvantaged communities, rather than being left to churches or market forces. However, their strong disavowals charity-only "ministry to" or "service for" approaches to poverty and economic inequality could give cover to—sometimes intentionally, usually not—conservative arguments against government welfare and antipoverty programs. This resonance may help explain the enthusiasm generated by two books—*Toxic Charity* and *When Helping Hurts*—that seemingly every evangelical I spoke with across the country had read or was reading during the time I was conducting my research.[58] There are philosophical currents within the Christian community development and asset-based community development movements that can be—and sometimes are—used to mobilize antigovernment and antiwelfare sentiments that effectively decouples grassroots nonprofit community development work in neighborhoods from the legislative and policy work of state and federal governments, to the detriment of greater advances towards ethical democracy.

There is also sometimes disagreement concerning the role of faith- or broad-based grassroots democratic organizing—which can and must be contentious at times in its mobilization and deployment of power in pursuit of democratic accountability, inclusion, and justice—within multicultural evangelical community development circles.[59] All embrace community organizing to some degree: some with and some without reservation. For those without reservation, community organizing is an essential tool for holding political leaders accountable to disadvantaged people and communities who are all too often subject to the exploitation and domination of elites whose interests are prioritized by those in power. For those with reservations, contentious community organizing is sometimes necessary but best avoided where possible in favor of more collaborative, "win-win" relationships with public officials and local government.

Richard, PCDA's founding director, was one such person. He was wary of leading with adversarial democratic organizing as a primary mode of engagement, in part because "it often does not lead to good long-term relationship. If you can come away from a project with everybody feeling proud, including the city, that's a win-win." He elaborated:

> We have used [community organizing], but our preferred mode is a development approach where you sit down with city leaders and say, "Let's put this vision together, what's in everyone's best interest, and find something we can all agree with and put all our efforts behind. That's optimal. Very often, community groups will be led by advocates who have an axe to grind and they start off in an adversarial role, which gets the bureaucrats on the defensive, and then it's just a power struggle. So we tend not to be advocates at all. We tend to be developers. Now where we'll mobilize a community is when there is a zoning issue and we need to get that junkyard out of here, or they are not keeping their agreements: then we'll mobilize folks to go down to their city council and show up and say this is bad. And that's important, that's good community development work. When the government is not doing its job, when it's either corrupt or not doing what it's supposed to. We just came through one of these . . . [where] it took community organizing and sit-ins and leveraging power from outside to get the mayor to bring something up the priority list and get it done. So yeah, it's an important tool

of community development. It's not one that you lead with; it's one that is necessary at times.

Preferring to cultivate more collaborative than contentious relationships with local political and economic elites whenever possible, Richard framed community organizing as a last-stop tool in the community development toolbox, rather than a go-to mode of engaging poverty and inequality.

No doubt this preference was shaped by Richard's insider status among local political and economic elites: an older, highly educated, white heterosexual male Christian in a Christian-majority context with significant connections and respect among local political, economic, and religious leaders. Other less advantaged multicultural evangelical research participants were quicker to lead with community organizing and less likely to view political and economic elites as potential allies in their work. For them, combating poverty and inequality was not just a matter of working "with" versus "for" economically disadvantaged persons and communities, it also often required working "against" existing power-holders and structures of authority who benefited from the existing economic and political order. It is also important to note the grassroots democratic organizers often develop collaborative—not just contentious—relationships with government officials and civic leaders as well.[60] Table 3.3 summarizes the degree to which different organizations emphasized contestation or collaboration, established durable reciprocal relationships across class lines, and contributed to the short- or long-term redistribution of economic and political resources and power between economically advantaged and disadvantaged citizens and organizational participants—along with the organizational types and scales at which they worked.

Finally, despite its negative assessment in asset-based community development rhetoric, working "for" disadvantaged persons and communities— to provide free medical and dental care to disadvantaged Portland residents (Healing Hands), for example, or lobbying legislatures against predatory lending and reduced funding to government anti-poverty programs (Christians for the Common Good), or developing "economic discipleship" Bible studies to educate and encourage middle-class members to limit consumption and collectively donate hundreds of thousands of dollars to effectively-run nonprofit organizations (Christian Social Justice Network)—can also advance the interests of ethical democracy. Such work

Table 3.3 Summary of Poverty and Economic Inequality Engagement Strategies

Location	Anchor Organization	Organizational Type	Durable two-way "bridging" relationships across economic lines*	Redistribution of resources / economic capital	Redistribution of power / political capital	Contestation Emphasis	Collaboration Emphasis	Scale / Level of Primary Work
Portland	Neighborhood Partners	Community Development	+	++	++	−	+	Neighborhood
Atlanta	Peachtree Community Development Association	Community Development	+	++	+	+/−	+	Neighborhood
Los Angeles	Together for Justice	Community Organizing	+	++	++	+	+	Neighborhood / City / Region
Boston	Neighborhood Solidarity	Community Organizing	+	+/−	+	+	+	Neighborhood
Portland	Christians for the Common Good	Political Advocacy	−	++	+/−	+	+	State
Boston	Christian Social Justice Network	Advocacy / Awareness	−	+	−	+	+	Churches / City
Portland	Serving the City	Public Service	−	+	−	−	+	City
Portland	Healing Hands	Public Service	−	+	−	−	−	Individuals / City

* Lichterman 2005

can function as a channel of economic redistribution while also debunking negative stereotypes and promoting class-bridging solidarity and empathic understanding. Of course, this work is inadequate in itself to bring about the changes to our political and economic order that ethical democracy demands. But the sorts of goods and practices generated by these initiatives are things we need more, not less, of, if we are to move towards the economic equity required of ethical democracy.

4

Engaging Politics, Culture, and Religious Difference

In racially, culturally, and religiously diverse nations such as the contemporary United States, practicing ethical democracy and seeking common goods often requires individuals, groups, and organizations to build bridges and partnerships across different types of difference and disagreement. The practical realities of democratic politics and pluralism also often require groups to negotiate compromises and boundaries that fall short of the highest ideals and aspirations of their deeply held convictions. Even in the best circumstances, this is not easy to do. In the increasingly polarized, partisan, and divided United States, forging bridging partnerships and negotiating acceptable compromises is even more difficult. Yet the historical and sociological record insists it is essential for the survival and flourishing of any democratic republic.[1] As central players in culture war struggles over gender and sexuality, science and secularism, racial integration and injustice, and the place of religion in public life, evangelical Christians have participated actively in the politicization and polarization of American public culture in ways that threaten ethical democracy.[2]

How do multicultural evangelicals, in light of these realities, engage religious, cultural, and political difference and disagreement in American public life, and to what ends? This chapter begins examining this question by first considering a long-running Buddhist–Evangelical dialogue series in Portland before introducing *particularist pluralism* as a mode of public religion that many multicultural evangelicals across the country—including those involved with the Buddhist–Evangelical dialogue series, Together for Justice in Los Angeles, and Christians for the Common Good (CCG) in Oregon among others—found appealing.[3] Subsequent sections examine how CCG—a faith-based political advocacy organization—engaged religious, cultural, and political difference and disagreement in their attempts to mobilize evangelicals and other Oregonians to "shape public policy for the common good" through antipoverty, health care, and environmental

Good News for Common Goods. Wes Markofski, Oxford University Press. © Oxford University Press 2023.
DOI: 10.1093/oso/9780197659694.003.0005

legislation.[4] The heart of the chapter offers an inside view of how CCG decided which issues and partnerships to become involved in, which ones to avoid, and why. It goes on to consider the language and methods CCG used to mobilize evangelicals and others around its policy platform and specific legislation, as well as how it communicated and worked with legislators, interfaith networks, partner organizations, and the general public. Finally, the chapter addresses the tensions and challenges that arose from CCG's unusual religious and political identity, including culture war issues relating to gender and sexuality in religious and political or public contexts. It concludes with a discussion of how the exceptional case method developed in this study illuminates important multicultural evangelical approaches to engaging religious, cultural, and political difference and disagreement that are too often obscured by taken-for-granted assumptions about evangelical Christianity and ethical democracy in America.[5] A final note points to the importance of postsecular particularist pluralism and the practice of social reflexivity across difference for the prospects of ethical democracy and reflexive evangelicalism in the United States.

Ethical Democracy and Religious Difference: Buddhist–Evangelical Engagement across Culture War Lines

In 2003, an African American woman named Kendra James was shot and killed by a white police officer in Portland, OR, sparking outrage and protests across the city's African American community. Black pastors and churchgoers were heavily involved in the protests and public meetings held in the aftermath of the shooting, demanding to know, "When will a Black woman's blood be viewed as being the same value as a white man's?"[6] In response to the unrest, the Portland Police Department partnered with the National Conference for Community and Justice to create a series of dialogue circles involving law enforcement officials and religious leaders representing different faith traditions. One of the religious leaders invited to these dialogues was Dr. Paul Metzger, a white evangelical theologian and seminary professor of influence in greater Portland's surprisingly robust white evangelical community. Another was Kyogen Carlson, a Buddhist priest and guide of a prominent Zen Buddhist center in Portland.[7] Paul found the discussions "enlightening" and "provoking," as they addressed "a long history of racial tensions in Portland, even though I think many in the white Christian community are seemingly unaware of this." It was in this context that Paul first met Kyogen, along with other Jewish, Buddhist, Black Protestant, mainline Protestant, and Catholic faith leaders from the greater Portland area.

These discussions unfolded over the course of 2003 and 2004, coinciding with the contentious 2004 presidential election campaign which saw George W. Bush reelected in part due to his support for the Defense of Marriage Act (DOMA). At the same time, Oregon voters were debating Ballot Measure 36, which amended the state constitution to define marriage as a union between one man and one woman before it was ruled unconstitutional in 2014. Kyogen's left-liberal Zen Buddhist center included many LGBTQ+ persons disturbed by Bush's reelection, the passage of DOMA and Ballot Measure 36, and the apparent "Religious Right takeover of America."[8] Paul's conservative evangelical community largely supported Bush, DOMA, and Ballot Measure 36. In this context of "intensifying culture war tensions in Oregon and Portland" (Paul, interview), Kyogen reached out to Paul "since we'd already known one another from this other conflict" and "asked me if we could come try and build greater understanding" between their respective religious communities:

> My friend was deeply troubled by the anger and fear in his own community concerning the religious and political divisions locally and nationally. . . . He hoped that we could work together—beginning in our own religious communities—to build mutual understanding and to foster civil discourse. I was struck by my friend's insight into the anger, fear, and pain . . . of [both our] communities, which the warring sides incite and inflict on one another through their overcharged and oversimplified rhetoric.[9]

After several months of one-on-one conversations, Kyogen and Paul initiated a series of "town-hall-like meetings" aimed at providing a "safe haven . . . to encounter one another" across deep political, religious, and cultural divides, "beyond what [we] stereotypically read and see and hear of one another from the headline news."[10] Over the course of nine months, evangelical and Buddhist lay persons met for a series of "dinnertime discussions" and a weekend retreat to—in the words of one participant—"chip away at the wall of separation and better understand the 'other.'"[11] The communities continued to meet periodically for over a decade, including a weekend retreat held a few days before I interviewed Paul and several other current evangel-ical participants in the Buddhist–Evangelical dialogue.

It is not particularly surprising or noteworthy for secular and interfaith re-ligious leaders to pursue "mutual understanding and to foster civil discourse" through interfaith dialogue. It is somewhat more surprising and noteworthy for white conservative evangelicals to be involved in such dialogue. However, the real interest of this case lies in the way Kyogen, Paul, and their respec-tive communities practiced intellectual humility and social reflexivity across difference on the basis of particularistic and often incommensurate reli-gious convictions.[12] As Paul put it, the discussions pursued mutual under-standing and civil discourse by "going through our convictions, not around them," which he found "much more enriching and meaningful" because of Kyogen and the Zen Buddhist community's willingness to "engage *through* our distinctives" rather than pursuing "this kind of namelessness approach, you know, some kind of vacuous middle space" that avoided the existence of real and deeply contentious difference and disagreement.

For Paul and his evangelical coreligionists, the discussions raised a cru-cial question about evangelical engagement across difference in America's pluralist, democratic public sphere, namely, "How can the [evangelical] Christian community engage in authentic dialogue in search of the mutu-ality so necessary for civil society and yet remain true to the particular truth claims of Christian faith?"[13] Why seek mutual understanding and solidarity across difference in the public arena? Why treat diverse or antagonistic reli-gious and political "others" with compassion? Paul found his own answer in a "Trinitarian model of authentic dialogue" according to which "the Christian community is called and enabled to pursue mutuality *because of* the particu-larity of Trinitarian faith."[14] In this view, authentic Trinitarian Christian faith compels evangelicals to exemplify the "compassionate suffering of Christ" in their interactions with diverse social others, which can "create[s] space for di-alogue, fostering and nurturing the beloved community."[15] Metzger pointed to Black civil rights leaders Martin Luther King Jr. and John M. Perkins as models of Trinitarian faith in public practice:

> In contrast to secularist historiography, which sees the beloved commu-nity program as a "secular movement that used religion to its advantage,"[16] King's vision of beloved community in which all people are one "was the-ologically specific: beloved community as the realization of [Trinitarian] divine love lived in social relation."[17]

Trinitarian faith points evangelicals toward "non-coercive" modes of public engagement that "does not compel worship or acceptance of its vision; rather, it embodies it."[18] The cruciform pattern of Trinitarian faith compels faithful evangelicals to recognize that, "Like Jesus before them, they gain political influence by losing it (John 12:24)."[19] At the same time, however, as King and Perkins demonstrate, Trinitarian faith also "supplies a fitting arsenal for resisting the enemies of justice [in this case Christian white supremacists] through Christ's compelling sacrificial love."[20]

In his Trinitarian model of authentic dialogue and public engagement, Metzger grounds the evangelical practice of social reflexivity across difference in particularistic religious convictions rather than secular reason and political philosophy.[21] For Metzger, the antidote to pathological expressions of public religion represented by the extreme religious right and other types of ethnoreligious nationalism is not a strident secularism but rather better, more faithful religion:

> The Religious Right could benefit greatly from reflecting upon Trinitarian orthodoxy and its accompanying practices, such as the compassionate suffering of Christ, King, and Perkins. Jesus did not marginalize liberals and lesbians, but instead identified with those that the dominant culture marginalized.... King and Perkins would not limit the beloved community to Christians. Nor would they say Christians alone aspire to compassionate forms of existence. For example, the Zen Buddhist tradition resonates with Perkin's particular brand of Evangelical Christian faith illustrated above. Both forms of faith affirm compassionate existence, patient acceptance, and identification with the other. Such communities should come together in solidarity in the present hour.[22]

Benefiting from experiences of sustained reciprocal contact with Black and Buddhist Americans under conditions of relative equality, Metzger discovered a rich trove of resources supporting the practice of transposable reflexivity and intellectual humility across difference in the public arena from within his own particularistic religious convictions, while also finding points of convergence between his own tradition and others.[23]

Other participants gave different answers to the question of "why a Buddhist would desire to sit and eat with a Christian, and why a Christian would desire to sit across the table from a Buddhist?"[24] On the evangelical side, participants saw sharing meals and conversation with left-liberal

Buddhists as an opportunity to "live the love of Christ" by "becoming involved with them in a loving relationship."[25] They contrasted such an approach with one motivated by "purely apologetic reasons, as an opportunity to prove that Buddhism is wrong and Christianity is right, hoping all the while to notch another mark upon their belt of winning souls."[26] Though the dinner discussions revealed "many areas of disagreement," evangelical participants resisted urges to focus on "wining arguments" or "proving others right or wrong," focusing instead on building "beautiful friendships," "irenic communion," and in the spirit of St. Francis, "seek[ing] not so much to be understood, as to understand."[27]

Zen Buddhist participants welcomed the opportunity to dine and dialogue with those "standing on opposite side of the battle line in a war for our country and culture" for different reasons, "even though, as a concept, it seemed counter-intuitive and intellectually and morally distasteful," under the assumption that "someone who believes [what evangelicals believe] can't possibly be loving, intelligent, kind, spiritual, flexible, interesting, moral, etc."[28]:

> Within our dialogue group, we had very real, very charged differences. Members of our group truly believe homosexuality is a sin, and one of the members of our group is a proud homosexual in a long-term, committed relationship. Members of our group believe abortion is murder, and one of our members had gone through two abortions with his wife. . . . At one point a Christian I had grown fond of and considered my friend looked me straight in the eye and said with a smile, "Yes, according to our belief you are going to hell. Sorry about that." We both laughed as I said, "Well, that's OK; according to our thinking you may be lucky enough to get it right in the next life.[29]

"Finding the Buddha-nature in such 'others'" turned out to be a "powerful affirmation of my faith" for Buddhist participants.[30]

Zen Buddhist priest Kyogen Carlson invoked Buddhist understandings of *sangha*, karma, and mandala as warrants for the practice of intellectual humility and solidarity across difference. *Sangha*, or community, "one of the three jewels of refuge in Buddhism," compels Buddhists to recognize that "all wounds are our own"—including those inflicted by the "outrageous," "unreasonable," "rhetorical extremes" taken up by culture warriors on both left and right.[31] "For Buddhists, community is sacred," and Carlson found in sangha motivation to "keep working to enlarge the way I think of *sangha* and community to include everyone."[32] Sharing his dialogue experience at a conference whose audience consisted mostly of white conservative evangelicals, Carlson affirmed, "I do feel that all of you are part of my larger community, and I hope we can heal the wounds we share."[33] This perspective, that "we are all of one community, one body," was represented for Carlson by the symbol of the mandala.[34] Rather than oscillating angrily between a "left-right divide" pitting "standards" or "accountability" on one (right) side of the balance and "compassion" or "tolerance" on the other (left) side, the mandala encourages all to seek balance while recognizing both sides are necessary parts of a larger whole.[35] Rather than asking "who started [the culture war], and whose fault is it?" the Buddhist view that "karma is beginningless" shifts focus from past blame to present action, for "although we [may] not know how it started, we can vow to stop it."[36]

In addition to ongoing Buddhist–Evangelical dinner discussions, Kyogen and Paul's collaboration spilled over into other initiatives, including a conference in the aftermath of the bruising 2004 election season, "Building Beloved Community: Calling for an End to the Culture Wars," hosted at the evangelical Multnomah Biblical Seminary in Portland. Along with keynote talks by Paul and Kyogen, the conference featured a self-described secular humanist author and former director of the Oregon Council for the Humanities, a journalist from a leading secular left-liberal periodical who wrote a viral hit piece on Portland's evangelical community, two white male evangelical professors from Wheaton and Multnomah Bible College, a female Unitarian Universalist pastor, a female Black conservative Protestant radio host, a best-selling white male evangelical author, and several other participants in the Buddhist–Evangelical dinner discussion series. Each of these speakers discussed the importance of seeking mutual understanding and civil discourse across difference and disagreement in public arena for the health of American democracy and society, but did so on different grounds.

For Black and white evangelical speakers, the question, "How do we work together, not going around our worldviews, but through them?" was paramount.[37] One solution, the move to a "secular public square" which demands that "religion should not enter public discourse" and "we leave all our worldviews behind when we enter the public square," was deemed at turns "naïve," "ludicrous," and "not helpful."[38] Instead, they argued, we must "reject stereotypes and straw man arguments" while searching for "common ground options" that allow diverse individuals and communities to "work together for the good of our city . . . without either one demanding that the other give up [their] basic worldview in the process."[39]

But why and how would one actually do this, to "get along" across deep religious, racial, political, and cultural divides?[40] Gospel singer and radio talk show host Georgene Rice leveraged what Patricia Hill Collins refers to as the "outsider within" perspective to address the challenges of pursuing social reflexivity and solidarity across difference in the American public arena:[41]

> As an African American, I have the advantage of observing the cultural divide from a unique vantage point—as both an outsider and an insider. . . . We overlook the complexity of the individual in favor of a more monolithic group approach. This tendency to oversimplify our neighbor and what [they] might believe makes "getting along" a much greater challenge. . . . The truth is, I know very little about you until I abandon my presumptions and we sit down and have a real conversation.[42]

Rice's description of how a "Christian worldview" informed her approach to culture war politics is particularly instructive:

> As a Christian, my faith informs my worldview. And while I am no authority on the subject of "getting along," there are several things from my faith tradition that I have found helpful as I navigate the cultural divide. . . . We need to practice humility, which is a major feature of the Christian faith. We need to be humble when we're right and humble when we're wrong. . . . Is it possible to disagree and yet have respect for your opponent? I think the answer is yes. In fact, I know the answer is yes. But it requires humility, a willingness to admit mistakes, and the intent to resolve conflicts quickly. We need to acknowledge our tendencies to want to be right all the time, to stick with the familiar, and to be defensive. We need to be flexible, willing to adjust our presuppositions. And we need to respect our opponent's right to disagree and be heard. If we are to "get along" in the 21st century . . . we must recognize that we are of equal value and each has a right to be heard. We must recognize that winning isn't everything, and certainly not winning at any cost, and to live civilly [when we lose]. We're called to be countercultural in the Christian tradition, not hostile.[43]

Like other multicultural evangelical individuals and groups to be discussed in Chapter 6, Rice's warrant for practicing intellectual humility, social reflexivity, and bridge-building across difference and disagreement was rooted in core evangelical theological doctrines regarding sin, the fall, forgiveness, the gospel, sacrificial love, and others.[44]

Conference participants noted that "getting along" in this sense does not mean that there is no place for "justified anger" or emotionally heated conflict in public discourse,[45] for sometimes "anger helps preserve our integrity and self-regard" while also providing necessary fuel for the difficult work of political activism and social change.[46] Rather, the important distinction to be made regarding justified anger, intellectual humility, and transformative civil discourse—as many wise community organizers and activists know—is "not between emotion and reason but between uncontrolled action and deliberate action,"[47] or between the "hot anger" of spontaneous reactivity, resentment, and revenge, and the "cold anger" of strategic collective action for justice and social change.[48]

The evangelicals and Buddhists who participated in the dinners, dialogues, and retreats organized by a popular evangelical theologian and Zen Buddhist priest did so for different reasons—reasons rooted in their particular faith traditions and religious convictions. They understood themselves to be creating a different sort of public space than those dominated by culture war politics and media technologies designed to exaggerate and amplify distrust and animosity across religious, political, cultural, and racial differences:

> We need to partner with others to recreate and cultivate again civic practices such as town-hall meeting places where everyone's voice can be heard. This historic enterprise has been missing from the current political and cultural landscape, driven away by the mass-market, mass media individualism and non-local virtual spaces of many internet chat rooms and competing blogs. We cannot afford to write one another off, nor allow the mass media to oversimplify respective movements and over-dramatize the differences . . . Beginning with these town-hall-like meetings involving our respective faith communities, we have begun to move toward the creation of more complex public spaces than simply the state or market to inhabit.[49]

In building such "complex public spaces," Buddhist–Evangelical dialogue participants sought to move beyond "mutual understanding" to "mutual persuasion," which they saw as the only way to combine "mutuality and particularity" in "authentic dialogue":[50]

For true mutuality to exist, we must seek after mutual persuasion. Neither Christians nor those from other persuasions have all that it takes. All of us are broken. And so, we should seek to persuade one another to go be-yond where we currently are. We should also invite the society at large, sec-ularist and non-secularist alike, to go there with us. While the Zen priest and I view the transcendent differently, our respective views on compassion help us affirm one another's dignity and show one another respect. . . . We may not persuade one another to become Buddhists or Christians. But we are persuading one another to go more deeply into our respective traditions in view of what we learn from one another in search of sources that will ad-vance further a compassionate form of shared existence . . . impacting our rhetoric and particular engagement of the other for the sake of building a civil society and world for all.[51]

For Buddhist–Evangelical dialogue participants, Buddhist and Christian convictions about compassion and love provided shared grounds for respect and solidarity as they practiced mutual persuasion amidst deep differences while recognizing that persuasion has limits even as it is necessary for learning and growth.

Particularist Pluralism and Religious Difference in Public Life

Paul, Kyogen, and other participants in the Buddhist–Evangelical dinners, dialogues, and conferences had a distinctive way of engaging religious, cul-tural, and political differences in public life that was neither strictly secular nor strictly conservative or fundamentalist. It was also distinct from typical interfaith approaches to religious difference in that, as Dr. Metzger noted, it involved "going through our convictions" rather than "around them," thereby avoiding "this kind of namelessness approach"—a religious homology to colorblind racial ideologies—that attempts to construct "some kind of vac-uous middle space" or "lowest common denominator" that avoids the ex-istence of real and sometimes contentious cultural and political difference rooted in distinctive religious, non-religious, or anti-religious traditions. Instead, these individuals and groups practiced a mode of public religion called "particularist pluralism," in which religious and non-religious actors are "invited to fully express the particular religious [or nonreligious] beliefs and corresponding value commitments" underlying their public and political standpoints.[52]

Recent studies of faith-based civic action can help us understand the appeal of particularist pluralism—compared to more common interfaith approaches—to engaging cultural and religious difference among evangelicals. Simultaneously, these studies challenge reductive characterizations of religion as essentially divisive in nature while highlighting the role it can play in providing cultural resources for bridging divisions and generating solidarity across different types of difference in the public arena.[53]

Faith-based democratic organizing groups, for example, often deploy collective prayer and spiritual reflection as a type of "bridging cultural practice" to generate solidarity across race and class divides in internally diverse organizational and social contexts.[54] While incorporating generalist interfaith practices can facilitate bridging across race, class, and religious difference, it can also "result in certain forms of exclusion" in different contexts, such as those involving theological conservatives of various traditions who "may not be comfortable with interfaith religious practices," on the one hand, or in secular contexts where "prayer may not be considered appropriate or unifying," on the other.[55] This helps explain why evangelicals often avoid participating in ecumenical or interfaith projects: they know that their particular style of religious belief and expression is unwelcome in such settings, and they worry that participating will compromise their theological and religious distinctiveness.[56]

The obstacles and discomforts that can arise when evangelicals participate in generalist interfaith settings are vividly illustrated in sociologist Paul Lichterman's account of a Religious Anti-Racism Coalition's response to a planned KKK march in a small Midwestern city.[57] After months of meetings and relationship-building centered on the group's common antiracist goals, coalition leaders came into conflict over whether to hold a "Christian" or "interfaith" worship service that would include non-Christian faiths. In pushing for an interfaith worship service, Lichterman notes, nonevangelical coalition members "envisioned a religious identity we might call inclusive—but it would end up excluding evangelicals."[58] Rather than uniting the group, the prospect of hosting an interfaith worship service was precisely that which divided it.

Does this mean that evangelicals are simply unwilling or unable to participate in religiously plural organizations or public settings? Not at all. Yet, many evangelicals do find the generalist interfaith mode of public religion problematic. Consider Naomi, the white evangelical neighborhood resident, nonprofit director, and organizing committee member of Together for Justice in greater Los Angeles we met in the Introduction. On our way to a planning meeting for an upcoming anti-trash-facility neighborhood canvassing event, Naomi discussed some of the challenges she's faced as a white evangelical in religiously diverse contexts:

> I've prayed and been asked to be more inclusive—you know, not use the J-word [Jesus]—in group prayers. But I've pushed back on that a bit with Jon [a local community organizer] and told him, "I think prayer is to God, not to the group, and whoever is praying should pray according to what they believe. I'm going to pray to Jesus, others can pray how they want to pray, but I don't want to do this common spirituality thing, like interfaith stuff on the campus." And Jon was like, "Ok, I guess I see your point." . . . It's interesting, the Catholic church [centrally involved in Together for Justice] is a charismatic Catholic church, so the [Hispanic] priest will sometimes say, "Let's pause for a minute in the presence of God," and he will use the J-word, but it's more acceptable, there's more leeway, because it's cross-cultural. When I do it as a white person, I get dirty looks, like, "Didn't you get the memo?"

Naomi and her fellow evangelical volunteers rarely engaged in overt religious expression in the Together for Justice context.[59] But as this quote exemplifies, when they did so, they preferred operating in a particularist pluralist rather than generalist interfaith mode. In this preference, Naomi and her coreligionists were typical of the other evangelical individuals and groups across the country I interviewed and observed while conducting research for this book. Multicultural evangelicals eagerly sought to collaborate with others across racial, religious, class, and cultural lines, but they wanted to do so as evangelicals, maintaining their distinctive forms of religious identity, belief, and expression while encouraging nonreligious people and people of other faith traditions to do the same.

According to Naomi and other evangelical leaders involved in Together for Justice, this particularist approach to pluralism was a significant reason they were drawn to the organization in the first place. Larry—a retired pastor and long-time champion of evangelical community organizing work who first introduced Naomi to Together for Justice—explained:

I like both ways broad-based organizing is lived out in [Together for Justice]. The first is that the organization itself consists of a wide spectrum of people's organizations. You've got unions, you've got churches, you have Jewish synagogues. You can have Buddhists. You can have the local rose-growers' society. And you even have businesses involved in it. . . . The second thing I like about it is it doesn't operate under the [interfaith] principle of least common denominator.

Larry then described a regional IAF [Industrial Areas Foundation] leadership retreat he had recently attended. Leaders were asked to share a reflection with the group on why they were involved in organizing work. A Jewish rabbi, Catholic priest, and evangelical pastor converged on the story of Exodus, explicating it from the perspective of their distinctive faith traditions. Jim, the head of the local teachers' union—who self-identified as Pagan—was (unsurprisingly) not drawn to the Exodus story as a source of political imagination. Instead, he focused on the Declaration of Independence. For Larry, it was "just awe inspiring":

He talked about the Declaration of Independence as his sacred text. That's the term he used . . . and in essence, exegeted it. And suddenly I understood Jim in a way I had never understood before—by having him share his depths. IAF organizing encourages that kind of sharing, not simply out of our commonalities but out of our particularities.

Though not unchallenged, the local IAF affiliate's embrace of religious particularity and difference—rather than a generalist interfaith blending or "watering down" of difference—appealed to evangelical sensibilities.

Other cases followed a similar pattern. As described in the Introduction, an East Boston anticasino coalition of racially, religiously, and linguistically diverse faith and community leaders found surprising success in defeating a public referendum supported by the mayor, the governor, and a multimillion-dollar corporate lobbying campaign. By fostering the expression of particularist religious language in a diverse multicultural setting marked by secular and religious plurality, the community was able to mobilize quickly and energetically against the big casino project, to surprising success.

In Portland, the progressive political advocacy organization Christians for the Common Good (CCG) brought together evangelical and mainline Protestant individuals and organizations who did not see themselves as sharing a common religious or political identity. As

Teresa—a thirty-one-year-old white evangelical female and CCG board member—expressed it, even when the organization appeared unified on an issue or identity position, the internal reality was that, "We're still diverse and we're still arguing about it [laughing]:"

> Different board members have different ideas about what it means to be a Democrat, a Republican, a liberal, a conservative, an evangelical, a mainline [Protestant]. I can't tell you how many conversations I've had with Ron [CCG board president and co-founder]—who considers himself a progressive—and I don't consider myself a progressive. And he's like, "You are so progressive, Teresa." And I'm like, "I don't consider myself progressive." All these terms are so loaded. People have baggage attached to it. All these things come out. . . . We've got Presbyterians, Episcopalians, Adventists, evangelicals, . . . Democrats, Republicans, and Independents. We have not done very well at keeping the Catholic community involved. I'm not exactly sure why that is. I think it's partly because they have a really strong tradition of social justice and have some of their own outlets for that. So I think there's less of a need for them to be involved. Whereas a lot of the evangelicals are like, "Oh my gosh, I needed this."

Although CCG restricted membership to Christians, it frequently partnered with secular, non-evangelical, and non-Christian organizations and individuals in a variety of ways. The organization's exclusively Christian identity was, like nearly everything else, a point of convivial contention within the organization.

Christians for the Common Good made frequent and explicit use of particularistic religious language in its outreach literature, legislative testimonies, and organizational communication, often articulating political positions in strongly Christ-centered, Bible-based, explicitly religious language. The organization entered the public arena intentionally and explicitly as a biblically-rooted Christian organization:

> We have a vision of a state transformed by a network of Christian citizens, rooted in the Word, active in the public arena, boldly proclaiming the fullness of Christ's vision for humanity, and empowered to work together to shape public policy for the common good.[60]

Note the distinctly evangelical flavor of the statement's references to being "rooted in the Word" [Bible] and "boldly proclaiming the fullness of Christ's vision for humanity," which capture widespread evangelical commitments to biblical authority and the bold proclamation of Christ: in this case referring to a Christ-rooted politics of common goods for all Americans regardless of religious background rather than a proselytizing appeal to personal conversion. When organizational staff and volunteers gave public testimony in support of specific legislation at the state capitol, they began their testimony by saying, "When I look at the life of Jesus, it is absolutely clear that he cared for children," or, "My own commitment to the environment is rooted in my Christian faith. In [the biblical book of] Genesis, I read . . . ." Rather than toning down particularistic religious expression in public settings, CCG explicitly and intentionally ratcheted it up in an attempt to influence public policy and mobilize Christians—and evangelicals in particular— around a progressive political platform centered on "care for the poor," "care for the sick," and "care for the environment" while actively challenging Christian Right hegemony over the public use and interpretation of scripture. Democratic and Republican legislators alike commented on how "refreshing" and "helpful" it was to hear biblical language being used to mobilize Christians in support of policy positions that protected the environment, opposed predatory lending, and expanded health care coverage for low-income children and families.

Early documents and vision statements highlight the organization's intentional efforts to mobilize evangelicals and shift the ground of religious discourse in American public and political life:

> Christians for the Common Good is dedicated to promoting public policy in Oregon which reflects the priorities of the ministry of Jesus Christ. As an organization, CCG gives voice to the values of Christians who feel that the current public and political face of Christianity has not represented their full reading of the Bible or their set of deeply held values. CCG seeks to promote a politics which transcends partisanship by placing a greater emphasis on the common good. . . . In living out our mission, we actively advocate on three issues which have both clear biblical roots and a prominence in the ministry and teachings of Jesus Christ:

> **Care for the Poor**
> Jesus cared for the widow and the orphan, the Acts Church shared material wealth, and all Christians are called to show compassion to those in need and to seek economic justice. CCG supports:

- Adequate funding for food and shelter for all Oregonians.
- Economic initiatives that strengthen families and create work opportunities for the poor.
- A state tax structure which builds a more equitable community by closing the gap between rich and poor sustaining a vibrant middle class

Care for the Sick

As Christians seeking to respond to God's call for healing we advocate for a fair health care system for all people. Health care must respond to peoples' needs rather than wealth or position in society. CCG supports:
- Affordable healthcare for all Oregonians.
- Access to healthcare for all Oregonians.
- Adequate healthcare for all Oregonians.

Care for the Environment

For Christians, a love for God and a commitment to stewardship of His creation are inseparable. We recognize that our relationship with the environment is a witness to the good news of God's promise for redemption and renewal. CCG supports:
- The production and use of renewable resources.
- Sustainable growth which respects the quality of life for every human being.
- Regulations which protect our shared resources: water, air, and public land.

The brochure concluded, "Join a network of Christians making positive change for the common good!", followed by a number of specific opportunities for individuals and groups to get involved. As with nearly all of the organization's public communications, both brochures also incorporated direct quotations from the Bible in central locations, along with an early organizational logo (later abandoned) that prominently featured an image of the cross.

In an early FAQ document for interested parties, CCG described itself as an ecumenical Christian organization "focused entirely on policy change for the common good," with a "clear focus on bringing together the full body of Christ . . . Catholics, Mainline Protestants, and Evangelicals" while "specifically reach[ing] out to individuals and faith communities who are new to living out their faith in the public arena."[61] At the same time, the organization partnered regularly with a wide range of secular, non-Christian, and interfaith religious groups in its advocacy efforts. Under the question, "Do you work only with Christians?" the document explained:

CCG works primarily with Christian groups and individuals across de-nominational boundaries. We work with Catholics, Mainline Protestants, and Evangelicals—anyone who claims Jesus Christ as the center of their moral universe. However, we gladly encourage partnership, collaboration, and involvement with those who do not self-identify as Christians, but who share our values.

In answer to the question, "It sounds like you are a 'political' organization. Is that legal?" the document stated, "CCG members do get involved in the po-litical arena, but this is completely legal":

The work of CCG is issue-based and completely non-partisan. CCG only gets involved in legislative matters and does not support candidates. CCG supports the separation of church and state.

The document closed with a popular Dr. Martin Luther King Jr. quote on the topic of church-state relations: "The church must be reminded that it is not the master or the servant of the state, but the conscience of the state."[62]

An internal draft of the document indulged in a rather more exasperated set of mock questions posed by secular progressive and conservative evangel-ical skeptics clearly intended to let off some steam, including, "It sounds like you may be trying to set up a theocracy—is this true?" (Answer: "Absolutely not.") and, "Aren't you just distracting people from the true message of Jesus—salvation?" CCG's efforts to navigate the tricky political and religious terrain implied by these questions, and its embrace of postsecular particu-larist pluralism, are examined more fully in the sections below.

Christians for the Common Good and Postsecular Pluralism: Partnerships and Policy

The Introduction describes a trip to Salem (Oregon's state capital) that I took with Christians for the Common Good staff and policy committee members to meet legislators and give testimony before the house judiciary committee

on behalf of a CCG-sponsored bill calling for the expungement of criminal records for minors charged or convicted of prostitution. The small bill
was unanimously passed by both the Oregon House of Representatives and
Senate and signed into law one month later, adding to CCG's list of legislative success stories. At the hearing, Mindy—the twenty-six-year-old white
evangelical head of the human trafficking arm of CCG's legislative policy
committee—began her testimony with a direct statement of CCG's religious
and political identity:

> Christians for the Common Good unites Christians to seek God's justice
> in Oregon. We base our personal and public values on the life of Christ as
> taught to us in the Bible and advocate for policies which reflect this care for
> the poor, the oppressed, and the most vulnerable.

Mindy's testimony belonged squarely in the center of typical CCG strategies
of legislative testimony and public communication, advocating for justice-
oriented "common good" policy proposals on the basis of particularistic religious beliefs and identity.

For example, when Teresa gave testimony on behalf of a CCG-sponsored
renewable energy bill alongside nonreligious and interfaith organizational
partners, she began:

> Each of us is here today because we care deeply for the Earth and wish to
> preserve it for generations to come. My own commitment to the environ-
> ment is rooted in my Christian faith. In Genesis I read:

> *"In the beginning God created the heavens and the earth. Now the earth was*
> *formless and empty, darkness was over the surface of the deep, and the Spirit*
> *of God was hovering over the waters. And God said, 'let the water teem with*
> *living creatures, and let birds fly above the earth and across the expanse of the*
> *sky.' And God saw that it was good.*

> *And God said, 'let the land produce living creatures according to their*
> *kinds: livestock, creatures that move along the ground, and wild animals, each*
> *according to its kind.' And it was so. And God saw that it was good. Then God*
> *said, 'let us make man in our image, in our likeness, and let them rule over the*
> *fish of the sea and the birds of the air, over the livestock, over all the earth.' God*
> *saw all that he had made and it was very good."* These Bible verses compel
> me to testify before you today.

Christians for the Common Good is a network of active Christian citizens, working together to promote Christ-centered values for the common good such as care for the poor, care for the sick, and care for creation. Care for creation is why we are here today.

Senators, environmental stewardship is a deep concern for the Christian community. We find spiritual communion in the words of Richard Cizik, Vice President of Governmental Affairs for the National Association of Evangelicals and the subject of recent specials on PBS, CNN, and ABC Nightline: "The climate change crisis that we believe is occurring is not something we can wait ten years, five years, even a year, to address. Climate change is real and human induced. It calls for action soon. And we are saying action based upon a biblical view of the world as God's world."

Stewardship of God's creation—here in Oregon and throughout the country—is a truly Christian concern. Senators, please support this renewable energy bill. We thank you for exercising good stewardship over the miracle of God's creation. In doing so you are also exercising good stewardship on behalf of the poor, the sick, and the hungry, and those communities most adversely affected by the unsustainable use of our God-given resources.

Note the remarkably direct, biblically anchored, decidedly evangelical flavor of Teresa's testimony in support of renewable energy investment to fight human-induced climate change before the Oregon state legislature.

On another occasion, Teresa gave the following statement on behalf of a state ballot measure to raise tobacco tax money to fund universal children's health care in Oregon:

When I look at the life of Jesus, it is absolutely clear that he cared for children . . . and recognized that God's intention was that they live a full and healthy and safe life. In our society based on politics and business and big money, though, kids are essentially voiceless in securing their own health and safety. Supporting this measure is the most effective, secure way that we can ensure our children experience the fullness of life that God intended. Give kids a chance to live the life they deserve and join us by Voting Yes.

CCG's official statement on the bill began with a Bible verse, Mark 10:14, and continued:

Christians, seeking to love one another as God loves us, understand that the abundant life God desires for all humanity includes physical and emotional well-being. This means that we take seriously the call to promote wellness, and to advocate for healing and wholeness for all people. It also means ensuring adequate and fair access to health care for all people, according to their needs rather than their wealth or position in society. Care for the lives and health of our neighbors is an extension and expression of God's love for us and of Jesus Christ's healing ministry. In light of Jesus' particular concern for children, we find it a moral imperative as Christians that we support Measure XX. It will give hope and healthcare to underserved and uninsured children in our state. Revenue generated by this measure will also offer health care to "the least of these,"[63] whom Jesus directed us to serve: the uninsured working poor and other Oregonians who are medically underserved. We urge our Christian brothers and sisters to respond to Jesus' call for compassion by casting a YES vote for children's health.

Once again, note CCG's adoption of directly biblical and religious language to motivate and justify its mobilization of Oregon Christians in support of expanded health care access. Advocacy campaigns encouraging Oregon Christians and the general public to support specific health care, environmental protection, criminal justice reform, anti-trafficking, and anti-poverty bills followed a similar pattern.

Christians for the Common Good was very active in promoting and shaping Oregon's participation in expanding health care coverage through the Affordable Care Act (a.k.a. Obamacare). Glossy postcard mailings with a picture of a sick child on the front framed by the words, "I BELIEVE CARE FOR THE SICK is a Christian Value," were distributed to constituents across the state for them to sign and send to their elected legislative representatives, stating, "As part of my Christian faith, I believe that God compassionately cares for the sick and desires a just health care system. Please consider the values of equality, affordability, and transparency when voting for health care reform this legislative season." A related brochure, titled, "When I was sick . . . a theological reflection and factual guide on Oregon Health Care,"[64] summarized the theological reasons for supporting the Affordable Care Act:

EQUALITY: Because people of every ethnicity, economic status, and with any medical condition or disability are equally created in the image of God and loved by God (Gen. 1:27, Jn. 3:16).

AFFORDABILITY: Because care for our basic human needs is required by our basic human dignity, freely given by God alone, not our ability to pay or social status (1 Jn. 3:17, Mt. 25:40).

TRANSPARENCY: Because God holds our society accountable for how we treat our most vulnerable members and we recognize the strong temptation for the powerful to benefit from unfair treatment of the weak (Ez. 34:3–4, Lam. 3:33–34).

The second half of the brochure, titled, "What You Can Do," suggested specific action steps under three primary headings, "Advocate: Promoting systemic changes," "Educate: Educating yourself and others," and "Serve: Direct care to those who are sick."

During the financial crisis and Great Recession, CCG worked to protect essential public goods and services from state budget cuts in the wake of plummeting tax revenues. A brochure titled, "Love Thy Neighbor: A factual guide & theological reflection" combined CCG's commitment to verified facts and theological values to summarize CCG's support for two state ballot measures aimed at increasing state tax revenue to protect essential public services. The front cover included a Bible verse, Micah 6:8, "And what does the LORD require of you? To act justly and to love mercy and to walk humbly with your God." Inside, pictures and text and unpacked what it meant to do so in Oregon's contemporary context:

Act JUSTLY: In a just society, Scripture states that those who have abundant resources are responsible (Luke 12:48) to allocate what God has given them to those who are poor and suffering . . . and those who may depend on the mercy of others (Leviticus 19:9–10; Leviticus 25).

Love MERCY: Jesus said to demonstrate mercy to children, the disabled, broken, hurting, sick, and poor, in both His words and actions (Luke 4:18–19). In the story of the Good Samaritan (Luke 10:25–37), Jesus asked, "[who] do you think was a neighbor to the man who fell into the hands of the robbers?" The expert of the law replied, "The one who had mercy on him." Jesus told him, "Go and do likewise."

Walk HUMBLY with God: In humbling ourselves to serve the humble, we reflect God's attributes (Proverbs 29:7; Philippians 2:1–8) as we love our neighbor.

The organization then summarizes its position, "CCG's reflection on Scripture and examination of Oregon's current fiscal situation and tax structure have led us to support [Measure XX and YY]. We humbly invite you to join CCG in voting YES."

In addition to CCG's bill-specific theological reflections, the brochure summarized the ballot measures and the organization's reasons for supporting them in several sections. In a section, titled, "Why Vote YES?" CCG answers:

These measures will modestly tax Oregon's top 2.5% wealthiest individuals (who earn over $250K) and will increase the $10 corporate minimum tax (for the first time since 1931). [This] will provide an estimated $1 billion that will support education, health care and human services, and public safety. These services affect the well-being of all Oregonians but especially the most vulnerable of us.

CCG also distributed carefully detailed talking points, Q&A fact sheets, and further theological reflections to pastors, church members, volunteers, and other interested parties in support of the measures. Both CCG-supported ballot measures passed.

In another effort, Christians for the Common Good joined forces with Ecumenical Ministries of Oregon, the Lutheran Advocacy Ministry of Oregon, and St. Vincent DePaul of Oregon, along with other faith-based and secular groups, to support a predatory lending bill capping payday loan and small consumer interest rates at 36 percent. CCG distributed a collaborative advocacy postcard featuring a cartoonish picture of a man-shaped shark in a business suit with briefcase overflowing with cash read, "People of faith in Oregon say: 'It's time to close the door on loan sharks,'" followed by a Bible verse, Proverbs 28:8, "If you make money by charging high interest rates, you will lose it all to someone who cares for the poor." In a separate communication, CCG stated its position to its own constituents and networks, which opened with a Bible verse, Matthew 25:40, "I tell you the truth whatever you did for the least of these brothers of mine, you did for me." The letter continued, "Dear friend in faith,":

Christians for the Common Good is asking for your help to put an end to modern day usury that is taking place with payday loans. . . . You and your congregation can make a difference. Together we can speak with a common voice in support of the payday loan act and bring an end to predatory lending. **As people of faith, we have an important voice in this vital moral issue**. Please join us today.

The mailing concluded with specific information and ways to reach out to legislators. Media reports and op-eds featuring CCG leaders and volunteers figured prominently in this campaign as in others. "As you can imagine, the payday loan and car title industry has deep pockets. . . . The moneylenders have a lot of resources, but we have our voices of conscience," wrote a former CCG director to a local newspaper, "Our support can drown out their dollars, but only if we speak out." This CCG-backed bill was passed. CCG was also active in pushing consumer protection laws in the mortgage industry, sending letters to Oregon legislators that began, "As a Christian, I am deeply troubled by the economic crisis Oregon families are facing due to the predatory lending practices in the subprime mortgage industry."

Criminal justice reform also captured the advocacy attention of Christians for the Common Good in several instances, including a movement to abolish the death penalty in Oregon that I will describe further below. An earlier effort opposed a state ballot measure that, as a CCG brochure on the bill read, "requires mandatory prison sentences for **first time** offenders up to **36 months** for property, drugs, and identity theft crimes" (emphases original). Titled, "Revisiting the Gospel: A factual guide and theological reflection on Measure XX," the brochure's cover featured a color photo of men in prison clothes lined up behind bars with an adjacent Bible verse. Following the standard CCG format, the inside brochure highlighted three theological themes, in this case "justice," "mercy," and "grace":

> JUSTICE is commonly associated with the concept of **retribution**, or "getting what you deserve." However, in the Hebrew Scriptures, the word *justice* is used in parallel with God's *righteousness*. **Justice** is doing things right with God and people. Unlike retribution, God's justice is also full of mercy with a desire to heal and restore lives.

> MERCY: In Matthew 18:21-33, Peter asks Jesus how often he should forgive someone. Jesus responds comparing the kingdom of heaven to a merciful king who, "*out of compassion*" (v.27) for his servant, releases and forgives his debt. However, this servant then turns to mercilessly demand the debt of another. When the king heard what his unforgiving servant did, he told

him, "*Should not you have had mercy on your fellow servant, as I had mercy on you?*" (v.33). Jesus' justice is **restorative**. Jesus especially cared for the poor, vulnerable, and outcasts of society (Luke 4:17-18) desiring all people to be redeemed regardless of their crime and be transformed into his perfect likeness.

GRACE: We were all prisoners of sin (Galatians 3:22) forgiven by the merciful justice of God and in turn should demonstrate God's righteous love to others in hopes for holistic restoration of our lives, families, communities, and society.

The section concluded that the ballot measure under consideration, "does not have room for grace." Finally, in a section on "impact," CCG argued against the measure's impact on:

FAMILIES. Women will be adversely affected by [this measure]. Separating mothers from their children for a minimum of 3 years would increase the burden on the already strained foster care system. Children of incarcerated parents are 7-8 times more likely to end up in prison themselves.

SERVICES. [This measure] would divert funding from vital social service programs that "defend the cause of the poor and needy" (Jeremiah 22:16).

STEWARDSHIP. [Oregon] spends a higher percentage of their general fund on prisons than any other state. [This measure] "increases [the] inmate population by 3,000 to 6,000 by 2011 at a cost of $200 million to $400 million a biennium." – The Oregonian, 9/15/08

PEOPLE. 84% of [this measure] will involve addiction related crimes. Prisons do not heal addictions.

To CCG's satisfaction, the measure was narrowly defeated.

Christians for the Common Good was also active in broad antipoverty advocacy efforts, including an effort to add "persons of homelessness" to 2011 hate crimes legislation. A brochure titled "Dignity" featured the photo of a homeless man who died in 2008 after having been set on fire, along with a Bible verse, Genesis 1:27, "So God created human beings in his own image, in the image of God he created them." It continued:

In the Spring of 2010, CCG's Poverty Advisory Committee held a listening session with persons without homes to hear what kind of laws they would like to see for themselves and their homeless community. Everyone said that they would like to be treated with dignity . . . like human beings. They began to share about the violence and abuse that they have experienced and have heard of. The committee then began to work with others to see about adding persons of homelessness to hate crimes legislation in 2011.

In addition to national and state-level statistics concerning violence against homeless persons, the brochure guided readers to several potential follow-up and action steps.

As demonstrated by the religious language and self-identification used by Christians for the Common Good in its advocacy efforts, the organization was intentionally explicit about its evangelical-infused Christian identity. Christians for the Common Good was also, however, extremely active in forming partnerships with other interfaith, secular, and non-Christian religious groups and organizations in its outreach and advocacy work. During a Great Recession–era attempt to cut the State Children's Health Program (SCHIP), CCG was part of a diverse group of almost forty organizations that mobilized support to fight for its continuation. CCG's director was quoted in local news stories on the subject with leaders of the Oregon Medical Association, the Oregon Association of Hospitals and Health Systems, and the Oregon Center for Public Policy. CCG co-sponsored a "discussion on environmental stewardship" hosted by Oregon's secretary of state, "Global Warming and The Impact on Oregon: What's Really Happening? What Can We Do?" alongside a local UCC (United Church of Christ) church, the Oregon Environmental Council, a local Presbyterian church, and a regional Unitarian Universalist group. The organization regularly supported, crafted, organized, and signed joint statements and campaigns on particular children's health, consumer protection, senior care, affordable housing, antihunger, and antipoverty bills with interfaith organizations. In one "interfaith forum" co-sponsored by CCG and Ecumenical Ministries of Oregon (EMO), "Building a Movement for Health Care Justice: An Interfaith Organizing Meeting for Yes on Measure XX," the organizations declared jointly, "We find it morally unacceptable that more than 100,000 Oregon children currently lack health insurance, and that health insurance has become unaffordable for many working Oregonians." An invitation flyer included endorsements from over 20 organizations and faith leaders representing a broad spectrum of Oregon citizens and communities, including Protestant and Catholic ministers, Jewish rabbis, Muslim faith leaders, and secular organizations such as the Oregon AFL-CIO, Oregon Business Association, Oregon Education Association, American Cancer Society, American Lung Association of Oregon, Oregon PTA, and Children First for Oregon, among others.

Christians for the Common Good was also an organizer and participant in Oregon's annual Interfaith Advocacy Day which brought hundreds of faith leaders and activists to the state capital every year for a day of talks, policy briefings, trainings, and meetings with legislators. In an invitation letter to constituents, CCG wrote, "Dear Pastor,"

> Many interest groups will lobby state leaders this year. Many of them will focus only on their own special interests. As one of the planners of *Interfaith Advocacy Day*, CCG is calling on the Christian community to lobby for something different. This is an opportunity to be a public example of Christian compassion, justice, and service. . . . Following Jesus's sermon in Luke 4, we will raise our voices proclaiming *good news* for the poor and suffering in our state. **We will ask our public leaders to do the most to help the least among us.** . . . Why are more Oregonians going without health care, especially children? Why do we allow families, living among us, to go hungry or homeless? Poverty and inequality are not just issues of charity and personal responsibility. They are also issues of *justice* and *public responsibility*.

Interfaith Advocacy Day brought together a wide range of faith and government leaders to focus on "hunger, health care, and housing," including the head of a prominent local Muslim Association, Jewish rabbi's and congregation members, Lutheran and United Church of Christ pastors and congregation members, Ecumenical Ministries of Oregon, the Oregon Faith Roundtable Against Hunger, Oregon Hunger Relief Task Force, Oregon Department of Human Services, and several legislators and legislative staff members, among others. The event was sponsored by fifty Muslim, Jewish, Catholic, Lutheran, Black Protestant, mainline Protestant, evangelical Protestant, Unitarian, Baha'i, Scientologist, interfaith, and religiously unaffiliated groups and organizations. Of the fifteen individuals who signed up for further advocacy leadership training with CCG and EMO, three were members of a prominent Portland evangelical megachurch, two came from an Evangelical Covenant church, three belonged to Lutheran congregations, and others to Catholic, Quaker, United Methodist, UCC, and nondenominational congregations.

CCG also helped organize an "interfaith letter" to an Oregon senator "opposing the use of torture by any U.S. Government Agency" in the wake of Abu Ghraib and other prisoner abuse crimes committed by US soldiers and intelligence officers against Muslim individuals and communities around the world. Along with the executive director and board members of Christians for the Common Good, the letter was signed by over 130 prominent Catholic, Orthodox, Lutheran, Jewish, Muslim, Black Protestant, evangelical and mainline Protestant, interfaith, Unitarian, Scientologist, and other/unidentified faith leaders in Oregon. It began:

> We are Oregon religious leaders representing many faiths, denominations and regions here in the state of Oregon. We write to express our moral opposition to the use of torture as a method of interrogation by any agency of the U.S. government....
>
> Torture is universally condemned by people of faith and conscience as contrary to our most deeply held values.
>
> For Christians, opposition is based, in the words of the National Council of Churches "on our fundamental belief in the dignity of the human person created in the image of God and the rights accorded to all persons by virtue of their humanity." This view is also expressed by the National Association of Evangelicals, which has an endorsed An Evangelical Declaration Against Torture. This Declaration is grounded in a Christian view of the sanctity of life, and in a commitment to human rights which finds expression in Christian sources dating to long before the Enlightenment....
>
> The Jewish Tradition also strongly condemns torture, and this has been expressed recently when 600 North American Rabbis signed the Rabbinic Letter Against Torture. . . . Strong statements opposing any use of torture by the U.S. government have also been issued by The Rabbinical Assembly (of Conservative Rabbis), the Reconstructionist Rabbinical Association, the Union for Reform Judaism and the Jewish Council on Public Affairs.
>
> The teachings of Islam are also quite powerful, "*Oh you who believe! Stand forth for Allah witnessing with justice. And do not let hatred of a people sway you into injustice, but adhere always to justice. That is true piety,*" (Qur'an, 5:8). The spirit of this Qur'anic decree calls for an end to torture and for the

universal guarantee of humane treatment and due process for all prisoners. For Muslims the use of torture under any circumstances is abhorrent.

The letter proceeded to argue against the use of torture under any circumstances on pragmatic and moral grounds, calling on the senator to support new anti-torture policies and congressional guidance for the US military and intelligence services.

Picking Issues and Partners: An Insider View of Christians for the Common Good Decision-Making

How did Christians for the Common Good decide what sort of organizations to partner with and what sort of bills to sponsor? Every community has boundaries, every identity entails exclusions, and every organization must make choices about the sorts of members, partners, and activities it will endorse and engage in, no matter how inclusive a community or organization aims to be.[65] Two core criteria guided CCG partnership decisions:

> Christians for the Common Good will evaluate the potential for partnership with another organization primarily based on two considerations:
> a. A clear commitment to the common good on the part of the potential partner
> b. A shared and authentic interest in a specific issue or set of issues

In addition to not "accept[ing] money or in-kind donations for support of another organization's mission or campaign," CCG's final criterion for partnership was, "Christians for the Common Good will proactively seek partners from a diverse set of political backgrounds," a commitment that was demonstrably evident in the organization's mission, membership, staff and board.

Regarding particular issues or bills, CCG's criteria outlined a "prophetic, political, and practical" approach to issue selection:

1. Prophetic
   a. Biblically-grounded
   b. Theological justification
   c. Christian precedent (on both sides)
   d. Build up the Body of Christ

2. Political
   a. State-level
   b. Issue specific (not partisan-specific)
   c. Intentional (Integrative?)
3. Practical
   a. Broadly and deeply felt (needs a super-majority: at least ½ of the Board must vote on an issue, and 80% of the Board must be in agreement)
   b. Solution must have a clear action opportunity
   c. Sustainable (within our capacity)[66]

The organization's official issue criteria statement ends with a quote from the Bible, Psalm 140:12, "For I know that the Lord secures justice for the poor, and upholds the cause of the needy."

CCG's issue criteria were fleshed out at a Board Retreat early in the organization's history:[67]

> It is clear from our mission statement that CCG intends to be actively engaged and involved in the political process in Oregon in an attempt to "shape public policy for the common good." It is also clear from our mission statement that we desire to be involved in advocating for systemic change to benefit Oregon's population by focusing on specific policy issues rather than simply being involved in charitable work. . . . To date, there has been general agreement on the types of issues on which CCG will become engaged in the political arena. Taking our cue from the life and ministry of Jesus Christ, as recorded in the New Testament, CCG has elected to prioritize the following issues, (a) advocating for those in poverty, (b) advocating for greater access to healthcare, and (c) advocating to protect God's creation—our environment. The issues we have prioritized to date are not intended to be an exhaustive list of the issues to which we are committed; as CCG is able to develop additional resources, we hope to expand our advocacy efforts into other areas that promote the common good.

In light of acute politicization and polarization of culture war issues involving sexuality and reproduction, Christians for the Common Good eschewed taking positions on abortion and LGBTQ+ issues. "Because other Christian organizations are already actively engaged on issues related to abortion and homosexuality," CCG's official position stated, "and because we felt that taking a position on these issues would compromise our ability to successfully advocate on our priority issues, we have formally decided not to taken an organizational position either of these two issues."[68]

Although it did not take an organizational position on policy issues related to abortion and LGBTQ+ rights, CCG did write a position statement on the subject:

> We believe sanctity of life is a "seamless garment", that all of life is sacred, and that, as Christians we are called to speak on behalf of all of God's creation. CCG exists to focus on the areas of life—the creation, the sick, the poor, the disenfranchised—that have been neglected by some in the body of Christ. We realized early on that if we took positions on abortion and gay rights, all the focus would again go to those two issues. We believe we are called to speak out on neglected issues, and if we were to take positions on abortion and gay rights, would lose our effectiveness in doing so for the following reasons:
>
> 1. While the causes are important, the rhetoric, tactics, and spirit of those who oppose abortion and gay rights has been less than Christ-like. These actions have led to divisions in the body of Christ, and to a compromised witness in the world. Because abortion and gay rights have, sadly, been so polarizing, were we to take a position on those issues, we would compromise our ability to call people of faith to the common ground around sanctity of life issues we advocate for.
> 2. Those opposed to abortion and gay rights have clearly aligned themselves with one political party, and in the minds of many people we want to reach with our message, that political party and religion are inseparable. We assiduously avoid being aligned with any political party, and therefore need to stay away from issues that both in reality and perception, have been the province of one party in such a way that has again, we believe, compromised the true gospel.

In its efforts to mobilize Christians around a "non-partisan" politics of the common good, Christians for the Common Good sought to avoid culture war politics to focus on environmental, economic, educational, human rights, and health-related policy advocacy rooted in "the teachings of Christ."[69]

As an example of how CCG's issue selection process worked, consider the Responsible Mortgage Lending Act, an Oregon Senate bill requiring increased transparency, disclosures, and enforcement of fair lending practices in the wake of the housing mortgage crisis. An internal document titled, "Housing Mortgage Crisis," justified CCG's decision to support the bill thus:

> CCG has a clear methodology for selecting issues it takes on and the actions its members take. Before moving forward, all issues and solutions must fit the following criteria: Prophetic, Political (but non-partisan), and Practical. CCG is supporting [this bill] for the following reasons:
>
> PROPHETIC: This bill is prophetic in that it speaks God's truth; that He wants us to be compassionate and fair in our financial dealings with our brothers and sisters. The Bible clearly shows a special concern for the poor and their vulnerability to usury. The Bible clearly sets up a moral standard that supersedes pricing based upon what is legal, customary, or "What the market can bear." Our actions recall Christians to this Biblical truth and urge them to reclaim this mandate.
>
> POLITICAL AND NON-PARTISAN: This bill is political but non-partisan in that it in no way strikes at pro-Democrat or pro-Republican issues. It does not hand out subsidies, cancel debt, or relieve individuals of the responsibility of their decision-making. . . . [It] will help secure a primary asset for middle class and working poor families struggling to emerge from poverty, provide education for their children, and participate effectively in the free market for capital investments.
>
> PRACTICAL: The housing bill is simple, clear, and easily implemented. It positively affects all income groups and constituents. We have the capacity to support it.
>
> STRATEGIC PLAN: Lastly, the bill fits clearly within CCG's strategic plan. It allows us to be a prophetic voice securing legal protections for the poor. It promotes partnerships across party lines. It is a vehicle for us gaining voice in the community. Lastly, it broadens the discussion of Christian values by providing a clear-cut case for how Christians should be active in supporting public policy for the common good.

This was followed by a "Biblical Support" section that provided a typed-out selection of scriptures that spoke to issues related to unjust lending and economic justice: Proverbs 31:8–10, Psalm 82:3, Jeremiah 5:27–29, Exodus 22:25, Leviticus 25:35–38 and 21–25, Deuteronomy 15:1–6, Nehemiah 5, Ezekiel 18:16–18, and Jeremiah 22.

Field notes from participant observation provide another lens through which to view CCG's issue selection process. I was a regular participant in all of CCG's legislative policy committee meetings in preparation for Oregon's first legislative session of 2012. I joined seven CCG members, staff, board members, and former executive director—all of whom were white evangelical or mainline Protestants—on CCG's Public Policy Committee, whose charge was to "meet and assess policy options for the 2012 legislative session focused on CCG's key issues."[70] Based on prior work of separate CCG policy committees and known priorities for the 2012 legislative session in Oregon, four issue areas were discussed at the first committee meeting: abolishing the death penalty, health care, human trafficking, and "poverty/economic justice."

On the first issue, CCG had recently been invited to add its name and support to a coalition of fifty-plus organizations calling on the state to repeal its death penalty. In its partnership appeal to Christians for the Common Good, the requesting coalition stated, "We feel from what we know of the progressive positions that your organization holds, it would be a consistent consideration signing on as a 'supporting organization' and for your organization to speak out in favor abolition." Quoting CCG's organizational mission statement, the coalition argued:

> As a network of Christians who care about creating a more just and equitable Oregon, we point out that the death penalty is not a public policy that supports that proposition. Christian teachings do not embrace the flaws with the death penalty:
> - The death penalty is biased against the poor.
> - The death penalty is biased against people of color.
> - The death penalty is NOT a deterrent to violent crime.
> - The death penalty is rife with mistakes, evidenced by the 138 exonerations of death row inmates.
> - The death penalty is very costly to maintain, at the expense of underfunded programs that your organization would support.
> - The death penalty puts the people of Oregon in the business of state-sanctioned killing.

After addressing further organizational details and requests, the letter concluded by "respectfully ask[ing] for your support in this effort."

The requesting coalition knew its audience. "It's sort of a no-brainer morally," said Harold, the fifty-plus-year-old CCG board member who brought the request to the committee, "it singles out minorities." The only question was whether taking action on death penalty abolition was practically sustainable and fit within Christians for the Common Good's core advocacy areas. On this point, a committee member answered Harold, "If the majority of people sentenced to death are single African American men, and a large percentage of them are poor, then the death penalty is also a poverty issue." After a cursory "theological reflection" about the request's biblical warrant, in which one committee member discussed how "Jesus changes the ethics of [capital punishment]" in Old Testament law, the committee unanimously agreed to recommend to the board that CCG become a supporting organization. Harold and Nancy—a fifty-plus-year-old mainline Protestant board member—volunteered to write a statement with supporting theological reflection to present to the board for posting on the organizational website.

The committee's discussion then turned to the issue of health care—a central CCG advocacy area in light of intensive state-level advocacy surrounding the Affordable Care Act and the presence of several physicians and health care policy experts on the committee. A CCG document on the biblical basis for universal health care was discussed. When Teresa—a thirty-one-year-old white evangelical CCG board member and former executive director—mentioned a recent interview in which a National Association of Evangelicals executive expressed support for legislation that extended health care services to undocumented immigrants—several members responded, "Wow!" and "Great!" Harold, the CCG board member leading the organization's death penalty abolition charge, added with conviction, "Health care is a basic human right. So undocumented status should not matter for care." George— another white fifty-plus-year-old board member—discussed the parable of the Good Samaritan in Luke 10 as biblical warrant for his position that the "conflict over citizenship shouldn't matter for care." The conversation turned to how the organization should position itself in relation to Oregon's rollout of Affordable Care Act health care exchanges. Noting insurance industry lobbying for existing condition clauses and higher premiums demands, a committee member noted that, "People are concerned that this might be good for middle class people, but not for the poor." The committee agreed to "advocate for a quality essential benefits package that is affordable and accessible to all Oregonians," while working to "eliminate insurance companies' pre-authorization activities."[71]

George took the lead on the final agenda item: poverty and economic justice. He opened with a personal comment on Luke 12:48, "From everyone who has been given much, much will be demanded; and from the one who has been entrusted with much, much more will be asked" (NIV), which he said formed the basis of his subsequent discussion. The financial crisis had created an extremely tight budgetary climate in Oregon, including the likelihood of a $250 million budget cut in January, such that "the only reasonable thing to get through might be elimination of the special deduction for people over 62," which allowed high-earning seniors and their households to deduct medical expenses from their tax returns. The committee proceeded to discuss their problems with a tax system that was working on "cutting the top tax rate while cutting education and health care spending." George discussed a number of CCG allies in the fight for progressive tax reform and, using language borrowed from Occupy Wall Street and Occupy Portland, added, "Our thrust will be getting on the 1% for the 99%," while admitting it was "dubious" to expect any significant tax revenue increases in the upcoming legislative session given the political and economic climate. Someone sighed and said, "If only the war on poverty were a real war. Then we would actually be spending money on it."

Health care, death penalty abolition, and the expunction bill—along with the organization's financial challenges—were the primary foci of the next CCG Public Policy Committee Meeting. Teresa, the committee's chair, was glad to report that the board had approved unanimously, for the first time, adding language about expanding health care to undocumented persons to its health care advocacy platform. Anti-trafficking committee members reported they were working on the language for an expunction bill with a state representative. Teresa subjected them to a tough round of vetting on about the bill's practicality and likelihood of success: "Would the district attorney's support it? Will it be done on time?" Answers were not forthcoming. Anti-trafficking committee members were encouraged to quickly remedy the lacuna by the following week.

CCG's board had also approved the committee's recommendation to make a public statement and join the death penalty abolition coalition. After several rounds of revisions by board and policy committee members, the final statement read:

> Christians for the Common Good believes that capital punishment is unjust and immoral. Jesus embodied an ethics of love and forgiveness, and taught that all humans, whatever their faults and crimes, are capable of redemption. Who are we to deny another person the opportunity to confess their sins and seek forgiveness? . . . The reality is that our judicial system is imperfect and flawed and may result in the ultimate injustice—taking the life of an innocent person. To the crowd around the woman caught in adultery Jesus said, "He who is without sin, let him throw the first stone" (John 8:7).

The committee also discussed new language for CCG's health care advocacy that built on past work while focusing attention on undocumented persons and racial disparities in health equity:

In seeking to respond to God's call to all creation for healing and wholeness, Christians understand that the abundant life God desires for all humanity includes physical and emotional well-being. We take seriously the call to promote wellness, and to advocate for healing and wholeness for all people. It also means ensuring adequate and fair access to health care for all people, according to their needs rather than their wealth or position in society. As Jesus took mercy on those who sought both physical and emotional healing, so we should be good neighbors to those who struggle with both mental and physical illness, ensuring their care and valuing their lives. Care for the lives and health of our neighbors is an extension and expression of God's love for us and Jesus Christ's healing ministry.

> We have consistently been a Christian voice in the health care conversations in Salem. The bills we choose to support are bills that lead to a more equitable health care system that does not neglect the vulnerable. We believe that health—and access to it—is imperative, and is a building block for strong families and communities. When 60% of all bankruptcies are directly related to medical debt, and many divorces are related to financial strife, it tells us that health equity is an important issue that Christians cannot ignore. CCG has historically prioritized health advocacy efforts around the three "A's": Access, Affordability, and Adequacy. Using these same principles to assess the current health reform, we will advocate that the reform efforts:

- Ensure that basic health services for all Oregonians are maintained and, when possible, expanded. We are especially concerned about the most vulnerable Oregonians including low-income individuals and families, children, seniors and people with disabilities. Any health package must be affordable, accessible and adequate.
- Address the serious health disparities that are experienced by certain populations due to race, ethnicity, or undocumented status. We will advocate that the health transformation initiative brings greater health equity to the entire system so all Oregonians can benefit from better health outcomes.
- Reduce medical costs. When medical procedures cost less, they become more affordable and therefore more accessible to all.

After considering the new language, the committee proceeded to discuss a recent Oregon Health Authority State of Equity Report on racial and economic disparities in health. "As a Christian, this is very important," Teresa affirmed in conclusion.

At the policy committee's final meeting before the first legislative session of 2012, the committee celebrated forward momentum on the expunction bill, death penalty, and health care expansion work. Regarding the expunction bill, Mindy remarked, "We have a lot of friends on trafficking. Republicans and Democrats. Eight legislators came to [a recent] rally. One of them reversed his opposition and supported [a previous bill] after University of Oregon InterVarsity [Christian Fellowship] students kept constantly calling him." We talked about who would travel to Salem to give testimony, whether to accept the drafting legislator's suggestion that CCG formally introduce the bill to the legislature as requesting organization, and other logistics for mobilizing CCG's Jewish, evangelical, and secular progressive partners, including an advocacy training day attended by over 200 members of a local emerging evangelical megachurch. After divvying up organizing responsibilities for the upcoming legislative session—writing op-eds, contacting constituents, meeting with legislators, and other responsibilities—the committee moved on to health care, economic justice, and, in conclusion, a positive report on the death penalty coalition's work: "The Governor said there would be no death penalty on his watch," Harold told us, "we've got 3,000 letters in support." The meeting ended with talk of how the upcoming wedding and childbirth of two prominent female CCG leaders would affect organizational capacity in the coming weeks— along with hearty laughter, celebration, and congratulations to one of the women who was present.

Christians for the Common Good and Postsecular Pluralism: Mobilizing Evangelicals and Others

In a rather direct way, Christians for the Common Good represents the sort of multicultural evangelical efforts to practice pragmatic postsecular pluralism in pursuit of common goods and ethical democracy described in the Introduction and Chapter 1 of this book. How did CCG go about mobilizing evangelicals in pursuit of this mission? How successful were their efforts? Organizational records and ethnographic observations of advocacy training and mobilization events offer insight into the approaches and outcomes of CCG outreach efforts.

"Legislators *want* to hear from Christians on these issues," Jill—a white thirty-one-year-old pierced and tattooed CCG operations manager—told several individuals who had braved the wet, frigid late fall evening to attend a CCG chili feed and thank you letter-writing event to legislators, "poverty and budgets and general governance, not just the hot-button issues." Erin—CCG's white twenty-nine-year-old director of communications and media—chimed in, "I advocate for disadvantaged people because it's what Jesus says to do." "As Christians, we should thank our legislators," Erin added while handing out thank you postcards for participants to write in to their legislators, "Be kind to them. Be grateful. They work so hard." Jill and Erin were evangelicals-from-birth who had recently begun attending an Episcopal Church led by an "amazing female pastor" (Teresa) after finding it increasingly impossible to reconcile their strong leadership gifts and gender egalitarian theologies with the restrictive gender norms of their former conservative evangelical churches.

Jill continued, "Ten years ago, there were no evangelicals involved in justice stuff." When evangelicals did get involved in poverty work, "they used to work in direct services. The Christians involved in advocacy work like what we do were *not* evangelicals. Patrick [Serving the City's executive director, whom we met in the Introduction] is the main reason evangelicals have gotten involved in justice issues in our city." She added, "I have to be honest: at first I was a little wary." Jill talked about worrying that mainstream evangelicals would take a "you have to listen to the gospel to get food" approach to their advocacy efforts, "that sort of thing. But now I'm pretty impressed." She cited Patrick and Serving the City's relationship with the mayor and other ongoing collaborations between Portland evangelicals and city officials to address homelessness, poverty, racial disparities, health care, anti-trafficking, and equitable education.

Still, Erin and Jill did acknowledge some frustrations. After listening to Jill lament how evangelicals sometimes "need to see us a handing a bowl to someone to justify [anti-poverty] work," a young white male in attendance responded, "You have to evangelize the churches about the value of politics." "Yeah, we do a lot of that," Jill answered. "Church leaders don't encourage political engagement; or they do it in the wrong way, on the wrong issues." She added that churches and nonprofit organizations "can't handle all the needs of the poor," but when CCG leaders and volunteers spoke at churches about the organization's successful anti-poverty work—"like the farm-to-table food for kids bill! I'm so proud of that one!"—Jill was discouraged that too often they "don't get excited. We do Bible studies, speak at churches, all that stuff," Jill continued, "but it's hard to motivate people. Or they're excited and positive when you come, but then there is no real action or follow up."

One month earlier, I had joined Jill, Erin, Sue (a thirty-five-year-old Korean American former executive director of CCG), and Wendy (a white regional organizer with Bread for the World, a national Christian antipoverty group) at a CCG-organized advocacy training event hosted by a local evangelical college. Thirteen people were in attendance—three men and ten women—most of whom had listened to Sue speak about CCG at morning chapel earlier that day. Erin kicked things off. "There's a lot of unrest in our country right now," she began, "and economic fairness is one of our core issues":

> Elected officials work for *us*. Mostly they hear from oil and pharmaceutical and other lobbyists who pay a ton of money to pass bills. Poor people don't have that, because they're just struggling to survive. CCG's focus is being that voice for those who are marginalized and vulnerable.

Her small audience nodded and appeared to be tracking with her, if scrambling somewhat to keep up with her rapid presentation of issues, data, policies, and rousing calls to action.

Wendy, the Bread for the World organizer, grabbed the baton from Erin with an opening vignette about Christians for the Common Good:

> I first got involved in social justice issues through CCG. They were working on the payday loan bill. The Bible tells us to take care of the widow and the orphan. I met a woman whose doctor told her she needed orthopedic shoes. They cost hundreds of dollars and she couldn't afford them, so she got a payday loan that almost doubled the cost. It made me mad; the Bible

says that's usury. I started calling people three nights a week. I went to give testimony before the state legislator in Salem. I'm Catholic, there was an Episcopalian, and a Baptist. A legislator called us later and said, "We did it, it passed! We'd tried before but it failed. It worked this time because [the faith community] had a united voice."

Wendy spoke quickly with great excitement, intensity, and passion, connecting personal stories to legislative advocacy work while those in attendance tried to keep up.

Sensing the need to slow things down a bit, Sue followed Wendy with a pastoral check-in, "How's everybody doing? Are you tracking? It's a lot of info." Sue spent a few minutes talking lightly with the group before transitioning to Jill, who began her discussion of federal budget priorities by stating, "What we want, what we ask, is that our government not balance the budget on the backs of the poor. As Christians, we've been called to do justice, and love mercy, and to protect the poor. That's our job as Christians." Jill proceeded to tell the group about a recent advocacy trip to Washington, DC, in which she discussed the power of storytelling to personalize abstract policy debates when speaking to legislators and the public.[72] "When I went to DC, I told them the story of my friend Mike, who will probably lose his housing" due to impending budget cuts, "and he will tell you he'll be a danger to himself and to others" if that happens. Jill and Erin then began working with individuals on how to tell their own stories in a way that connected urgently to a current policy issue. After overhearing one individual discuss inadequate education and health care support for military veterans, Erin responded, "Yes! That's not justice, and that's why it bothers us! I know justice because of how angry I get at injustice." She reminded the group of how Jesus cleared the Temple in anger over religious taxes on the poor,[73] "Don't be afraid to be bold and call it out. Anger at injustice is Christian!"

One month later, I joined Jill, Erin, and others at the waterfront in downtown Portland to enact a symbolic "Circle of Protection" in defense of federal antipoverty programs against drastic budget cuts as local television cameras rolled. In the shadow of gleaming corporate towers adjacent to the World Trade Center Portland, a group of fifty gathered at noon down by the river on a grey rainy day to raise their voices on behalf of the "hungry, poor, and disadvantaged." The event was co-organized by Christians for the Common Good, Sojourners, and Bread for the World; it drew Catholic, mainline Protestant, and evangelical Protestant pastors and laypersons—predominantly but not exclusively white—to read short poems, prayers, scripture, and speeches to increase awareness and pressure legislators to protect federal anti-poverty programs. Holding signs that read, "Cut Military Spending," "Budgets are Moral Documents," "Matthew 25 Christians," and the like, participants took turns speaking into cameras and microphones while standing in a circle admonishing each other and their audience to contact legislators and protect the interests of the poor and disadvantaged. "As Christians we are called to love and care for people; that's why we are here, and why we must speak on behalf of the poor and hungry." "President, you have failed. Congress, you have failed. Republicans and Democrats, you have failed." The opposite of a raucous street protest, the group's style was forceful but measured—an orderly, media-coordinated, middle class, multigenerational version of grassroots political pressure.

A related "faith-based call to action" event focused on "hunger and the budget crisis" drew a similar but somewhat larger crowd to participate in a half-day of talks, advocacy workshops, letter writing, and action planning to defend federal antipoverty and health care programs from being slashed in the name of "balancing the budget" after the Great Recession. Organized by Bread for the World in partnership with Catholic Relief Service, the Oregon Food Bank, the Oregon Center for Public Policy, Ecumenical Ministries of Oregon, and others, the event featured a panel discussion in which Erin— CCG's director of communications and media—joined four other policy, economic, and advocacy experts who gave prepared talks and answered questions from the audience about poverty-related economic policy. Deep dives into economic data, policy, budgeting, aid, development, and federal programs were framed by up-front faith-based language from each of the primary speakers, such as the need for a "collective Christian voice" to fight poverty and economic inequality; adherence to the "gospel of Jesus Christ, the sanctity of life," and government that treats people according to "need, not creed"; the power of stories to "tell policy makers, as people of faith, to remember their responsibility to the people they represent, and to God!" while "overcoming partisanship and denominational divisions"; and an evangelical college economics professor "envisioning a Christ-centered community" committed to anti-militarism, anti-poverty legislation, and ending hunger.

Christians for the Common Good also cultivated relationships with greater Portland's evangelical community through an array of conferences, summits, talks, advocacy trainings, Bible studies, chapter meetings, book studies, church visits, and other well-attended events. The organization was born out of a gathering of over 2,000 Oregon Christians who came out to hear popular evangelical left author and speaker Rev. Jim Wallis, an early indicator of "a high level of interest and energy among local Christians for a fresh vision on faith and values in American life" that CCG sought to cultivate and amplify.[74] The following year, CCG sponsored its own summit on faith and American values featuring Rev. Wallis and local evangelical theologian Dr. Paul Metzger that was attended by over 800 hundred evangelicals and others, with several hundred attending the subsequent year's summit featuring evangelical left author and speaker Dr. Ronald J. Sider. In 2010, CCG partnered with a local evangelical college to host Shane Claiborne—another popular evangelical left and new monastic author, activist, and speaker—for a 600-plus person event that brought sixty contacts and over a dozen new members to CCG. The organization also cosponsored and participated in national "faith and justice" advocacy and organizing events in Washington, DC with evangelical left and ecumenical Christian organizations such as Sojourners, Bread for the World, and others.

In greater Portland, Christians for the Common Good was an ongoing presence at multiorganizational theological, educational, service, and worship gatherings involving hundreds of evangelical and mainline Protestant churches and religious organizations—often co-hosting or co-organizing such events as organizational capacity allowed. Organizational staff and board members spoke at fifty-plus churches, colleges, conferences, and events annually—a majority of which identified as evangelical. Congregations, colleges, homes, and pubs across greater Portland, Salem, and other Oregon communities hosted Bible studies, advocacy trainings, educational forums, and chapter meetings attended by dozens or hundreds and led by CCG staff, congregational leaders, and network members. Prominent city and state newspapers and media outlets regularly featured CCG activities in positive earned media coverage. State legislators knew, appreciated, and respected the organization's professionalism, leadership, and mission.

During one conversation, Erin recalled one of Oregon's US Senators referring to CCG as "one of the most effective advocacy organizations in Oregon." "Just getting that recognition is really awesome," Erin recounted, "Getting thank you letters or just having people say, 'Thank you for calling me about something besides abortion. It's nice to have Christians caring about a wider range of issues.' Our [US] Senators—they know us, they have relationship with us, we check in with them. It's really neat." CCG was also invited to provide curriculum and advocacy training for Serving the City (described in the Introduction), which coordinated the relationship between the city of Portland and over 500 Portland-area evangelical churches. The net effect of all this activity and exposure had yielded a modest but enthusiastic list of over 130 dues-paying members and 1,200 newsletter and action alert recipients whom CCG called on to make their voices heard during legislative sessions and advocacy campaigns.

Christians for the Common Good and Multicultural Evangelicalism: Tensions and Challenges

Despite Christians for the Common Good's significant legislative, advocacy, and outreach successes, however, the organization faced many challenges. First and foremost among them was funding. Like many nonprofits, CCG struggled to keep the lights on:

> I think part of what we're really struggling with at CCG is figuring out what our mission and purpose is and how we're going to operationalize that. We've been in survival mode for so long that we're focusing more on, "How do we stay afloat?" rather than "How do we shift the tide?" . . . We've had so much turnover with our staff—our staff is so stretched, I mean, God, bless their hearts . . . and so much turnover on our board too. (Heather, board member)

CCG's financial challenges were reaching acute levels during my time with the organization, at times causing stress and tension among staff and board members. At the beginning of one public policy meeting following a recent CCG board meeting, one member commented, "Usually the public policy piece is most contentious" item on the agenda of monthly board meetings, "*finances* are most controversial and difficult right now." CCG staff had been informed the organization currently had funding "through the end of the year; maybe February," but things were uncertain after that. A founding board member was leaving the organization due to burnout, and the executive director position was temporarily vacant. Upcoming births and marriages were likely to further reduce short-term organizational capacity at a time when staff were already stretched extremely thin. CCG's active board, which along its two to three person staff provided much of the organization's energy and hands-on leadership, had shrunk by half. Three former board members had agreed to return to increase stability and leadership—a source of strength and encouragement to beleaguered staff—but the organization was clearly in a trough, at risk due to financial challenges and greater-than-usual executive leadership turnover.

Aside from the usual challenges of small nonprofit organizations, Christians for the Common Good's financial challenges reflected the organization's delicate positioning among liberal mainline and evangelical Protestant communities, progressive secular and faith-based nonprofit organizations, and non-partisan and partisan actors and issue agendas. The theological and cultural diversity of the organization's internal leadership, constituents, and organizational partners—while contributing much to organizational vitality—also created funding and outreach dilemmas that challenged organizational stability. One of these dilemmas involved balancing CCG's educational and outreach goals with practical financial and organizational sustainability considerations. Put simply, the organization received most of its funding from liberal mainline Protestant and secular individuals, groups, and institutions, but attracted most of its individual members—and targeted much of its outreach—to evangelicals. CCG's evangelical members were often highly enthusiastic and active in organizational activities, but they also tended to be "young and broke" (Jill), and thus unable to provide the organization with a sustainable source of funding through membership dues or donations. As Rachel, a thirty-three-year-old white evangelical board member confirmed,

> I think one of the things that has been difficult for CCG funding wise is that most of the people who are really excited about the work that CCG is doing and really want to get behind it and get involved are all under the age of thirty-five and poor.

Moreover, unlike many Catholic and mainline Protestant churches and denominations, evangelical churches do not have a history of financially supporting or contributing to US-based social service, social justice, or advocacy work as congregations, preferring instead to support international and domestic missionaries and letting individual members decide on their own which parachurch or nonprofit workers and organizations they chose to support financially. The net effect was, despite investing heavily in outreach to evangelical churches and organizations, CCG received very little from the evangelical community in terms of financial support.

CCG's mission and methodology—faith-based non-partisan political advocacy for the common good—further complicated matters:

> Funding has never been an easy thing for us. We're a faith-based organization: that narrows our pool. We're a predominantly *evangelical* faith-based organization: that narrows our pool even more. We're a *progressive* evangelical organization: narrows the pool even more. And we're not doing actual charity work. We're doing public policy. But people want to give to programs. They want to contribute to my HIV program or they want to do food donations. Public policy is so much more ambiguous. So our pool is really tiny. (Rachel)

Even progressive evangelical churches, Heather observed, were hesitant to support CCG "as a church. They might contribute some money here and there, but they're not going to become a member necessarily—and certainly not if it's something that might reek of politics." She explained, "Some of the progressive evangelical churches are especially intentional about wanting to put distance between themselves and the Christian Right, like, 'The church was so involved with *this* kind of politics, we don't want to be involved with *any* kind of politics.'"

This was true despite CCG's avoidance of taking positions on "hot-button" (Teresa) political issues relating to abortion and sexuality, and despite achieving widespread recognition for its successful anti-human trafficking work "before anyone was talking about it" (Sue), for which there was strong support in the evangelical community:

> One disappointment has been seeing how [evangelicals] choose to only care about human trafficking but not care about or take up the other issues we feel are biblical justice issues. People want CCG to come and talk about human trafficking all the time—but even that doesn't make them open their wallets or decide to become members. It's like, it's "scintillating," but it doesn't really move them to actually throw their weight behind what needs to be done to really stop this. Not all of them, but a lot. So that's been super discouraging. People are not that interested in the environment, they're not that interested in health care. These are areas to me where it's a real struggle to go up against kind of how, you know, right wing Republican Christianity has coopted that stuff and made Christianity a champion of capitalist values (Jill).

Despite ongoing efforts to link evangelical enthusiasm for antitrafficking work to antipoverty, health care, immigration, and other issues of "biblical justice" and equity, organizational leaders lamented evangelicals' outsized focus on antitrafficking work in comparison to other issues.

Whereas CCG's work on antitrafficking legislation was a source of significant positive attention and support from the organization's evangelical constituency, other legislation sometimes had the opposite effect. Teresa, a former executive director and board member whose work with CCG predated its official founding, described two such cases at length, along with the challenge of balancing the consensus-oriented "bridge-building" and prophetic "truth-speaking" aspects of CCG's mission:

> We try to pick issues that are bridging the gaps. So human trafficking is a great one. The environment, sometimes, depending on the issue, is a really good one. We try to pick issues that bridge communities, and focus on areas of consensus for the most part. That build the body [of Christ], as best we can. Although that's hard too, because we also feel like we have a role of speaking truth to the community. So there can be tension around, What issues do you take on? And how do you take on those issues? We got involved in—well, two pretty contentious issues. One was a tax measure, which we supported, and one was about incarceration [both bills are described above]. Those are hard tensions: when evangelical gets mixed up with being Democrat or Republican. Conservative evangelicals didn't like the position we took on the tax measure. But we felt very, very strongly as an organization that is focused on justice and poverty in our community that we had to support it. We did a lot of thought and debate on that one. The tax measure was a really big, contentious issue that there was a lot of argument about. "We try to build consensus, this isn't building consensus, should we take a position on this, is it important enough?" We had a lot of those conversations. We learned that when you start to take positions on issues like taxes, you start to get backlash. So that was really hard.

When I asked Teresa if the organization lost members as a result of its position, she answered,

> We did lose some from that one, yeah. More so from the tax one than the incarceration one. With the tax measure, we took quite a bit of backlash. But we also got support from other people. I don't know if collectively it was up

or down. But we definitely got push back and lost churches, lost supporters from that. Lost some big [evangelical] foundation support. . . . I think they felt like we were pushing too far. Like that was too political, you know, "It's fine for you to talk about the other stuff. But when you start talking about money, now you're talking politics." So that was a big deal. . . . There were some very wealthy individuals who are a part of that [foundation] who were not happy with our position. It led [a large evangelical organization] to step back and say, "We thought we knew who you guys were." Those were hard losses. I think it set us back a lot.

Teresa's comments were corroborated by interviews with members and partners of the large organization in question along with several emerging evangelical megachurch leaders closely connected to them, who told me that—despite "good relationships" and a number of successful partnership ventures—some of their colleagues had become "*very* wary" of CCG and other "Sojourners-type" groups. Teresa continued:

I think it changed the dynamics a little bit. And I think different CCG board members and staff members would feel differently about that: some would look at that as a good thing, some as a bad thing. Some people would feel, I think, that we were not of one mind on that: both on our decision to support the bill and the fallout of some of those decisions. Sometimes it's made us more cautious and sometimes it's made us more aggressive. Because some people are like, "Well, who cares what they say? This is the point of why we exist!" And other people say, "Look what happened. We can't [take positions that cause us to lose crucial support]." And we haven't had any resolution on that.

As Teresa's comments suggest, despite its attempts to avoid hot-button partisan culture war issues, CCG's attempts to bridge gaps and build consensus around a common good politics could not shield it from having to make difficult practical and ethical judgments about whether or not to take positions on specific issues or bills—or from the practical and financial consequences of those decisions.

This created tension at times among staff and board members who held different views on the value of continuing to devote large amounts of the organization's limited resources to reaching out to the white evangelical community in light of its limited substantive and financial support for much of its work. Teresa's summary of these debates were echoed by every CCG staff and board member I spoke with:

> How much time do you spend reaching out to a community and trying to build relationship? How much time? And to be honest, a lot of the challenges have been around funding, because evangelicals don't want to fund it. Secular people want to fund our work sometimes more than Christians want to fund our work. Most of the money comes from progressives. Most of the marketing goes to evangelicals. So that's been a tension point.

Indeed, though no longer involved, the organization's primary funding for the first several years of its existence came from secular progressive sources who would not have been eligible for membership in the organization. Recent years had seen diversification and growth in support from evangelicals and other funding sources, representing both "uber-left" and "uber-right" organizations (Rachel), but the organization continued to draw most of its financial support from "progressive Christian," liberal, and mainline Protestant individuals and groups.

As a result of these tensions, after years of intensive mobilization and outreach efforts, some CCG members were reevaluating the organization's focus on the evangelical community. "CCG is floundering," one older mainline Protestant board member exclaimed at a public policy meeting, "we're not terribly good at connecting with evangelical churches" (Harold). Erin, CCG's younger evangelical director of media and communications, made a similar point somewhat more hopefully:

> I feel like the work of CCG is really more to be a lighthouse: a light that's shining, that's there for [evangelicals] to come to. I don't know if our work really should be to go and evangelize the evangelicals. I think there are a lot of evangelicals who respond to us and are like, "I have been looking for something like this!" That's who we're for. We don't have the capacity to go and really do a full spread attempt to reach [all evangelicals]. To challenge that right wing, you know, Republican Christianity message just takes so much.

Though not all CCG leaders agreed with Harold and Erin's recommendations, Erin's image of Christians for the Common Good as a lighthouse drawing "like-minded" politically progressive evangelicals and others together in community and common cause was echoed in the reflected experiences of her fellow evangelical CCG staff and board members (Erin, Jill, Teresa, Rachel, Mindy, Sue, Becca), who spoke about their deep sense of relief, gratitude, and community upon discovering "my people" (Erin) through their active involvement in the organization.

CCG's intentionality about cultivating political and religious diversity within its leadership and membership, while often experienced as a strength, could also be a source tension and weakness depending on one's point of view. Founding staff and board members included registered Democrats, registered Republicans, and political independents representing evangelical and liberal mainline Protestant traditions. All agreed on the need to challenge Christian Right narratives of religion and politics and held broadly shared progressive views on the organization's core issue areas. All were interested in mobilizing white evangelicals and others towards a different sort of political engagement rooted in a politics of the common good. CCG's original founders and funders, however, had different reasons for becoming active in launching the organization, differences that continued to shape the organization's identity, prospects, and priorities into the present. According to organizational documents and interviews with founding organizational members, allies, and potential competitors, there was significant divergence in the agendas and vision of several leading figures in CCG's founding.

During an interview in his office, Evan—a fifty-one-year-old white mainline Protestant executive director of an established interfaith advocacy organization that often partnered with Christians for the Common Good— reflected on the diverse identities and agendas individuals brought to CCG's founding:

> I was thinking about the early days of CCG. I was involved in conversation even before the organization got created. There were some people—one fellow in particular—from the Adventist church. There was a professor who was a United Methodist. There were a few other younger evangelical social justice folks. And then there were a couple of other players: particularly an agnostic or atheist Democratic attorney in town and some other folks. I think their agenda was much more how to capture a more progressive or moderate evangelical vote for the Democratic Party. I remember sitting in that meeting thinking, "There's too many—there's a lot of different agendas

here." . . . That political agenda in the early days—I don't think it was hidden or anything. I do think it was sort of the elephant in the room in a way.

An early founding document clearly reflected this more explicitly partisan agenda, describing a new organization whose mission would be to "promote consistent progressive Christian messages" and "true progressive Christian values" by "mobilizing and galvanizing support among a progressive [mainline Protestant and Catholic] Christian base and expanding support among right-of-center churches (evangelicals)." While the document made frequent mention of the "common good" along with "bringing together leaders from diverse backgrounds" and "building bridges between Christian communities and political leaders," it also prominently highlighted directly partisan objectives as "long-term action priorities" that included "help[ing] secure Democratic seats," "cultivate support for Democratic presidential candidate," "promote dialogue between Democratic candidates and the religious community (particularly evangelicals and right-of-center churches)," putting "pressure on conservative political leaders," and "support[ing] new progressive leaders in conservative districts." According to multiple interviews, at least one of the organization's early funders was driven primarily by this more partisan political agenda, and one of the organization's founding board members was an active state-level Democratic party organizer in addition to being a prominent voice on CCG's board and policy committees.

By all accounts, this early partisan focus had lost out to the organization's dominant bridge-building, bipartisan political and religious identity, including severed financial ties with more partisan-oriented early funding sources. As Evan put it, echoing others:

> That partisan political piece, I think it's—I don't see that anymore. I think the funding ended and things like that. Some of that might have been expectation on deliverables. But what we were trying to point out early on is if a group like CCG is true to its values, it will need to be nonpartisan. And it's probably not going to deliver what that more progressive Democratic group wanted. . . . It really became a lot more about collaboration.

CCG's current membership included "some Republicans"—including a founding board member and former executive director—though "not very many," "a lot of independents" who "would identify ideologically" as nonpartisan, and many Democrats (Teresa). "In general, we're pretty progressive. I have all my little red flags that go off when I say that. But I mean, we're going to be frankly more Democrat than Republican. We're going to be more progressive on [core] issues. That's one of the reasons we exist." CCG's attempts to be both a "prophetic voice" and "bridge-building" transpartisan advocacy organization that could mobilize evangelical Christians and others behind a politics of common goods involved a host of sticky practical, financial, ethical, religious, and political issues that were not easily managed or resolved.

Christians for the Common Good and the Culture Wars: Gender and Sexuality

As noted above, CCG's attempts to build bridges across religious and political divides in order unite Christians and partner with others to "shape public policy for the common good" involved avoiding polarizing culture war issues relating to gender and sexuality. On these topics, CCG recognized the impossibility of reaching consensus either within the organization or in the diverse field of Christian congregations and organizations it sought to mobilize. While staff and board members vigorously discussed and debated the issue—particularly in the organization's early years—most accepted the substantive and strategic reasons for not taking action on abortion and LGBTQ+ issues. This included board members with divergent personal positions and experiences. While discussing conservative blowback against CCG's advocacy for progressive tax and incarceration reform bills, Teresa recalled how "there was a lot of argument—not bad argument, but discussion—around the gay marriage and abortion stuff, from people who took different positions on the issues":

> At the beginning, we had a guy who was a gay man on the board. And those were hard discussions. And again, people were never afraid to speak up, and there was a lot of love, you know, in the group. But at that time, those are hard conversations: for someone to say, "I don't believe in that, I think that this is sinful." How do you deal with that?

One primary way CCG members dealt with it was to create an organizational culture that focused on areas of agreement while avoiding areas with potential to threaten the group's ability to work together:

I do think because we've maintained denominational differences, we have different perspectives on scripture and theology, and one of the ways that we've stayed together is by focusing on the things that we agree on. And that was something we always kind of decided. It gets tricky when you're talking about a specific policy decision. But in general, you know, we don't sit around talking about Calvinism or predestination, or all these other things that people talk about in the Christian faith. We're just like—we don't talk about it. We don't talk about those things. We are here because we care about our communities. We're not saying those things aren't important. They're very important and you should talk about them in your church, with your community. But here, we're working together. We're trying to do things together. So that was a very strategic choice.

And we've actually had people call that out in meetings, like, "We don't talk about that here." . . . There are people who disagree about women in leadership on our board. There are people who disagree about gay marriage on our board. I know those two are big. And abortion. There are people who definitely disagree about that.

I: But those are not discussed in the context of the organization?

Teresa: Yeah. You've probably heard this, but that's one of the other lines in the sand—we don't talk about abortion or gay marriage. We're all kind of breathing a sigh of relief that it's not going to get on the ballot for next fall, because it would've gotten really contentious. And there are people we know who have very different perspectives on that. And so we just say we don't—our position is that we don't have a position and we don't talk about those issues.

I: What do you say about why that's the case?

Teresa: What we have said historically is that there has been so much attention on those two issues from the Christian community that we feel like one of our roles is to put voice to other issues. So that doesn't give a theological answer. It's one of the whole reasons we exist as an organization: to show that there are other issues Christians care about. But also, practically, it would tear apart our group. Because people don't agree. And those two things have been difficult for funders too. We've had people who say, "We would have funded you if you would have taken a [supportive] position on abortion." Or, "How can you say you're a Christian organization and not be pro-life?" Or, "How can you be a Christian organization and not support gay marriage?" We just say we don't do that.

Like many other faith-based community organizing coalitions,[75] in order to focus on mobilizing evangelicals and other Christians around its core environmental, economic, and health care platforms, CCG opted to remain neutral on partisan-polarized culture war politics.

While generally accepted by organizational staff, board members, and volunteer organizers, CCG's neutrality position was not without contention. Heather, a thirty-three-year-old white evangelical pastor and CCG board member with lifelong experience in both evangelical and mainline Protestant congregations, had recently become a dissenter. When I asked Heather, "How would you describe CCG's mission?" she responded:

How would I describe CCG's mission? I'm feeling a lot of conflict over CCG's mission. I think one of those reasons, in full disclosure, is that CCG hasn't been willing to take a stand around gender and sexuality. I get why, but it's hard for me.

I: Makes sense.

Heather: I also think there's a lot of difference of opinion on the board as to what the purpose and mission of CCG are. What I find compelling about CCG or what drew me to the work has less to do with the actual work that CCG does in terms of policy, and more to do with the work that CCG does in terms of shifting the dialogue among evangelicals. I told you that story about my mother calling and crying with relief when I told her, "I think I'm a feminist. I'm a feminist."[76] Gordon [College, a prominent evangelical college that several CCG leaders had attended] was really foundational and eye opening for me in the sense that, before attending, I legitimately didn't realize that committed people of faith could think differently than the Christian Right. Because the message I had heard with my Brethren community was that those Presbyterians I hung out with weren't really Christians. And then suddenly at Gordon I was surrounded by these evangelicals who were definitely Bible-believing people who read scripture differently, with different implications. So for me, what is life giving and exciting about the work of CCG is opening that door for other people. The policy work is great and it's important. I work in social services so I see how policy impacts real people every day. But what is most exciting is that shifting of dialogue.

Heather gave an example from her work as social service provider at a non-profit HIV positive health center:

One of the things that evangelicals do really well is storytelling. Our preachers preach for hours—God, they preach for hours, they have four-point sermons and whatever. But they're full of stories. I think Erin's digital storytelling project about health care gaps and disparities is one of the things that has been most encouraging and exciting to me about CCG, and this idea of telling stories. . . . It has also been really encouraging for me to hear people—I work in the HIV community, and I was at this public policy meeting with all of the executive directors and public policy directors of the social service organizations in [Portland]. And mind you, the church does not have a very good reputation in this community for some pretty good reasons. So there was a piece of legislation that [CCG] had signed onto last year involving cultural competency training in medical professions. So the public policy director for one of those organizations was talking about his experience with the Oregon Health Authority and how there's this coalition of organizations coming together to push this policy forward. And he said, and, "You know, it's kind of strange, Christians for the Common Good are the ones pushing this." And then he goes on and he makes this whole big disclaimer, like, "I know that that name sounds like this [right-wing conservative group], but they're really all about this, this, that, and the other thing." And people around the table are talking and reacting surprised in a good way. Nobody knows that I'm affiliated with the organization they're talking about. And I'm like, "Good, this is good. We're putting out a different message. A different face of Christianity." And people are hearing that and seeing that faith in action. That's really encouraging to me.

What was not encouraging to Heather, however, was CCG's decision to maintain organizational neutrality on issues of gender and sexuality:

I think some of the things that have been hard is CCG's desire to not take polarizing issues. . . . It's hard for me to sit here and say we're a justice organization, we're talking about embracing the full humanity of people, yet in our desire to be neutral, we are leaving out this entire part of our community. I was at the Wild Goose Festival [a progressive evangelical gathering] last summer. . . . they had these tiny little sessions, or what were supposed to be tiny little sessions, on sexuality. And strangely not about gender. Very interesting. Lots of stuff about race and sexuality but nothing about gender. Still the silent thing in the [evangelical] church. But they had these tiny little breakout sessions in the schedule for conversations or presentations around sexuality. And those sessions ended up being the most well attended of the conference. People were bursting at the seams. There were spontaneous new sessions that came about because people wanted to continue the conversation. That was telling to me. And I came back to CCG after that and was like, "There is a movement of people within the evangelical church for whom this is—whether or not we want this to be an issue—it is. And it is going to be in our face before we know it." . . . Which again, I can appreciate and understand [avoiding polarizing issues]. But I also feel like it's, well, I was rereading Martin Luther King's "Letter from Birmingham Jail" last week, and he tells [white Christian leaders], "You all say that there will be a time and we have to wait for the right timing. But the timing is always right to do what is right." And I was thinking about that and just feeling like there's some incongruency there. I'm not exactly sure what to do about that. I understand that it's messy and it's complicated. But that's been personally hard for me.

Heather's personal "wrestling" with issues of gender and sexuality in her personal faith and work life were making it increasingly difficult to agree with CCG's position of neutrality.

Like a number of other female CCG staff and board members, the conservative evangelical church's restrictive view of gender equality was also pushing Heather to explore Christian traditions that were more affirming of female authority in religious and public life:

My own faith journey has changed a lot in the last five years, such that my [current] evangelical church might not be the most logical place for me. Most recently I've been exploring the Episcopal community. . . . A big part of it has to do with my own wrestling about gender in the church, which was a really early conflict in me because I felt a clear call to ministry when I was in high school that my PCUSA church very much encouraged and empowered and provided opportunities for me. I was a deacon in the church and I preached. But I felt a lot of conflict around that in terms of my [conservative] evangelical roots. . . . I was part of a women's group that really encouraged me to pursue and wrestle with that question . . . and I came to back to Portland and had to wrestle with it again in my evangelical church here. It's been really draining, and I finally came to a place of real resolution. I think in the past I was always able to separate my intellectual life from my spiritual life in the sense of, yes, logically, intellectually, I fully embrace women in ministry, but somehow that doesn't apply to me. Or in terms of feminist theory and race, class, and gender—those were things I was looking at but were not yet coming to fruition in my own life. I started wrestling with that more in graduate school, and then I came back home and finally reached some resolution or integration of all that. And my evangelical denomination, while it is officially embracing of women in ministry, the reality is that women aren't really pastors. They're in parachurch ministries, they're in denominational leadership. They're not actually pastors. So that is one piece.

The other piece is that I work with the HIV+ and LGBT community in my job, and I've had several very close friends and family members in my life recently come out. So I've been wrestling with gender and wrestling with sexuality. I think there was a place in time where I was content to be someone who was fighting for change from the inside—both in terms of gender and sexuality—but I reached a point where I was like, "I can't do that." I'm thankful for those people that can fight for change from the inside, but I can't be one of them. I need to be in a community that embraces women. And I think I'm feeling similarly around sexuality. Perhaps because it's not "my issue" I'm more positioned to fight for that from the inside—to fight for change or to be an ally. But I just feel whereas, there was a point in time I could say it wasn't necessarily my issue, I don't think I can say that anymore. So I'm feeling like, you know, it might be time for me to head back to the mainline church in terms of those pretty big issues.

Despite her deep biblical and evangelical roots, Heather's exhausting struggle with sexism and heterosexism in evangelical churches—even the relatively affirming church she had most recently served as pastor—was leading her to consider other options.

She was not alone. Jill grew up in a "dysfunctional" home-schooling conservative evangelical family in which "my dad did his own thing and my mom was responsible for raising the children." She read Rush Limbaugh books for home school and served as a page for the Republican Women's Convention:

> I got super pissed at the church. I'm still really pissed at the church. I've got some issues when it comes to the church . . . which doesn't help when you work there [laughs]. I have to constantly pray for patience [laughs]. . . . I had gone to Bible college for a little while, That's where it started. Like, "Are you kidding me?" Because when you're a woman, you don't—there isn't equality. And believe what you want, Wes, but I have a real problem, I have a serious problem with the inequality that exists within the church.

I: Mm-hm. Gender in particular?
Jill: Exactly. Well, gender, yeah. Personally, not as a spokesman for CCG.
    Because I consider myself to be a feminist, and as a feminist, I don't
    feel like you can advocate for one group of people and not advocate
    for all groups of people. . . . I don't like to be oppressed; I don't like to
    see people get oppressed.

The bad taste in Jill's mouth—which she attributed to race, class, sexuality, and gender inequity in the white evangelical churches of her youth—led her to "kind of leave the church and come back to the church and leave the church and come back to the church," despite always experiencing a "really unshakeable connection with Jesus."

Like several other female CCG leaders who had spent their entire lives in evangelical churches, Jill had recently occasionally begun "going to an Episcopal church, because I don't know where I belong [laughing]." During a CCG office conversation with me about the biblical view of power, she elaborated:

> I think as a woman, I want to hold [power] even closer because I have less than you. And I know that. I think I feel it more in this job than a lot of other jobs I've had, because I'm going into churches. I know that you're not, as a dude, you're not going to listen to me the same as you listen to a man. Or you're going to question the things I say, so I'm going to have to know twice as much. I've experienced that on a regular basis. That is just the way it is. I think men have to change that, and I don't know if that's going to happen. For a while I hoped it would. But what I'm seeing, and this is separate from any issue with CCG, but just as far as power goes, what I'm seeing more and

more is women just leave the church, or go to churches where they are accepted. That is the only reason I go to an Episcopal church: because I want
to be in a place that's affirming. That's unfortunate for the body of Christ.
Because it's not like I'm not the only person doing that.

Indeed, among CCG board and staff members, Jill was one of several strong
female white evangelical leaders who had recently begun attending local
Episcopal churches led by women.

Teresa was another. Like Jill and Heather, she had grown up in conservative evangelical churches—Baptist, in Teresa's case—before becoming frustrated and migrating to an Episcopal Church where she was mentored by a
Black female Episcopal pastor for whom she had high regard. When I asked
the source of the frustration that led her away from her Baptist roots, she
answered:

> I think one of the things that happened is I started growing professionally.
> And I started encountering difficulties and questions, like, "Why can I be
> a leader in the community but I can't speak at the church?" In my church,
> I can't give an announcement, right? Because I'm a woman. But I can give a
> speech at the capitol. So I just started really having some tensions internally
> with that. That was one of the drivers for me to look at the Episcopal church.

Teresa spent five years in the Episcopal church before moving back to a
charismatic evangelical church with more progressive views on gender and
women in leadership.

Peachtree Community Development Association in Atlanta, like
Christians for the Common Good in Portland, was also home to a strong collection of female leaders—including several women of color in senior leadership positions—who struggled at times with the conservative perspectives
of some of their organizational partners on issues relating to gender and sexuality. Elena, a Latina woman in her early twenties, repeatedly returned to
the themes gender and race during a long coffeeshop conversation in East
Atlanta about her experiences with PCDA-affiliated churches and organizations. Elena had recently returned from sitting on a panel discussion featuring
women of color in leadership in Christian organizations—including several
Black female PCDA leaders—at a local university. Elena spoke extensively of
the challenges of working in the majority-white and male-dominated traditional evangelical landscape:

It's really isolating. Especially for Sofia—she's from India, she came over when she was 13—she's the only person of color in her [intentional living community]. That's rough, because there's a lot of stuff that goes on.... As women of color engaging in diversity work, one of the hardest things to do is us letting go of our anger enough to come to the table while still being a strong Mexican woman. How do you live that out? That's really hard. I think it's a whole other ball game with women of color in some of these settings. It's really hard.... I've been leading this team and working with another director, Jack, who is a white guy from the Midwest. We have had really hard conversations about race and our relationship. What it has showed me is you've got to trust people, and that I hear things differently than he does, and that it's really hard . . . learning how to speak out for myself to my co-leader, and then trusting that my co-leader is going to engage in the process with me and we are going to learn some things together has been really, really hard. We've had lots of conversations. Sometimes they involve yelling. But it has been a gift, showing me what a reconciled relationship looks like.... I've talked with Leonard [the organization's Black president], about what it would look like to have more women of color in leadership, or with Josh, a [white] program director in Chicago, about how we need more people of color on staff. And all of our staff is committed to this. It's just really hard to do this job without being able to relate to [other women of color in leadership].

Elena was excited about new hiring and support initiatives for women of color in leadership in the organization, including a new leadership intern position in which half of the newly hired staff were women of color.

Despite these welcome steps, Elena spoke of the significant challenges she faced as a Latina evangelical woman in leadership. The multiracial, mixed-gender intentional community house Elena was currently leading included three white men from the Midwest between nineteen and twenty-six years old and three women of color—a Chinese-American, Mexican-American, and a biracial Canadian French-Chinese woman—between nineteen and twenty-two years old. Elena observed that although "we all came to the house and organization for the same sort of reasons, our understanding of what we were getting into is very different":

My guys had never talked about the fact that they are white and what that means, and I was really nervous to be their leader, because our program really smacks you in the face with the reality and experience of white privilege—this privilege that only exists for you, that your neighbors or your housemates don't have—and asks why that is. Oh my gosh, that's a really hard thing, and some people fight it, and that fight can get really ugly. I've been like, "Man, this is going to be tough."

As much as Elena welcomed the opportunity as a woman of color to lead her community, she wrestled with the cost of what prior experience told her she was likely to encounter as she led the young white men in her house through the organization's immersive experiential learning program.

Elena, who grew up in a conservative evangelical church and was currently attending an Evangelical Covenant church, also discussed how recent experiences had shifted her religious and political views regarding sexuality and other topics:

> My [Evangelical] Covenant church is really great, but sometimes when my pastor talks about the Bible or salvation, I just don't agree. I don't talk about all my religious beliefs because I think they would get angry. I think some people in my [organization] would get mad too. But I blame them! A lot of my intentional community team members, who are my closest friends, came out this year while in the program. That really changed my views on sexuality and identity and what it means to love people. Another friend who spent a year with our organization six years ago recently came out. Hearing his story and their stories—when you really put a name to a story, a face to a story, it changes the way I speak, and it changes the way I vote, because I want to honor my friends. Because they have loved God, and we did this program together, and they've had to live with all these lies. And when you hear their stories—I mean, how can you say, "That's wrong" or "that's just a demon" or "that's un-Christian" or "they just need to work harder" [to resist same-sex attraction]? I can't. It changes the way I look at everything.

Like many of her multicultural evangelical peers across the country, Elena was deeply engaged in wrestling with the personal, religious, and political ramifications of traumatic experiences and changing views on gender and sexuality in evangelical churches and religious organizations. Chapter 6's discussion of transposable reflexivity will consider further examples and lessons from the experiences of women of color in leadership in multicultural evangelical settings, and their implications for ethical democracy and the practice of social reflexivity across different types of difference.

Conclusion

Christians for the Common Good and the other organizations and groups described in these chapters bring together organizations, people, and perspectives that are not often brought together: Democrats and Republicans, left-liberal Buddhists and white conservative evangelicals; white evangelical pastors and progressive secular political leaders; Bible-quoting evangelicals and progressive political advocacy groups; liberal mainline and evangelical Protestant churchgoers; evangelical feminists and committed complementarians, gender traditionalists and LGBTQ+ persons and allies; evangelical churches and interfaith networks; Black, white, Indigenous, Asian, and Hispanic Americans; committed secularists and committed evangelicals; and so on—positions and people who are often positioned as opponents (or enemies) in the race and culture wars roiling the streets and public institutions of contemporary American democratic life. As such, these are "exceptional cases" in which multicultural evangelicals are engaged in somewhat unusual and potentially promising efforts to advance ethical democracy in America, cases with potential to problematize taken-for-granted classificatory schemes and normative categories (such as, in this case, the tendency to conflate evangelicalism with across-the-board conservatism, right-wing politics, and whiteness), highlight new classes of social objects and categories (such as, in this case, multicultural evangelical modes of public religion), and make previously invisible or overlooked patterns of relations more visible and legible (such as, in this case, relations among multicultural evangelicals and diverse social, religious, political, and cultural others engaged in ethical democratic projects across the United States).[77]

The exceptional nature of these unusual patterns of relations, ideas, people, networks, and organizations does not come without challenge, conflict, or instability. The pages above witness individuals moving in and out of organizations, networks, identities, churches, jobs, religious convictions, and political affiliations as they challenge established shibboleths, explore new horizons, and test out new ideas and practices while simultaneously holding on to cherished beliefs, values, relationships, convictions, and spiritual experiences. These are not easy waters to navigate. The complex fault lines of American racial, cultural, and religious politics are fraught; the consequences of judgment for "heresy" of various types increasingly brutal. Sometimes the tensions threatened to pull them, or their organizations, apart. Yet they endure, even in the post-2020 political landscape, and in so doing, present a vision of new configurations of public religion and politics in the United States beyond the ruthlessly polarized and increasingly violent—both culturally and materially—zero-sum struggles of today's partisan race and culture wars.[78]

Such a vision requires what German social philosopher Jürgen Habermas calls "complementary learning processes" among religious and secular citizens who have increasingly come to distrust and often despise one another and their respective visions of democracy in America.[79] More broadly, it requires social reflexivity across different types of difference.[80] In place of rigid secularist and religious fundamentalisms, Habermas advocates a new "post-secularism" that takes the deeply held convictions of religious and nonreligious people and groups alike seriously as potential sources of public inspiration, communication, legitimation, mutual recognition, understanding, and critique across deep difference.[81] Particularist pluralism is one mode of public religion whereby organizations such as Christians for the Common Good attempt to enact this vision.[82]

In today's polarized US public sphere, however, there is much shouting and little listening, much trench-digging and little bridge-building, much power-clinging and little power-leveling, much self-righteousness and little self-reflection, much opportunity hoarding and little equitable redistribution, much finger-pointing and little openness to honest critique. As sociologist Michele Dillon laments:

> The idea that religious believers and secularists "can live together in a self-reflective manner" as Habermas envisages,[83] is attractive but hard to imagine. It is not the living together but the reflexive self-reflection—and the new political and cultural outcomes that it might produce—that is more elusive.[84]

Such an environment spells trouble for ethical democracy. Building on the stories and experiences of publicly-engaged multicultural evangelicals described in these chapters—along with new data—Chapters 5 and 6 investigate further what a more reflexive evangelicalism in particular might look like, and what lessons it might hold concerning the practice of social reflexivity and the advancement of ethical democracy in America.

5

Reflexive Evangelicalism

Learning from Experience and Scripture

As demonstrated by Christians for the Common Good and the Buddhist–
Evangelical dialogues described in the previous chapter, multicultural
evangelicals draw on both the religious authority of the Bible and pragmatic lessons from experience and interaction with diverse social others
in their efforts to embody a more reflexive evangelical spirituality with respect to religious pluralism. We have seen similar dynamics at work in
multicultural evangelical approaches to race (Chapter 2), poverty and inequality (Chapter 3), and politics (Chapter 4)—processes that can be further
illuminated by listening to research participants' own stories of learning
through experience and scripture. The first section of this chapter explores
multicultural evangelical approaches to multifaith collaboration and evangelism, a defining feature of evangelical religious identity. Rather than inflexibly applying the evangelical imperative to proclaim the gospel in
triumphalist zeal and reductive certainty when engaging secular and religious others, multicultural evangelical research participants practiced social reflexivity by critically examining and adjusting evangelistic expression
while interacting across different types of organizational and public settings.
Subsequent sections investigate reflexive evangelical approaches to (1) politics and culture war, (2) poverty and economic inequality, and (3) racial difference and inequality. A final section explores the biblical and experiential
meanings and motivations of strategic relocation, given its significance as an
intensive case of multicultural evangelical approaches to racial justice and
integration.[1] In light of widespread white evangelical support for Trumpian
racial and culture war politics, economic and social conservatism, and strong
Republican Party affiliation, this chapter focuses on whether and how the
perspectives of white evangelical interview respondents in particular grew
or changed through their involvement in faith-based public service, political advocacy, community development, and community organizing groups
across the United States.

Good News for Common Goods. Wes Markofski, Oxford University Press. © Oxford University Press 2023.
DOI: 10.1093/oso/9780197659694.003.0006

Reflexive Evangelicalism: Evangelism and Religious Difference

As this book's title and first chapter attest, one cannot talk about evangelicalism without talking about evangelism. Emerging from the "great commission" given by Jesus to his disciples found at the conclusion of the book of Matthew, evangelism—the practice of sharing the gospel or good news of Jesus Christ with others—is central to the identity and practice of evangelical Christians in the United States and around the world.[2] For many observant evangelicals, practicing evangelism is the most important form that living out one's faith in public life can take: more important even than voting or political activism, excelling at work or educating children, promoting morality or influencing culture, feeding the hungry or serving the poor.[3] For these evangelicals, practicing evangelism is the highest expression of Christian love and witness.[4] In Chapter 4 and prior chapters we observed multicultural evangelicals interacting closely with nonreligious persons and those from different religious traditions in secular and multifaith settings where the practice of evangelism would be highly contentious. How do multicultural evangelicals navigate the tension between a controversial imperative of evangelical faith and their desire to participate in common good collaborations with diverse religious and irreligious people and communities?

We have already seen examples of how multicultural evangelicals navigate the tricky terrain of religious pluralism and evangelical particularism in the preceding pages. Many of these approaches involve recognition by evangelical actors of the different settings in which public religious engagement and civic action occurs, along with a willingness to interact flexibly across difference in diverse secular and multifaith contexts.[5] Serving the City, for example, which mobilizes a large proportion of the total evangelical church population in greater Portland, adheres to a firm no proselytizing agreement while engaging in annual public service projects at the behest of the city of Portland. Healing Hands similarly refrains from evangelistic communication while conducting its free medical and dental clinics across greater Portland. These examples align with the findings of other sociological studies of evangelical public engagement in which evangelical actors eliminate or reduce overt religious talk and expression while operating in secular or multifaith contexts.[6] This "secular" approach to public religion when operating in multifaith contexts is surprisingly common among evangelical groups and organizations across the United States.

Adopting a secularist mode of public religion in this manner does not, however, involve repudiation of distinctive evangelical religious identity or disavowal of the importance or appropriateness of evangelism in other settings. Patrick, director of Serving the City, described the organization's approach in an interview while discussing behind-the-scenes conversations among skeptical evangelical pastors and a gay mayor beleaguered by scandal:

There are a handful of suburban evangelical churches, a very small handful, that are more on the real kind of hard-core evangelism side. I met with one of them last week. I'd gotten a more direct hint from them that, "We don't get or trust this relationship with [Portland's mayor]. We don't feel comfortable with that. We don't hate him, don't get us wrong, but we don't see what good that's doing. How is that furthering the Gospel?" So I met with the senior pastor. And I told him some behind the scenes kind of things about the relationship and how when the mayor—the reason he showed up at [an event] in front of 500 evangelical pastors and leaders about a month after his election and about two weeks after the exposure of the affair and his admitting it and all that—was that two weeks before when the whole thing blew up, Jim [an evangelical pastor and Serving the City partner] met with him for a couple hours. Jim was one of two people he met with that whole first weekend, because of this trust that had developed. And without going into details about what the conversation was, it was everything that any evangelical would dream of in any one-on-one situation with a person in crisis who was genuinely saying, "I don't get it. How could I have allowed myself to do this? I'm a smart person." And Jim being able to just say, "Well . . . you're Episcopalian. So as you know, the Bible says the heart is deceitful and desperate." Just shared the basic gospel.

So some things you can say more quietly one-on-one and say, "Look, we're an evangelistic organization. We're very bold about that, when it's appropriate, and you need to know that." In public schools? Absolutely not. We affirm to the principals and teachers and superintendents, "You can trust us in the evangelical community. We're not going to tape tracts to the undersides of kids' desks or inappropriately take advantage of it. Yet you need to know our heart is for the Gospel." That's why I tell people we call this a Gospel movement, to use a Tim Keller phrase. It's not just about the [public service]. We see it as a Gospel movement. We want to look back ten years from now and say fifty new churches were planted and followers of Christ are thriving and growing. We're not ashamed of that. Again, we haven't hid that from city leaders. We want to see people come to Christ. I don't care what church a person goes to, but we want people to have a relationship with Christ.

Rather than practicing an inflexible, setting-insensitive approach to evangelism, Patrick describes a flexible, setting-specific approach that differentiates between "appropriate" and inappropriate contexts and ways in which to engage in more overtly religious or evangelistic communication. Serving the City thus remains committed to evangelism and its distinctive evangelical religious identity while simultaneously engaging in an ongoing secular public service collaboration with progressive Portland city officials, a collaboration that "remains a message-neutral genuine service primarily done by evangelical churches."

Whereas Serving the City and other evangelical groups and organizations practiced a "secularist" mode of public religion that restricted overt religious or evangelistic talk in nonreligious or multifaith settings, other groups—such as Christians for the Common Good and the Buddhist–Evangelical dialogue series—embraced particularistic evangelical religious expression while refraining from directly evangelistic talk in such settings.[7] In the former case, Christians for the Common Good engaged in distinctly evangelical modes of communication—including public quotations of scripture, Bible-based theological justifications of political positions,[8] prayer and public religious self-identification, and frequent use of distinctively Christian symbols and imagery—in both public and private organizational settings and communication. In the latter case, participants in the Buddhist–Evangelical dinner discussions explicitly engaged religious differences and distinctiveness while prioritizing "beautiful friendships" and "learning" over "winning arguments" or "winning souls."[9]

In addition to interacting flexibly with respect to evangelism and religious difference across different types of multifaith settings, multicultural evangelical research participants also described a sort of division of labor among different parts of the "body of Christ" [a Pauline metaphor for Christian churches], some of which are more "wired" for evangelism while others are more wired for justice advocacy or community organizing work.[10] Cooper, the thirty-seven-year-old white evangelical pastor and East Los Angeles strategic relocator we met in Chapter 2, expressed this view while describing his training in Industrial Areas Foundation (IAF)-style democratic community organizing work:

> I learned that I am definitely an apostolic person. I am definitely a church planter. I am that guy. I want to see people love Jesus. We have people that are more fired up and wired for the community organizing. Now they're doing it. But because of how I'm wired, I'm really grateful that my training was presented in such a strong biblical tone. Bob Linthicum was the guy that trained me. . . . He just takes scripture, and it's like getting a new education. I think it was just very easy for me to say yes; to kind of go: people are made in the image of God. And shalom is the great purpose of God in this earth. And the only way to appropriately work with the urban poor is to work in a way that recognizes and calls out the image of God. And if you try to shortcut that and just do evangelism stuff, you're just carrying all these preconceived stereotypes and issues, like, "*I* have something to bring to *you*." So it was very easy for me to digest. Now, my personality is such that sometimes it's too slow for me. And that's just my brokenness. That's just me repenting and going, "God, I just want to see people converted. That's my heart. Let's get a church going." But I also realize that the people that have really stuck in our church are the ones that came while they were organizing. You really see it. And you see that real, lifelong change comes as people are really given a voice.

For Cooper, community organizing was simultaneously a foundational expression of God's purposes on earth as written in scripture, a specific vocational call for some individuals, and a corrective to arrogant and shallow evangelism-only styles of evangelical public engagement. In each of these instances, it was also a potential site of Christ-centered witness while working alongside "some very liberal folks" in the broad-based community organizing field:

> One thing I disagree with around some organizers is the lack of Jesus-centeredness. For those that are not Christian, I've got no problem with that. That's just where they're at. It's the ones who say they are Christian but never talk about Jesus—or who don't really have any thought of using it to pull people into communities of faith or into challenge with God— obviously, I disagree with that. In my own personal work with [community

organizing], I think it is important to prioritize and work with biblical priorities. . . . People reconciling with Jesus, even in a simple way, is the priority. But the discipleship process has to include the whole holistic shalom-oriented kind of thing. So I think folks that move in as missionaries into a community for thirty years and don't really ever mention the name of Jesus and just work on all these social projects—I think they are missing the priority. If we keep that clear, then I think everything is good. . . . We've got to at least make sure that Jesus is in that equation, so that if you work in a community that's not going to really say yes to any significant social change, that they at least have a chance at [receiving] the gospel. That's just how I try to hold all that in tension.

While most (though not all)[11] research participants viewed situation-sensitive evangelism as an important element of Christian witness and the teachings of scripture, Cooper was unique in voicing support for the prioritization of evangelism over other forms of public religious engagement in the manner of dominant American evangelical perspectives—though he did so circumspectly, recognizing that his own personal "wiring" and vocation was not shared by all.

Across the board, when multicultural evangelical research participants discussed nonreligious persons or those belonging to other religious traditions, they did so respectfully, as bridge-builders and potential collaborators rather than triumphalist proselytizers or religious chauvinists. This stands in contrast to dominant expressions of white American evangelicalism often marked by a combative, high-boundary approach to religious identity and difference; strong suspicion of secular and religious others; and a "pietistic idealism" that refuses to partner with anyone who does not share their distinctive theological and moral standpoints.[12] For a variety of reasons, evangelicals have a long history of being unwilling, unable, or un-interested in participating in common good collaborations with secular and religious others. At a Seattle conference on "collaboration and community transformation" I attended with Neighborhood Partners staff, however, I was surprised by the strong, univocal support given by conference speakers and participants in favor of "inclusive partnerships" with religious and secular others for "community transformation" and the "common good":

"Jesus got in trouble for inclusivity, not exclusivity."—*Former missionary*

"If we're talking about community transformation, every worldview should be at the table."—*Conference speaker*

"We must work with followers of Jesus *and* with all people and leaders of good will. Put a fork in the sacred-secular dichotomy. It's all sacred."— *Conference speaker*

"There are only two singers in the universe: death or life. . . . Nowhere in scripture do we find support for people inside the church judging people outside."—*Conference speaker*

The consensus view was summarized by a keynote speaker's closing remarks—"All truth is God's truth"—by which he meant that, when it comes to partnering with others on issues such as reducing hunger, poverty, violence, racism, pollution, or injustice, there is no need for theological litmus tests or religious bouncers to expel the doctrinally impure. Since "all truth is God's truth," evangelicals should work with Muslims, Hindus, atheists, other Christians, or anyone else on common good collaborations for their neighborhoods, cities, and nations.

The consensus view at the Seattle conference was also the consensus view of my multicultural evangelical interview respondents, all fifty of whom expressed unequivocal support for partnering with religious and secular others on projects of shared interest and concern.[13] Their reasoning is instructive:

I: What do you think about Christians or churches working with other religious groups, non-Christian groups, secular groups, or others on justice issues?

R: All for it. I think you have to know who you are and stay true to your values, but if they're passionate about the same justice issues, the same values, however we can get this done, let's get it done. And hopefully in that, they'll realize what motivates us is Christ's love and redemption. But I don't think you ever shut doors.—*Deb, 34-year-old white evangelical, Atlanta*

R: I think it's good to work with anybody, really. If they're doing work that is going to help get rid of poverty and going to help prevent inequality, then that's a really good thing. So even if they believe differently or have a different motivation, I think that's okay. The more hands working towards a good thing, the better. I don't really have a problem working with people from other faiths. I don't think it changes what I believe or why I do what I do.—*Carrie, 32-year-old white evangelical, Atlanta*

R: I definitely think Christians should be doing things that benefit everyone and figuring out what that looks like in different contexts. Interfaith, working across religious difference—I've seen that done really well. In LA in particular, I was connected to CLUE [Clergy and Laity United for Economic Justice] and worked with them and some others a little bit. . . . just using immigration reform as an example: you need all the people you can get. It doesn't matter. I'm doing it because I'm motivated by my Christian faith. But you're not going to turn away people who are motivated for other reasons. I think that's just something that, you know, God accomplishes his purposes however he wants to.—*Sandy, 30-year-old white evangelical, Atlanta*

R: I think diversity in everything we do is valuable and important. I think we have a lot to learn from groups from a different background and different faith. For me, ultimately, it's about the betterment of who we're serving, and not about our own self. How do we best serve the person we're looking to serve? And if that means that a Jewish or Islamic or secular group can serve that person better, then I have no problems with that. I think it makes us stronger and also shows the world that it's not about us, it's not about Christianity. I'm willing to share with you why I believe what I believe, but let me show you by my actions that I can actually get along with someone and do something together, versus fight and bicker.—*Dave, 34-year-old white evangelical, Atlanta*

Research participants described an array of reasons to work with secular and religious others, including learning from people of different religious traditions, practicing humility, discovering the most effective ways to help people, increasing numbers and effectiveness, and achieving important objectives such as immigration reform, equitable access to education, racial justice and equity, and reducing poverty and inequality.

Multicultural evangelical research participants highlighted other benefits of multifaith collaboration as well, such as building Christian unity across denominational or confessional lines, reducing animosity and distrust rooted in religious or political difference, and forging solidaristic bonds for mutual benefit in local communities:

The work of community development is not only loving God and loving neighbor, but also bringing the saints together. When you bring together people in a [community] of Catholics and Protestants and evangelicals and charismatics and Baptists and others—when you bring them together not as different denominations but as community members—they realize that they really need each other in order to accomplish the greater good of loving our neighbors. And when the saints—who have been un-Christianizing each other and are on opposite sides of the political spectrum—when the saints come together and start working together and actually developing friendships and affectionate relationships, there is power that is released that leads to conversations within the [community]: "Do you see what's going on? They've been political enemies, but do you see what's going on?" So evangelism is a byproduct of the two prior commands of loving God, loving your neighbor, and loving each other. It's a byproduct. It's not an end in itself, it's a result. When I answer that question, "How do you bring Jesus into this?" I say, "We go first with the fundamentals [loving God and neighbor] that Jesus said we should be about."[14]

Richard—turning conventional evangelical idioms of evangelism priority and "fundamental" doctrine on its head—affirmed ecumenical and multifaith collaboration as faithful obedience to Christ and the commands of scripture concerning evangelism.[15]

Like Richard, Doug (thirty-five-year-old white evangelical, Peachtree Community Development Association [PCDA]) strongly affirmed the importance of working with religious and secular others in "dignified interdependence" for the "common good" as a central feature of Jesus's teaching concerning the "kingdom of God," while also challenging "condescension" and "arrogant" approaches to evangelism and religious difference:

I: Do you think that it's appropriate for Christians or Christian groups to work with interfaith groups or secular organizations?

R: Absolutely. It's the common good, it's the kingdom. . . . Reciprocity. Honoring people's dignity . . . You can work with interfaith [groups] for the common good. This is where—coming from Liberty [University, where Doug attended college]—people are like, "People need to be saved. You need to present the Gospel to them as soon as you meet." Well, no. I think that's been done way too much. People already have a really bad idea of what it is to be an evangelical Christian.

What if we just humbly work together and actually reflect the life of Christ, and serve, and love, and didn't say anything about evangelism? Just respectfully worked together. And Christians: we're very arrogant about our faith. Particularly in America. Christians are starting to get pushed to the margins. And for many Christians, that's hard. And what's our response? For many, it's to get up in arms, get really mad. "We're losing our rights!" Okay, what rights? What about the common good? I understand protecting our rights and freedom of speech, but I'm so quickly reminded of the fact Christianity has always done best on the margins.

Rather than engaging in "arrogant" and combative approaches to evangelism or politics, Doug believed American Christians ought to put greater effort into pursuing common goods alongside secular and religious others in humility, service, and love. Like other evangelical research participants, Doug did not disavow evangelism or the hope of seeing people come to faith in Christ. "As a Christian," he averred, "drawing on what Paul says in the book of Philippians, I would say the ultimate goal is . . . that we come together as 'partners in the Gospel.'"[16] But such was not a prerequisite or primary purpose of engaging in "respectful" and "humble" multifaith collaboration for the "common good" in one's neighborhood or nation.

Evan, a twenty-eight-year-old white evangelical practitioner of strategic relocation in Portland, echoed Doug, Richard, Elena, and other interview respondents' critiques of conventional evangelical approaches to evangelism and religious difference while emphasizing his community's "place-shaped" practice of Christian spirituality in a working-class southeast Portland neighborhood:

I'm very curious about working with Buddhists, atheists, and Muslims in my neighborhood towards the city's healing and flourishing. I've derived a lot of value from having friends who are sort of capital P practicing Pagans. I've learned about truth and faith through that. There's a real possibility of cross pollination. I've learned that the Spirit is at work all over the place. And I have very vigorous disagreements with plenty of other things. But I can't deny that God is up to good things through people of other faiths. I don't monopolize truth. God is a little bit less uptight than I think we've been told. So, like, one of the neighbors is a witch. And we've worked with her on a variety of things. And it's charitable, you know.

I: Does she know who you are?

R: Oh yeah. Oh yeah. There's no ill will. The challenge is, again, in this
moment in history, it feels like a lot of people that join a community like ours are reacting strongly against certain ways of relating to
other faiths, or evangelism, or—what is it called—apophatic or negative theology: that we're defined by what we're against. . . . So it's this
real challenge where we don't want to be like that, but we do want
to be able to give a good answer for the hope that we have, the actual reasons we live the way we do, beyond just being "good Portland
liberals" [laughs].

Evan's allusion to 1 Peter 3:15, "Always be prepared to give an answer to everyone who asks you to give the reason for the hope that you have. But do this
with gentleness and respect,"[17] aptly captures the modal approach to evangelism and religious difference practiced by multicultural evangelical interview
respondents and their respective groups and organizations.

By limiting evangelism or gospel proclamation to appropriate settings;
recognizing legitimate differences in how, by, and to whom evangelism is
ethically and pragmatically practiced; affirming positive nonevangelistic
interaction with religious and secular others in multifaith public projects
and common good collaborations; and critiquing arrogant and inflexible
approaches to evangelism and religious difference, multicultural evangelicals
engage in the sort of social reflexivity that philosophers, psychologists,
sociologists, and theologians have found essential to the practice of ethical
democracy under conditions of religious and cultural pluralism—a point to
which we will return at length in Chapter 6.[18] By simultaneously affirming
and critically adapting a core element of evangelical religious conviction to
diverse pluralist and public settings, multicultural evangelicals demonstrate
how religious actors can combine intellectual humility and religious conviction in their interactions with secular and religious others in public life.[19]

Reflexive Evangelicalism: Politics and Culture War

When I asked multicultural evangelical interview respondents whether or
not their political views had shifted at all since becoming involved in their
current faith-based public service, political advocacy, community development, or community organizing work, over half answered affirmatively.

Given the strong correlation between evangelicalism and conservative politics in the United States, it is perhaps no surprise that in every case, interview respondents reported their political views moving toward more left-liberal positions. Peter, the forty-seven-year-old white evangelical working with Neighborhood Partners in Portland whom we met in the Introduction and Chapter 3, is a typical example. "I grew up in pretty conservative circles," Peter told me, before adding he had developed "a deeper sense of social responsibility, and a relational approach to things, that made a Democratic [Party] approach make a little more sense." Not every multicultural evangelical research participant I spoke with had changed their partisan political identification, but those who did shifted from Republican to Independent or Democratic Party affiliation as a result of changing views on race, poverty and economic inequality, immigration, gender, sexuality, and other issues.

Doug did not even let me finish my question when I began asking, "Have your political views changed at all since you—," cutting me off to respond, "Oh, drastically":

Growing up, I went to a small Christian school in "Bumpville." So come on. The sort of place that said, "If we can just get enough people in power, we can change America for the better." All sorts of Republican Christian speakers would come. So yeah, absolutely. Where you live definitely changes everything. Did I agree with all Obama's policies? No, absolutely not. But it's like, once you live and share life with African American people, people that have been oppressed, and finally one of their own is president . . . . It gives you perspective. And it's so easy—I tell my dad and anybody else—it's so easy to sit there and watch Fox News and have your ideologies reinforced, until you actually come face to face with people. When you actually move and come face to face with a person that is experiencing the effects of these ideologies, people experiencing racism or oppression, it changes things.

Raised and educated in a deeply conservative white evangelical community, strategic relocation to a majority Black neighborhood while working with PCDA had "drastically" changed Doug's political views and personal engagement with racism and electoral politics.

Ada—the thirty-year-old white female neighborhood resident and PCDA-affiliated strategic relocator we met in Chapter 2—mirrored Doug and others in discussing their journey away from the conservative political views of their childhood and families of origin:

I: Have your political views shifted at all?

R: Oh my gosh. Drastically. My parents would probably disown me now. I'm from a very Republican household. My mom's a Republican, my dad's a Libertarian. He's very brainy. He's the practical brain side of the family. My brother is a Libertarian just like my dad. So I came out of high school very Republican. Where I'm at now, I view myself as an independent. I really hate the parties, I hate both political parties, I hate the song and dance we have to do politically. But I definitely lean towards the Democratic end now, as far as a lot of things go. And my frustration towards the political parties has increased. The attachment to the Republican Party by the Christian church really bothers me. I don't know when it became true that Jesus was a Republican. He's not. Jesus, let's be honest, he's not a part of our framework. He wasn't an American. I don't know why we try to put him in a box. So it's really frustrating to me that we're going to take one or two issues as our platform and ignore everything else. That doesn't make any sense. And what makes those issues—not that they're not important—but what makes them more important than anything else? It's very frustrating. . . .

I think a lot of the reason for that is, in my own experience, people are only exposed to narrow, one-dimensional political information. So they keep holding onto those few things they "know" are right or wrong and they don't listen to anything else. And the more exposure I have to diversity and to people of all walks of life: it changes everything. That changes the ballgame all together. You realize it's not a Republican versus Democrat issue, it's a people issue. It's a justice, equality, people issue. Jesus was about people, equality for the people. Didn't matter if they were gay or straight, didn't matter if they were Black or white, didn't matter if they were Muslim. You're going to fight for those people because they're people, they're God's people, God created them. So how do we—I don't see how you can fight for, like I said, one group or one dimension of humanity and not all the others. If you're going to fight for one, you have to fight for them all. You can't pick and choose. And if you go too far with one party or the other, that's what you're doing. You're leaving out large groups of people that you should still be fighting for. So I don't know. It's a continually frustrating system that we're part of.

Ada attributed her changing political views to racial integration and strategic relocation while voicing a "consistent ethic of life" position common among evangelicals and Catholics who occupy a "contradictory cultural location" between secular progressives and religious conservatives.[20]

Sandy (thirty-year-old white evangelical) also grew up in a conservative evangelical Republican family before coming to question her political upbringing and perspective on power and political leadership more generally:

> When I [first started practicing strategic relocation] I was, like, voting for George Bush via mail. And now I'm like, "What on earth?" Although I will say—and I'd guess this is not uncommon—I'm becoming increasingly frustrated with politics in general. I grew up in a hardcore Republican home. I was out canvassing the streets for the Christian Coalition when I was like eleven: passing out pamphlets, standing on street corners protesting abortion and those kinds of things as a child. I will say I'm so thankful for that now—even though I kind of almost role my eyes because it's so stereotypically evangelical—but my parents taught me if you don't agree with something, you say something about it. You have a voice. You use the tools we have in the [United] States to protest and all that. So yeah. I mean, ironically, so much of evangelicalism takes this stance of, "Don't be political." But it was very political. I would say in some ways, I'm still political, but I've kind of swung so that now I'm a Democrat....
>
> I'll tell you directly: I no longer believe that just because people are given a position of power in the society that they're using that for good. You see that with police officers. It's been interesting. Police officers are a very sore or very touchy subject. Because in certain circles in my life, a police officer is always right. I think the paradigm shifting that has to occur before people recognize that police corruption could and does exist—it's almost so unsettling some people can't fathom it. And I think that has translated politically for me as well. I don't assume that just because you're leading us, you're doing the right thing. In fact, I'm willing to believe that you may be doing some really evil things, whether or not your motivation is evil. What you're doing may be creating evil. And so I think that kind of relationship to authority has been almost the basis of that shift politically....
>
> I mean, there's definitely power dynamics in the Bible and you often see Jesus on the side of the folks that are not in the societal realms of power. I believe wholeheartedly that white privilege exists. And I think—I don't know—I feel like Jesus is pretty direct about going against the powers of the

day, confronting powers, turning things upside down. And the things he does often don't make sense or follow convention. And I think sometimes, that's a little tough. How do I interpret that and follow Jesus as a Christian who has power due to my nationality? Due to my race? My socioeconomic class? How do you interpret what it means to follow Jesus when Jesus often seems to be against the people who have societal power? And I think a lot of that has come around to those questions of, "How do I best submit my privilege to God?" How do I figure out ways to use that privilege not just for the benefit of myself and my family? You can't pretend power doesn't exist or you're just playing right into it. You have to acknowledge it's there. And seek ways to confront it and turn it upside down.

Breaking with family tradition, shifting partisanship, reckoning with race and whiteness, expressing frustration with the political and religious status quo: Sandy's narrative represents a particular flavor of the general experience of my white evangelical interview respondents across the country.

While Sandy and other research participants expressed frustration at various aspects of partisan politics in the United States, they also reported increased political awareness and activism as a natural consequence of their work. Nick, a thirty-five-year-old white evangelical PCDA leader and strategic relocator, responded to my query about whether his political views had shifted or not by discussing his increased commitment to political activism and bridge-building across partisan divides:

I would say yes in the sense that my heart for political advocacy has grown or increased because of things that I've experienced or seen firsthand living in Atlanta, and connecting with people in lots of other cities who are facing similar situations. Just seeing that there is a place to raise a voice to address issues of policy and decision-making politically—no matter which side of the fence that people fall on—in our attempts to understand and pursue God's heart as far as we can understand or see. I've also become even more passionate about trying to call people together, rather than just pick a side and stay on it. . . . I have friends on both ends of the [political] spectrum. And I think sometimes politically, as Jesus followers, we can find ourselves in a political bubble, believing that our way is the only way to attempt to follow Jesus. And I get concerned about that. Because the spirit and the approach of Jesus followers in a lot of other hard places globally don't have that perspective and aren't taking that approach. Having said that though, and living in this context, there are definitely cases where it's necessary to pick a side: whether it's signing a petition, trying to voice a concern in Washington, attending a rally in our city or sending a hundred faxes through our neighborhood council to the city of Atlanta to address abandoned houses in our neighborhood or whatever.

Previously a largely apolitical evangelical,[21] Nick described how strategic relocation had elevated his political awareness and activism while also increasing his desire for greater transpartisan communication and cooperation among followers of Jesus across the political spectrum.

Reflexive Evangelicalism: Poverty and Inequality

Several clear themes emerged when I asked multicultural evangelicals whether their views of poverty and inequality had changed since becoming involved in faith-based public service, political advocacy, community development, or community organizing work. Deb, the white, thirty-four-year-old senior PCDA leader and strategic relocation veteran we met in Chapter 2, described a growing focus on macroeconomic issues:

> The longer I've done it, the older I've gotten, I've just gotten more passionate about the economic side of everything. Delivering true economic change. No matter how many kids you've loved on and how many good after school programs you have, how much housing you've done, I keep returning to, "How do we create larger economic change? How do we change the economic landscape? How do you do that justly?"

Deb's up-close engagement with poverty and economic inequality as a neighbor and PCDA leader over time helped her see the importance of scalable approaches to economic equity and opportunity for racial and economic justice.

Carrie and Evan, on the other hand, focused on how their thinking about poverty and inequality "had become more personal in a lot of ways" (Carrie) as their experiences had put "a face to it" (Evan)—often in ways that sharply challenged their own assumptions, attitudes, and self-righteousness. Evan discussed his experience living in a Christian intentional community in a working class Portland neighborhood:

I think for me a lot of the poverty thing before was about not buying certain products, not shopping at certain places. And I still try and practice that broadly. Or it was sort of the poor in abstraction. Now, I get a little wary talking too much in those abstractions. It changes when you have a face to it. I think that's just one of the hardest parts about how we talk about anything in this culture—whether it's poverty or war or sexuality—is, you know, when you have a living, breathing, crying person, human, in front of you, it changes things. And so for me, it's been much harder to really own my favorite [Bible] verses about poverty. My neighborhood is not grindingly poor, but there's a low-income apartment building right across the street. Poverty in Portland tends to just get piled up into apartment complexes, and just can get exponentially crazier because of that. But as I just get to know people who are thoroughly different from me, it's hard. A lot of the culture in my neighborhood is more like "white trash." As a "good Portland liberal," it's hard for me to deal with that. Like, I can rail against the intolerant right. But then I realize how intolerant I am of the veteran that lives next door, or the gun toting libertarian, or the guy that just has seven cars in his front yard because he just loves cars. Suddenly, I'm like, "fuck the poor. That guy's being a real jackass." I thought that I believed that, you know, I see Jesus in the poor. I thought I believed! It's a lot harder to live it out with actual people. It's a hell of a lot harder. And it requires, it means it's not just a series of opinions. Like being for Jubilee is not—it's easy to be sentimental and fiery about it. It's a lot harder to live into. Remarkably harder.

Evan's response traces a common theme among multicultural evangelical research participants of moving from idealism to realism, abstraction to personalization, and self-righteousness to critical self-reflection in their understanding of poverty, inequality, and difference.

Carrie, like Evan, emphasized how her understanding of poverty and inequality had "become more personal in a lot of ways" while also discussing new perspectives on how poverty and economic inequality are linked to race and politics in the United States:

It's more prevalent or just there in my face every day, instead of being something that we just talk about or see occasionally. Those issues: you can't push them aside. You have to wrestle with them and think about them because they're not going anywhere. I think I had a better understanding of global poverty [before becoming a strategic relocator] but not as good of an understanding of poverty in the United States. I think poverty here is really—I mean, it's complex everywhere—but I do think there's a lot of racial history that plays into it. I've become a lot more aware of how race and class interact. You see how things are interconnected: schools and segregation, racial segregation in neighborhoods—even though we're all supposedly integrated now. Yet there are still neighborhoods that are mostly white, and neighborhoods that are mostly Black or mostly Hispanic. And you start to notice, you know, some of those neighborhoods are poor, and their schools are poor, and there's a cycle—just kind of making those connections. I would say that's been sort of an ongoing process.

I think I've just become a lot more aware of it, and aware of my own identity as a white person. I think I had a hard time—I think a lot of white people have a hard time realizing that there is a white culture, that you have a racial identity, and that it's different. It's not just "normal," you know? So I've kind of gone through that. My first year, all my coworkers where I was volunteering were African American. Everybody in my church was African American. All of a sudden, I would have an opinion, and I would realize I was only one voicing that opinion and everybody else had the opposite opinion. And I would say, "Okay, maybe there's some sort of racial factor happening here." Maybe there's something I've experienced as a white person that makes me think this way, and nobody else had that same experience. I kind of had that broken down a little bit.

Somebody in my church asked me at one point, after I'd been here for a few years, "At what point did you realize that you were white?" And I was like, "What do you mean?" And he said, "Well, whenever I go out anywhere and it's all white people, I realize that I'm Black. I feel like I'm Black. But when I'm around all Black people, I just feel like I'm me." So he was asking, "When did you have that experience?" And it was definitely true, though I had never thought about it in that way. So I think that's just been sort of an ongoing process. And I think race is really complicated. So I think it's constantly learning and figuring stuff out, how does that impact relationships with people and dynamics in neighborhoods and things like that. Yeah. Still learning.

I: Do you remember any specific examples of, "I'm voicing this perspective and I'm the only one?" Do you remember any of those details?

R: I think politics was a big one. My family was always pretty staunchly Republican. And pretty much everybody else was Democrat. When talking about presidents and decisions and things like that, I was like, "This is different."

I: Have your political views changed or shifted at all as a result?

R: Yeah. I think I've always been somewhat moderate anyway but I definitely lean more on the Democratic side at this point.

I: And that wasn't the case?

R: No. I would say I was more Republican. But I don't think I really knew what I was talking about anyway. And I think I'm still just starting to know what I'm talking about.

I: All right. So why that shift? Has it been easy or difficult? For some people, that's a pretty big bracing shock to realize not all Christians are Republicans and to some it's not a big deal.

R: [laughs] That's true. It would really shock my grandmother. For me, it wasn't super shocking. I don't think I ever thought that one party was actually the Christian party even though there's that sort of perception. I think it's just been, I think as I've seen some of the ways that decisions that Republicans have made actually impact people that I know or people that I work with, it's hard to get behind some of those decisions.

As with multicultural evangelical research participants in the previous section, Carrie's political views changed while witnessing first-hand the perspectives and fallout of policy changes that were "hard to swallow" because of their negative impact on "people I know or people that I work with" across race and class lines. As we will in the next section, Carrie's "ongoing process" of awakening to her own racial identity and privilege while "constantly learning" more about the intersections of race, poverty, inequality, and politics in the United States closely mirrored those of other white evangelical strategic relocators.

Traci, a thirty-four-year-old white evangelical PCDA-affiliated relocator, also spoke of her changing views on poverty and economic inequality through an intersectional lens:

I grew up in a low-income family. One parent. And we lived in a tough neighborhood like the one I currently live in. But I probably wouldn't consider myself poor now. And I think most of that is around my whiteness and my privilege. Because I mostly live and work in contexts where people of color are in the majority . . . for me, when I think about poverty I think about the connection between power and privilege and poverty. While I understand that there are poor white people, I think that if you put a poor white person and a poor Black person in the same room, the Black person is still poor because of the ways that societal structures are established to disadvantage them. And so my understanding of poverty is very connected to my understanding of race and racism.

Along with a greater understanding of the systemic causes of racialized poverty, Traci, like Evan and others, also discussed wrestling with structural and personal aspects of generational poverty:

I think when I first moved to Philadelphia especially, I just couldn't understand how the people I was living around were poor, because they had much nicer cars and much nicer things than I did. . . . But I come back to this realization of just the fact that I'm white. Even in my immigration here. I had the wrong visa at one point and so was actually technically here without the right documentation. But because I had a job, because my job would sponsor me and pay for some of it, because my job paid me and I was able to pay for some of it as well, I was able to get legal help. When I went to the immigration office, they would respond to me and talk to me kindly because I could speak English or because my skin was white. I now have a green card and have access to the United States for ten years. So, you know, just this realization that the structures and injustices in the world keep people in poverty. I'm not sure it's always people that keep themselves in poverty. I think my understanding is much more structural than anything else. I think people make really bad choices as well and that's always really hard to watch.

Traci's experiences with immigration and strategic relocation as a white woman from a low-income background helped shift her understanding of poverty in more race-conscious and systemic directions, without thereby erasing personal responsibility and agency.

Ada joined Carrie and Traci in identifying a growing systemic, personalized, and intersectional understanding of poverty and economic inequality in the United States:

Yes. [My views have changed]. I came from a Christian background in very rural upstate New York. Looking back on it, I feel like I was very far removed from reality. I mean, there was rural poverty, but we didn't even really talk about that in my church. Very middle class. Oblivion. Middle class oblivion. It really was. The more I think about it, the more disappointed I get that's so common.... Now I see it as systemic, race and class, all these things that go into the reason poverty still exists to such an extent in this country.

Ada proceeded to give a concrete example of a "surface problem"—inadequate public transportation—that she saw as arising from underlying issues of racial and socioeconomic inequity:

MARTA [Metropolitan Atlanta Rapid Transit Authority] here is a surface problem. But MARTA is a result of the dysfunction of public transportation in the city. It's a result of everything that's gone down racially and economically. It's really frustrating when you see how it's connected with everything, to the idea, "That person needs to pull themselves up by their bootstraps." That's painful when I hear that. I'm like, "You don't even know." You're saying that as a white suburban or rural person who has never experienced what it's like. That's completely different—a completely different scenario. Yes, maybe in that scenario, people can pull up their bootstraps and do their thing. But here: the schools. The jobs. The power. It's completely different.... So yeah, [relocation] has drastically changed my views of poverty. Especially in this country. Especially in the context of Christianity. Because I feel like as Christians we kind of brush it under the table here: "[Poverty] is not big enough or extreme enough," or we make excuses for why city poverty exists. "Oh, they're not deserving." Or the underlying racism behind some of it, which isn't even acknowledged as racism....

I: You said MARTA is one of the surface problems. Tell me about that.
R: MARTA is like the worst public transportation system you could possibly experience. I could walk most places faster than I'm going to get there on MARTA, even if it's three, four miles. Because if I take MARTA, it's going to take me an hour and a half, and cost me $2.50, which is the same price as New York City right now. And then you have the racial divide on MARTA. In general, this is a huge generalization: I nanny and work part-time at Barnes and Noble, where I come into contact with higher income white people. So I know a lot of people outside of the neighborhood. And my general perception of what they think about MARTA is that it's high crime, they don't want to ride it, it takes too long. So people with money are not going to use

it, because they're not going to risk safety, and they even go as far as saying [negative] things about people who ride MARTA. Not everybody but some people. So you have this divide. And then you have the people with money in the city say we're not going to vote to give money to MARTA money for those same reasons.

All these people think, "Why would we put money into MARTA when we could just build more highways?" Instead of realizing that, number one, MARTA serves an underprivileged population. But also, for your city to thrive, you need public transportation. But I don't feel like people care enough about the underprivileged in this city to do anything. They would rather get what they want, the upper class would, than to care about the city's collective success. The old Southerners who live here are very much like, "We like our cars, we like to drive everywhere, we're not giving that up and we're not going to take MARTA anyways. And you're not going to tax me for it." And they don't want to vote for the tax because their view is, "I'm not going to pay for something I'm not participating in." So then MARTA is privatized. So it's lacking money. The prices keep going up. They keep cutting routes. And often when they cut the routes, it's routes in the low-income neighborhoods. So our bus is always, it's packed whenever I'm on there. You know. So then the bus is packed and your bus driver's grumpy because people are crazy. It's cyclical. It's very frustrating to see such a small, rich part of the population running everything and not caring about the collective good at all. Like, even logically—it would be nice if you actually cared about people. But even logically speaking, if you want your city to survive, you need public transportation! But they don't care. They just don't care. They're going to keep adding highways, which is what they're doing.

So MARTA: people in this neighborhood use MARTA. That's how people get around. My house can barely afford cars. They're never going to be able to afford a car. Or they get a car and then it breaks down on them. And MARTA has been known to be not dependable. So you have people getting up at 3:00 in the morning to get to their job, because MARTA takes an hour and a half. Or people get there a whole route ahead, so if something goes wrong, you're still on time. Things like that: there's good evidence that we just, as a city, don't care about poor people who use MARTA. "Too bad, you need to find your own way to get to work." Because there's just no investment in it whatsoever.

From Ada's perspective as a low-income resident of a low-income, majority Black neighborhood, Atlanta's ambivalence and opposition to adequate funding for public transportation—including its privatization, service cuts, and lack of reliability and usership—represented a shameful callousness towards low-income Atlanta residents, driven largely by latent and overt racism, elitism, and affluent Atlanta residents' short-sighted neglect of how they themselves benefit from the collective good of public transportation.

Multicultural evangelical interview respondents who lived and worked in multiracial contexts found it difficult to discuss poverty and economic inequality without also talking about white privilege and racism. The next section turns directly to the question of whether or how research participants reported changes to their views on racial difference and inequality through their involvement in faith-based public service, political advocacy, community development, or community organizing work, beginning with a brief of examination of prior sociological research on race and religion in the United States.

Reflexive Evangelicalism: Race and Reflexivity

Despite periodic surges in evangelical social activism aimed at promoting "racial reconciliation" among Black and white Americans,[22] challenging racialized poverty and inequality,[23] and creating multiracial communities and congregations,[24] the historical and sociological record suggests that American evangelicals are more likely to reinforce than to challenge racial inequity and division in the United States.[25]

In their landmark study of evangelical religion and race relations, *Divided by Faith: Evangelical Religion and the Problem of Race in America*, sociologists Michael O. Emerson and Christian Smith find that the "cognitive building blocks" through which white evangelicals understand race relations "make it difficult for evangelicals to construct racial issues in social-structural terms, and also doom concrete attempts at race-bridging to failure."[26] White evangelicals, Emerson and Smith argue, tend to:

> (1) minimize and individualize the race problem, (2) assign blame to Blacks themselves for inequality, (3) obscure inequality as part of racial division, and (4) suggest unidimensional [spiritual-individualist] solutions to racial division.[27]

In a related article, "Race-Bridging for Christ? Conservative Christians and Black-White Relations in Community Life," sociologists Paul Lichterman, Prudence L. Carter, and Michele Lamont concur with Emerson and Smith's "pessimistic prognosis" concerning evangelical race-bridging efforts in light of their "color-blind" approach to racial issues, which undermines race-bridging efforts for a number of reasons: it "downplays racial differences" and "steers people away from publicly acknowledging racial categories and racial inequality, which may be necessary to change attitudes," it "often devalues religious and cultural practices associated with African Americans," it "cultivates unequal relationships that are at odds with the civic ideal" of ethical democracy, and it "does little to weaken the sense of distance that many white conservative Christians have in relation to African Americans."[28] If—as sociologist Korie Edwards and other leading studies of multiracial religious organizations have found—multiracial religious congregations tend to discourage open discussions of racial inequality and difference, cater to white members, and reproduce internally the same racialized power hierarchies which exist in American society at large, it is questionable whether even these more integrated race-bridging institutions have much to offer by way of challenging racial inequity and division in the United States.[29]

Despite the generally gloomy picture that emerges from sociological research on the subject, studies of evangelical race and religion in America do offer a few glimmers of hope. Nonisolated white evangelicals—evangelicals whose neighborhoods and social networks afford them opportunities for regular, reciprocal interactions with people of color—are significantly more likely to "see," be troubled by, and offer structural or systemic explanations for racial inequality than are racially isolated evangelicals, suggesting that white evangelicals' reliance on spiritual-individualist, color-blind, or white supremacist understandings of race relations can be modified through regular exposure to more diverse social experiences and contexts under the right conditions.[30] "If white evangelicals were less racially isolated," Emerson and Smith conclude, "they might assess race problems differently and, working in unison with others, apply their evangelical vigor to broader-based solutions."[31]

Han and Arora, for example, find that evangelical participants in racial justice courses led by a Black evangelical pastor of a large multiracial, majority white evangelical megachurch are significantly more likely to engage in racial justice action and cross-racial perspective taking over time, consistent with prior findings that cross-racial relationships and personal exposure to racial injustice are key factors in generating antiracist action among whites.[32] Similarly, some multiracial evangelical religious organizations manage to be both "Christ-centered and socially reflexive," retaining an evangelical emphasis on Christ-centered spirituality and identity while simultaneously encouraging open and critical discussion of race relations inside religious organizations and challenging racial inequity outside of them.[33] By institutionalizing "difficult" ongoing conversations about race, cultivating theological justifications for multiculturalism, encouraging white congregants to listen and learn from people of color, and subverting racialized power hierarchies in organizational leadership structures, such groups are able to "make racial identity itself an object of critical reflection, rather than to focus on racially blind Christ-centeredness."[34]

The racial perspectives of white evangelical research participants in Portland, Atlanta, Los Angeles, and Boston corroborate the importance of immersive experiences in multiracial settings for increased awareness and investment in pursing racial justice and practicing racial reflexivity. When I asked white evangelical research participants whether or not their views on race had changed at all since becoming involved in their current public service, advocacy, community organizing, or community development work, 89 percent of white strategic relocators responded affirmatively.[35] In mirrored contrast, 87 percent of white evangelical nonrelocators responded negatively to the question of whether their views on race had changed since becoming involved in their current work. Immersive experiences in multiracial neighborhood and organizational settings enabled by the practice of strategic relocation were strongly associated with changing perspectives on race matters among white evangelicals.

"I think a lot of white people have never had to deal with their whiteness," Sam, a mid-twenties white evangelical strategic relocator in Atlanta told me in his small chaotic kitchen over the din of a young child, "I grew up fairly poor and never felt privileged at all. But I'm learning to deal with the privilege that comes from just being white." Deb (thirty-four-year old white evangelical in Atlanta) reported that her ideas about race or racial issues had "definitely" changed since becoming a strategic relocator and joining PCDA:

My world growing up was pretty homogeneous. I didn't have a lot of interaction with people of other races. Certainly not at an intimate level. I think
race plays into all of this, unfortunately: it's played into a lot injustice. It

plays into economics and poverty. . . . It's always there. It's a very present factor in everything. You can't ignore the privilege, everything that goes with being white. You can't ignore any of that. You've got to bring it to the table almost every single time.

Twelve years of living and working in multiracial, majority-Black contexts had helped Deb develop deep race-bridging friendships and change such that "sometimes, I'm very hopeful. But then I'm like, do I live in a bubble?" In the end, Deb summarized how her experiences had shaped her current views on race, "We've got a long, long ways to go."

Chuck, a twenty-eight-year-old white evangelical relocator and Neighborhood Partners volunteer in Portland who grew in a conservative rural community in the mountain West, was frank:

I've more or less just come to grips with the fact that I do have some prejudices. I might be a bit of a bigot. . . . And it's wrong. And I need to work through that stuff. I never—I've always thought of myself as not a racist, not a bigot. But I think there's evil within me. And it comes out. I need to confess that. I think we all are. I think I'm privileged just because of where I'm from and the color of my skin.

After growing up in small town where there was "zero diversity; no ethnic people" (sic), Chuck's relocation to a more diverse Portland neighborhood, participation in the Buddhist–Evangelical dialogues described in Chapter 4, and involvement in asset-based community development work in his neighborhood had convicted him of his participation in the "evil" reality of individual and systemic racism.

Whereas Chuck was a relative newcomer to strategic relocation, "white Dave"—whom we met in Chapter 2—had relocated to a disadvantaged, majority-Black neighborhood in Atlanta over a decade ago. When I asked Dave if his "views of racial issues had changed over the years as you've been in the neighborhood and done this work," he responded:

Yeah, they definitely have. I'm obviously more aware of racial issues and how they play a part in everyday life. If you had asked me when I was twenty-one, "Dave, are you racist?" I would have said, "No!" Emphatically, I would have said no. Now I would recognize . . . you judge people often based on things that are learned, contexts that you know, places that you're in. I've realized that just saying that emphatic, "No, I could never be racist!"—that's not solving anything. It's better to honestly talk about that struggle, which hopefully leads to a better place. I've realized that racism is more than just someone saying, "I hate Black people" or "I hate brown people" or "I hate whoever." It's about realizing how that plays out in society as a whole. It's more than just an interpersonal thing. It's a systemic thing that filters out throughout society. Just because the civil rights movement is over doesn't mean that we as a nation have come to, are at a place of, reconciliation, by any stretch of the imagination. So yeah, I think of systemic stuff.

Further examples of how white Dave's racial views were challenged and transformed through strategic relocation are considered in Chapter 6.

Like Chuck, Dave, and others, Ada (thirty-year-old white female evangelical strategic relocator in Atlanta) discussed her growing awareness of the ubiquity and complexity of racial division and inequity in American Christianity and society:

I've learned that racial issues are complex. I think way more people are racist than think they are racist. I definitely didn't know that, or even really realize how much you're at an advantage and part of a system just by being white. Just because of that. You're part of a racist system. The realization of that was really hard. And the continual reminder of that. And seeing it sometimes, and being pissed about it. That's hard to realize, and to know what to do with it, and to know how to move forward: this realization that racism is just way deeper. I feel like the general opinion in America has been, "Oh, we've moved on, racism doesn't exist anymore," or, "It's only in certain areas." Or, we say, "Oh, we know it's still a problem," but we don't really believe it. We just kind of brush it under the rug. And I feel like we want—the majority white population wants—people of color to just stop talking about it. There's this misunderstanding. How are they going to stop talking about it if it still exists? If it still exists, we're always going to be talking about it. Just recognizing those things and how big they actually are still. Very, very big.

And seeing that in things like public transportation or schools; seeing both sides of it. Nannying for people with kids of privilege who send their kids to private schools. Or if they find a public school, they're going to bus them all the way across town to get them there. The dissonance of wanting the public school system to be better but not enough to really fight for it. And not wanting your kids to be in there with all those other kids that live across town. Well, I feel if we were really reconciled, our kids would be able to play together. Our kids would be going to school together. That would be something important enough where you care about other people's kids too. If they were your sister or brother's kids, you're going to want their kids to have a good education. You should want that for everyone.

And it also goes back to the Christian bubble. I feel like we're a middling, complacent Christian church in America. Somehow our culture got so infused into Christianity, the American dream has become the Christian dream; like it's all one. But should we really become comfortable if our neighbors aren't comfortable? However you want to define your neighbors. If other people's kids in this country aren't starting at the same starting line as our kids—as my kids if I had kids—how are we okay with that? And it always just happens to be people of color. So that would probably mean— that we are racist. Realizing that reality and how ignorant we are—myself included—and a lot of people, especially, surprisingly, in the church, you would think we would be more, I don't know, progressive in discovering that we are racist and doing something about it. But we're not. So I've gone through that discovery and that frustration. Or how racially divided churches are, and the handful of people I know who have tried to build [racially integrated] churches—it's been really hard to try to have multicultural churches. There are very few that are successful. And most of the time, the stress of it is going to override sticking it out for the community of it. So most of the time, people quit. "Well, I don't understand them, they don't understand me, we're just going to go our separate ways and let it be." So. Yeah. All of that about racism has been really hard.

Ada traced out a "very hard" and "complex" years-long experiential learning curve relating to the problematic conflation race and poverty (and of Christianity with the American dream), the complacent self-satisfaction and self-justifying morality of class-advantaged white Americans, the complicity of American churches in systemic racism (along with a glaring lack of racial integration and reconciliation), and white Americans' lack of awareness and motivation to combat deeply rooted inequities, injustices, and hierarchical divisions relating to race. She did so not as an enlightened prophet of wokeness, but as a lamenting and "pissed off" beneficiary of an American racial order that harmed people she cared about and for which she found no religious or moral justification.

Based on extensive ethnographic and interview data, strategic relocation had a transformative impact on white evangelicals' understanding and response to racial difference and inequity.[36] As noted above, nearly all strategic relocators reported significant changes in their understanding of both personal and systemic racism. On the other hand, hardly any white evangelical non-relocators reported changing racial views since becoming involved in their current work. Jack—the forty-six-year-old white evangelical director of PCDA-H—was an exception. Over the course of a nearly two-hour interview in his office, Jack recounted how his own racial views had changed over time—despite not being a strategic relocator—through this work with PCDA-H before I asked any questions on the topic:

> PCDA has helped with race. I think before coming to work for PCDA I would have said, "Yeah, I'm not racist. Yes, I'm white, but I don't think I'm driving people away." Now I can put language to that view that I had and say, "That's the thought of somebody from a dominant racial group, who doesn't have to think about racism today, who doesn't see himself as even having a racial [identity], who has no idea how structures have been set up in such a way that every privilege goes to them." So it never would have occurred to me that my schooling, for example, starting in grade school and through high school and then into college and my work—I was fairly successful in the retail environment I was in, managing different stores and being asked to go to stores to help them recover—it never would have occurred to me that I benefited from those [education and economic] structures. For example, if I was competing for a job with somebody that had the exact same skill set, but wasn't white, knowing that ninety percent of the time I'd get the job. I couldn't put words to that or think from that direction.
>
> So when I came to work with PCDA, you are in the neighborhood regularly. On my very first day, I came to the neighborhood with Nick. We went to his house. We get out of the car and walk up the driveway and go up the steps to the porch of his house and he goes into his house thinking I'm following him. But he has—he has a pretty big dog. I'm not a big dog guy. And it was standing there waiting for me to walk up the steps. I know this dog knows I'm scared of it—and that makes it the alpha dog, right? I just stopped, froze,

and Nick went into the house. So Nick's in the house and me and the dog are staring each other down. And his dog's sweet as could be.

I: But you didn't know.

R: I didn't know if I was breakfast or what right there. I happen to hear some guys laughing, and I turn around and there is there's four young African American men, I'm gonna say twenty-somethings, sitting on the stoop of the house across the street. It was the first time I had the experience where I thought, "I'm white. I don't fit in." That's the first time I ever felt my race. That alone was a huge, sort of watershed moment for me: to learn that I'm white, right? Nowhere else in my life had I had to worry about that. But in the neighborhood, I carry that, right? I know I'm white.

I have a Korean American friend that I go to church with. He leads music. And I asked him after this experience, "Do you carry your race on Sunday morning when you come in?" And he said, "Jack, as much as I love this church, and I love leading music and worship at this church, there is never a moment that I do not feel Korean. I know that people see me differently." And so, that lesson sort of blossoms out, and you begin to recognize, "Okay, there are some real issues. There's structural injustice." And this is part of what we do in housing. We feel like we are dealing with structural sin—that's what we call it at PCDA-H. Compared to PCDA as a whole, at PCDA-H, we don't talk about social justice as much as we talk about social mercy. Justice is getting what we deserve. None of us wants just what we deserve; we want mercy too. We use that language internally. We are trying to achieve structural justice in the neighborhood but applying social mercy to what we do. And back to race—I couldn't talk about race and structural justice like that before. I don't think that I could have led the church that I led in the direction we were going [Jack was a former evangelical pastor] without my PCDA experience, because I would have been doing what every person from a dominant race does when we go into a neighborhood and we think we can fix everything. We don't have any respect for tradition, or for the reality that just because a neighborhood may be low-income doesn't mean there is not already a huge mix of diverse gifts that God has already placed there. And the question from a community development standpoint is, "How do I come alongside of that and help it grow?", rather than sort of infusing myself so that I'm leading it or taking credit. I couldn't have done that sort of thinking four years ago.

Jack's increased awareness of racial inequity and his reflections on white privilege and structural advantage were similar to those experienced by white evangelical strategic relocators across the country. Despite not living in the neighborhood, Jack's professional and personal networks, daily work environment, and larger organizational context within PCDA were highly integrated racially. He also worked for an organization that was explicitly committed to racial equity, integration, and resource redistribution, and he worked alongside Black colleagues of equal and greater professional status and authority within the organization. As such, Jack's social context satisfied key conditions relating to the potential positive effects of racial integration and intergroup contact, with expected results.[37]

Reflexive Evangelicalism: Meanings and Motivations of Strategic Relocation

Strategic relocation, while no panacea for all of what ails democracy in America, is nevertheless instructive as an intensive case of social learning processes enabled in part by socioeconomic and racial integration aligned with ethical democratic principles.[38] It is also a central strategy of faith-based activism for justice and social change in a number of multicultural evangelical movements and organizations across the country, including— as we saw in Chapters 2 and 3—several organizations in this study. In light of its prominence as a strategy of public engagement among these groups, it is worth exploring the meanings, motivations, and experiences of strategic relocation further in order to better understand why and how strategic relocation "works" as a pathway to increased social reflexivity, integration, and justice. What motivates multicultural evangelicals to practice strategic relocation across racial and socioeconomic divisions? How do they understand what it is they are doing? What do they hope to accomplish? What sorts of experiences does the practice of strategic relocation lead to, and how do relocators give meaning to and learn from these experiences—if at all? While previous chapters and sections address some of these questions, this section features white evangelical research participants' own reflections on their understandings and experiences of strategic relocation for the purpose of building bridges and seeking change across race, class, and religious lines.

Pastor James, founding director of The Food Co-op, spoke about strategic relocation as the expression of a spiritual calling and an alternative to dominant American (and American Christian) lifestyles and worldviews. Contrasting strategic relocation with "church charity" that often "seems to be about salving our consciences without really having to know people or to create risks," Pastor James "felt led to move into areas where there was poverty. I didn't really want to do something 'for' people. I really wanted to do something 'with' people." As described at length in Chapter 3, Pastor James's commitment to reciprocal engagement and solidarity—rather than exploitation, avoidance, or charity—across class and race lines marked a lifetime of personal and organizational learning and growth. Richard—PCDA's founding director—described his movement towards strategic relocation in similar terms:

> I started working with kids first, and then I realized to be very effective you've got to work with the families . . . and finally realized if you are really going to change an environment that was negatively impacting families, you need to be a part of the community. So we moved into the city. And that pretty much changed everything. It changed our paradigm of ministry— obviously, we became personally involved in everything from education to crime on the streets to real estate issues—and so that began a switch from kind of personal ministry to community development.

When I asked Richard whether there was a theological framework or biblical principle that inspired his own practice of strategic relocation, he responded:

> I certainly think that you can build a theological case for relocation: incarnation, love of neighbor . . . I certainly think that it's pretty easy to build a theological case for it. But it was more pragmatic than theology. It was realizing that the commuting [person] doesn't have anywhere near the power, the credibility, the *gravitas*, that a neighbor does. It had political strength. Relocation implies some permanency, and so at lots of different levels that kind of consistency becomes very important. It had authenticity—"where your treasure is, there will your heart be also"[39]—so when *your* kids are in this neighborhood and in this school, it's part of your treasure, and your heart's gonna be there. So, for a lot of reasons, relocation, there's a good case to be made about it.

Multicultural evangelicals engaged in strategic relocation drew on a rich theological language rooted in the life and teaching of Jesus to ground their efforts. However, like Richard, they were more likely to cite general and practical considerations than particularistic religious ones to describe the origins and implications of their work. Practical experience, rather than the rote application of Bible passages, led Richard and others towards the practice of strategic relocation through the sort of iterative action-reflection-adjustment cycles practiced by democratic community organizers and described by pragmatist theories of action.[40] Among my research participants, the practice of strategic relocation emerged from a reflexive, experience-based approach to public engagement that combined religious principles and practical learning in reflexive chains of ethically motivated action.

Sounding themes from Tocqueville and the field of broad-based community organizing,[41] Deb—PCDA's Chief Operating Officer—discussed strategic relocation as an intentional choice to tether natural human self-interest to a larger religiously inspired vision of racial and economic justice and reconciliation:

> I think it [relocation] legitimizes everything that you do. It says, "I'm truly invested in this community and the people who are here." And when we—when it's our community—we serve it, we take care of it. Because we all take care of our own—no matter how sacrificial we want to be—we always take care of our own first. So when our own is what we're trying to do, we just always do a better job of that. And [relocation] just lends itself to reconciliation more. I mean, it definitely can be very hurtful and misunderstood and a lot of [difficult] things can happen. But it allows relationship. And very authentic and normal—not stressed and artificial—kinds of [relationship]. . . . I think there's also something about our longevity of relocation. People begin to trust you so much more when you're not going anywhere. And then it's not even like "them" and "us." It's "all of us." It's funny now, living in the neighborhood for twelve years, I've lived here longer than a lot of people. . . . So it's not just like, "Oh, the new people." We're not the new people anymore.

Like other strategic relocators, Deb did not disavow or diminish the religious motivations that drew her to PCDA and helped sustain her work, but she was more likely to emphasize practical interpersonal and political reasons for engaging in strategic relocation.

Alexei—the thirty-year-old husband, father of four, and PCDA bike shop founder we met in Chapter 2—likewise emphasized the importance of relocation for building trust and solidarity with neighborhood youth and their families over time:

> Without being philosophical about it . . . you basically say, "I'm here with you." . . . There's a lot that happens in that emotional, heart-to-heart space, just that presence. I don't even know how to describe. The fact that you're sharing the space, sharing the air. That you're with somebody beyond any program.

Ada—a single thirty-year-old white female youth worker living in a new monastic community in the neighborhood—sharpened Alexei's point further, asserting, "I have no business serving here if I'm not going to live here":

> You just can't be a neighbor from far away. You just can't do it. There's just such a different level of understanding and compassion and desire for deeper relationships. You just start taking on things. I'm not saying that I want to do something because, "I'm trying to help you." I'm saying that I want to improve things because it's my neighborhood too. So let's do this together. Instead of it being "us versus them," it's very much us together, all of us together. Let's move forward together.

Research participants described increased solidarity, reciprocity, trust, legitimacy, personal investment, justice, understanding, and friendship as some of the many reasons for practicing strategic relocation across race and class lines.

Along with these practical reasons, research participants also cited theological and spiritual motivations for their practice of strategic relocation, though with somewhat less emphasis and frequency. The Christian doctrine of the incarnation was the most commonly cited ground for the religious dimension of strategic relocation.[42] For example, Deb discussed "the incarnation of Jesus coming to the earth" as an exemplar calling Christ-followers to more local, embodied, place-based expressions of Christian spirituality in public life:

> I think we are living incarnationally with people. Not that we're like "saviors" or anything. But it's a model of being among the people. And of

course the book of Acts as well, where you live and you share everything that you have.[43] I just think proximity and location: Jesus was always very aware of those things. Where he was and who he was around. I don't think we can ignore that power of place.

In addition to the incarnation, research participants frequently cited the early church in Acts and Jesus's teaching about the upside-down nature of power in the "kingdom of God" in the Sermon on the Mount (Matthew 5–7) and elsewhere as religious warrants for practicing strategic relocation. Like Nick, however, they did so with a circumspect focus on mutual recognition, reciprocity, and the "dual" vision of personal and social transformation they hoped to realize in their lives and work:

> The kingdom of God is meant to be a "beloved community" in Christ that crosses the barriers that in this country are historically set up and structured to keep people [racially and economically] isolated.[44] That's not even close to what God originally intended. So wanting to live out beloved community is a major motivation, and wanting to contribute to the process of restoration, regeneration, transformation in . . . under-resourced communities, and believing that's God's heart. So there is an aspect of need. But the "need" isn't just external. I think the other motive is internal: I am being changed and transformed in the process. So it's a mutual, dual process, knowing, okay, there are some things God is asking me to contribute to. And there are also some things that I know are there—or that I might not even know are there—that need to change in me as well.

Without exception, strategic relocators described how strategic relocation involved one inexorably in ongoing learning processes that arose from encountering new, perplexing, challenging, and rewarding experiences across race and class lines. Nick spoke at length about the "systemic" and "personal" learning experiences he had been continually challenged by since leaving a high-profile pastoral position in the Midwest to relocate to a disadvantaged majority-Black Atlanta neighborhood with his young family:

> Since moving to Atlanta, my understanding of systemic racial inequality and economic inequality has increased dramatically just based on living in the South and the context and history behind this community and this neighborhood. Seeing the effects of decisions that were made decades ago

and how it's still, all these years forward, impacting the lives of people now. So systemically, my views have changed, definitely.

And personally, my views have changed, most definitely. Because I think the longer we "do life" and live with people [across differences], if we're intentional—I love Richard's quote "relocation doesn't guarantee reconciliation," meaning you can relocate and still live in a bubble—but if we're actively "doing life" alongside of our neighbors in the process of relocating, then absolutely.[45] Because relationships are alive, and if we're alive and we're living life with people, then the learning never ends. The relationships will always have the opportunity to grow. And it takes work. . . .

If people are willing and intentional about working through chaos and conflict, there can be a self-emptying where people mutually say, "We're going to let go in order to move toward each other." And through that self-emptying, that's the spark when authentic, real community, real relationship happens. But then the cycle happens all over again. And we can easily revert back to pseudo-community—sort of that fake surface stuff—unless we work through the cycle again and again and again. So as long as we're openly attempting to live life through that process, then we have the opportunity to always change and always grow, on so many levels. And I think, also . . . a big part of the change and the growth is just hanging out, doing life, celebrating, having fun. Challenging each other with ridiculous horseshoe championships on our block or whatever. Just doing life. And being okay with being yourself. And being open. . . . Just learning to be present with each other in normal life ways.

Growth, process, learning, choosing experiences, the importance of routine interaction and communication across difference: Nick's reflections on the experience of strategic relocation resonate deeply with pragmatist theories of action, democracy, and social ethics.[46]

Like Jane Addams and her fellow progressive era pragmatists and democratic reformers, Nick and other strategic relocators talked frequently about learning from new, challenging, or perplexing experiences. But what sorts of experiences were they talking about? Some, like Alexei, involved dramatically direct experiences of white privilege while interacting with law enforcement and government agencies:

So I showed up at the Atlanta Housing Authority. I was there as a homeowner that entered through a [government aid] program. But because of the color of my skin, they were like, "Oh, you're a landlord. You go stand in that line." But I'm not a landlord. A lot of assumptions are made. Another time a house alarm goes off and I walk through the front of the driveway. A police officer shows up assuming I'm supposed to be there, that I'm checking on the house. Right? I'm like: "You need to write down the number from my ID! You need to know that you saw me here. You can't take my word for it!" I get frustrated. There's a lot of that goes on.

For Alexei, experiencing firsthand preferential treatment from law enforcement and city officials because he was white served as bracing tangible evidence of systemic racial bias in the contemporary United States, while challenging him to grow in his understanding of it:

It's still a learning kind of deal. It's a complex world. Try following the links and relationships. You go deeper and deeper with the legal system for example. You become familiar with how many more African American people are in jail than white people—disproportionate to population percentages. You start to see there's a lot of that going on: a lot of flat-out racism.

Alexei also learned by making mistakes in interpersonal and social media interactions with Black friends and neighbors. During one such experience, Alexei got into trouble for "putting our neighborhood in a bad light" in a Facebook post while asking for prayer about a difficult interaction:

I thought I could say it in such a way that I wouldn't offend anybody. But it backfired. Sometimes people will find things in your words that you did not think you were saying. It can be very painful. Because when you make a mistake publicly, folks will correct you publicly. And not necessarily correct you but respond publicly. You can start questioning a lot of things, or think, "I'll just go back to my hole and not try."

In this interaction, Alexei was reminded firsthand how difficult it can be to establish solidarity and trust across racial lines in the context of US race relations, where, "Before you even start talking, on your face, is the history of what white people have done to Black people. That's tough to overcome. It can be paralyzing if you allow it." However, "the encouragement in that," Alexei continued, recognizing the challenge of practicing ideal communication under inequitable conditions, "is if you're not making constant mistakes, you're probably not trying hard enough."

For Alexei and other relocators—in contrast to the experiences of most white Americans, whose racial privilege and isolation can make it easy to ignore race under most circumstances—ignoring race is impossible for people immersed in racially integrated neighborhoods, organizations, and social networks. For them:

> The topic of racism is right in your face. A lot of what happens is interpreted through race. If my neighbor yells at the kids in our street, it's very different than if I say those same words to those same kids. There's so much that gets filtered through race. And it's a natural response when you unpack the history. You can't be in this neighborhood and not be aware of the history. Or rather, that's one thing you *should* be aware of—the history, and that there are issues you need to be sensitive around. And there's a lot of tension. Like Dr. Perkins says, you know, racism is an environmental issue. It's in the air, it gets on you. You've got to purposely clean yourself of it. And I've seen that's a continuous process, where your own assumptions surprise you, and also when the assumptions of your close [Black] friends and neighbors can come out of nowhere and surprise you. Like, "You thought that's what I was saying?" There are times—it's a surprise. You want to say: "Hey, we're on the same team!" So that's been a surprise. You can imagine that, "Yes, race is going to be an issue," you know, but . . . experiencing it is another thing.

> Also experiencing the redemptive relationships where somebody of a different skin color tells you, "You're like a brother to me." I have a friend like that. He's twenty years older than me, African American, and he might be my closest ally. And God forbid somebody tries to do something to me when he's around. He will be there for me. And he's been there for me many times. He's a neighbor. We shared a twenty-three-year-old truck for eight months. He wanted to buy it. We were just waiting for the right financial opportunity for him. But he needed the vehicle to get to work and back, so I made an extra key and that's what we did. We shared the truck. It confused the hell out of people. . . . You see a Black guy or a white guy driving this truck at different times, and it's aggravating. You don't know whose truck it is, you know! We joked about that. But it was living out redemption. Those are the beautiful things you experience.

Living and working as conspicuous minorities in majority Black contexts, Alexei, Nick, and other white PCDA relocators were regularly confronted with opportunities to engage and learn from—rather than avoid or shut down—difficult encounters involving racial difference and inequity, while also enjoying and learning from positive race-bridging relationships and experiences made possible in part through the practice of strategic relocation.

Like Nick and Alexei, research participants noted the countless ways that practical experiences afforded by strategic relocation dramatically increased their understanding of racial and economic inequities while also recognizing, as Ada did, that, "I'll never fully understand where [my neighbors] are coming from." In light of the challenges of authentic encounter understanding across difference, Ada, Alexei and other relocators learned through experience the importance of open, critical, and reflexive communication:[47]

> I feel like the only redemptive way to get out of where we are is to talk about it. And sometimes you can see on [peoples'] faces, like, "Are we really openly talking about racism across racial lines?" And that feels very redemptive, to be able to discuss and explain and own up to that.

Such communication is hard to come by in the contemporary United States, where, as Nick lamented, "so many of us live in isolated spaces: culturally, economically, whatever the line is." Still, citing his own experience with strategic relocation, Nick held out hope in "believing that if we're being changed by crossing some of those lines, and learning across that space, we can begin to collaborate with others across those dimensions."

If, as discussed at length in Chapters 1 and 6, ethical democracy requires bridging social capital,[48] and bridging social capital requires social reflexivity,[49] then these white evangelicals' experiences of critical growth and change through strategic relocation—alongside the redistributive practices chronicled in Chapters 2 and 3—provide some evidence of its ethical democratic potential.

Recall Deb's observation that "when it's *our* community—we serve it, we take care of it . . . because we all take care of our own first," or Richard's comment about how strategic relocation "changed everything" because it helped him and fellow relocators to "put their own skin in the game" by sending their children to disadvantaged public schools, or dealing with negligent or biased city officials and law enforcement, or watching people they personally know and care about react with pain and anger to incidences of racial bias and violence on their streets and across the country. When the political becomes personal, emotions kindle action, urgency to challenge inequity is heightened, and solidarity coalesces in the face of shared challenges.[50]

For some of my research participants, solidarity in the face of shared challenges was experienced with particular acuity and intensity. Sandy, a thirty-year-old white evangelical woman, for example, met, fell in love with, and married an undocumented Latino man from Central America while working in Los Angeles as a program coordinator for community-based urban ministry courses at a Christian liberal arts college. For years Sandy was deeply involved in immigration reform activism while working through the fraught, plodding process of seeking legal immigration status for her partner. "But," Sandy reflected ruefully, "as we've become more socially isolated from those experiencing [immigration-related] injustice most intensely, our urgency on the matter has waned." After years of anxiety and struggle alongside other undocumented families and individuals, her husband became a legal resident and, eventually, a US citizen by marriage. The couple had a child, moved across the country, and began slowly to lose touch with their undocumented friends and neighbors in LA. Reflecting on this and other experiences arising from her experience as a white strategic relocator in a majority Black neighborhood, Sandy explained why she had come to believe that "relationships are key for sustaining justice work long-term":

> I am convinced we need relationships that cross boundaries of race, ethnicity, religion, and socioeconomic status now more than ever. We were [recently] reminded of the tragic death of 12-year-old Tamir Rice. He was playing with a toy gun in the park, and an officer shot him within two seconds of arriving on the scene. Seeing his photo, I cannot help but think about the boys on my street. When we moved here almost seven years ago, they were mostly around eight years old, knocking on our door to borrow our air pump (yet again). We watched them go through their own awkward tween years, when they were twelve-year-old boys playing outside. And I can't help but mourn young Tamir....
>
> Relationships with those who have different life experiences than our own make an impact. We are *all* changed when we have the opportunity to share life and see situations from multiple perspectives. As the news continues to prey on our fears of those who are different, we must be counter-cultural. We need to reach out and connect with others, experience our shared humanity, and learn from our unique experiences.[51]

Through new relationships and first-hand experiences of racial injustice, strategic relocation and cross-racial friendships increased the urgency and intensity of white evangelical research participants' efforts to combat race, class, and citizenship-based drivers of inequality.[52] Changing their perspective—the physical and social locations from which they viewed the US racial order[53]—helped white relocators "see" and be troubled by race, class, and other inequities in new ways.

Conclusion

In this chapter we have heard multicultural evangelicals describe how their understanding of race, poverty and economic inequality, politics, evangelism, and religious difference changed over time through strategic relocation and participation in faith-based public service, political advocacy, community development, and community organizing work. Their experiences highlight the necessity of learning, growth, and change through intentional experience and reflexive action alongside diverse social others. In this, they exemplify pragmatist understandings of ethical democratic action while extending prior research on the importance of social reflexivity for the practice of ethical democracy amidst deep difference.[54] They also raise further questions about the relationship between experience and scripture, conviction and humility, and faith and reason in the pursuit of ethical democracy, and about the possibilities and limits of evangelical practices of social reflexivity across different types of difference in American public life. It is to these questions we turn in Chapter 6.

6

Ethical Democracy and Four Modes
of Social Reflexivity

Previous chapters have examined multicultural evangelical approaches to engaging racial difference and inequality; poverty and economic inequality; and politics, culture, and religious difference, approaches that point to the possibility of a more reflexive evangelicalism than is commonly observed or practiced in the contemporary United States. Drawing on previous chapters and newly presented data, the heart of this chapter defines and gives examples of four distinct modes of social reflexivity practiced by multicultural evangelicals across the United States. Though emerging from research on multicultural evangelicals, these concepts offer a potentially generalizable framework applicable to other groups and settings. The next section discusses the relationship between social reflexivity, ethical democracy, and post-secular pragmatism, while a concluding section examines how the practice of intellectual humility and social reflexivity across different types of difference is supported by traditional evangelical interpretations of the Bible—and why that is important.

Ethical Democracy and Postsecular Pragmatism

Ethical democracy, as it is understood in the early American pragmatist and republican traditions, calls on individuals and groups to actively cultivate cognitive and embodied habits of "mixing on the thronged and common road where all must turn out for one another, and at least see the size of one another's burdens," lest "we grow contemptuous of our fellows . . . and not only tremendously circumscribe our range of life, but limit the scope of our ethics."[1] Empirical studies of democracy and grassroots organizing likewise highlight the central importance of social reflexivity and bridging social capital for successful democratic projects and the pursuit of ethical democracy's

Good News for Common Goods. Wes Markofski, Oxford University Press. © Oxford University Press 2023.
DOI: 10.1093/oso/9780197659694.003.0007

elusive dream of liberty and justice for all—a diverse and open society "in which all share and to which all contribute."[2]

I have argued that the early American pragmatist tradition is a useful reference point for sociological inquiries into the nature and workings of democracy in America. There is at least one way, however, that Deweyan pragmatism in particular requires modification in order to better recognize and respond to deep difference and disagreement in American public life. Unlike his approach to some other dimensions of difference, Dewey and his intellectual heirs did not seek to accommodate religious diversity so much as to exterminate and replace it with a common, secularized social-democratic faith.[3] More generally, the subject of religion has remained curiously absent from leading intellectual debates and discourses concerning diversity and democracy in increasingly multicultural Euro-American contexts.[4] This absence is all the more remarkable in the United States, where the prominence of religion in public life and political discourse has never been in doubt.[5] Whether this disjuncture between public and academic discourse concerning the role of religion in public life is due to a "secularist" bias, antipathy toward religion among Euro-American intellectual elites, or something else,[6] it remains that—as Rogers Brubaker remarks in Grounds for Difference— "discussions of diversity . . . often proceed in striking indifference to religion, as if the diversity that mattered were exhausted by race, ethnicity, gender, and sexuality."[7]

It is understandable in this context why the post-secular turn of German pragmatist social philosopher Jürgen Habermas caused such a stir.[8] Habermas's growing "awareness of what is missing" from strictly secularist accounts of constitutional democracy led him to reconsider the role of religion in democratic civil society and the public sphere.[9] Where once he roundly dismissed religion's democratic and communicative possibilities,[10] Habermas now defends public religion's potential for offering "key resources" of "normative truth," "moral intuition," and the "creation of meaning and identity" which may otherwise elude secular society and secularist reason.[11] In doing so, Habermas newly upholds the rights of citizens to use religious language and make religiously based political arguments in the public sphere, and has become a critic of "rigid secularism," "Enlightenment fundamentalists," and antireligious prejudice—perhaps with an eye toward his own earlier work.[12] In a much publicized debate concerning the "pre-political moral foundations in the construction of a free civil society" with Cardinal Joseph Ratzinger (later Pope Benedict XVI),[13] Habermas acknowledges legitimate "doubts as to the ability of the constitutional democratic state to renew its existential foundations from its own resources, rather than from [an alternative] philosophical and religious . . . undergirding."[14] Habermas's descriptive recognition and provisional embrace of a "postsecular" age that better accommodates secular and religious pluralism—and its resonance and reverberations in public and academic discourse across the globe—is indicative of a turning point in Euro-American understandings of the relationship between religion, secularism, and democratic society.[15]

Habermas's vision of postsecular democracy depends on religious and secular citizens engaging in a "complementary learning process" through which they come to encounter one other as equals and afford each other the "mutual recognition which is constitutive of shared citizenship."[16] With respect to religion, ethical democratic principles of mutual recognition require that "secular citizens in civil society and the political public sphere must be able to meet their religious fellow citizens as equals," overcoming the secularist bias which views religious communities as "archaic relics of pre-modern societies" and religious adherents as "not to be taken seriously as modern contemporaries."[17] For religious citizens, this complementary learning process manifests as a "shift from the traditional to a more reflexive form of religious consciousness"—a shift Habermas counts as indicative of post-Vatican II Catholicism and German Protestantism.[18]

Habermas's strong commitment to the secular state and secular reason makes the learning processes required of religious citizens' rather more steep than those of non-religious citizens: religious citizens must learn to "accept the priority that secular reasons hold in the political arena" and defer to the "institutionalized monopoly of modern scientific experts" and secular knowledge in the public sphere, while also learning how to respectfully treat rival religious traditions and worldviews as legitimate (without however necessarily abandoning their own exclusive religious truth claims).[19] The development of these "epistemic attitudes" among the religious cannot, however, be imposed from above by secular elites or the democratic state, rather, they can come only through the "arduous work of hermeneutic self-reflection" within religious communities themselves, lest the learning process forfeit its ethical democratic legitimacy.[20]

Many Americans, for whom it is commonplace to hear politicians and public officials use religious language to describe, justify, and frame policy positions and political deliberation, will find even this "post-secular" Habermas to offer a quite restrictive view of the role of religion in public and political life—for good or ill.[21] Nevertheless, Habermas's explication of the reflexive epistemic and communicative learning processes that religious and nonreligious citizens must embrace in order to recognize each other as equal and legitimate participants in a shared democratic society offers a welcome philosophical touchstone for investigating the relationship between social reflexivity, ethical democracy, and difference that does not exclude religion.

Perhaps the closest sociological analogue to Habermas's notion of the reflexive learning processes required of participants in pluralist postsecular democracies is found in Paul Lichterman's work on religion in civic action.[22] Drawing on Tocqueville and the classical American pragmatist tradition— Jane Addams and John Dewey in particular—Lichterman first developed the concept of social reflexivity to help explain why some religious groups are able to build two-way bridges across different types of difference while others struggle to do so.[23] According to both the pragmatist and neo-Tocquevillian traditions, people's capacity to build bridges of empathy, trust, solidarity, and reciprocity across difference in public life is a necessary component of democratic flourishing.[24] Whereas Lichterman's original conceptualization focuses on the communicative practices of groups, I define social reflexivity more broadly as people's capacity to think and interact flexibly and self-critically in relation to diverse social others and situations.[25]

Four Modes of Social Reflexivity

While conducting research across a wide variety of multicultural evangelical groups, organizations, and settings in Portland, Los Angeles, Atlanta, and Boston, I observed evidence of four distinct modes of social reflexivity being practiced by actors across different types of difference: namely, *segmented reflexivity*, *transposable reflexivity*, *deep reflexivity*, and *frozen reflexivity*.[26] Individuals and groups practice *segmented reflexivity* when they think and interact flexibly and self-critically with respect to one type of social difference but not others. Segmented reflexivity is reflexivity restricted to one domain.[27] In contrast to segmented reflexivity, individuals and groups practice *transposable reflexivity* when they think and interact flexibly and self-critically across multiple types of social difference. Transposable reflexivity is reflexivity across domains. Individuals and groups practice *frozen reflexivity* when they think and interact self-critically, but partially and inflexibly, with respect to identities, groups, settings, or traditions with which they are involved. Frozen reflexivity is self-critical, but truncated and at times dogmatic. In contrast to frozen reflexivity, individuals and groups practice *deep reflexivity* when they demonstrate iterative capacity for flexible and self-critical

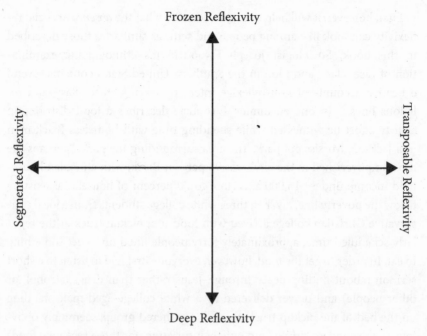

Figure 6.1 Axes of Social Reflexivity

thought and action across difference whilst recognizing the inescapably partial and fallible nature of their efforts. Deep reflexivity is reliably recursive
and fallibilist; it seeks understanding whilst recognizing the impossibility of
a perfect fusion of horizons even amidst genuine encounter.[28]

As demonstrated in Figure 6.1, the concepts of transposable, segmented,
frozen, and deep social reflexivity are not merely four ad hoc categories
pulled out of a sea of undifferentiated conceptual space. Rather, they are four
categories that can fully elaborate the space of possible types of social reflexivity by depth (y-axis) and range or breadth (x-axis). This gives us the ability
to heuristically locate particular concrete practices of social reflexivity on a
two-dimensional continuum that accounts for both the depth and breadth
of socially reflexive practice, advancing the analytic depth and clarity with
which we can explore the impact and limits of different types of social reflexivity across difference in public life. Though emerging from research on
multicultural evangelicals, these concepts offer a potentially generalizable
framework applicable to other groups and settings.

The following sections draw on original ethnographic, interview, and textual data to define and give examples of the individual and collective practice
of each of these four types of social reflexivity.

First, however, it will help to briefly describe what the *absence* of social reflexivity can look like among people and settings similar to those described in this book. Sociologist Joseph Ewoodzie Jr.'s ethnographic examination of race, class, and food in the Southern United States contains several evocative accounts of non-reflexive interaction across race, class, and religious lines.[29] In one encounter, Ewoodzie describes a food distribution charity effort he witnessed while spending time with homeless Black men in a Jackson, Mississippi park. The area surrounding the park, "perhaps the most impoverished in the city," was 98 percent Black, with a median household income under $15,000 and close to 70 percent of households existing below the poverty line.[30] When three white college students from a local conservative Christian college arrived with food in a pickup truck at the regularly scheduled time, approximately forty people lined up to get something to eat. In order to get the food, however, everyone first had to listen to a short sermon (about finding peace through Jesus rather than drugs, alcohol, or other people) and prayer delivered by a white college-aged male standing on the bed of the pickup truck above the gathered group, seemingly oblivious to the condescending (and quietly infuriating, for those receiving food) overtones of the interaction.[31] This scene is contrasted by one later in the book in which a different white male, affiliated with the Southern Poverty Law Center, addressed a group of fifty Black mothers and grandmothers at a local BBQ restaurant. Here, Ewoodzie observes that "most of the women knew [the man] well and trusted him, an interracial trust that is hard to come by in their Mississippi."[32] "He had a white man's convictions," Ewoodzie elaborates, "but he also acquiesced when members of his audience challenged and corrected him. That is how he earned and kept [their] respect."[33] The white conservative Christian actors in the first scene typify non-reflexive interaction across race and class difference; the second scene describes interactions marked by social reflexivity, with predictable consequences for each in terms of their success at building bridging relationships across difference in pursuit of racial justice.[34]

Segmented Reflexivity

As defined above, individuals and groups practice *segmented reflexivity* when they think and interact flexibly and self-critically with respect to one type of social difference but not others. Segmented reflexivity is reflexivity restricted to one domain.

Neighborhood Partners and its director Kent offer an illustrative case of the practice of segmented reflexivity. Kent and his fellow Neighborhood Partners staff combined remarkable flexibility and self-critical aware-ness of the dynamics of economic inequality in their work with unhoused and economically disadvantaged persons in the "other Portland" with an equally vivid incapacity to reflexively engage issues of racial difference and inequality.

Kent, for example, would invariably critique the condescending "othering" language often used by religious volunteers while communi-cating to, or about, the homeless persons and economically disadvantaged neighbors with whom they interacted. He also engaged in critical self-reflection and changed behavior in response to his own frequent, ongoing interactions with unhoused persons. In one example, Kent became friends with Donnie, a "super, super mad" homeless man he met on a freezing cold February afternoon two years earlier. Across multiple encounters Donnie repeated the same mantra to Kent: "I'm done. I'm so sick of this. The system is so broken. I've wanted to get off the streets for so long, but it just won't happen." Within several months, Kent connected Donnie with a housing advocate who was able to help Donnie find housing and a job. Donnie also met the formerly homeless pastor of the church described in the Introduction, started to meet with him daily, eventually became a Christian, and began going with this formerly homeless pastor of un-housed persons to homeless camps in order to build relationships and offer support to others. Kent was excited. "[Donnie] called me at my home one day and said, 'I just gotta tell you how thankful I am,'" Kent told me, "It was thrilling."

Eight months later, however, Kent spotted Donnie while hosting a mobile overnight hospitality center for homeless persons: "He came walking up with his old clothes on and his scowl. And he just was back to his old self. He didn't really want to talk to me." Later Donnie did talk to Kent and explained to him that he had "felt guilty because his people were still living outside while he was comfortable." "He spent twenty years outside," Kent elaborated, "and it just didn't feel natural to him. And he felt lonely because his people—he wasn't with his people. So he just quit his job and went back outside." Kent recalled Donnie telling him, "Kent, guys like you, you're fine and good and everything and thank God for you: but you don't know anything. Come out here. Live with me for a couple months. And then you'll have something to say." "And who can argue?" Kent reflected:

I just thought: you're right. In this arena, I don't know anything. That was very impactful and I carry that around a lot. Cause I am a know-it-all. I'm sorry to say. But I've come to the realization that's just true. I think I know everything. But then I meet guys like Donnie and I go, "I don't really know anything." And it's helpful.

Rather than sanctimoniously blaming Donnie for wasting his chance to get off the street, Kent reflected self-critically on his own middle-class assumptions and expectations about his presumed right to determine what was best for Donnie and the cognitive limitations that his own social context and experiences placed on his ability to fully understand Donnie's life choices.

More generally, Neighborhood Partners seminars and training modules were almost obsessively focused on the necessity of developing reciprocal relationships of mutual recognition and benefit across socioeconomic lines, rather than the usual one-way charity relationships in which middle class individuals or groups periodically donate goods, services, or time to "help the poor" while maintaining their social distance, economic privilege, and sense of superiority. Kent and his fellow Neighborhood Partners staff were highly sensitive to the linguistic, religious, political, and institutional mechanisms whereby evangelical Christians and other affluent and middle-class Americans kept the poor at arm's-length: whether through dehumanizing "othering" language, distant and condescending charity programs, blame-the-victim religious and political ideologies, or by closing themselves off to learning and receiving things of value from economically disadvantaged persons.

Whereas Kent and Neighborhood Partners routinely demonstrated the capacity to think and interact flexibly and self-critically with respect to class and economically disadvantaged others, this was generally not true of their engagement with racial difference and inequality. One example is particularly illustrative. A white evangelical community activist and good friend of Kent's had become involved in a weekly gathering of Black pastors and civic leaders from across the city. His friend strongly encouraged Kent to begin attending the gathering, telling him, "You need this. It will be good for you." Eventually, Kent relented. "And I've got to tell you," Kent reported back to me after attending the meeting, "I had a hard time." I asked him why. He told me that he had felt attacked, under siege. During the meeting, Black leaders took turns sharing their experiences of anti-Black racism in the city and wider church community. They angrily denounced aggressive race-based police tactics and gentrification policies that were pushing poor Black residents out of North Portland. They lamented the historical legacy and ongoing ramifications of racial oppression and discrimination on their communities.

The longer the meeting went, the more frustrated Kent became. "I just don't get it," he recalled thinking, "Why are you all still so angry?" For Kent, the whole affair seemed "pointless" and "inefficient." He wondered why the group insisted on "rehashing the past" and focusing on particularistic racial experience instead of "just getting on with it," by which he meant working together across racial difference to build capacity for everyone in disadvantaged neighborhoods without focusing on their racial history and makeup. Kent wondered why they insisted on making race the center of discussion, which to his mind simply fostered anger and divisiveness.

In this case—unlike his response to Donnie and issues of poverty and homelessness—rather than interacting flexibly or reflecting self-critically on his perplexing experience, Kent shut down reflection and opted out of further experience. "I didn't go back," Kent told me, without regret. Nor did race typically enter into Neighborhood Partners' discussions of poverty, economic inequality, grassroots democracy, or religion, which were otherwise rife with sophisticated and self-aware analyses of the problems and potentialities of faith- and community-based social and political activism. While Neighborhood Partners effectively collaborated with a wide range of secular and religious individuals and organizations, their organizational partners tended to be overwhelmingly white, and I observed little reflexive self-critique or intentional effort to change this state of affairs. Kent and Neighborhood Partners practiced a segmented social reflexivity capable of attending to issues of class, but not racial, inequity and difference.

Another organization in Portland, Christians for the Common Good (CCG), practiced segmented reflexivity by thinking and interacting flexibly and self-critically with respect to political and religious, but not racial, difference and inequity, with a few exceptions. Detailed readings of years of organizational staff and board meeting minutes demonstrated a remarkably high capacity for deep deliberation, disagreement, and critical self-reflection with respect to individual and group religious identities, political identities, and relations with diverse religious and political others. Passionate arguments, consensus-challenging disagreements, institutionalized practices of personal and collective self-reflection, extended deliberation over policy recommendations and the political meanings of biblical passages, regular reformulations of public messaging and identity, and crit-ical self-evaluation of organizational culture and operations: these were all standard fare and corroborated by extensive ethnographic, interview, and other documentary data, as described at length in chapter 4. Internally, ex-pansive discourse about religious and political difference abounded within CCG organizational culture.[35] Externally, while focusing a large proportion of its marketing and mobilizing energies on evangelicals, the organization worked with a wide variety of secular, interfaith, mainline Protestant, and evangelical people and organizations to promote their vision of the common good in Oregon through legislation and public advocacy. These broad and diverse public partnerships were made possible by organizational members' capacity to communicate and interact flexibly with respect to deep religious, political, and cultural differences.

However, similar to Neighborhood Partners, Christians for the Common Good did not regularly extend their practice of social reflexivity to racial difference and inequity at the organizational level. Apart from Jill (white) and Sue (Asian American), it was rare to hear CCG staff or board member address racial inequality and difference—whether in the form of focusing directly on issues of racial equity through legislation and public advocacy work, or developing partnerships with organizations and communities of color, or increasing the racial diversity of organizational staff and board members. While observing meetings, conducting interviews, and talking with CCG volunteers, staff, and board members, race did not typically enter the conversation unless or until I explicitly raised a question about it, and re-search participants did not have much to say on the matter once it was raised. Board members frequently gave inchoate, floundering answers when asked whether and how the organization attempted to address racial issues, saying things such as, "I wish we had more people of color on our board," or "Yeah, I don't know, we just haven't really known how to engage those people." As Teresa acknowledged:

> That's one of the big areas where I'm sad that CCG has not done a better job.
> I wish we would do more. I wish we'd prioritize it more, which we could.
> I don't know what it is. But we haven't. The woman who mentored me here
> from the Episcopal church is an African American female pastor. I learned
> a lot from her. But I don't think [we've focused on race] as much with CCG.
> I think that's one of the biggest areas we should be involved in, and we're not
> doing a great job.

Whereas Christians for the Common Good spent an enormous amount of time, energy, and resources thinking and interacting flexibly and self-critically with diverse religious and political others both within the organization and with organizational partners, it demonstrated limited capacity for flexible and self-critical thought and action with respect to racial difference and inequity, despite expressing antiracist convictions at the individual level. In this respect, Christians for the Common Good practiced a segmented variety of social reflexivity.

It is noteworthy that both of these examples of segmented reflexivity involved white evangelical (and, in the case of CCG, white mainline Protestant) failures to practice social reflexivity with respect to racial difference and inequity. It is also noteworthy that, in both cases, the racial composition of organizational leadership, staff, partners, and settings of operation were overwhelmingly white.

Other evangelical individuals and groups practiced segmented reflexivity in different ways, interacting and flexibly and self-critically with respect to race but not gender or sexuality, politics and religion but not class, gender and sexuality but not race, race but not class or gender, and so on.

Transposable Reflexivity

In contrast to segmented reflexivity, individuals and groups practice *transposable reflexivity* when they think and interact flexibly and self-critically across multiple types of social difference. Transposable reflexivity is reflexivity across domains.

Sue—a Korean American woman and former CCG executive director—represents an illustrative case of the practice of transposable reflexivity at the individual level. In both talk and action, Sue combined tour-de-force awareness and recognition of race, class, gender, and global inequality and difference with deep critical insight into the majority white evangelical religious culture of which she was a part. During one conversation with Sue in her campus office at a local Christian college, we began talking about her perspective on the "justice conference" phenomenon among evangelicals and, more generally, the explosion of interest and talk about social justice in evangelical circles across the United States in the early 2010s. Sue was often asked to attend and speak at these events, about which she was deeply ambivalent:

There are good folks that you have interviewed here and they want to do great things. So they'll put on a justice conference. I've been to so many of these. And they'll host them at a Black church, they'll have a Black speaker. Maybe sprinkle in another couple minorities. But the leadership and the power always remains with the powerful rich white males. Always. And if you look at the demographic of the people that will attend: privileged, educated, rich, white. And I think that a lot of justice conferences—now that it's become a little bit more popular, popularized—the conversation tends to be coming from white males who are engaging in something that's popular but not coming from their own experience of poverty or pain or oppression. So they're, in a sense, telling another's story. Whereas I think the people who've lived those stories are just as competent and capable of telling their own stories, in their own voice. That's bringing dignity, I think. The true sense of justice is not hoarding and keeping your power and privilege and position but empowering those who society has not allowed to have that.

So this is a little bit of my disengagement of some of the justice conference stuff. 'Cause I was on that circuit of speaking and going to conferences and everything, and I was just like, "Oh good God. I'm in the circus now." I was asked to be on the board for a big justice organization, a national one. And the guy who was the director of that, he's like, "I'm in the justice circus. It's all the same people, the same conferences. Same thing." That's how I felt with Q [a trendy gathering of cosmopolitan evangelicals of some renown]. I went to a Q Conference. One, it's outrageously expensive. But then it's like: if I see another rich white male at a justice conference talk about all the great work they're doing in Rwanda, and pat themselves on the back [pause]: It's like, use your freaking money and bring a damn Rwandan here and have them tell their own story! With great force and dignity and power. Instead, you are still hoarding and keeping all power for your own gain and glory. And it sickens me; it's using the poor to get fame. And that's what I continue to see. So I decided consciously to not choose that.

On the one hand, Sue had gone to seminary in order to learn about biblical justice and work toward educating and mobilizing evangelical pastors, church leaders, and churchgoers around social justice issues. In that regard, the explosion of evangelical discourse and interest around social justice concerns was a welcome development. On the other hand, Sue's involvement in the evangelical "justice circus" had left her disenchanted with the lack of critical self-awareness concerning issues of power and privilege which, ironically to her, lie at the very heart of the meaning of social justice. From Sue's perspective, evangelical justice conferences more often than not simply reproduced the very same problems of race, class, gender, sexuality, and global inequities that they were purportedly trying to challenge.

Sue's practice of social reflexivity was not merely a matter of talk, but of power and action. To my knowledge, she was the only CCG leader who ever brought one of the disadvantaged individuals on whose behalf the organization served as advocates with them to the state capitol in order to let them "tell their own story" to legislators—rather than having someone else tell their story for them. Sue brought Eve—a mentally ill homeless woman and former prostitute angry about experiences with gender inequity and domestic violence—to speak to a crowd at the state capitol during a CCG political mobilization. "You asked me for a success story," Sue said, "That, I think, by far, probably trumps anything. . . . She told me, 'I learned that I can speak for myself and I have the right to live in a clean safe environment.' She learned she had a voice." Despite identifying as and working for an organization rooted in outreach to evangelicals, the fact that Eve was a former drug addict whose concern about domestic violence stemmed in part from experiences with her female partner did not deter Sue from recognizing that Eve deserved the right—and possessed the capability—of educating hundreds of smart and powerful people gathered at the state capitol to bring attention to issues of homelessness and domestic violence. By thinking and interacting flexibly and self-critically across multiple categories of social difference, Sue practiced a transposable social reflexivity capable of attending to intersectional social difference and inequity.

While Sue offers a glimpse of transposable reflexivity practiced at the individual level, Peachtree Community Development Association (PCDA) consistently practiced transposable social reflexivity at the collective level. Take PCDA's directors' meetings, where a multiracial, intergenerational, mixed gender group of department heads gathered monthly to discuss important business. These meetings were unfailingly rich with critical, reflective, expansive deliberation about local and translocal racial problems, race- and class-based dilemmas of gentrification, intra- and extraorganizational issues relating to gender and sexuality, and the organization's relationship with diverse evangelical and nonevangelical religious others. Still, as I note in the Introduction, while PCDA's presence in the neighborhood was by invitation and overwhelmingly well-received, it was not without detractors. Prior to one particular director's meeting I had been spending a lot of time with some disgruntled residents and former PCDA employees who were critical of the organization for not doing a better of job of finding ways to support everyone in the neighborhood.[36]

Ayesha, a twenty-eight-year-old Black female and former PCDA thrift store employee who had moved to the neighborhood twenty months earlier, had the ear and limited trust of the source of PCDA's strongest—though small and disorganized—opposition in the neighborhood:

> Older males—thirties to forties—there's nothing here [PCDA] for them. Nothing at all. They really have trust issues. They have ego, they have pride. They didn't understand how I could be on this side [spending time with PCDA people and places] one day and their side the next day. I'm like, "Whoa, I'm just kind of learning both sides, you know?" But there was a point in time where they basically told me I had to choose a side, that, "I couldn't be on both sides. So what are you going to do?" So now I sit with the men. I just sit with them and listen. They started trusting me. I'm still working on it. For a long time they thought I was police, because I just came in, I spoke "properly" and just sort of appeared or sprouted out of nowhere, and it was, "I think she's with the white people. I think she's a white girl. We can't trust her. She's with the feds, that's how the feds send them in." I sit amongst them and just take in their conversation. They just need gainful employment and to feel like a man, whatever that looks like. That's it. To feel loved, because, you know, "I'm a human. Don't be afraid of me. I am a human being. I am person and at the end of the day. I'm not going to do anything to you unless I have to, so just understand that, and stop being afraid."

Ayesha confirmed this subset of men as PCDA's main critics in the neighborhood, and she shared her perspective on why that was the case, along with some hypothetical advice to PCDA leaders and others doing similar work:

> The male is the head of the household ultimately, so if you come into a place and you are not helping the head of the household, what are you really doing? You are not building anything, and really, that's what we need. We need stronger men. That's what we need, and if you really want to help and conquer a problem, build up the men and everything else will fall in place. But that's not what's being done. They are afraid of them, which is quite understandable, because they are quite scary. They are angry. You have to understand that they are just mad, and I would be mad too, if I were

them. I would be really mad. Especially around here in the South. There are so many things stacked up against them, and people view them as just scary, angry, lazy people. They are not lazy. They just don't have any other choices except to do what they do, so how can we judge or shy away from them or anything like that? You can't. But it seems like [PCDA's work in the neighborhood] is still going along and creating problems, because they are helping women, they are helping children, and some men, but they are also creating division because they're not helping everyone. Instead of going down to the bottom and nourishing that, they kind of start at the midpoint and everyone under that midpoint just gets swept under a rug and pushed out, and that doesn't help anything. You are just moving the problem somewhere else, and then someone will go to that place and just do the same thing. So, I don't know: maybe they [PCDA] shouldn't be here.

I understand that there are some addiction issues . . . but just because someone is smoking a crack pipe in the middle of some broken down hole in the floor doesn't mean God is not in the middle of that. So you need to go in there and just—at first you won't be comfortable, because no one is comfortable in situations they've never been exposed to at first. But just trust God is there. And maybe you're the light to get them out of there. Maybe you are not the light to get them out of there. Maybe you are just the light to give them love in that moment. There's nothing wrong in that. It's nothing to be ashamed of. Just be quiet and sit down and listen. There's really nothing that you can do. It's just something that we have to do for ourselves, and that's it.

As described in Chapter 2, Ayesha and her confidantes accurately perceived an intentional PCDA emphasis on providing support and opportunity for single mothers and youth in the neighborhood, along with the fact that PCDA did not have capacity to equally reach everyone in the neighborhood. They also perceived a lack of focus or support for some people—particularly low-income older Black men with criminal records—who were angry and struggling with racial discrimination and distrust, unemployment, substance abuse, mental health, and lack of opportunity.

Soon after this conversation with Ayesha I arrived at a PCDA director's meeting, at which the conversation shifted from the usual discussions of organizational business to a police incident that had occurred in the neighborhood the previous night. An intoxicated, mentally ill man with whom some were familiar had been arrested after discharging a firearm several times while staggering down an abandoned street in the middle of the night. At first the conversation focused on the details of what had happened: where and when the incident occurred, which streetlights may have been shot out, the experiences of neighbors living near the incident who heard the shots, shouting, police response, and the like. Soon, however, the conversation turned to what the incident meant for PCDA's work in the neighborhood. One person said they weren't doing enough to reach out to ex-convicts, people struggling with substance abuse, and mentally ill neighborhood residents. "It's a real weakness of ours," another said. Members nodded their heads in agreement and began discussing possible solutions: raising money to hire a mental health specialist, finding people who had expertise in the area with whom to partner, strengthening substance abuse recovery and support programs, and finding new ways to build rapport and relationship with middle-aged male ex-offenders living in the neighborhood. For over 45 minutes, the group tabled business as usual for an expansive, self-critical, action-focused discussion of who they were and weren't reaching effectively in the community. It was as if Ayesha and her fellow PCDA critics were in the room with us discussing their problems with the organization's work in the neighborhood.[37] It was actually quite remarkable—spooky even— how closely the director's meeting discussion mirrored the criticisms and concerns I was hearing while spending time with PCDA critics.

Although it did not always take such clear and dramatic form, individual and group practices of transposable social reflexivity were ubiquitous in the PCDA context. Whether interacting with race/class/religion diverse neighborhood residents and community leaders, gay and lesbian neighbors and former organizational members, disadvantaged Black neighborhood youth and their parents, or organizational members experiencing crises of faith and doubt, PCDA staff and volunteers habitually demonstrated capacity to think and interact flexibly and self-critically in relation to diverse social others and situations across a wide spectrum of race, class, gender, LGBTQ+, religious, and political divides. Other individuals and groups did the same, practicing transposable reflexivity across diverse social situations and categories of difference.

Frozen Reflexivity

Individuals and groups practice *frozen reflexivity* when they think and interact self-critically, but partially and inflexibly, with respect to identities, groups, settings, or traditions with which they are involved. Frozen reflexivity is self-critical, but truncated and at times dogmatic. It involves a capacity to find flaws and errors within one's self, group, situation, or tradition; however, this critique is wielded with rigidity. Frozen reflexivity is not mere dogmatism—wherein there is no room for self-critique or critical engagement of any kind—but shares with dogmatism a degree of insensitivity and inflexibility with respect to engaging diverse social actors and settings. Sometimes such inflexibility can be an asset—a helpful intransigence to refuse compromise or dilution of core principles. Often, however, it is a liability—resulting in reduced influence, distorted perceptions, and failure to bridge differences and achieve important social or political goals.

Peter, a white evangelical community activist and asset-based community development (ABCD) trainer with Neighborhood Partners, is an illustrative case. As a deeply engaged citizen who led or participated in a remarkably wide-range of neighborhood initiatives, citizen committees, non-profit boards and activities, and community development projects, Peter had developed an extremely fine-tuned sensitivity to class inequality and power imbalances in local decision-making. A true believer in the asset-based community development model of inclusively mobilizing the gifts and energies of all members of a community for social change, Peter was obsessively committed to the principle of participatory decision-making, and an indefatigable critic of top-down, outside-in, problem-centered, or needs-based paradigms of public engagement.

Peter's strong commitment to participatory decision-making processes and heavy critique of existing modes of political organization and public engagement did much to push local political, civic, and religious leaders and groups toward more inclusive modes of public planning and collective action. Under Peter's influence, disadvantaged neighborhood residents became board members and committee leaders with real decision-making power, rather than passive subjects of top-down projects led by local political, economic, and religious elites. Peter kept city officials on their toes with his sharp critiques of bureaucratic power and planning processes that were unaccountable and inaccessible to ordinary citizens. These are all unalloyed goods from the perspective of ethical democracy. However, Peter also frequently found himself alienating allies, getting kicked off planning committees, and losing influence due to his incessant criticism and rigid insistence on applying ABCD principles to even the tiniest minutiae of public interaction.

Take, for example, the following scene. When the city of Portland decided to invest millions of dollars in long-term incremental tax financing to fund neighborhood initiatives across the city similar to the Greenbush Initiative,[38] it was a major victory for Peter and for Neighborhood Partners. Hundreds gathered to hear the mayor and city officials announce the initiative to the press. Angel, the Greenbush Initiative's lead organizer, was excited. "We were just talking at our last meeting how we needed to get some good press for our neighborhood! This is *great* press!" she gushed. She was right: the press corps was out in full force, interviewing neighborhood leaders and residents for what were sure to be positive stories about community involvement and investment in some of Portland's rougher neighborhoods.

Peter, however, was unimpressed: "Yeah, it's great to get together to talk about all the *needs* and *problems* we have," he responded sarcastically, despite the fact that neither the mayor nor any of the other event speakers had actually done such a thing. "And that hospital director—it's surprising she wasn't more sensitive to problematic language, what with health care becoming more and more about preventive medicine, community-based prevention and such," he added, despite the fact that the hospital director had given an unremittingly positive and cheery little speech suited to the occasion. Angel looked incredulously at Peter, her mentor and supervisor in the early days of the Greenbush project. "She said *solutions*, too!" Angel pushed back, barely concealing her annoyance while shaking her head and walking away to give an interview. Undeterred, Peter carried on with his criticism. As one high-ranking Portland Development Commission manager told me, the event marked a watershed moment for a "more grassroots, less top-down" approach to public engagement in low-income neighborhoods: one that was well-funded and modeled in part on the Greenbush Initiative's successes. Yet Peter perceived it as just another example of top-down bureaucratic management and problem-based discourse—all evidence to the contrary.

While Peter practiced frozen reflexivity in relation to grassroots democratic politics and public decision-making, Anders—one of Peter's white evangelical Neighborhood Partners colleagues—practiced frozen reflexivity with respect to religion. Anders had developed a strong, systematic critique of white American evangelical strategies of proselytizing public engagement, bemoaning evangelicals' insistence on prioritizing evangelism and gospel proclamation over other forms of public engagement, their moral and religious triumphalism, and their often paternalistic styles of engaging with the poor and non-Christians. As a vocal critic of his own religious tradition,

Anders hammered away at what he perceived to be the many shortcomings and blind spots of traditional evangelical strategies of engaging the public and the poor. While leading training seminars in asset-based community development, Anders pilloried one-way charity programs and paradigms of public engagement for which evangelicals are known during formal presentations and informal conversations with seminar participants. While facilitating the reading/discussion component of a service-learning class on community development and urban ministry with students from a local Christian college, Anders colorfully constructed and annihilated caricatures of white evangelical gospel proclamation and community engagement. While helping lead local and out-of-town church groups in short-term urban outreach projects, Anders doggedly undermined traditional evangelical interpretations of scripture and the gospel at seemingly every turn.

In many respects, Anders's critique of traditional American evangelical styles of engaging the public and the poor was sophisticated, penetrating, and warranted. It was also rigid, repetitive, and overly self-assured. Anders's communication style with students, interns, seminar participants, and visiting churchgoers was more soapbox than dialogue, more preacher than partner, a one-way bullhorn more than a back-and-forth discussion—which was somewhat ironic in light of his deep commitment to ABCD first-principles of "listening," "dialogue," and "partnership" that this communication style sometimes appeared to violate. Still, despite these inconsistencies, it is important to note that the frozen reflexivity reflected in Anders's fixed critique of his own religious tradition remains distinguishable from the triumphal and unreflective ministrations of religious (or nonreligious) dogmatism per se, which ignores context, refuses compromise, and assumes its own infallibility as an a priori fact.

Deep Reflexivity

In contrast to frozen reflexivity, in which initially positive self-critique and flexibility hardens into self-congratulatory perspectives that hinder bridge-building and iterative reflexive action, individuals and groups practice *deep reflexivity* when they demonstrate iterative capacity for flexible and self-critical thought and action across difference whilst recognizing the inescapably partial and fallible nature of their efforts. Deep reflexivity is reliably recursive and fallibilist, recognizing the inescapably partial and fallible nature of all human efforts to bridge differences, fight inequity, and practice solidarity across different types of difference.

A deep capacity to adjust beliefs and practices over time in response to critical assessment, new information, and changing social contexts was evident across a wide range of individual and collective practices at the Food Co-op and PCDA. For example, a PCDA-affiliated church's efforts to distribute clothing through a standard "clothes closet" charity that tended to reinforce, rather than challenge, race and class divisions evolved into the establishment of a neighborhood thrift store with a greatly expanded selection of goods that employed low-income neighborhood residents at fair-market wages. Later, after years of trying, and failing, to persuade a major grocery store chain to open a branch in their neighborhood—which sat in the middle of a food desert—PCDA shifted gears and converted their resale store into a neighborhood food market providing fresh, healthy, affordable, in-demand foods within walking distance of neighborhood residents. The Food Co-op was born out of the ruins of a local church's charity-based food pantry transformed into a member-run food cooperative providing extremely low-cost food, leadership opportunities, employment, community-based health and social service education, social capital, emotional support, and spiritual uplift to members. As described at length in Chapters 2 and 3, Food Co-op and PCDA programs and practices changed over time in response to challenges and input from neighborhood residents and program participants, to critical reflection and assessment of past and current organizational practices, and to changing social conditions and circumstances.

The practice of deep reflexivity is characterized by a demonstrable fallibilism that recognizes the inescapable limits and failures inherent in all efforts to bridge differences, fight inequity, and practice social reflexivity across difference. PCDA staff and volunteers frequently demonstrated this component of deep reflexivity at both the individual and collective level. I have already noted one example in the PCDA directors' meeting response to a neighborhood shooting in the pages above. An even more dramatic example of PCDA's fallibilism in this regard is how veteran organizational leaders spoke of the catastrophic failure of an ambitious community development project they had been invited to participate in another disadvantaged majority Black neighborhood decades earlier. After a promising start, the venture collapsed in on itself amidst a sea of racially tinged accusations and recriminations of greed, deceit, and mismanagement. According to various accounts, a fatal combination of poor communication, word-of-mouth contract agreements, unsecured loans, changing market dynamics, externally imposed time pressures, inexperience, petty interest, and racial mistrust led to a complete unraveling of the project amidst million-dollar losses. "It went bad real fast, real fast," Richard lamented, "and it set race relationships back a good two decades." Making no attempt to put a positive spin on the project or minimize the damage it had done, Richard directly and openly addressed the project's failures, lamented its deleterious effects for racial and economic equity, and reflected on lessons learned for subsequent work.

At the individual level, Kaito and Leonard's reflections in Chapter 2 on the limits of their communities' practice of strategic relocation—and strategic relocation in general—as a strategy of combatting racial and economic inequity are exemplars of deep reflexivity, while Deanna's reflections on Christian community development and youth programs in race and class disadvantaged neighborhoods—and her ongoing reconstruction of PCDA summer and after-school programs—demonstrate the practice of deep reflexivity at the individual and organizational levels.

Deep reflexivity also involves acknowledging the limits of a person or group's capacity to bridge differences and fully comprehend the experiences and perspectives of diverse social others. "White Dave"—the PCDA leader we met in Chapter 2 whose nickname derived in part from his incorrigible cultural "whiteness"—is an apt example. White Dave did not seem to make it through many days without unintentionally alienating on of his Black coworkers, clients, and customers. But he owned his mistakes, learned from them, accepted his outsider status, and just kept plugging away at his work and relationships in the neighborhood. "White Dave" made a few enemies in the neighborhood, but he won the respect and appreciation of many more for his sincere and often effective participation in work to combat racial and economic inequity in his community.

One vivid example of White Dave's demonstrated capacity to both learn from and accept the limits of all human attempts to build understanding and solidarity across difference can be seen in his reflections on the Trayvon Martin shooting. While many white Americans in 2012 remained ignorant or unmoved at the shooting death of the young Black male, Dave offered a different perspective while reflecting on the incident in a letter to supporters:

> My hopes and dreams for moving to [this neighborhood] included living a life with my neighbors and sharing in their hopes, dreams, sorrows and fears. . . . Fast forward several years and I never would have imagined

that I would have grieved as much as I have over the past few days. If I am honest with myself though, the reason for my grief is what is the most shocking to me. I came here to share in life with my neighbors, but the events of the weekend showed me that no matter how hard I try; I can never fully understand what my neighbors, and now friends, are really going through.

White Dave reacted to the unaccountable shooting of another young Black male with visceral outrage and grief, grief that was compounded by the suffering and anger of his Black neighbors and colleagues that he could not fully participate in. White Dave went on to give a sophisticated lament in solidarity with his Black friends' and neighbors' experiences of pain, anger, and fear that their own children might just as easily fall victim to the violent consequences of racial threat and stereotyping by police officers and anti-Black vigilantes, while at the same time describing why it was impossible for him to fully enter into their experiences. By seeking change while recognizing the inescapably partial and fallible nature of his own efforts to understand and combat racial inequities, white Dave represents an illustrative case of the practice of deep social reflexivity with respect to race at the individual level.

Social Reflexivity and Scripture

In addition to advancing an empirically rooted and theoretically useful set of concepts concerning the general practice of social reflexivity across different types of difference, these findings also suggest that evangelicals can, in fact, be both "Christ-centered and socially reflexive" under certain conditions.[39] That is, contrary to common liberal secularist assumptions (or those of many evangelicals themselves), evangelicals don't have to stop being evangelical or abandon core religious convictions in order to practice deep and transposable social reflexivity across different types of difference and disagreement in public and political life.

There are several reasons for this. First, a large body of research suggests that evangelical practices in general—and those related to social reflexivity in particular—are often conditioned more by social and contextual factors than by explicitly "religious" ones. Second, evangelicalism is not a monolith, a single point on the map of American religion; rather, it is an internally diverse and contested field of agreement and struggle over a wide range of religious and political standpoints and strategies of action.[40] While much of what passes for evangelical Christianity in the United States demonstrates a clear lack of social reflexivity across different types of difference,[41] such positions are frequently contested, not least by other evangelicals holding alternative religious convictions more conducive to the practice of deep and transposable reflexivity in public life. Third and related, perhaps the most important reason to suppose that evangelicals can practice social reflexivity across difference while holding fast to particularistic religious convictions is that their sacred scriptures demand it. The highest source of intellectual and moral authority in the evangelical faith tradition—the Christian Bible read through an evangelical lens—provides a rich and authoritative resource for the evangelical practice of intellectual humility and social reflexivity across difference.

This is important, because, as a postsecular Habermas has come to recognize, making a priori demands that religious believers ground the substance and style of their engagement in public life in strictly secular or universally accessible terms is unnecessary, unproductive, and unethical from the standpoint of ethical democratic theory.[42] It is unnecessary because traditional or orthodox religious individuals and communities of all persuasions have demonstrated capacity throughout history for practicing religious reflexivity in the public arena—to "consider one's own faith reflexively from the outside and relate it to secular views"—whilst remaining rooted in their own particularistic religious tradition and convictions.[43] It is unproductive because it unnecessarily alienates large swaths of people who find it difficult or impossible to articulate reasons for their political views in nonreligious terms for various reasons, and because it helps fuel hostility and distrust between religious and secular citizens (or between religious citizens and the secular state) that threaten baseline requirements of solidarity, trust, and civility necessary for healthy democratic functioning.[44] Finally, it is unethical because it undermines normative democratic commitments to self-determination and inclusive participation in the democratic public sphere for all citizens, including religious ones, which "empowers them to be the authors of laws to which as its addressees they are subject."[45] As such, religious and secular proponents of ethical democracy alike have reason to welcome particularistic religious reasons and motivations for the practice of social reflexivity in public life, even when they themselves do not find such reasons persuasive, compelling, or authoritative.

For evangelicals, the Christian Bible interpreted through an evangelical hermeneutic offers many such resources. The first is the evangelical doctrine of sin and human weakness.[46] "All have sinned and fall short of the glory of God," writes Paul in the book of Romans (3:23, NIV). Lest his readers think their identity as Christ-followers exempts them the universal scope of this claim, the writer of 1 Timothy (v.15, NIV) elaborates, "Here is a trustworthy saying that deserves full acceptance: Christ Jesus came into the world to save sinners—of whom I am the worst." According to traditional evangelical readings of scripture, who is the person requiring the highest levels of critical scrutiny, moral circumspection, and reflexive self-examination? Oneself. Who is most subject to critical evaluation, scrutiny, and correction after oneself? The community of believers or the church, as described in 1 Corinthians 5. While dealing with a case of church discipline in Corinth, Paul draws a distinction between the community of believers and the general public: "What business is it of mine to judge those outside the church? Are you not to judge those inside? God will judge those outside" (1 Corinthians 5:12–13). Paul's discussion here echoes the teachings of Jesus as recorded in Matthew 7:1– 5. It is not others, but oneself; not outsiders, but insiders; not the stranger, but the friend; not "the world," but "the church"; that must be subject to the most rigorous moral and intellectual criticism and self-scrutiny according to classic evangelical readings of scripture.

This evangelical understanding of sin and self-scrutiny is closely tied to the theological doctrine of the fall and resulting partial corruption of human faculties of reason and will. We must be slow to trust ourselves, our motivations, and our understandings, the prophets say, for, "the heart is deceitful above all things . . . Who can understand it?" (Jeremiah 17:9, NIV). We are all inveterate self-idolaters, prone to exaggerate our own person or groups' merits while casting shade on others. Faith in Christ brings forgiveness and the possibility of renewal, but "the flesh" is beyond redemption— only death and resurrection can cure it, as Paul argues in chapters seven and eight of the book of Romans. Until then, all our knowledge—not least religious knowledge—is "partial and incomplete," for "now we see through a glass, darkly" (1 Corinthians 13:9, 12, KJV). As such, Christ-followers are called to a vigilant moral and intellectual humility, acknowledging the fallible and partial nature of all human knowledge and moral striving—including first and foremost their own.

This intellectual and moral humility in the face of sin and human weakness is most directly expressed in the practice of repentance. In evangelical parlance, repentance, or *metanoia*, means to change one's mind, to concede mistakes, to admit one's fault, to turn around, to take a new direction—as anyone with passing familiarity with popular evangelical homiletics might tell you. By necessity in light of the fall, repentance is a routine expectation and commitment of everyday life, a mundane—if exceedingly difficult—practice of daily spiritual discipline, a pillar of evangelical piety. Repentance marks the beginning of every evangelical's spiritual journey and is their constant companion thereafter, for it is the call of every believer to "be transformed by the renewing of your mind" and thus "not think of yourself more highly than you ought, but rather to think of yourself with sober judgment" (Romans 12:2–3, NIV). It grows more, rather than less, prominent in the lives of authentic religious leaders—who come to recognize themselves as "foremost of all" sinners (I Timothy 1:15, NASB) and "very least of all the saints" (Ephesians 3:8) the nearer they approach God (Isaiah 6:1–7).

Another central pillar of evangelical theology—the doctrine of incarnation, that God became flesh in Jesus of Nazareth—further amplifies the evangelical religious warrant for intellectual humility and social reflexivity across different types of difference. As described in the second chapter of Philippians, the doctrine of *kenosis*—the self-emptying incarnation of God in the person of Jesus—calls Christ-followers to renounce privilege, practice humility, prioritize others' interests and perspectives, and reach across difference with love in the manner of their incarnate and crucified God (Philippians 2:3–8). Evangelical research participants invariably cited the incarnation as a primary religious motivation for strategic relocation.

Research participants also frequently invoked Jeremiah 29:7 (NASB): "Seek the welfare of the city where I have sent you into exile, and pray to the LORD on its behalf; for in its welfare you will have welfare." Beyond presaging Tocqueville's doctrine of enlightened self-interest, this passage and others like it have shaped multicultural evangelical community activists' pursuit of collaborative solutions to public problems for decades.[47] "What does the Lord require," ask the prophets (Micah 6:8)? "To do justice, love mercy, and walk humbly with your God." According to my research participants and long-time multicultural evangelical urban activists, this involves working alongside "people of good will" across the social, political, and religious spectrum for the common good of one's city, neighborhood, or nation. For God causes the "sun to rise on the evil and the good, and sends rain on the just and the unjust alike" (Matthew 5:45, NLT). In this view, the goodness of

God, God's creation, and God's authority extend beyond the boundaries of the individual believer or church to include all people, all nations, the entire cosmos. As such, to quote one evangelical community leader in Portland, "all truth is God's truth," regardless of whether it is spoken by a Muslim, a Hindu, an atheist, an evangelical, or a liberal Episcopalian. Finally, seeking the welfare of one's city or nation involves loving one's enemies (Matthew 5:44), and, "if it is possible, as far as it depends on you," to "live at peace with everyone" (Romans 12:18).

These evangelical doctrines of sin, the fall, repentance, incarnation, *kenosis*, creation, the common good, and the nature of God's kingdom and character constitute a set of powerful and authoritative religious resources supporting evangelical practices of intellectual humility and social reflexivity across difference and disagreement in the public arena. Moreover, these doctrines and traditions of biblical interpretation are not foreign or peripheral to mainstream evangelicalism; rather, they are central pillars of traditional evangelical belief and self-understanding. To the extent that the "big tent" of American evangelicalism is collapsing with the erosion of these pillars, it is not for lack of their biblical or theological support.

We see these endogenous cultural resources being put into practice in Neighborhood Partners' adoption and framing of asset-based community development (ABCD) strategies of public engagement in theological terms. For example, prior to their weekly "community listening" ventures in the "other Portland," Neighborhood Partners staff subversively led outreach groups through Bible studies based on Philip the Evangelist (Acts 8:26–40) to encourage them to engage people by "listening before speaking" and looking to "hear the voice of God" through the people and settings they encountered. Neighborhood Partners staff also discouraged groups from proselytizing during these outings, in both verbal and written instructions discussed on the Bible study guide given to each participant: "We're asking you to practice listening tonight. Because we believe our natural tendency is to speak before we've really listened well, we're asking that for tonight, you really resist the urge to TELL." Neighborhood Partners staff and volunteers frequently admonished their fellow evangelicals to "*discover* the gospel *in* their neighborhoods," rather thinking of themselves only as "*bringing* the gospel *to* their neighborhoods" (emphases original).

These activities were supported by a robust theological framing that creatively rooted asset-based community development principles in core evangelical doctrines. In addition to day-long ABCD workshops for secular and religious nonprofits, neighborhood residents, and public officials, Neighborhood Partners offered twelve-to-eighteen-month hands-on education and coaching experiences for churches as part of its School of Neighborhood Transformation. Each phase of these Neighborhood Transformation Courses began with teaching on the theological underpinnings of core asset-based community development practices.[48]

In the first phase, participants learn that Christian public engagement ought to be marked by a spirit and practice of "relational reciprocity" which reflects how "true relationship affirms the value and contribution of the other." This principle was justified theologically based on an orthodox evangelical understanding of Trinitarian theology, which establishes "relational precedence and harmony" as constitutive of the very nature of God and thus also a regulative principle for legitimate evangelical public engagement. Not just a matter of cognition or belief, course participants learned that Trinitarian theology also called evangelicals to "affective heart change," from fearful isolation and triumphalism to "togetherness and humility" with diverse social others.

Phase two focused on the core ABCD principle of "searching for assets," which involves "finding the latent assets in every neighborhood and person." Rather than describing people or communities first in terms of their problems or deficits as defined by external actors and authorities, asset-based community development begins with a search for the positive "gifts of head, hands, and heart" that are assumed to exist within every person, community, neighborhood, or situation—nonChristian and Christian alike. This principle was rooted theologically in an evangelical understanding of the "*missio Dei*," or mission of God, interpreted as a "love motivated search for people" initiated by God and imitated (*imitatio Christi*) by his followers. Proper understanding of the *missio Dei* required an "affective heart change" from judgmental moral and religious superiority to that of "loving search."

In phase three, course participants learn about "collaborated solutions" enabled by "facilitating a culture of mutually discovered" problem-solving and collective action. Neighborhood Partners staff rooted this principle in the *imago Dei*, the Christian doctrine that all people are sacred and made in the image of God, which carries the implication that "God [is] in everyone inside and outside the church." The affective heart change motivated by the *imago Dei* and facilitated by the search for collaborative solutions to social problems is the unconditional "hope and dignity" of all people, no matter their religious, moral, economic, racial, or social status.

The principle of "relocation," the focus of phase four of the Neighborhood Transformation Course, encourages evangelicals toward "moving out of our comfort zone to become *of* the other." As discussed above, the evangelical doctrine of "incarnation," God's own "sacrificial identification with the Other" in Jesus Christ, provides the theological warrant for the practice of relocation. Beyond mere physical or cognitive relocation, incarnation calls for an affective heart change toward "sacrifice and being OF the Other (sic)" in a spirit of radical solidarity and cruciform love.

Finally, in the fifth phase, course participants explore "social justice," which requires "advocating for equity" in the public and political arenas. Evangelical commitment to social justice is predicated on God's desire for "shalom"—Hebrew for peace or flourishing—as exemplified in the "prophetic kingdom culture" described in the gospels and Hebrew prophetic tradition rooted in the major and minor prophets of the Hebrew Bible or Christian Old Testament.[49] For the evangelical follower of Christ, pursuing shalom through action for social justice requires an affective heart change that seeks justice and social "righteousness for ALL (sic)," not just one's own family, tribe, self, community, or nation.

Conclusion

Neighborhood Partners' School of Neighborhood Transformation demonstrates how evangelical religious convictions can provide powerful and authoritative endogenous cultural resources for grounding evangelical practices of intellectual humility and social reflexivity across difference in public life. More broadly, the empirical evidence presented in this and previous chapters suggests that these convictions are sometimes put into effective practice when multicultural evangelicals enter the public arena. None of these religious convictions are grounded in secular reason or universally accessible language, but they are no less effective for that. In fact, if the role of motivation in de-biasing thought is as important as the psychological literature suggests,[50] we might expect particularistic religious convictions to be more effective at persuading religious individuals and communities to practice intellectual humility and social reflexivity across difference in public life than secular reasons, given the powerful emotional, social, and cognitive functions religion plays in the lives of many individuals and communities. For such individuals and groups, denigrating religion or insisting that religious persons abandon religious reasons when entering the public square may undercut the very motivations for bridging differences and practicing social reflexivity that advocates of ethical democracy must seek to encourage.

Conclusion

Multicultural Evangelicalism and Democracy in America

There has been a lot of bad news about evangelical Christianity and democracy in America in recent years.[1] In its understandable ubiquity and alarm, this litany of bad news threatens to drown out the voices of multicultural evangelicals whose understanding and practice of evangelical Christian faith can constitute good news for common goods and ethical democracy in America. The social and political orientations of these "other evangelicals"— representing millions of Black, Asian, Hispanic, Indigenous, and white Americans—bear little resemblance to standard depictions of evangelical politics and religion in America.[2] Unlike many of their white conservative evangelical coreligionists, multicultural evangelicals reject white Christian nationalism and rising antidemocratic currents inside and outside their faith communities in the United States.[3] This book offers a window into the sorts of beliefs, activities, groups, and organizations through which multicultural evangelicals across the United States are engaged in living out their understandings of what Lisa Sharon Harper calls the "very good gospel,"[4] the "good news" of Christ for all the earth. In the multicultural evangelical understanding of scripture, the gospel or good news does not sanction racial or religious nationalism, imperialism, colonialism, or triumphalism, but rather invites Christians to build "creative community for the common good,"[5] treading the "uncommon ground" of "living faithfully in a world of difference"[6] alongside religious, racial, cultural, and political others while seeking common goods and ethical democratic approaches to pluralism, inequity, division, and democratic self-governance.

In its ideal typical expression, multicultural evangelicalism reflexively engages difference in both internal religious and external public contexts, practicing social reflexivity as a natural outgrowth of evangelical religious commitments to humility, repentance, and self-giving love. Multicultural

Good News for Common Goods. Wes Markofski, Oxford University Press. © Oxford University Press 2023.
DOI: 10.1093/oso/9780197659694.003.0008

evangelicals are reflexive evangelicals, interacting flexibly and self-critically in relation to diverse social others and situations, albeit imperfectly. They are also often bridge or boundary-crossing evangelicals, moving back and forth across evangelical and nonevangelical organizations, settings, and sensibilities. As such, multicultural evangelicals frequently operate along edges of evangelicalism, retaining core evangelical religious distinctives and network ties while exploring alternative expressions and identities that sometimes put them at odds with dominant expressions of evangelical Christianity in America.[7] At other times, multicultural evangelical perspectives converge closely with those of the larger evangelical field. Multicultural evangelicalism, like evangelicalism more broadly, is not a monolithic standpoint but rather a multivocal field, containing significant internal diversity and contestation across multiple dimensions regarding the legitimate expression of biblical Christianity in public and religious life.[8]

Some multicultural evangelicals are across-the-board progressive evangelicals, aligning with left-liberal positions on racial and economic equity, gender equity, religious and cultural pluralism, LGBTQ+ issues, and partisan politics. Others are mosaic multiculturalists, combining a bricolage of conservative and left-liberal perspectives across various dimensions of difference and disagreement in American public and religious life. Many multicultural evangelicals occupy a contradictory cultural location between the secular left and religious right, at odds with the binary political grammar and partisan polarization of contemporary US politics and public life.[9] Their practice of social reflexivity across different types of difference reflects this variation, sometimes extending across domains as in the practice of transposable reflexivity, sometimes restricted to one domain as in the practice of segmented reflexivity.

While this book's depiction of different types of social reflexivity emerged from first-hand observations of multicultural evangelical approaches to engaging racial difference and inequality, poverty and economic inequality, gender and sexuality, and political, cultural, and religious difference, it is not restricted to any particular social context or identity. Transposable reflexivity, segmented reflexivity, deep reflexivity, and frozen reflexivity can be practiced by any individual, organization, or group across any dimension of difference. They are general concepts not limited to multicultural evangelicals alone. This book extends previous research demonstrating the importance of social reflexivity for building bridges across difference, and the importance of bridging social capital for the advancement of ethical democracy.[10]

Any person or group can practice social reflexivity and bridge building across difference, but their reasons for doing so are not always the same. Multicultural evangelical practices of intellectual humility and social reflexivity are authorized by particularistic religious beliefs rooted in scripture that other religious and secular groups do not share. This is not a problem for ethical democracy. Unlike varieties of religious or secular fundamentalism, pragmatic postsecular pluralism recognizes the legitimacy of diverse secular and religious motivations and modes of public discourse and political engagement. This book offers examples of what a pragmatic post-secular pluralist approach to ethical democracy and the pursuit of common goods amidst deep difference and disagreement can look like in practice.

As we have witnessed in the preceding chapters, there is no biblical or practical reason that evangelicals cannot or should not partner with diverse social others across race, class, religious, political, or cultural lines to advance common goods in their neighborhoods, cities, nation, and world. Theologically, the ground has already been cleared for a distinctly evangelical approach to public religion, multifaith collaboration, and multiculturalism consistent with ethical democracy and evangelical faith.[11] Sociologically, this book demonstrates how multicultural evangelicals across the country are already practicing the sort of reflexive evangelicalism best equipped to contribute to ethical democratic projects across a range of public problems, issues, and concerns. Like all such endeavors, their efforts are limited and imperfect, requiring ongoing critique, adjustment, and reconstruction. But that is just to say that multicultural evangelicals reflect the fallible human condition like everyone else—something that evangelicals of all people ought to readily recognize according to their own core religious convictions.[12]

Conversely, there is also no moral philosophical or political reason that secular progressives and people of different faith traditions cannot or should not partner with evangelical Christians to advance common goods in their neighborhoods, cities, nation, and world. Culture wars are not one-way affairs.[13] Just as ethical democracy calls for a more reflexive evangelicalism than has been heretofore ascendant in the United States, so too does it call for a more reflexive secularism and progressivism. There are better ways for secular and progressive Americans to approach religious conservatives than treating them as eternal enemies of ethical democracy who, "because of their religious mindset, are not to be taken seriously as modern contemporaries."[14] Mutual recognition and genuine encounter—not the elite condescension of an illiberal secular progressivism, nor the populist fury of an intolerant religious authoritarianism—are what ethical democracy requires.

The call to ethical democracy and a renewed politics of common goods is not an argument against political critique, anger, argument, or conflict in general, but rather a call to remember the shared humanity and citizenship that motivate our democratic ideals and passion. Accepting pluralism, practicing social reflexivity, and seeking common good collaborations across deep difference and disagreement does not require abandoning strongly held identities, beliefs, and values—or fighting fiercely and fairly for them. It is not a refusal of conviction. Politics is messy; change is hard. It sometimes requires us to steel ourselves against distracting lies, unacceptable compromises, and false accusations of our opponents—with searing focus and unshakeable conviction that our cause is right and just—in order to sustain energy, justify sacrifices, and mobilize support for necessary change. There is no progress without struggle, and often, the struggle is fierce.[15] Nevertheless, we can all commit to recognizing one another as fellow citizens and humans worthy of respect, dignity, and fairness, to treating political opponents as current adversaries rather than mortal enemies, and to practicing collaboration and compromise when conditions merit—no matter what the other side may be doing. If ethical democracy is as much about culture and public life as it is about power and political life, then the means whereby we pursue ethical democracy will always be as important as our ends.

* * *

While evangelicalism is historically a predominantly white religious tradition in the United States, this is not true globally, and it is becoming ever less true in the United States.[16]

As Korean American evangelical pastor and author Soong-Chan Rah argues, the "next evangelicalism" must reconstitute itself as the fully multiracial and multicultural movement it professes to be.[17] This will require significant change and commitment from majority-white evangelical institutions and communities to embrace racially reflexive practices, perspectives, and politics that wed evangelical religious conviction to transposable and deep social reflexivity across difference. Those white-dominated evangelical institutions and communities that fail to do so will only further isolate themselves from their multicultural evangelical siblings and others seeking to advance ethical democracy in America.

But why, one may ask, if the Bible-backed evangelical warrants for social reflexivity, racial and ethical democracy, and common good collaborations across difference are as strong as the multicultural evangelicals described in this book suggest, do we see so many examples of American evangelical public and political engagement that violate, oppose, or undermine ethical democracy, racial justice, and social reflexivity across differences? The large body of research on white conservative American evangelicalism suggest a variety of answers. These include persuasive arguments that white evangelicalism, like white America in general, has continued to harbor implicit and explicit racism whose eradication in the post–Civil Rights era has been greatly exaggerated.[18] These views, in turn, fuel an ethnoreligious "white Christian nationalism" in which racially, religiously, and culturally diverse Americans are not "real Americans" and do not truly belong.[19] In its secularized, politicized, Trumpified form, evangelicalism is reduced to a tribal identity marker, a "political identity denuded of ethical" or "explicitly religious content," as seen in Trump's exaggerated appeal among white evangelicals with weak religious attachments across a variety of indicators.[20] White evangelical racial isolation,[21] status resentment,[22] culture war mobilization,[23] and top-to-bottom partisan political polarization[24] further undermine conservative white evangelical commitments to ethical democracy, racial equity, and social reflexivity across difference. The multivocal, polysemous nature of biblical interpretation makes room for misuses, abuses, omissions, honest differences, and culturally conditioned appropriations of scripture that can violate ethical democratic and multicultural evangelical commitments.[25] Finally, a combative, populist, high-boundary style of theology and religious practice helped fuel American evangelical identity and growth over the last 100 years,[26] supporting a "pietistic idealism" that is suspicious of outgroups and resistant to boundary-crossing collaboration in public and religious life.[27]

The multicultural evangelicals described in this book are all well acquainted with these powerful currents in the field of American evangelicalism; many of whom grew up and remain intertwined in conservative evangelical contexts and relational networks. What, then, might account for the different ways that multicultural evangelicals approach racial difference and inequity, poverty and economic inequality, religious and cultural pluralism, and ethical democracy, in addition to the obvious fact that many multicultural evangelicals are people of color?[28] The ethnographic findings

presented in this book offer some clues. Racial integration; strategic relocation; urban residence; diverse social networks; affective kinship or close interpersonal relationships across difference; belonging to multiracial religious
organization (particularly those with empowered people of color in senior
leadership positions); participation in racially, religiously, politically, or culturally diverse political or community organizations; firsthand encounters
with poverty, racism, and gender or sexuality-based discrimination; mentorship experiences under evangelical and other leaders of color; participation
in education and training opportunities for engaging across difference; extended cross-cultural experience or subaltern identity status; and embodied
attachment to particular elements of classical evangelical theology and biblical interpretation are among them. These observations are not causally de-
finitive, but they are suggestive and resonant with prior research.[29]

It remains, however, despite significant institutional support and links
to mainstream evangelical institutions,[30] that multicultural evangelicalism
is a minority position within the field of American evangelicalism, and recent events—the 2016 and 2020 presidential elections, the storming of the
US Capitol building on January 6, 2021, conservative evangelical reactions
to the COVID-19 pandemic and racial justice movement in the wake of
George Floyd's murder in Minneapolis—have put American evangelicalism,
not to mention American democracy, into crisis.[31] The ranks of disaffected
evangelicals of color, #exvangelicals, postevangelicals, deconstructing
evangelicals, exiting leaders, and evangelical migrants to other Christian
traditions continue to grow.[32] It would seem that evangelicalism's big tent
is collapsing. And yet, just as the continuing prominence of religion in the
modern world has frustrated the expectations of secularization theorists
and proponents for centuries, American religion—and evangelicalism in
particular—continues to do the same.[33] American evangelical religious affiliation has proven remarkably steady, even among evangelicals of color and
anti-Trump evangelicals.[34] Assuming the imminent decline of evangelical
spirituality in America—or

caricaturing evangelicalism as an exclusively white, racist, reactionary,
antidemocratic engine of right-wing authoritarianism—continues to be politically unwise and sociologically inaccurate. Evangelicalism will remain
with us for the foreseeable future; so, too, will multicultural evangelicalism.
It behooves us all, for the sake and survival of democracy in America, to find
better ways to relate to one another.

APPENDIX

The Exceptional Case Method

This appendix describes the sociological methods and data used to investigate how multicultural evangelicals across the United States are attempting to engage racial difference and inequality, poverty and economic inequality, religious and cultural difference, and political polarization and partisanship through diverse organizational and interpersonal expressions of public religion. It also introduces the primary and supplementary public service, political advocacy, community development, and community organizing groups and organizations with whom I conducted participant observation research for this book, and discusses my ethnographic relationship to the groups and places under investigation. I describe the benefits and limits of my exceptional case method and multisite ethnography for conducting sociological ethnography, and explain the empirical, theoretical, and normative reasons behind my methodological approach.

Exceptional Case Method

This study focuses on exceptional cases of evangelical public engagement: cases in which evangelicals are engaged in relatively unusual and potentially promising efforts to promote ethical democracy and engage racial difference and inequality, poverty and economic inequality, and political, cultural, and religious difference in the United States.[1] In this book I develop and deploy an *exceptional case method* designed to contribute to our empirical, theoretical, and normative understanding of multicultural evangelicalism and ethical democracy in the United States.[2] Empirically, studying exceptional cases advances sociological knowledge by focusing attention on varieties of evangelical public engagement which are often overlooked in the sociological literature.[3] More generally, exceptional cases—defined broadly as "objects of consideration" that "stand apart" from other cases by virtue of appearing to contradict some widely recognized pattern, classificatory scheme, or set of causal relations—carry unique epistemic potential for contributing to social and normative theory.[4] The exceptional case method combines a focus on exceptional cases with a normative case study approach.[5]

Exceptional cases offer three specific epistemic potentialities I make use of to explore the relationship between multicultural evangelicalism and ethical democracy in America. First, exceptional cases carry potential to problematize taken-for-granted classificatory schemes and normative categories, such as, in this case, the tendency to conflate evangelicalism with across-the-board conservatism, right-wing politics, and whiteness. Second, exceptional cases carry potential to exemplify paradigmatic characteristics of new classes of objects or social categories, such as, in this case, multicultural evangelicalism and different evangelical modes of public religion which we may be particularly interested in for theoretical and normative reasons.[6] Third, exceptional cases carry potential to make previously invisible or overlooked patterns of relations visible, such as, in this case, new relations and practices among multicultural evangelicals and diverse social others engaged in different types of ethical democratic projects across the United States.[7] In brief, "an exceptional case [or set of cases] has the potential to challenge standard categories, to epitomize a new class of objects and to disclose new sets of relations."[8]

The exceptional case method shares with Michael Burawoy's more familiar extended case method a theory-driven logic of ethnographic case selection that facilitates causal and interpretive explanation, but differs in its heightened attentiveness to culture and its engagement with multiple theoretical frameworks within a single ethnographic study— as opposed to restrictively rooting ethnographic investigation in a single favored research paradigm or theoretical approach.[9] The exceptional case method also makes use of standard grounded theory techniques of iterative coding and "constant comparison" across emerging categories of interest while insisting that the ethnographic research process inevitably presupposes and requires engagement with existing bodies of theory— both folk and scientific—from beginning to end.[10] This book centers the descriptive, interpretive, and normative elements of the exceptional case method, and foregrounds a composite rather than comparative analytic approach to my topic and cases for reasons described below. However, by combining theory and grounded observation to construct well-defined objects of comparison and contrast within and across ethnographic cases, the exceptional case method can also facilitate the discovery of partially generalizable, middle-range social mechanisms via contrastive explanation.[11]

Finally, against positivist and materialist philosophies of social science, the exceptional case method rejects the strict demarcation of idiographic and nomothetic, interpretative and explanatory, and scientific and normative knowledge, insisting instead that all modes of social-scientific inquiry involve fallible, interpretive, concept-dependent, case-based— and typically, normative—reasoning.[12] In its deployment of the exceptional case method, this study thus offers an example of how multisite ethnography can contribute to interpretive knowledge,[13] explanatory theory,[14] normative theory,[15] and public sociology.[16]

Despite its considerable potentialities, the exceptional case method is not without limitations. The individuals, groups, and practices under investigation in this study do not constitute "average" or "typical" expressions of American evangelicalism.[17] Nor are they representative of the full range and scope of multicultural evangelicalism in the United States. White evangelicals, for example, remain slightly overrepresented in my sample, while Asian and Latino evangelicals are underrepresented. Applying lessons from these cases to other expressions of American evangelicalism is thus complex and fraught. However, neither are these cases singular outliers.[18] By studying these cases, we expand significantly our understanding of the full range of evangelical modes of public religion and political engagement, and of the possibilities and limits of multicultural evangelical contributions to ethical democracy in America.

Multisite Ethnography: Case Selection and Description

I selected Portland, Atlanta, Los Angeles, and Boston as research sites for several reasons. First, they are home to leading community organizing (Los Angeles and Boston), community development (Atlanta), public service and transpartisan political advocacy (Portland) efforts involving evangelicals in the United States. Second, the selection of these sites allowed for comparisons of multicultural evangelical modes of public religion and political engagement both within and across organizational types, as well as comparisons across different types of institutional and individual "bridging" relationships.[19] Third, the relative lack of research on multicultural evangelicalism and ethical democracy suggested the need for a broad, cross-regional analysis rather than settling for a narrow focus on one or two organizations within a single city or region.

Participating intensively as a volunteer with multiple organizations in each city, I observed culture in action and interaction across a wide range of public and private settings: organizational staff meetings, legislative testimonies, volunteer trainings, fundraisers, community events, public meetings, religious celebrations, informal gatherings, and more.[20]

Guided by my research questions, the acquisition and coding of interview transcripts, organizational documents, and fieldnotes involved special attention to the nature and quality of relations developed across different types of difference; to signs of the presence or absence of intellectual humility and social reflexivity; to the use (or absence) of religious language in different public and private settings; and to the construction and maintenance of group boundaries and identity.[21] I selected cases in which I was able directly to observe and interview race, class, and gender diverse evangelicals interacting with diverse social others across multiple settings and social contexts—an important feature of my research design given that religious actors may talk and act differently across different types of public and private settings.[22]

While conducting research for this study, I canvassed neighborhoods, listened to speeches, attended organizer trainings, and hung out with activists in a low-income Hispanic neighborhood in greater Los Angeles as they fought the construction of a large waste transfer station in their heart of their community. I witnessed another diverse immigrant community celebrate victory in a shockingly successful campaign to block the development of a major casino resort in East Boston. I attended community meetings, backyard barbecues, and neighborhood fundraisers with lifelong residents and strategic relocators in a disadvantaged historically Black neighborhood in Atlanta's urban core. I sang Black spirituals and helped fill cardboard boxes with food in a church basement alongside participants of a member-run food cooperative—the first of its kind in the nation—in another predominantly African American neighborhood in urban Atlanta. I traveled with young progressive white evangelicals from Portland to Salem to meet legislators and watch research participants give testimony before the Oregon state legislature. I participated in the public policy and strategy meetings of a state-level lobbying organization composed of evangelical and mainline Protestants, observing the internal and external conflicts that arose from organizational efforts to mobilize evangelical and liberal Protestants together around a progressive political agenda. I spent countless hours observing, listening, and studying multicultural evangelicals interacting with their neighbors, allies, skeptics, and partners in coffee shops and community centers, progressive dinners and planning meetings, conferences and long car rides, fundraising concerts and late-night street talks, homes, and workplaces.

All ethnographic fieldwork and interviews for this study were conducted between August 2011 and August 2012. I spent approximately six and one-half months in Portland, three and one-half months in Atlanta, and one month each in Los Angeles and Boston. The amount of time spent in each location varied so as to achieve a rough equivalence of depth and breadth of engagement with each of my central cases, which are depicted in Table A.1 below.[23]

These four cases—each anchored by an evangelical-identifying organization and including the people, places, and institutions with which it works—constitute the primary research sites from which the majority of ethnographic data found in this study are drawn. To be classified as evangelical, research participants had to both, (1) be embedded

Table A.1 Central Cases

Location	Anchor Organization	Organizational Type	Religious Composition (Organization)	Religious Composition (Partners)	Racial Composition (Organization)	Racial Composition (Context)
Portland	Christians for the Common Good	Political Advocacy	Evangelical-Mainline Protestant	Evangelical-Mainline-Secular	Majority White	Majority White
Portland	Neighborhood Partners	Community Development	Evangelical	Evangelical-Secular	White	Majority White
Atlanta	Peachtree Community Development Association	Community Development	Evangelical-Mainline-Black Protestant	Secular-Evangelical-Mainline-Black Protestant	Black / White	Majority Black
Los Angeles	Justice in the City / Together for Justice	Community Organizing	Evangelical / Multifaith	Multifaith / Secular	Multiracial	Majority Hispanic

in evangelical-identifying organizations and networks, and (2) self-identify as evangelical or express adherence to evangelical beliefs, practices, and relationship with God.[24] In the spirit of relational ethnography, it is the constellation of individuals, institutions, and social spaces in which these evangelical-identifying organizations are embedded—and not simply the organization itself—which constitute each of the "cases" under investigation.[25] Along with these central cases, I also collected significant—though less extensive— interview and ethnographic data at several other research sites which constitute a set of supplemental cases as depicted in Table A.2.

In addition to gathering extensive ethnographic data from each of these cases, I also conducted ninety-two in-depth interviews (with ninety individuals) ranging from one to three hours with key organizational staff and volunteers; neighborhood residents; community leaders; and organizational partners and opponents; intentionally sampling for diversity across race, gender, religion, and "strategic relocation" to allow for comparisons across these theoretically significant categories (Table A.3).[26]

Finally, along with ethnographic and interview data, I also collected and analyzed extensive print and digital organizational document data for the anchor organizations of each of my central cases, including annual reports and budgets; organizational mission statements and strategic planning documents; newsletters, brochures, and marketing materials; written transcripts of board meetings, staff meetings, and policy meetings; fundraising reports; donor and partner communications; legal documents and bylaws; internal memos, meeting reports, and monthly reports; newspaper articles, essays, blog entries, and thought pieces; recorded talks and PowerPoint presentations; along with other documents.

All of the central and most of the supplemental cases that constitute the empirical core of this study are introduced in the ethnographic vignettes of the book's Introduction. Below I provide an overview of each of the study's central and supplemental cases, which are described in greater detail at appropriate points throughout the book.

Central Cases

Peachtree Community Development Association (Atlanta, GA)

A pioneer in the "Christian community development" movement since its inception in the late 1970s,[27] Peachtree Community Development Association (PCDA) has evolved into an urban collective of distinct but related community organizations, ministries, nonprofits, and housing initiatives working to "create healthy places in the city where families flourish and the Shalom of God is present."[28] With approximately sixty staff members, fourteen divisions, and $6 million annual budget, PCDA is one of the largest Christian community development organizations in the United States. A multiracial Christian organization, PCDA works by invitation in economically disadvantaged neighborhoods, participating with residents in the work of "transforming distressed urban neighborhoods" according to three guiding principles: dignity, empowerment, and neighboring.[29] Over the course of its thirty-five-plus year history, PCDA has been invited by residents and neighborhood leaders to work in five disadvantaged neighborhoods in Atlanta. As Richard told a group of neighborhood leaders at one PCDA training event, "We only go where we're invited, and sometimes they kick us out."[30]

Peachtree Community Development Association has been working in its current neighborhood since 2001. Committed to "strategic relocation"—the intentional,

Table A.2 Supplemental Cases

Location	Anchor Organization	Organizational Type	Religious Composition (Organization)	Religious Composition (Partners)	Racial Composition (Organization)	Racial Composition (Context)
Portland	Serving the City	Public Service	Evangelical	Evangelical-Secular	Majority White	White / Multiracial
Portland	Healing Hands	Public Service	Evangelical	Evangelical-Secular	Majority White	White / Multiracial
Boston	Christian Social Justice Network	Advocacy / Awareness	Evangelical	Evangelical-Mainline-Secular	Majority White	Majority White
Boston	Neighborhood Solidarity	Community Organizing	Evangelical / Multifaith	Multifaith / Secular	Multiracial	Multiracial / Hispanic

Table A.3 Interview Respondent Characteristics

Location	Portland	Atlanta	Los Angeles	Boston	—
	39	30	14	7	
Religion	White Evangelical	Black Evangelical	Asian / Hispanic Evangelical	White Mainline Protestant	Other / Unknown
	50	10	6	8	16
Gender*	Male	Female	White Female	Female Person of Color	—
	48	42	26	16	
Race	White	Black	Asian / Hispanic	—	—
	63	19	8		
Strategic Relocation	Yes	No	—	—	—
	32	58			

* Gender identification based on open-ended self-categorization; no respondents identified as gender nonbinary or other.

invitation-based practice of moving into disadvantaged contexts in order to learn from and participate with residents in projects of social empowerment and transformation—dozens of Black and white individuals and families have put down deep roots in this predominantly African American neighborhood:[31] buying homes, sending their children to local public schools, participating in neighborhood association events, working in local businesses, and trying to be good neighbors. Through various PCDA-related programs and initiatives, they helped build a new neighborhood coffee shop and community center, family thrift store, bike repair shop, and coworking space employing neighborhood residents. PCDA-affiliated residents have also developed popular after school and summer programs for local youth, established a new multi-ethnic neighborhood church, and built or renovated over seventy neighborhood homes under various federal and private affordable home programs, opening new pathways to Black homeownership and cutting into the neighborhood's 25 percent stock of vacant properties.

The religious and racial composition of core Peachtree Community Development Association board, staff, and volunteers is diverse. White evangelicals are well-represented, as are evangelically identifying mainline and Black Protestants. PCDA works with a wide range of partner organizations and institutions, including a large network of evangelical, mainline, and Black Protestant churches, denominational bodies, local neighborhood associations, and city and federal government entities. The neighborhood in which PCDA currently works is predominately (over 80 percent) African American.

Justice in the City/Sunrise Community Church/Together for Justice (Los Angeles, CA)

Justice in the City is a twenty-plus year-old interdenominational evangelical nonprofit organization consisting of over seventy-five staff and forty interns living and working in disadvantaged urban shantytowns and neighborhoods across the globe—including three major US cities. The organization has an annual budget approaching $2 million through which it aims to participate in the "transform[ation] of urban poor communities" through church planting, community organizing, community and economic development, health care, political advocacy, and education programs in collaboration with local residents and community partners.[32]

Sunrise Community Church is a small, multiracial evangelical church located in a low-income, majority-Hispanic neighborhood in greater Los Angeles where a contingent of current and former Justice in the City staff and interns also dwell. Over 75 percent of Sunrise's regular attendees live within one mile of the church, having intentionally relocated from other—often more affluent and white—areas. In addition to being an active founding member in its broad-based community organizing network, the church launched a nonprofit organization that runs a popular after-school program and community garden among other initiatives.

Sunrise is a founding member of Together for Justice, an Industrial Areas Foundation (IAF)-affiliated broad-based community organizing coalition that has twenty member institutions, one full-time organizer, and an annual budget of $160,000.[33] Together for Justice has been involved in initiatives ranging from job creation and new worker education programs to sustained grassroots political actions for increased environmental and undocumented immigrant protections. Together for Justice is racially and religiously diverse, consisting of predominantly white, Asian, and Hispanic Catholic, evangelical, mainline Protestant, Jewish, and secular member institutions and leaders.

Neighborhood Partners (Portland, OR)

Neighborhood Partners is a small ($100,000 annual budget) community development organization based in southeast Portland, founded and staffed by white evangelicals—a director and three part-time staff volunteers—committed to "spiritual and social transformation":

> We do this by equipping and resourcing churches to engage in community partnerships
> ... with people of goodwill, agencies, nonprofits, and schools, to create sustained, positive change, socially and spiritually, in their neighborhoods.[34]

Neighborhood Partners works in the "other Portland"—the one that isn't featured on the hit show *Portlandia*—where residents complain about the city spending all its money on luxury bike routes and $10,000 solar-fueled self-compacting garbage cans downtown, while in the other Portland—where most people of color, immigrants, and working class whites live—residents live without access to basic amenities such as sidewalks, street lights, and clean, safe bus shelters.[35]

Neighborhood Partners practices and trains individuals and organizations—both secular and religious—in asset-based community development (ABCD), an approach to neighborhood change and sustainability popularized by John McKnight and colleagues.[36] Neighborhood Partners' regular day-long training workshops on ABCD methodology was reflected by the organization's full schedule of training events and workshops for secular nonprofit, government, and religious partners.

Neighborhood Partners has also supported and supervised several nonreligious AmeriCorps workers in disadvantaged neighborhoods nearby. While working with Neighborhood Partners, one of these AmeriCorps workers became the lead organizer of a grassroots neighborhood development initiative called Greenbush, whose success helped convince the city of Portland to invest millions of dollars in long-term incremental tax financing to support similar initiatives in other low-income neighborhoods across the city. Initially launched as a community-based policing response to a year-long spike in criminal activity culminating in several homicides, the Greenbush Initiative developed into a broad, grassroots collaboration among neighborhood residents, local businesses, churches, nonprofit agencies, and community police liaisons. It involves a range of activities including youth programs, gang outreach, community markets and art events, public safety initiatives, neighborhood visioning gatherings, and the construction of a new community meeting space.

Neighborhood Partners is also involved in additional programs and activities aimed at developing collaborative partnerships for grassroots community empowerment and transformation. These include helping facilitate the homeless outreach initiatives and free neighborhood medical clinics described in the Introduction, along with an intern program and service-learning class for local college students, an ABCD-based outreach program to low-income urban apartment dwellers, urban ministry training and experiences for out-of-town church youth groups, and regular "community listening" ventures in disadvantaged Portland neighborhoods. Neighborhood Partners works with evangelical churches, religious and secular non-profits, neighborhood associations, local colleges and universities, and residents of disadvantaged southeast Portland neighborhoods. While the Portland neighborhoods in which Neighborhood Partners works are more racially diverse than most in the city, the large majority of the organization's partners, donors, and volunteers are white.

Christians for the Common Good (Portland, OR)

Christians for the Common Good (CCG) focuses on educating and uniting Christians in support of common good and social justice-oriented public policy at the state level, sponsoring or cosponsoring state legislation on issues ranging from criminal justice reform and expanded health care coverage for children and low-income adults to increased environmental protections and predatory payday loan regulation. It is a relatively small operation, consisting of one full-time director, two part-time staff, and a $100,000 annual budget drawn from a mix of personal donations, church contributions, and foundation grants. Extremely active board members and volunteer policy committee members drawn from local churches supplement the efforts of organizational staff members to "seek God's justice and the common good in Oregon."[37]

Christians for the Common Good was founded by a small group of progressive-leaning evangelicals and mainline Protestants who in 2006 felt that "the current public and political face of Christianity has not represented [our] full reading of the Bible or [our] set of deeply held values,"[38] which "reach beyond traditional 'moral values' issues' to encompass 'care for the poor,' 'care for the sick,' and 'care for the environment.' "[39] While focused largely on mobilizing evangelical churches and organizations, mainline Protestant churches are more regular sources of funding—despite the organization having an active network of individual evangelical donors and volunteers, most of whom are younger than their mainline counterparts. In its early years the organization also received funding from secular progressives who shared the organization's legislative and advocacy priorities and were disgruntled with the presidency of George W. Bush and the Christian Right more generally.

While Christians for the Common Good describes itself as an ecumenical Christian organization, it was founded specifically to unite, educate, and engage evangelicals in political advocacy on behalf of the poor, the sick, and the oppressed in the name of "biblical justice."[40] Christians for the Common Good is an overwhelmingly white organization working in majority white contexts in Portland and greater Oregon. Organizational staff, board members, and policy committee members are a mix of mainline Protestant and progressive evangelicals. CCG has made some effort to engage Catholic, Black Protestant, and Hispanic Christian churches and organizations in their advocacy efforts, but to little effect. However, Christians for the Common Good does work with a wide range of secular, Christian, non-Christian, and interfaith groups and organizations in its advocacy efforts on behalf of "the poor, the sick, the environment, and the vulnerable."[41]

Supplemental Cases

Serving the City (Portland, OR)

Initiated by a group of pastors representing fifty evangelical churches in the greater Portland area, Serving the City began by asking the mayor of Portland how they could best mobilize the evangelical community to serve the city. Within months and at the mayor's request, Serving the City mobilized 26,000 volunteers from over 400 evangelical churches to participate in 278 city-designated volunteer projects, including public school maintenance and beautification projects, anti-hunger and health and wellness initiatives, services to the city's homeless population, and free meals and mentoring support for low-income students among others.[42] Originally conceived of as a one-time event, Serving the City has become an ongoing partnership that mobilizes over 25,000 volunteers annually from 500 evangelical churches to address a list of city-identified public concerns.

Neighborhood Solidarity (Boston, MA)

Neighborhood Solidarity—a hastily organized racially, religiously, and linguistically diverse coalition of faith and community leaders in East Boston—formed in opposition to a multimillion-dollar casino project and corporate lobbying campaign targeting East Boston neighborhood residents. A small, predominantly white group of evangelical young professionals who lived in East Boston joined the coalition and lent support through event planning and participation, postering and picketing, and social media campaigning among other avenues. Neighborhood Solidarity involved Catholic, Muslim, mainline and evangelical Protestant, Pentecostal, and religiously unaffiliated individuals, churches, businesses, neighborhood leaders, and community groups united in opposition to the casino project.

Healing Hands (Portland, OR)

Founded in 2005 by an evangelical pastor and a recent Bible college graduate, Healing Hands is a faith-based nonprofit organization that sponsors free one-day medical clinics led by coalitions of neighborhood churches across the city of Portland—almost all of them evangelical—by mobilizing volunteers and donations from local churches and businesses to provide free medical, dental, and chiropractic care to underinsured neighborhood residents. Healing Hands annually facilitates approximately twenty free one-day medical clinics involving 200 churches, 3,500 volunteers, and $475,000 of free medical services provided to over 4,500 people across the city.[43]

Christian Social Justice Network (Boston, MA)

Founded in 2006 by a multiracial group of evangelical and mainline Protestant Christians in their twenties and thirties, the Christian Social Justice Network (CSJN) describes itself as a "grassroots, ecumenical community of Christians seeking social justice as an expression of faith," one that "unites and mobilizes Christians to alleviate poverty and promote stewardship through personal, community, and policy change."[44] The group sponsors events and develops curriculum aimed at sharpening American Christians' awareness of, concern about, and personal financial investment in combating global and domestic poverty and economic inequality through enhanced charitable giving, lifestyle changes, policy advocacy, and "economic discipleship." Organizational initiatives have included organizing an ecumenical, multiracial group of Christian churches to promote passage of a fair trade resolution through Boston City Council; to hosting local conferences, learning opportunities, and advocacy events for diverse Christian congregations seeking to combat local and global poverty and economic inequality; to publishing an "economic discipleship" Bible study curriculum used by 40 groups with over 300 participants in its first several years—mostly "middle-class, college-educated Christians in their 20s and 30s"—who collectively donated $500,000 to "fight hunger, poverty and injustice at home and abroad in the name of Christ."[45]

Ethnographic Identity and Representation

Ethnographic identity is not fixed. The ethnographer's identification and relation to research participants during fieldwork depends on the shifting situations they find themselves in and shifting identities of the persons with whom they interact in the field.[46] My ethnographic identity shifted between insider and outsider depending on which people, organization, neighborhood, event, and interaction I found myself in. As an ecumenical Christian with evangelical-charismatic roots and extensive ethnographic and personal experience working with faith-based organizations similar to those in this book, I was often positioned as a relative insider with respect to organizational gatekeepers and staff despite having no prior relationship with any of the persons or organizations involved in the study, and despite my status as an outside observer whose participation was driven by academic research rather than personal commitments or the achievement of organizational goals.

I found this status to be an advantage for several reasons. First, because the multisite construction of my research object involved participant observation in communities across the United States, gaining the entrée and access necessary to gather valid triangulated data at each site was a challenge.[47] Time was of the essence; my relative insider status enabled me to quickly gain access and establish trust with key actors at each site. Second, my extensive experience in similar settings enabled me quickly grasp the communication styles, social practices, and complex organizational dynamics at each site. This allowed me to efficiently select settings and direct attention for effective participation observation, construct useful interview questions, find essential organizational document data, ask probing and verifying questions, and efficiently test tentative findings from internal and external data sources.

In many settings and situations, however, I was an outsider. A white man in his thirties from the upper Midwest, I was often a conspicuous outsider while living and working in East Boston, south and east Atlanta, Los Angeles and LA's inland empire, and some neighborhoods in north and southeast Portland. In my frequent ongoing interactions with Black, Hispanic, Asian, and white neighborhood residents, community leaders, and organizational partners and critics of the primary organizations with whom I conducted participant observation work, I was positioned, and positioned myself as, an outsider. This included both my racial and nonresident status as well as my connection to the organizations with whom I worked most closely while conducting ethnographic fieldwork.

I found this status, too, was often an advantage. During formal interviews and informal conversations in public work and private home settings, organizational staff, leaders, volunteers, and participants took advantage of opportunities to raise doubts and concerns about their work, to question organizational priorities or procedures, to process frustrations and failures, to point out areas of tension or struggle among organizational participants and partners, and to share their sustaining vision and inspiration for the frequently challenging work and lives they had committed themselves to. I was also welcomed and treated well, if sometimes curiously, by the overwhelming majority of residents of the neighborhoods in which I lived and worked, despite my status as a racial outsider and neighborhood newcomer. I found them eager to talk to someone about what they "really thought" of the people, activities, and organizations with whom I was conducting participant observation research. They generously shared their time and knowledge, and they frequently put me in contact with other community members who shared their concerns and perspectives whom I would not have otherwise met. Organizational partners were also quick to air their misgivings or disagreements, along with their respect or admiration, for the groups and organizations with whom I interacted most closely.

As a method of social enquiry, ethnography can produce valid, but not reliable in the technical scientific sense, information about the social world. Due to complexities of its temporal and embodied nature, no ethnography can ever be reliably "reproduced" under the precise conditions of initial data collection. The passing of time changes the fabric a community, the texture of interactions, the social structural context, the cultural symbols and meanings, even the demographic makeup of any given research site such that ethnographic "revisits" are better understood as a type of longitudinal data or robustness check than as a reliability retest.[48] The embodied nature of ethnography leads to similar conclusions. As Princeton sociologist and ethnographer Matthew Desmond succinctly notes about the inescapably personal and embodied nature of the ethnographer as research instrument,

> Everything about you—your race and gender, where and how you were raised, your temperament and disposition—can influence whom you meet, what is confided to you, what you are shown, and how you interpret what you see. My identity opened some doors and closed others. In the end, we can only do the best we can with who we are, paying close attention to the ways pieces of ourselves matter to the work while never losing sight of the most important questions.[49]

The embodied nature of ethnography interacts with multisite ethnography to advantage and disadvantage in this study. Because I was solely responsible for collecting and interpreting all ethnographic data at each field site, every interaction and setting was filtered through the lens of a single ethnographic perceiver. Thus, whatever filters or biases I carry with me as an ethnographer were active in equal measure and standard across field sites, in contrast to team-based multisite ethnographies involving different ethnographic researchers assigned to different sites, each with their own unique set of filters and biases at play. On the other hand, the embodied nature of ethnography limited the amount of data I could collect at each site in comparison to team-based multisite ethnographic projects, or in comparison to single-site ethnographic research projects.[50]

Finally, this book uses pseudonyms in place of the real names of individuals and organizations as a default. The use of pseudonyms has been a topic of debate among sociological ethnographers in recent years in light of increased critique and scrutiny of the veracity and reliability of ethnographic research, with some ethnographers calling for the end of pseudonymous research and others defending the practice.[51] A good bit of this debate has involved comparing sociological ethnography to journalism. There is a real and useful distinction, however, between sociological ethnography and journalism that accounts for their different approaches to writing, evidence, fact-checking, representation, and the use of sources.[52] Responsible sociological ethnography is no less committed to factual accuracy and veracity than responsible journalism. However, unlike journalism, sociological ethnography aims to contribute to general social scientific theory and understanding by focusing on the underlying processes, relations, social mechanisms, and interpretive meanings involved in their investigations. This creates a different set of objectives and ethical obligations—and a different set of relations to research participants, textual representation, and public audiences—than is true of journalists.

In addition to standard arguments for the protection of research participants' confidentiality while conducting sociological research, I elected from the beginning to use pseudonyms for a variety of reasons. First, the use of pseudonyms allows research participants to speak more freely, vulnerably, and, if they so desire, critically of the organizations and institutions of which they are a part than they would be likely to do if their real names and identities were on record. While this practice makes ethnographic revisits and reliability checks nearly impossible, it enables the collection of much more penetrating, comprehensive, and critical data than would typically be possible were the use of pseudonyms abandoned. The same argument holds true for organizations. While not always necessary or useful depending on one's research project, using organizational pseudonyms can allow for much greater organizational access and openness, yield more penetrating and accurate information, reduce incentives for inflationary organizational self-regard, and shield organizations willing to participate in the work of social scientific research and knowledge production from potential unintended consequences or negative harms that might potentially arise as a result of their participation. For these ethical, evidential, and social scientific reasons, all individual and organizational names in this study are pseudonyms unless stated otherwise.

Notes

Introduction

1. John 1:46, NIV
2. E.g., Bean 2014; Miller, Sargeant, and Flory 2013; Offutt 2015; Reynolds and Offutt 2013; Smilde 2007; Swartz 2012.
3. E.g., Emerson and Smith 2000; Ecklund 2008; Mulder, Ramos, and Marti 2017; Thomas 2021; Wong 2018.
4. Smith 2000:13.
5. Balmer 2017 et al.; Gorski 2020a; Gorski and Perry 2020; Marti 2019, 2020; Whitehead et al. 2018; Whitehead and Perry 2020.
6. Markofski 2015a; Gorski and Perry 2020; Whitehead and Perry 2020.
7. Bielo 2011; Markofski 2015a; Marti and Ganiel 2014; Sparks et al. 2014.
8. Campolo 2008; Swartz 2012; Wallis 2005.
9. Lindsay 2007; Gasaway 2014.
10. Ecklund 2008; Harper 2008; Kim 2004, 2006; Mulder, Ramos, and Marti 2017; Wong 2018.
11. NAE stands for the National Association of Evangelicals; *Christianity Today* is the flagship evangelical periodical founded by Billy Graham and associates.
12. Markofski 2015a:143–144.
13. On ethical democracy, see Wood 2002; Wood and Fulton 2015; Markofski 2015b; and Chapter 2.
14. Markofski 2018b.
15. Arsenault 2013a; Morrison 2014.
16. Arsenault 2013b, 2013d, 2013e; Seelye 2013; Kamp 2013.
17. Arsenault 2013c, 2013e; Seelye 2013.
18. Arsenault 2013a, 2013d, 2013e.
19. Arsenault 2013e.
20. Arsenault 2013f.
21. The central selling point of the East Boston-Revere casino project was the promise of 4,000 new jobs for the community, along with increased tax revenue and mitigation agreements to improve roads, address increased traffic flow, and support popular neighborhood charities such as the local Boys and Girls Club.
22. Sheppard 2014.
23. Arsenault 2013e; Jonas 2013; Arsenault 2014; Arsenault and Estes 2014.
24. Pending the outcome of litigation: the casino development bidding process generated a barrage of lawsuits against the Massachusetts Gaming Commission, the Massachusetts Bay Transit Authority (MBTA), and various casino developers and city officials (Pyles 2014; Dumcius 2015; Arsenault 2015).

25. Pineo 2013.
26. Arsenault 2013a; Pineo 2013; Steger and Steger 2014.
27. Reilly 2013.
28. Pineo 2013.
29. Pineo 2013.
30. Sheppard 2014.
31. Gardner 2011.
32. Testa 2011; Roberts-Fronk and Engdahl 2011.
33. Rodriguez 2012.
34. Rodriguez 2012.
35. E.g., Patillo 2008, 2013.
36. On the paradoxical simultaneous under-policing and over-policing of low-income Black and Latino neighborhoods, see for example Rios 2011.
37. Café mission statement and Oldenburg 1989; see also Ewoodzie 2021; Putnam 2000; and Sampson et al. 1997, 1999, 2002.
38. E.g., Corbett and Fikkert 2014; Lupton 2011; Markofski 2015a; Ewoodzie 2021.
39. 2014 Annual Report.
40. Healing Hands brochure, n.d.
41. Mesh 2009.
42. Rios 2011.
43. Harris 2011.
44. Harris 2011.
45. Markofski 2015b; Mesh 2009.
46. On social reflexivity, see Lichterman 2005; Markofski 2019; and below.
47. See the Appendix for a full description of the organizations, cases, and methodological considerations that form the empirical substrate of this book's central arguments.
48. E.g., Markofski 2015a; Steensland and Goff 2013.
49. E.g., Lichterman 2005; Markofski 2019.
50. In addition to its obvious audiences, this book also engages central topics and research in political and democratic theory, political theology and ecclesiological ethnography, urban sociology, race and ethnicity, gender and sexuality, sociological theory, and ethnographic methodology.
51. Collins 1986, 2019.
52. Abbott 2016; Brubaker 2015; Collins 2019; Fiel 2021; Go 2021; Monk 2022; Robinson 2000; Tilly 1998.
53. Anderson 2010; Emirbayer and Desmond 2015; Markofski 2015b; Wood 2002.
54. Table 3.3.
55. Markofski, Fulton, and Wood 2020.
56. Lichterman 2005; Markofski 2019.

Chapter 1

1. Wright 2010:46.
2. Cf., Acts 10:34–35; Romans 2:11; Galatians 3:26–28.

3. As Shane Claiborne quips in *The Irresistible Revolution*, "People do not get crucified for charity. People are crucified for living out a love that disrupts the social order, that calls forth a new world. People are not crucified for helping poor people. They are crucified for joining them" (2006:129).

4. E.g., Harper 2016.

5. Balmer et al. 2017; Gorski 2020a, 2017; Marti 2020; Whitehead et al. 2018; Whitehead and Perry 2020.

6. Bean and Martinez 2014; Coley 2018; Burke 2014; Gallagher 2003, 2004.

7. On dominant and dominated positions in the American evangelical field, see Markofski 2015a.

8. Whitehead and Perry 2020; Whitehead, Baker, and Perry 2018; see also Gorski 2017, 2020a; Marti 2020.

9. Bean and Martinez 2014; Coley 2018; Markofski 2015a; Moon, Tobin, and Sumerau 2019.

10. Dreher 2017; Markofski 2015b; on evangelicalism prioritization, see Markofski 2015a:182–183.

11. Markofski, Fulton, and Wood 2020.

12. Dewey 1988 [1927].

13. Markofski 2019.

14. Aristotle 1980 [1925]; Plato 1991.

15. Locke 1988 [1698]; Rousseau 1997.

16. Rawls 1971, 1995; Walzer 1983.

17. Doering 1994.

18. MacIntyre 1988.

19. Bretherton 2015 and Zaman 2004.

20. Braunstein 2017; Bretherton 2015; Stout 2010:34–44.

21. Cf. "Vote Common Good" n.d., "New Evangelical Partnership for the Common Good, About Us" n.d., Pally 2011; Skillen 1994; Slade et al. 2013.

22. Barber 2016; Harper 2016; Keller and Inazu 2020; Meador 2019; Wallis 2014.

23. Mouw 2016; Volf 2011, 2015.

24. Bretherton 2015:307n16; see also Volf 2011 and Bretherton 2019.

25. Thurman 1971.

26. 2.11.12 fieldnotes.

27. 2007 Vision Statement.

28. 2007 Board Retreat Minutes.

29. Alexander 2006; Anderson 2010; Bretherton 2015; Dahl 1989; Stears 2010; Young 2011.

30. E.g., Young 2011 and below.

31. Mouffe 2013.

32. Alexander 2006; Habermas 1991.

33. Alexander 2006; Hunter 2010.

34. Catholic Church and McDonagh 2016:I.23; see also Matthew 5:45.

35. Catholic Church and McDonagh 2016: chapter One, I.25.

36. Catholic Church and McDonagh 2016:VI.54.

37. Catholic Church and McDonagh 2016:VI.53.

38. On the difference between particularist and exclusivist modes of public religion, see Markofski, Fulton, and Wood 2020. On varieties of religious and political exclusivism, see Volf 2015:137–160.

39. Catholic Church and McDonagh 2016: Chapter 4, IV.156; see also *Caritas in Veritate*.

40. Catholic Church and McDonagh 2016: Chapter 4, IV.157–158.

41. Rawls 1985:42–43:139.

42. Rawls 1971:14–15, 91.

43. See for example, the biblical book of James and the Hebrew prophetic tradition of Isaiah, Micah, Jeremiah, etc.

44. Note also the universal in each instance is motivated by different underlying principles—liberal rationalism on the one hand and scripture or religious tradition on the other.

45. Hussain 2018.

46. Hussain 2018.

47. Cohen 1986, 2009; Habermas 1992; Rawls 1971.

48. Dillon 1999, 2010; Habermas 1992; Rawls 1971.

49. Benhabib 1992, 2006; Fraser 1992, 1995; Mahmood 2015; Neuhaus 1984; Salomon 2017; Young 2011.

50. Anderson 2010; Young 2011.

51. Mahmood 2015.

52. Fraser 1995; Young 2011.

53. Neuhaus 1984; Habermas 2006, 2008; Volf 2011, 2015.

54. Bretherton 2015:307n15, 16; see also Bretherton 2010. On "ethical democracy" and faith-based community organizing, see Wood 2002; Wood and Fulton 2015; Markofski 2015b and below. On democratic experimentalism and the American pragmatist tradition, see Bohman 2013; Dorf and Sabel 1998 and below.

55. Wood and Fulton 2015.

56. Bretherton 2015; Stout 2010.

57. On the broader field of faith-based or broad-based community organizing, see Wood and Fulton 2015.

58. Bretherton 2015:86; see also Stout 2010:34–44.

59. On social movement frames, see Benford and Snow 2000. On "deep difference," see Brubaker 2015 and Inazu 2016.

60. Elgot quoted in Bretherton 2015:89.

61. Bretherton 2015:83.

62. Bretherton 2015:85.

63. Reflecting on London Citizens and the grassroots democratic organizing tradition represented by Saul Alinsky and the IAF, theologian and ecclesial ethnographer Luke Bretherton distinguishes between two "interrelated and symbiotic forms of civic life: a hospitable politics and the politics of a common life," in which the tradition of broad-based community organizing practiced by the IAF, Faith in Action, and others represents the latter (Bretherton 2015:9; see also p.101, 307n16). In speaking of a "faithful form of secularity," Bretherton means to evoke developments in "post-secular" philosophical and theological discourse—which build on the post-secular

framework of German social philosopher Jurgen Habermas—in which "'religion' and 'secular' politics . . . are now seen as intertwined, both in theory and in practice" (Bretherton 2015:8–9; see also Habermas 2006, 2008; Sigurdson 2010). On Bretherton's accounting, "Both a hospitable and a common life politics can constitute performances of democratic citizenship and faithful secularity" (Bretherton 2015:9; see also p.307n16).

64. Bretherton 2015:306n5, 307:n16, 188, 190–192, 200.

65. Bretherton 2015:15 (and n40); see also Dewey 1988 [1927].

66. Bretherton 2015:85; see also 84–86, 94–96.

67. Inazu 2016:132; see also 15, 141n1.

68. Inazu 2016:131.

69. On arbitrary domination as a violation of democratic principles, see Stout 2010:141–143. On the "tyranny of the majority," see Tocqueville 1966 [1835/1840].

70. "Those relationships," Inazu recognizes, "are not always possible—sometimes the best we can do is coexist. But in many cases, we can work together toward common ground in spite of our differences. These common efforts may not actually bridge our ideological differences—we may remain uncompromising or unchanged in our own views. That's not to say that either compromise or change is impossible. But it does suggest that meaningful relationships for the sake of shared interests do not depend on either one" (Inazu 2016:12, 116–124). See also Stout 2010.

71. Bretherton 2015:96. On civic action, see Lichterman and Eliasoph 2014. On "re-neighboring" and strategic relocation, see Chapter 2.

72. Bretherton 2015:95. There is, of course, no guarantee it *will* emerge, and the possibility of shared stories of belonging and shared social and political life across difference has real limits. Even if they obtain, they will coexist alongside stories of belonging and normative frames for social and political that are decidedly *not* shared, and likely never shall be so. See also Sparks et al. 2014 and the "new parish" movement in the United States.

73. Indeed, attending to the spatial dimension of a politics of common goods—focused on the preservation, inclusive access, equitable organization, and creative expansion of "public spaces" against the onslaught of neoliberal privatization and economic commodification—is a hallmark of emerging social movements and theories of the "commons" across Europe, Latin America, and beyond (Bretherton 2015:156–157; Stavrides and Verlic 2016:49–50. See also Brown 2017; Hardt and Negri 2009, 2012). These commons-based theories and movements share affinity with a long tradition of sociological research and advocacy that centers civic action, civil society, and the public sphere as privileged sites of democratic practice and social empowerment in the face of ever-growing threats to human freedom and flourishing from late modern economic and political behemoths (Alexander 2006; Emirbayer and Noble 2013; Lichterman and Eliasoph 2014; Wright 2010). Against the insatiable demands of state and market, "public sociology" points to civil society as a primary site and source of social solidarity and democratic empowerment—albeit a frequently divided and hierarchical one (Burawoy 2005; Markofski 2015b; Stavrides and Verlic 2016:52; Wright 2010).

New theories and practices of "commoning"—activities and relationships through which diverse citizens and movements "make the commons" together (Hardt and Negri 2012:105–106; see also Hardt and Negri 2009:250–260)—highlight the importance of inclusive "spaces of commoning" in efforts to "sustain common wealth through democratic participation" (Baldauf et al. 2016; Hardt and Negri 2012:105–106). Space is conceptualized here in simultaneously social-relational and concrete-physical terms: referring to both a "network of relations . . . formed by social interactions" and "concrete places in which rules of use are always contested" (Stavrides and Verlic 2016:49–50; on purportedly objective or universal rules that exclude marginalized actors from full participation in the public sphere, see for example Fraser 1992). In these movements, acts of "commoning" or making the commons—such, as "the ability to create social bonds with each other," to "communicate through differences," and to build "capacity for democratic political action"— are seen to be "foundational and necessary for constituting a democratic society based on open sharing of the common" (Hardt and Negri 2012:105–106). Such open sharing requires recognition of both commonality and difference: "Commoning should not be considered as a homogenizing set of social practices and institutions but, on the contrary, as the making of shared worlds crafted by people who decide to explore common grounds exactly because they are different and difference matters" (Stavrides and Verlic 2016:52).

Note the making of shared worlds through "commoning" is articulated here as "craft," the application of practical intelligence to the pursuit of common goods and public problem-solving through any number of activities, including what Dewey (1988 [1929]) calls the "practical arts." "Commoners" make the commons together through community organizing and community development; through public education and public service; through cooperative businesses and crowd-sourced local start-ups; through nonprofit health centers and public media ventures; through art and architecture, music and theater; through social and technological innovation; through urban communes and rural off-grid intentional communities; through scientific research and open-access knowledge dissemination; through municipal movements and utopian encampments; through theatrical performances of politics and rituals of democracy; that is, through any activity oriented to the pursuit of goods in common (Hardt and Negri 2012:105; see also Alexander 2004; Bretherton 2015:156–168; and Burton et al. 2016). Note also the recognition and necessity of "encounter" across difference in creating a commons that does not reduce, exclude, homogenize, suppress, or marginalize dissenting voices or minority perspectives and persons (Hardt and Negri 2009:252; see also Stavrides and Verlic 2016 and chapter 2 below. On the difficulty of constructing an inclusive "we" that does not exclude an outside "they," see for example Stavrides and Verlic 2016:50–52; Alexander 2006; and Mouffe 2013).

74. Inazu 2016:120.

75. On the scalability of various local or place-based practices of democratic organizing, see for example Wood and Fulton 2015 and Stout 2010. On nations as "imagined communities," see Anderson 1983.

76. Sociological ideal types are empirically based analytic concepts that accentuate logico-typical features of a given set of empirical phenomena (e.g., Weber 1949 [1904]).

77. Rah 2009.

78. Markofski, Fulton, and Wood 2020.

79. Markofski 2015a; Smith 1998.

80. Lindsay 2007; Merritt 2016.

81. Merritt 2016.

82. Lindsay 2007:221.

83. Merritt 2016.

84. Lindsay 2007: back cover.

85. Lindsay quoted in Merritt 2016.

86. Balmer et al. 2017; Merritt 2016; Stetzer 2016; Wehner 2016, 2020.

87. Markofski, Fulton, and Wood 2020.

88. Emirbayer and Desmond 2015:296–301.

89. Alexander 2006; Appiah 2006; Benhabib 2006; Emirbayer and Desmond 2015; Kymlicka 1996; Taylor 1994; Young 2011.

90. Emirbayer and Desmond 2015:276.

91. Lindsay 2007:221, 310.

92. Lightly, as in facile universalist, ironic, detached cosmopolitanism or "color-blind" approaches to difference; or destructively, as in fascist, totalitarian, or virulent expressions of xenophobic ethnoracial or religious nationalism.

93. As Green (2013) notes, populist evangelicals diverge from ideologically conservative Christian Right evangelicals in their support for government action to reduce economic hardship, address perceived social problems, oppose narrowly self-interested foreign policy, and protect the environment.

94. Gorski 2020a; but see Markofski in Balmer et al. 2017.

95. Campolo 2008; Gasaway 2014; Pally 2011.

96. Gasaway quoted in Miller October 27, 2015; see also Balmer December 1, 2019; Gasaway 2014; Swartz 2012.

97. Wallis quoted in Lampman March 12, 2008; Campolo 2008:15–17; Harper 2008; Sider January 18, 2020.

98. Markofski 2015a; Gasaway 2014; Swartz 2012.

99. Bean and Martinez 2014; Coley 2018; Markofski 2015a.

100. Campolo 2008.

101. Campolo 2008:15.

102. Campolo 2008; Claiborne 2006; Harper 2008, 2016.

103. Steensland and Goff 2013.

104. "Black Americans who are Evangelical Protestants" n.d., Cox and Jones 2012; Edwards 2016, "Latinos who are Evangelical Protestants" n.d.; Wong 2015, November 1, 2018.

105. E.g., Bretherton 2015:188; Wallis 2005.

106. Alexander 2006; Benhabib 2006; Habermas 2008:24–26; Kymlicka 1996; Taylor 1994; Young 2011.

107. Alexander 2006; Young 2011.

108. Alexander 2006; Anderson 2010:1–2,110,188,190; Habermas 2008; Young 2011.

109. Emirbayer and Desmond 2015:301.

110. Anderson 2010:1. For an evangelical version of the "rise of the diversity expert," see Marti and Emerson 2013.

111. Or any groups for that matter.

112. Emirbayer and Desmond 2015:300; Habermas 2008:25–27; Taylor 1994. Nancy Fraser solves this problem arbitrarily by fiat, granting legitimacy only to those groups who affirm rights "of the sort usually championed by left-wing liberals" (1995:70fn2), which is really no solution at all.

113. Sullivan quoted in Emirbayer and Desmond 2015:301. See also Brubaker 2015; Hunter and Wolfe 2006; and Inazu 2016.

114. On the necessity of subjecting all types of majority and minority persons and groups to mutual democratic deliberation and critique, see Anderson 2010; Emirbayer and Desmond 2015; Habermas 2008; Wood and Fulton 2015:4–10.

115. Tilly 1998; see also Anderson 2010; Brubaker 2015; Fraser 1995; Kymlicka 1996; Wood and Fulton 2015. On the Black evangelical argument for "reconciliation, relocation, and redistribution," see Perkins 2007.

116. Markofski 2015a.

117. Jenkins 2011; Miller 2013; Offutt 2015; Rah 2009; Reynolds and Offutt 2013; Swartz 2013.

118. Cox and Jones 2017. Using a slightly different denomination-based coding scheme, Pew Research Center data puts the number of white evangelicals at 76 percent, Hispanic evangelicals at 11 percent, Black evangelicals at 6 percent, Asian evangelicals at 2 percent, and 5 percent as mixed or other race (Masci and Cox 2018). For similar data using National Association of Evangelical (NAE) criteria for defining evangelical, see Earls 2016.

119. Wong 2018:6.

120. Cox and Jones 2017; see also Masci and Smith 2018.

121. Cox and Jones 2017; see also Masci and Smith 2018; Moon November 13, 2014; Wong 2018.

122. Moon November 13, 2014; Lehman and Sherkat 2018; Shelton and Cobb 2018; Sherkat 2014; Steensland et al. 2000, 2018; Woodberry et al. 2012.

123. Shelton and Cobb 2018:737.

124. Masci and Smith 2018; Moon 2014.

125. Martinez and Smith 2016.

126. Steensland quoted in Moon 2014.

127. Markofski 2015a; Markofski 2018.

128. Wong 2018; Cox and Jones 2017; Martinez and Smith 2018; Masci and Smith 2016, 2018.

129. Cox and Jones 2017.

130. Greeley and Hout 2006; Green 2013; Markofski 2018b.

131. Markofski 2015b.

132. See the Appendix and Markofski 2015b.

133. Addams 2002 [1902]; Dewey 1988 [1939]; Gorski 2017.
134. Addams 2002 [1902]:7–8.
135. Addams 2002 [1902]:7–8 Or, as Dewey put it, "Democracy is more than a form of government. It is primarily a mode of associated living, a conjoint communicated experience" 1980 [1916]:87.
136. Wood and Fulton 2015:8.
137. Anderson 2010:89 and Anderson 2006.
138. See discussion of pluralism and agonistic democracy below.
139. Wood and Fulton 2015:8.
140. While Tocqueville and his later followers called attention to how civic associations and democratic "mores" or "habits of the heart" make democracy possible (Tocqueville 1966 [1835/40]:287; see also Bellah 1996; Perrin 2014; Putnam 1993, 2000), the civic and religious republican traditions reaching back through the American founders to ancient Hebrew and Greek sources likewise call attention to the necessity of an active, engaged, self-governing, politically educated and organized citizenry as bulwark against political oppression and tyranny (Alexander 2006:45; Bush 2015; Cooper 2016 [1892]; Gorski 2017; Stout 2010).
141. Dewey 1980 [1916]:376; Gorski 2017. Critics would argue that it is the interests and ideological constructions of powerful elites which govern law, politics, and policy in real world democracies, rather than the moral and cultural characteristics of ordinary citizens and civic institutions. A critical pragmatist approach to democratic theorizing must take account of both (cf., Emirbayer and Schneiderhan 2012).
142. Alexander 2006:4,37; see also 39–46.
143. Alexander 2006:13–22, 398–402.
144. Alexander 2006:4.
145. Alexander 2006:9; see also Cooper 2016 [1892].
146. Alexander 2006:4.
147. Alexander 2006:42. Of course, Alexander's particular understanding of the civil sphere and the solidaristic "structures of feeling" (43, 70) on which it rests diverges significantly from pragmatist conceptualizations of democracy in other ways (such as the stability and binary construction of democracy's civic codes or the role of abstract principles versus practical experience for generating effective democratic solidarity and problem-solving ability), and the extent to which either Alexander or the pragmatists accomplish their task is a matter of considerable debate.
148. Wright 2010; see also Fung and Wright 2003. In *Envisioning Real Utopias*, Wright discusses micro-, meso-, and macro-level instantiations of "real utopian" practices and institutional arrangements in government, economy, and civil society. On the "peculiar convergence" of Wright's (Marxian) and Alexander's (Durkheimian) democratic imaginary, see Emirbayer and Noble 2013.
149. Wood 2001:183–185; see also Markofski 2015b; Stout 2010; and Wood and Fulton 2015. Some organizing coalitions (such as the Alinsky-founded Industrial Areas Foundation, or IAF) prefer the term broad-based community organizing (BBCO) because of the growing involvement of non-religious organizations (such as public school teachers and labor unions) in their work; others (such as Faith in Action

(formerly PICO)), retain the traditional faith-based community organizing (FBCO) designation to acknowledge the centrality of religious organizations and inspiration in the history and current practice of this style of grassroots democratic organizing (Stout 2010; Warren 2001; Wood and Fulton 2015).

150. Seigfried in Addams 2002 [1902]:ix.

151. Wood 2001; Stout 2010.

152. Wood and Fulton 2015:95; see also Wood 2001:183–184 and Stout 2010.

153. Wood 2001:184. On the rare racial and socioeconomic diversity of the field of faith-based community organizing compared to other public and political institutions in the United States, see Wood and Fulton 2015.

154. Whimster 2004; Wood 2001:183–194. On the "enlightened" self-interest ("self-interest properly understood") that incorporates collective/communal as well as individual interests, see Tocqueville 1966 [1835/1840]:525–529.

155. Wood 2001:186,189.

156. Bretherton 2015; Stout 2010; Wood 2001:183–194; Wood and Fulton 2015.

157. Wood and Fulton 2015; see also Anderson 2010 and Young 2011

158. Anderson 2010; Benhabib 1992, 2002; Fraser 1992; Kymlicka 1996; Taylor 1994; Young 2011.

159. Alexander 2006; Anderson 2010; Benhabib 2002; Habermas 2008.

160. Emirbayer and Desmond 2015:301–307; see also Anderson 2010 and Cooper 1892. On "color-blind racism," see for example Bonilla-Silva 2003.

161. Anderson 2010:2, 110, 177–191; see also Emirbayer and Desmond 2012, 2015.

162. Habermas 2008:29 and Habermas 2006:4.

163. Anderson 2010; Brubaker 2015; Inazu 2016; Tilly 1998.

164. Alexander 2006; Anderson 2006, 2010; Habermas 2006, 2008. Even Iris Marion Young (2011:188–189), strong multiculturalist that she was, recognized the necessity of forging collaborations and coalitions across difference in shared pursuit of rights and goods beyond narrow group boundaries and self-interest.

165. Wood 2001:184–185, 192–193; Wood and Fulton 2015:139; Alexander 2006, 2010; Bretherton 2015:158–173; Emirbayer and Desmond 2015:305–306; Fraser 1992; Markofski 2019; Stout 2010:210–234; Young 2011.

166. Alexander 2006:409.

167. Anderson 2010:190; see also 95–102.

168. Anderson 2010:98. Whether congressional hearings in the contemporary United States are typified by "relatively sober talk" of the rational-deliberative variety is another matter.

169. Anderson 2010:98 and Anderson 2006.

170. Mouffe 2013; see also Connolly 1991, 2005; Honig 1993. Stephen White (personal communication, March 24, 2020) objects to my turn to Mouffe, rather than Connolly or Honig, as an exemplar of agonism, on the grounds that Mouffe represents an "imperializing" version of agonism (adopted from Carl Schmitt's friend/enemy distinction) that demonstrates insufficient grounding in democratic norms of equality and justice (White 2021). I find Mouffe's reconstruction of Schmitt less problematic and more committed to democratic norms of justice than does White. For example, White sees Donald Trump's trampling of democratic norms as a natural outgrowth

of Mouffe's (and especially, Schmitt's) "imperializing" version of agonism; I see it rather as an example of just the sort of antipluralist, norm-destroying "antagonistic" treatment of political "enemies" that Mouffe's formulation of agonism warns against. Like White, my incorporation of agonism as a component of ethical democracy is intended to supplement, rather than replace, Habermasian theories of democratic deliberation and justice (cf. Chapter 6); unlike White's more fine-grained analysis, my incorporation of agonism is general and makes no distinction between Mouffe's variety and others.

171. Mouffe 2013:XII. On the relationship between democratic community organizing and agonistic pluralism, see Bretherton 2015:14–15, 191–192, 214–216, 388n142. On the benefits of religious and agonistic pluralism for American democracy, see Wuthnow 2021.

172. Mouffe 2013; Alexander 2006.

173. Mouffe 2013: 6–7. And, I would add, with democratic norms of equality and justice (e.g., Alexander 2006; Habermas 2006; White 2021).

174. Mouffe 2013: 7.

175. Mouffe 2013: 6–7. Here, Mouffe approaches White's (2021) insistence on the "moral equality of voice" as a necessary feature or supplement to agonistic theories of democracy.

176. Inazu 2016; Hunter 1994, 2010.

177. Dillon 2010; Habermas 2006.

178. Mouffe 2013:8.

179. E.g., Brubaker 2015; Hunter and Wolfe 2006.

180. On the other hand, given the durable human propensity to turn arbitrary differences and honest disagreements into hierarchical distinctions and full-blown acts of war, perhaps it is not so difficult to imagine after all.

181. Mouffe 2013:8.

182. Habermas 2006:10; see also Markofski 2019.

183. With respect to its handling of "deep difference," Inazu's (2016) construction of "confident pluralism" is, in this regard, preferable to Mouffe's conceptualization of pluralism, as is the post-secular Habermas (2006). See also Bretherton 2015:214–216 and Wuthnow 2021.

184. Alexander 2006:43.

185. Stout 2010:9.

186. Wood and Fulton 2015:1; see also Stout 2010:240–259.

187. Brown 2017; Habermas 1998; Honig 2017; Stout 2010.

188. Gorski 2017:24–26; see also Anderson 2010; Brubaker 2015; Sharkey 2013; Stout 2010:134–147.

189. DuBois 1999:78–92; Stout 2010:6–14, 240–259; Tucker 1978.

190. Stout 2010; Wright 2010; Dreher 2017. On the refusal of representative democracy and temptation to opt-out of actually existing democracy given its myriad flaws, see for example Markofski 2015a:215–224; Mouffe 2013:XVI; and practitioners and theorists of the Italian Autonomia movement, for example.

191. Markofski 2019; Markofski, Fulton, and Wood 2020; Marsden 2014:151–178; see also Chapters 4 and 6.

192. E.g., Markofski 2015a:194–224, 2019; Pally 2011.
193. Gorski 2017:17; Gorski and Altinordu 2008.
194. E.g., Harper 2016; Mouw 2016; Pally 2011; "Uncommon God, Common Good" n.d.; Volf 2011, 2015; Wolterstorff 2010.
195. "National Association of Evangelicals, About Us" n.d.; "New Evangelical Partnership for the Common Good, About Us" n.d.
196. Mouw 2016.
197. Slade et al. 2013.
198. Wallis 2014.
199. Marsden 2014:170; see also Mouw 2011, 2016; Seiple 2018; Skillen 1994.
200. "Center for Public Justice, About the Center" (n.d.).
201. Pally 2011; see also Harper 2008; Keller and Inazu 2020; Markofski 2015a; Steensland and Goff 2013.
202. Bretherton 2015:9, 2010, 2019.
203. Bretherton 2015:9; see also 2015:306n5, 307n16, 17; Bretherton 2010:18–19; Bretherton 2019.
204. Volf 2011:xvii; see also 119–138 and Volf 2015:137–160.
205. Volf 2011:xvi, 144.
206. Volf 2011:xvii.
207. Volf 2011:145.
208. Marsden 1997:45–46.
209. Bretherton 2015:9.
210. My argument affirms pragmatist antifoundationalism with respect to democratic politics and the necessity of a pluralistic interpretation of the common good(s) and public life; it does not affirm pragmatist antifoundationalism in epistemology or ethics per se (nor, in resonance with Gorski's (2017) construction of "living tradition" and the simultaneously secular and religious roots of the American democratic project, is my argument strictly antitraditionalist or ahistorical).
211. Marsden 1997:45.
212. James quoted in Marsden 1997:46.
213. Marsden 1997:46.
214. Marsden 1997:46. It is certainly true, as Phil Gorski notes concerning Dewey's often intemperate statements on the subject, Dewey was a fierce critic of traditional religion who had little sympathy for traditionally religious persons or communities (Phil Gorski, "Philosophy without Ontology? Pragmatism and 'Metaphysics' in Dewey and Putnam," Pragmatism and Sociology Conference, August 21, 2015). See also Marsden 2014:151–178. In this, Marsden's views are similar to Bretherton 2015, 2019; Volf 2011, 2015; Wolterstorff 2010; Neuhaus 1984; and even Habermas 2006, 2008. See also Markofski 2019 and Chapters 4 and 6.
215. Dewey 1934.
216. Marsden 1997:46.
217. Cf. Habermas 2006, 2008; and Chapter 6.
218. Lichterman 2005:15, 45, 52–55; Lichterman and Reed 2015. Lichterman's definition of social reflexivity draws heavily on his own prior work with Nina Eliasoph

on how culture is expressed through the customs and habits of group interaction. In Lichterman's conceptualization, social reflexivity is a matter of collective discursive practice in group settings, with a particular focus on how a group's communicative practices reveal implicit customs regarding the boundaries, bonds, and speech norms that define membership in a group and its relation to outsiders (Lichterman 2005:54).

219. Lichterman 2005:15.

220. Lichterman 2005:45.

221. Lichterman 2005:42–52; Putnam 1993, 2000.

222. Lichterman 2005; Markofski 2019. My expanded definition of social reflexivity incorporates Lichterman's original conceptualization as a subset of social reflexivity—call it *collective communicative reflexivity*—which focuses on the practice of socially reflexive communication in groups. Whereas Lichterman's (2005) formulation foregrounds communicative and collective practices (cf. Lichterman and Reed 2015), my formulation involves both cognitive and communicative habits observable at the individual and group level.

223. E.g., Dewey 1988 [1927]:147; Addams 2002 [1902]; and Chapter 6.

224. On the rooted revisability and dynamism of living "traditions," see Gorski 2017:4–7.

225. Smith 2011.

226. Locke 1988 [1689]; "United States Declaration of Independence," 1776; "Universal Declaration of Human Rights," 1948.

227. Sen 1999; Nussbawm 2000.

228. Smith 2015; Volf 2015; Wright 2010.

229. In keeping with pragmatist theories of action, the pragmatic postsecular pluralist conception of ethical democracy described here does not distinguish formally between process and outcome or means and ends; rather, both processes (means, procedures, or "equal opportunity") and outcomes (ends, consequences, or "equality of welfare or resources") must be evaluated with respect to democratic ideals (Sen 1980; Roemer 1998).

230. Hunter 2010; Stout 2010; Tocqueville 1966 [1835/1840].

231. MacIntyre 1988.

232. Niebuhr quoted in Inazu 2016:33.

233. On the inevitability of conflict over divergent perspectives on the "sacred" and "horrendous" in democratic life, see for example Stout 2010:118, 210–234, 317n102, 319n110; and Hunter and Wolfe 2006.

Chapter 2

1. Patterson 1997.

2. Anderson 2010. By "directly tests," I mean to invoke a critical pragmatist, rather than positivist, understanding of scientific and practical-democratic learning (e.g., Burawoy 1998; Dewey 1988 [1929]).

3. Marsh 2005; Perkins 2007; Slade et al. 2013.

4. This chapter focuses more on the observed practices and interactions side of the coin; Chapter 5 focuses more on the beliefs side of the coin.

5. Lichterman 2005; Lichterman et al. 2009; Markofski 2019.

6. Bonilla-Silva 2004; Tran 2021.

7. Lichterman 2012.

8. The house and its occupants are discussed further in Chapter 3's section on "gentrification with justice."

9. July 2012 neighborhood association minutes.

10. cf., Duncan and Magnuson 2005; Duncan et al. 2017; Edin and Shaefer 2015; Sharkey 2013.

11. I describe a related director's meeting experience in Chapter 6.

12. Mervosh 2021.

13. Anderson 2010; see also Emirbayer and Desmond 2015.

14. Anderson 2010:21.

15. Anderson 2010:16; see also Emirbayer and Desmond 2015; Tilly 1998; Young 2011. An even more fully relational theory of group inequality would go beyond Anderson's definition of relationality as "processes of interactions" to include non-phenomenologically realized "structures of positions" as well (e.g., Bourdieu and Wacquant 1992).

16. Tilly 1998; see also Brubaker 2015.

17. That is, according to both nonideal political theorizing and empirical social-scientific evidence.

18. Anderson (2010). On assimilation and critical whiteness theory, see for example Alexander 2006; Edwards 2008b; Jennings 2020; Tranby and Hartmann 2008; Young 2011.

19. Anderson 2010:134; see also 43 and elsewhere.

20. Wacquant 2010:81.

21. Brubaker 2015:29.

22. E.g., Brubaker 2015; Emirbayer and Desmond 2015; Tilly 1998. For a somewhat more nuanced account of the causes and consequences of segregation across social contexts, see Fiel 2021.

23. Fiel 2021:134.

24. Fiel 2021:186–188; see also Walton 2021a, 2021b.

25. Alexander 2006:450; see also Walton 2021b.

26. Alexander 2006:116.

27. Anderson 2010:123; see also Allport 1954; Pettigrew and Tropp 2006, 2008.

28. Emerson 2011:318; see also Edwards et al. 2013. Anderson (2010) makes passing references to racial segregation in churches on pp. 26, 34, 43, and 189.

29. See Brubaker (2015) and Chapters 1 and 6.

30. Anderson 2010:94.

31. E.g., Balmer et al. 2017; Becker 1998; Yukich and Edgell 2020; Edwards 2008a, 2008b; Edwards et al. 2013; Emerson and Smith 2000; Emerson and Woo 2006; Flores 2013, 2018; Perry and Whitehead 2019; Perry et al. 2019; Tranby and Hartmann 2008; Whitehead et al. 2018.

32. Edwards et al. 2013 and Banks 2020.

33. Edwards et al. 2013.

34. Edwards et al. 2013 and Emerson and Woo 2006.

35. Wood et al. 2012:10 and Braunstein et al. 2014.

36. Balmer et al. 2017; Brint and Schroedel 2009; Butler 2021; Edwards et al. 2013; Lichtman 2008; Emerson and Smith 2000; Markofski 2015a; Tisby 2020.

37. Anderson 2010:116–117; see also Wilson and Taub 2007.

38. Massey and Denton 1993; Massey and Tannen 2015; Rothstein 2017.

39. Wilson 1987; Sharkey 2013.

40. Schelling 1969, 1971; Bayer and McMillan 2005.

41. Massey and Denton 1993:49. This despite the fact that self-segregation sometimes enables nondominant groups to consolidate resources, autonomy, and leverage for challenging racial injustice and categorical inequality (e.g., Fiel 2021; Morris 1986; Young 2011).

42. Hwang and Sampson 2014; Massey and Tannen 2015.

43. Edwards 2008b; Fiel 2021; Walton 2021a, 2021b.

44. Given the pervasive racialization of inequity in the contemporary United States, racial equality can at best be relative, even in local settings where Black coworkers, residents, and partners share equal or greater socioeconomic status, positional authority, cultural capital, and demographic numbers relative to white Americans.

45. Markofski 2015b.

46. Perkins 2007; Slade, Marsh, and Heltzel 2013.

47. Gordon and Perkins 2013; Perkins 2007; Slade et al. 2013.

48. Killian 2017.

49. Markofski 2015a; The Rutba House 2005.

50. Sparks et al. 2014.

51. Markofski 2015a. Chapter 5 discusses the biblical and spiritual roots of multicultural evangelical practices of strategic relocation in detail.

52. Whereas spatial integration involves the "common use . . . of facilities and public spaces," social integration additionally "requires intergroup cooperation on terms of equality" (Anderson 2010:116).

53. Anderson 2010; Lichterman 2005; Putnam 2000.

54. Coy 2021.

55. See below and Chapter 3.

56. Desmond May 9, 2017; Johnson 2010; Massey and Denton 1993; "Reducing the Racial Homeownership Gap," (n.d.); Shapiro et al. 2013.

57. Besbris and Faber 2017; Desmond 2016; Faber 2013, 2018; Faber and Ellen 2016; Massey & Denton 1993; Patillo 2008; Rothstein 2017; Sharkey 2013.

58. Hwang and Sampson 2014; Patillo 2008.

59. Brummet and Reed 2019; Hymowitz 2019; Pitts 2007; The Inquirer Editorial Board 2019.

60. "PCDA-Housing Impact on [neighborhood]," n.d.

61. Habitat for Humanity, an Atlanta-based international housing nonprofit, is particularly active in Atlanta.

62. Richard, PCDA training weekend, March 29, 2012.

63. Richard, PCDA training weekend, March 29, 2012

64. Jack, PCDA training weekend, March 30, 2012.

65. Faber 2013, 2018.

66. Deb (personal interview).

67. For more on PCDA's provocative discourse concerning "gentrification with justice," see Chapter 3 and Hymowitz 2019; The Inquirer Editorial Board 2019.

68. Morenoff et al. 2001; Sampson et al. 1997, 1999, 2002.

69. For different perspectives on the relationship between local indigenous and external resources in community development, organizing, advocacy, and justice work, see Chapter 3.

70. E.g., Desmond et al. 2015; Desmond and Perkins 2015; Desmond and Shollenberger 2015; Desmond 2016.

71. Besbris 2020

72. Or, alternatively, allowing the historic pattern of systemic disinvestment, surveillance, subjugation, and abandonment in disadvantaged Black communities to continue unabated (cf., Wacquant 2009).

73. Of PCDA-H's sixteen most recent home sales, for example, fifteen were sold to Black homeowners.

74. This estimate slightly exceeded my own ethnographic observations, which noted the presence of twelve white households in the neighborhood with current or past affiliation with PCDA.

75. Ada, personal communication, June 11, 2012.

76. Patterson 1997.

77. Lichterman 2005.

78. See also Chapters 5 and 6.

79. This, of course, does not mean that there were none, just that they were likely infrequent as reported consistently by Black and white research participants alike.

80. Emirbayer and Desmond 2012; Markofski 2015b.

81. Deanna, PCDA training event, March 30, 2012.

82. Deanna, PCDA training event, March 30, 2012, emphases original.

83. Deanna, PCDA training event, March 30, 2012, emphases original.

84. A biblical reference to Matthew 25:40.

85. On moving from a "youth-control complex" to a "youth-support complex" for disadvantaged Black and Latino youth; see Rios 2011.

86. On public schools as a significant site of grassroots democratic organizing, see for example Warren and Mapp 2011.

87. Markofski 2015a:190–193.

88. For more on the evangelical doctrine of the incarnation of Christ as theological warrant for the practice of strategic relocation, see Chapter 6.

89. Erik Olin Wright, in *Envisioning Real Utopias* (2010), discusses these three indicators of the transformative potential of social democratic movements and institutions.

90. Anderson 2010; Fiel 2021; Young 2011.

91. Anderson 2010.

92. Lichterman 2005; Markofski 2019; and Chapter 6.
93. Paxton 2002; Putnam 2000; Sampson et al. 1997, 1999, 2002.
94. Anderson 2010; Emirbayer and Desmond 2015.
95. Perkins 2007.

Chapter 3

1. Wright 2010.
2. Nussbaum 2000, 2011; Sen 1999; Smith 2011; Stout 2010; Wright 2010.
3. On this point, the pragmatist, republican, and democratic-socialist traditions are in agreement (e.g., Addams 2002 [1902]; Gorski 2017; Wright 2010).
4. That is, "Never do for others what they can do for themselves" (Stout 2010:136).
5. "The Food Co-op," n.d.
6. Pastor James, personal communication, April 5, 2012.
7. Patillo 1998.
8. "Feeding Dreams," October 13, 2014.
9. Pastor James, May 1994 letter to supporters.
10. On the impacts of social isolation in disadvantaged neighborhoods, see Klinenberg (2020). On juggling food, rent, utilities, school supplies, and other basic expense budgets in disadvantaged households, see for example Edin and Shaeffer 2015 and Desmond 2016.
11. Hale 2019:11.
12. "The Food Co-op," n.d.
13. Ibid. On the limited food choices of low-income Black Southerners, see Ewoodzie 2021.
14. "Food Co-op Program Evaluation," 2018.
15. "Food Co-op Program Evaluation," 2018.
16. "Food Co-op Program Evaluation," 2018.
17. "Food Co-op Program Evaluation," 2018.
18. "Feeding Dreams," October 13, 2014.
19. The language of recognizing and empowering the manifold gifts present in disadvantaged neighborhoods and communities is common in asset-based community development circles in which The Food Co-op participated.
20. "Feeding Dreams," October 13, 2014.
21. On probation, police surveillance, system avoidance, and the importance of faith-based groups and organizations for social bonding and attachment among ex-felons, see for example Brayne 2014; Flores 2013, 2018.
22. "The Federal Bonding Program: A US Department of Labor Initiative," 2013.
23. See also Chapters 1, 5, and 6.
24. Edin and Shaefer 2015; Desmond 2016.
25. E.g., Desmond 2016: 215–226, 377–379, 389–390.
26. November/December 1998 newsletter.

27. "Feeding Dreams," October 13, 2014.
28. Hale 2019: 184–185, 190–191, emphasis original.
29. Desmond 2016.
30. "Asset Based Community Development Strategies Worskshop," n.d.
31. Bretherton 2015; Chambers 2003; Linthicum 2006; Stout 2010; Wood 2002.
32. "Greenbush Initiative," n.d.
33. "Things are Happening in Portland Neighborhoods," n.d.
34. Perkins 2007; Slade et al. 2013.
35. For other perspectives on gentrification with or without justice, see for example Brummet and Reed 2019; Hwang and Sampson 2014; Hymovitz 2019; Patillo 2008; Pitts 2007; and The Inquirer Editorial Board 2019.
36. On collective efficacy, see Morenoff et al. 2001; Sampson et al. 1997, 2002. On the imperative of integration for racial equity, see Anderson 2010. On racial residential segregation and generational poverty, see Anderson 2010; Massey and Denton 1993; Sharkey 2013.
37. On concentrated disadvantage and generational immobility in race and class disadvantaged neighborhoods, see for example Sharkey 2013 and Wilson 1987.
38. As noted in Chapter 2, Deb's depiction was accurate: fifteen out of PCDA's sixteen most recently restored affordable houses were sold or rented to Black residents.
39. Cf. Desmond 2016.
40. In this, PCDA echoed John Perkins writing and teaching, which often criticized forms of welfare and charity for creating relationships and habits of "dependency" rather than interdependency among the privileged and the poor.
41. Edin and Shaefer 2015; Sharkey 2013.
42. Massey and Denton 1993; Desmond 2016.
43. Patillo 2008, 2013.
44. Mitchell, CSJN Executive Director, August 2012 personal interview and "Lazarus at the Gate goes to the Slow Food Summit!", April 12, 2012.
45. Pastor James supplements his reflections on the Lazarus parable and its implications for Christian approaches to poverty and inequality with other scripture references including Luke 8:3; Luke 10:27, 14:13–14; Matthew 19:23–24; Matthew 25:31–40; 1 Corinthians 11:17–24; and James 2:1–9.
46. CSJN economic discipleship curriculum:9–10.
47. CSJN economic discipleship curriculum:12.
48. CSJN economic discipleship curriculum:14.
49. On the importance of biblically-justifiable religious and political standpoints and strategies of action in the evangelical field, see Markofski 2015a.
50. "CCG's Theological Foundations Project," March 31, 2010 Draft.
51. Of the 50 evangelicals I directly asked these questions (Table 3.1), 40 identified as white (17 female, 23 male), 4 identified as Black (2 female, 2 male), 3 identified as Hispanic (3 female), and 3 identified as Asian American (1 female, 2 male). In addition to these evangelicals, I also directly asked 8 white mainline Protestants (2 female, 6 male) these questions, all 8 of whom took strong "progressive" positions of the biblical view of poverty and inequality, and of both the church and government's obligation to actively combat poverty and economic inequality.

52. Deuteronomy 15:11.

53. Emerson and Smith 2000; Markofski 2015a.

54. Chapters 5 and 6 explore further how the practice of strategic relocation related to increased social reflexivity as observed and reported by multicultural evangelical research participants across different dimensions.

55. Jane Addams' (2002 [1902]) classic depiction of the "charity visitor" is a dramatic example of the type.

56. Rios 2011; Wacquant 2009.

57. On the possibility and importance of scaling up grassroots democratic community organizing efforts to combat poverty and inequality, see for example Wood and Fulton 2015.

58. Corbett and Fikkert 2014 and Lupton 2011.

59. On the importance of civic groups having cultural resources for both contestation and compromise for effective ethical democratic organizing, see Wood 2002.

60. Wood and Fulton 2015.

Chapter 4

1. The literature is vast; see Addams 2002 [1902]; Alexander 2006; Putnam 1993, 2000; Tocqueville 1966 [1835/1840] and Chapter 1 for a sample.

2. Balmer et al. 2017; Butler 2021; Emerson and Smith 2000; Gorski 2020a, 2020b; Hunter 1991, 1994; Markofski 2015a; Tisby 2020; Whitehead and Perry 2020.

3. Markofski, Fulton, and Wood 2020.

4. Christians for the Common Good mission statement, n.d.

5. On the exceptional case method, see Markofski 2015b and the Appendix.

6. Metzger 2006.

7. Paul Metzger and the late Kyogen Carlson are not pseudonyms but rather published authors and public figures. In interviews Paul requested his real name be used; Kyogen passed away in 2014.

8. Metzger 2006.

9. Metzger 2006:57.

10. Metzger 2006:58–59.

11. Sater and Farlow 2006:71.

12. Markofski 2019.

13. Metzger 2006:51.

14. Metzger 2006:51, emphasis original.

15. Metzger 2006:56.

16. Marsh 2005.

17. Metzger 2006:54.

18. Metzger 2006:53.

19. Metzger 2006:55.

20. Metzger 2006:54.

21. See Markofski 2019 and Chapter 6.

22. Metzger 2006:56.
23. On transposable reflexivity, see Markofski 2019 and Chapter 6.
24. Sater and Farlow 2006:71.
25. Sater and Farlow 2006:73.
26. Sater and Farlow 2006:73.
27. Sater and Farlow 2006:74.
28. Sater and Farlow 2006:71.
29. Sater and Farlow 2006:72.
30. Sater and Farlow 2006:71.
31. Carlson 2006:64–66.
32. Carlson 2006:66.
33. Carlson 2006:66.
34. Carlson 2006:62.
35. Carlson 2006:62–63.
36. Carlson 2006:65.
37. Harper 2006:16.
38. Harper 2006:16.
39. Harper 2006:15–16.
40. Rice 2006:41.
41. Collins 1986.
42. Rice 2006:41–42. Georgene Rice is not a pseudonym.
43. Rice 2006:43–45.
44. On the authoritative theological warrants undergirding evangelical practices of intellectual humility and social reflexivity, see Markofski 2019 and Chapter 6.
45. Gee 2013.
46. Nichols quoted in Baxter 2006:31; see also Wood 2018.
47. Nichols quoted in Baxter 2006:31.
48. Rogers 1990.
49. Metzger 2006:56, 58.
50. Metzger 2006.
51. Metzger 2006:57–58.
52. Markofski, Fulton, and Wood 2020. Particularist pluralism bears some resemblance to Inazu's description of "confident pluralism" discussed in Chapter 1.
53. Braunstein, Fulton, and Wood 2014; Lichterman 2005; Smidt 2003.
54. Braunstein, Fulton, and Wood 2014.
55. Braunstein, Fulton, and Wood 2014:721.
56. Bean 2007; Perry 2017; Smith 1998.
57. Lichterman 2005.
58. Lichterman 2005:242.
59. Markofski, Fulton, and Wood 2020.
60. Early organizational mission statement.
61. "Frequently Asked Questions about CCG" draft, August 16, 2007.
62. King 2019.
63. Matthew 25:40.

64. "When I was sick," is a reference to a series of Jesus's parables about salvation, mercy, justice, and judgment as recorded in the book of Matthew chapter 25, verse 43 in particular, "I was a stranger, and you didn't invite me into your home. I was naked, and you didn't give me clothing. I was sick and in prison, and you didn't visit me."

65. Alexander 2006; Braunstein 2017; Braunstein et al. 2014; Lamont and Molnar 2002; Smith 1998.

66. "Criteria for Partnerships," n.d.

67. "Christians for the Common Good Policy Statement on Lobbying and Political Activity, Prepared for February 22-23 Board Retreat," n.d.

68. "CCG Positions on abortion and gay rights," n.d.

69. "CCG Policy Statement on Lobbying and Political Activities," n.d.

70. "CCG Public Policy Committee Update," November 28th, 2011.

71. Ibid.

72. On the power of storytelling in advocacy, see for example Braunstein 2012, 2017; Braunstein and Yukich 2014; Bretherton 2015.

73. Mark 11:15–18.

74. "CCG Background Information," 2006.

75. Wood 2002; Wood and Fulton 2015; Stout 2010.

76. Here's the full interview excerpt: "Gordon was sort of the first place that I realized that Christians could think differently about things. That they didn't have to be uber-conservative. I remember one morning my mother called me on a Saturday morning. It must've been really late because my mother always sleeps in really late and we're three hours ahead. And she asked why I had been up so late, because I said I was up all night. And I was like, well, I was having this conversation, mom, and I think I'm a feminist. And my mom got so excited and she started crying. And she said, 'Oh my god, you know, I really thought when we let you go to that [evangelical] school that you were going to come out just like Pat Robertson.' So needless to say, I did not come out like Pat Robertson—perhaps because I'm contrarian, as my mother likes to tell me."

77. Ermakoff 2014; Markofski 2015b; and the Appendix.

78. Hunter 1994, 2010.

79. Habermas 2006, 2008.

80. Lichterman 2005; Markofski 2019.

81. Habermas 2006.

82. Markofski, Fulton, and Wood 2020.

83. Habermas 2008:12.

84. Dillon 2010:152.

Chapter 5

1. Miles and Huberman 1994.

2. Matthew 28:18–20.

3. On the prioritization of evangelism in the American evangelical field, see Markofski 2015a:182–184 and elsewhere.

4. Cf., 2 Corinthians 5:18–21; John 3:16; 1 Timothy 2:3–6; Romans 3:21–28; Romans 5 and 8.

5. Lichterman 2012; Lichterman and Eliasoph 2014; Markofski 2019; Markofski, Fulton, and Wood 2020.

6. Lichterman 2005; Markofski, Fulton, and Wood 2020.

7. Markofski 2019; Markofski, Fulton, and Wood 2020.

8. On political position-taking and the Bible across various movements in field of American evangelicalism, see Markofski 2015a.

9. Sater and Farlow 2006:73.

10. Cooper, referring to 1 Corinthians 12:12.

11. Whereas Cooper sat at one end of the evangelism spectrum among my research participants, Elena sat at the other end. "I don't really agree with evangelism to begin with," Elena told me while discussing her journey away from the "really conservative theology" of her youth, "it doesn't feel right for me to force a belief on someone." In completely disavowing evangelism and framing it is an effort to "force a belief on someone," Elena was even more of an outlier than Cooper among my research participants.

12. Perry 2017:9–11; see also Hunter 1987; Markofski 2015a, 2018a; Smith 1998.

13. On the demographic makeup of these interview respondents, see Table 3.1 and Chapter 3, n.42.

14. Richard spoke of Jesus's summary of the "Greatest Commandment" recorded in Matthew 22:36–40; John 13:34.

15. This interview excerpt focuses on collaboration among Christians; Richard also affirmed positive examples of collaboration with Muslim, Jewish, and nonreligious individuals and groups.

16. Philippians 1:5.

17. 1 Peter 3:15, NIV.

18. E.g., Braunstein 2019; Markofski 2019; Habermas 2006, 2008.

19. Braunstein 2019; Lynch et al. n.d.; Markofski 2019.

20. On the "consistent ethic of life" position, see for example Markofski 2015a and Steensland and Goff 2013. On the "contradictory cultural location" of many "other evangelicals," see Markofski 2015a and 2018b.

21. Regnerus and Smith 1998.

22. Emerson and Smith 2000 and Lichterman et al. 2009.

23. Elisha 2011; Emerson and Smith 2000; Steensland and Goff 2013.

24. De Young et al. 2003; Christerson et al. 2005; Emerson and Woo 2006; Edwards 2008; Edwards et al. 2013; Marti 2012.

25. Balmer et al. 2017; Butler 2021; Gorski 2017, 2020a; Gorski and Perry 2022; Marti 2020; Emerson and Smith 2000; Jones 2020; Tisby 2020 and Chapter 2.

26. Lichterman et al. 2009:200.

27. Lichterman et al. 2009:170.

28. Lichterman et al. 2009:214–215.

29. Emerson and Woo 2006:131–157; Edwards 2008; Edwards et al. 2013.

30. Emerson and Smith 2000:83–86, 106–113; see also Allport 1954; Anderson 2010; Pettigrew and Tropp 2006, 2008.

31. Emerson and Smith 2000:132; see also 125–133.

32. Han and Arora 2022 and Warren 2010.

33. Lichterman et al. 2009:212–213 and Rehwaldt-Alexander 2004.

34. Lichterman et al. 2009:213; see also Lichterman 2005; Christerson et al. 2005:151–185; Emerson and Woo 2006:168–169; and Fulton, Oyakawa, and Wood 2019.

35. I asked this question directly to 18 white evangelical strategic relocators (16 affirmative, 2 negative responses) and 15 white evangelical non-relocators (2 affirmative, 13 negative responses). The stark difference in responses is suggestive if not statistically robust.

36. In addition to participant observation data, this includes both white evangelical self-reports and in-depth interviews with Black, Hispanic, and Asian American neighbors and coworkers.

37. Anderson 2010. My research participants' experiences exemplify a core aspect of pragmatist social and democratic theory: namely, that human learning, growth, and habit-transforming creative agency typically emerges as a result of new, difficult, or perplexing experiences with diverse social others and situations. As Jane Addams argues in *Democracy and Social Ethics*, speaking from a position of privilege, "we are under moral obligation in choosing our experiences, since the result of those experiences must ultimately determine our understanding of life" (Addams 2002 [1902]:7). While not everyone can, or ought, to practice strategic relocation, there are myriad other avenues whereby individuals, groups, and institutions can take up our "moral obligation" to pursue better understandings and responses to racial inequity and division through multiracial relationships, experiences, and learning.

38. Miles and Huberman 1994.

39. Matthew 6:21.

40. Addams 2002 [1902]; Chambers 2003; Dewey 1988 [1939]; Linthicum 2006; Mead 1934, Wood 2002.

41. Stout 2010; Tocqueville 1966 [1835/40].

42. E.g., John 1; Philippians 2:1–11.

43. Acts 2:42–47, 4:32–35.

44. The "beloved community" is a reference to the life and work of Martin Luther King Jr.

45. Cf. Walton 2021b.

46. Addams 2002 [1902]; Dewey 1980 [1916], 1988 [1939]; Habermas 2006, 2008, West 1989.

47. Hart 2001; Lichterman 2005.

48. Anderson 2010; Braunstein et al. 2014; Putnam 2000; Wood 2002; Wood and Fulton 2015.

49. Lichterman 2005; Lichterman and Reed 2015; Markofski 2015b; and Chapter 6.

50. See also Han and Arora 2022 and Warren 2010.

51. "Why we need different friends now more than ever," January 11, 2016.

52. Han and Arora 2022 and Warren 2010.

53. Emirbayer and Desmond 2015.

54. E.g., Lichterman 2005; Markofski 2019.

Chapter 6

1. Addams 2002 [1902]:7–8.
2. Dewey 1988 [1939]:229; see also Putnam 1993, 2000; Paxton 2002; Wood and Fulton 2015; Wood 2002; Stout 2010; Warren 2001; Hart 2001; Lichterman 2005; Braunstein et al. 2014; Schneiderhan and Khan 2008.
3. Dewey 1934; see also James 1985 [1902]; Gorski 2017; Marsden 1997.
4. Brubaker 2015:5–6.
5. E.g., Bellah 1967; Gorski 2017; Habermas 2006:1–3.
6. Habermas 2008; see also Brubaker 2015; Smith 2003.
7. Brubaker 2015:6. To be sure, prominent sociologists of religion have addressed the role of moral and religious difference in organizing political struggles in the United States (e.g., Hunter 1991, 2010; Wuthnow 2005), but for the most part these inquiries have not made their way into dominant philosophical or sociological discourse concerning diversity and democracy, being relegated instead to discussion among small and marginalized pockets of conservative scholars.
8. E.g., Dillon 2010; Gorski et al. 2012. On Habermas's relation to classical American pragmatism, see, for example, Shalin 1992; Ray 2004.
9. Habermas et al. 2010; see also Habermas 2006, 2008; Dillon 2010.
10. Dillon 2010:146; Habermas 1992.
11. Habermas 2006:10; Habermas 2008.
12. Habermas 2008:25–29; Dillon 2010.
13. Nemoianu 2006:23; Habermas and Ratzinger 2006.
14. Habermas quoted in Nemoianu 2006:24–25.
15. Habermas 2008; see also Asad 2003; Casanova 1994; Gorski et al. 2012; Mahmood 2015; Menchik 2015; Salomon 2017. In calling attention to the Euro-American context, my aim is to not normatively or theoretically center "the West" but rather to provincialize and historicize it while avoiding the sort of false universalisms that too often accompany discussions of democracy, religion, and secularism.
16. Habermas 2006:4; Habermas 2008:29.
17. Habermas 2008:29; Habermas 2006:15.
18. Habermas 2008:27–28.
19. Habermas 2006:14.
20. Habermas 2006:14; see also Habermas 2008:28. This is true of both the "internal" or "subjective" legitimacy of the learning process from the perspective of religious communities as well as its "external" or "objective" legitimacy from the perspective of ethical democratic requirements of mutual recognition and non-coercion.
21. E.g., Bellah 1967; Gorski 2017. Habermas (2006) himself recognizes this example of "American exceptionalism" among contemporary Euro-American nations in terms of the vitality of both public and private religion.
22. Lichterman 2005, 2012; Lichterman and Potts 2009; Lichterman and Reed 2015.
23. Lichterman 2005:15, 45; Lichterman and Reed 2015.
24. Addams 2002 [1902]; Dewey 1980 [1916], 1988 [1939], 1997 [1938]; Paxton 2002; Putnam 1993, 2000; Tocqueville 1966 [1835/40].

25. Lichterman 2005; Markofski 2019.

26. I initially described this variety as *dogmatic reflexivity* to capture the dogmatic rigidity of criticism inherent to this mode of social reflexivity: it could reasonably be used as an alternative nomenclature. However, while I appreciated the oxymoronic nature of the phrase, I discovered that many readers found it difficult to distinguish between dogmatic reflexivity and dogmatism per se, and thus renamed the category. One benefit of this shift is that the antipodal pairing of *deep* and *frozen* reflexivity evokes the naturalistic image of a frozen lake in winter, with rigid ice on the surface and fluid water at the depths, an image that this book's fellow Northern readers in particular may appreciate.

27. I thank Mustafa Emirbayer for his help in naming this category.

28. Gadamer 2013.

29. Ewoodzie 2021; see also Lichterman 2005.

30. Ewoodzie 2021:80.

31. Ewoodzie 2021:80–86; see also 59–64, 73–76. As Ewoodzie notes, clients of religious charities that view their work as a "means to a more important end" (such as religious conversion or personal reform) often find "religious incorporation [to be] a hindrance to the services provided and, at times, an invasion of their faith preferences" (82, 85). In one study of homeless recipients of faith-based service provision, a third of respondents believed the religious efforts of these organizations to be "hypocritical," while one half viewed the religious content of such organizations as "coercive and forced" (85). Such is the fruit of non-reflexive religious charity work.

32. Ewoodzie 2021:153.

33. Ewoodzie 2021:153.

34. E.g., Lichterman 2005; Markofski 2019.

35. On the importance of expansive discourse and group communication for successfully bridging differences and sustaining social movements over time, see Hart 2001; Lichterman 2005; Lichterman and Reed 2015.

36. Or—as I quote Ayesha in the Introduction—for working primarily with "women and youth, and lighter-skinned people, but not men. Not those who really need help." Whether Ayesha's criticism was fair is questionable. I did not observe any evidence of colorism (Monk 2014, 2015) while working with PCDA staff and employees—many of whom were "darker-skinned" African Americans—nor did I hear anyone else echo Ayesha's critique. It is also questionable whether "women and youth" were more privileged or less disadvantaged than men in the neighborhood as a general rule, and thus that they did not "really need help" or increased access to opportunities, resources, and support made possible in part through PCDA's work in partnership with local residents.

37. Neighborhood residents did in fact directly discuss with PCDA leaders—who were also often their neighbors—their views on the organization's work in the neighborhood frequently in settings ranging from formal neighborhood council meetings to chance encounters on the street.

38. The Greenbush Initiative is discussed in the Introduction.

39. Lichterman, Carter, and Lamont 2009.

40. Markofski 2015a.
41. Balmer et al. 2017; Markofski 2019.
42. Habermas 2006, 2008.
43. Habermas 2006:9–10.
44. Habermas 2006, 2008; see also Gorski 2017; Hunter 1991; Mahmood 2015; Neuhaus 1984; Putnam 1993, 2000; Wood and Fulton 2015.
45. Habermas 2006:10. Habermas, of course, maintains an "institutional translation proviso" requiring religious citizens and groups to translate their concerns and reasons into universally accessible secular language in formal political environments and while conducting official state business.
46. Jacobs 2008; Plantinga 1995.
47. Bakke 1997; Lupton 2005; Markofski 2015b; Perkins 2007; Sider et al. 2008.
48. The following quotes come from a one-page brochure describing each phase of the school.
49. Gorski 2017.
50. Lynch et al. n.d.; Markofski 2019.

Conclusion

1. Balmer et al. 2017; Butler 2021; Gorski and Perry 2022; Gorski 2020a, 2020b; Jones 2020; Marti 2020; Stetzer November 2, 2016; January 11, 2021; Tisby 2020.
2. Markofski 2018b.
3. Balmer et al. 2017; Butler 2021; Gorski and Perry 2022; Gorski 2020a, 2020b.
4. Harper 2016.
5. "Creative Community for the Common Good," n.d.
6. Keller and Inazu 2020.
7. Bender et al. 2012; Markofski 2015a.
8. For a Bourdieusian field analysis of significant movements within American evangelicalism, see Markofski 2015a.
9. Markofski 2015a, 2018b.
10. Braunstein, Wood, and Fulton 2014; Lichterman 2005; Paxton 2002; Putnam 1993, 2000; Markofski 2015b, 2019; Smidt 2003.
11. E.g., Bretherton 2019; Keller and Inazu 2020; Mouw 2016; Volf 2011, 2015.
12. E.g., Plantinga 1995 and chapter 6.
13. Hunter 1991, 1994, 2017.
14. Habermas 2008:29.
15. Andrews 2004.
16. Jenkins 2011; Miller et al. 2013; Offutt 2015; Swartz 2020 and chapter 1.
17. Rah 2009; see also McCaulley 2020.
18. Balmer et al. 2017; Butler 2021; Tranby and Hartmann 2008.
19. Whitehead and Perry 2020 and Gorski 2020a; see also Gorski and Perry 2020; Lichtman 2008.
20. Gorski 2020a; see also Delahanty et al. 2018; Gorski and Perry 2020.

21. Edwards et al. 2013; Emerson and Smith 2000.
22. Balmer et al. 2017; Wald et al. 1989.
23. Balmer et al. 2017; Du Mez 2020; Hunter 1991.
24. Balmer et al. 2017; Bean 2014; Liebman and Wuthnow 1983.
25. Markofski 2015a.
26. Smith 1998.
27. Markofski 2018a; Perry 2017.
28. E.g., Green July 7, 2021 and Griswold December 26, 2018.
29. E.g., Allport 1954; Pettigrew and Tropp 2006, 2008; Anderson 2010; DeYoung et al. 2003; Edwards 2008; Edwards et al. 2013; Emerson and Smith 2000; Emerson and Woo 2006; Fulton and Wood 2017; Fulton et al. 2019; Han and Arora 2022; Han et al. 2021; Warren 2010; Wood and Fulton 2015.
30. These include institutions such as the National Hispanic Christian Leadership Conference, the National Latino Evangelical Coalition, the National Black Evangelical Organization, the Asian American Christian Collaborative, *Christianity Today*, the National Association of Evangelicals, the Evangelical Covenant Church, Fuller Theological Seminary, Gordon College, Eastern College and Seminary, Wheaton College, InterVarsity Christian Fellowship and InterVarsity Press, the Christian Community Development Association, the Voices Project, The Witness: A Black Christian Collective, Freedom Road, Undivided, Civil Righteousness, the Parrish Collective, Red Letter Christians, Multifaith Matters, and thousands of individual congregations and other religious organizations across the country. This is not an exhaustive list.
31. Brooks February 4, 2022; Green July 7, 2021; Griswold December 26, 2018; Robertson March 9, 2018; Stetzer January 11, 2021; Wehner October 24, 2021.
32. Campolo 2008; Chastain August 28, 2021; Gushee 2017; Plummer 2012; Kight September 19, 2021; Labberton 2018; McAlister August 7, 2018; Onishi April 9, 2019.
33. Casanova 1994; Gorski and Altinordu 2008; Markofski 2015b; Smith 1998; Finke and Stark 1988.
34. Burge March 21, 2019; Shellnutt September 16, 2021; Smith September 15, 2021; Wong 2018.

Appendix

1. On exceptional cases, see Ermakoff 2014.
2. On the potential contributions of empirical sociological case studies to normative theory, see Thacher 2006.
3. Markofski 2015a:16–18, 2015b.
4. Ermakoff 2014:6,8.
5. Ermakoff 2014 and Thacher 2006.
6. See also Markofski 2015b; Markofski, Fulton, and Wood 2020.
7. Ermakoff 2014:18; see also Thacher 2006.
8. Ermakoff 2014: 18.

9. Lichterman and Reed 2015:3. On the necessity of theory in ethnographic case selection see also Burawoy 1998; Desmond 2014; Ragin and Becker 1992. On the need for heightened attentiveness to culture in the extended case method, see Lichterman and Eliasoph 1999. Note that the exceptional case method also departs from Burawoy's (1998) "two sciences" epistemology of social knowledge production.

10. Glaser and Strauss 1967; Strauss 1987; Tavory 2016; Timmermans and Tavory 2009, 2012. On the ubiquitous use of constant comparison even among different ethnographic research paradigms, see Lichterman and Reed 2015:6, 41fn.9.

11. Lichterman and Reed 2015 and Gorski 2009.

12. Gorski 2004, 2013a, 2018; Lichterman and Reed 2015; Reed 2011; Steinmetz 2004; Thacher 2006.

13. Reed 2011.

14. Steinmetz 2004 and Lichterman and Reed 2015. My position is similar to Reed's (cum Weber) "interpretive realism" (Reed 2011:91n2), albeit with less skepticism than Reed concerning the possibilities of a more robustly interpretive postpositivist "critical realism" (Bhaskar 1998 [1979], 2008 [1975]; Gorski 2013b, 2018; Steinmetz 1998).

15. Thacher 2006.

16. Burawoy 2005 and Markofski 2015b.

17. Markofski 2015a, 2015b.

18. E.g., Gasaway 2014; Markofski 2015a; Mulder, Ramos, and Marti 2017; Steensland and Goff 2013; Swartz 2012; Thomas 2012; Wong 2018.

19. Braunstein, Fulton, and Wood 2014; Lichterman 2005; Lichterman et al. 2009; Putnam 2000; Wuthnow 2003.

20. Eliasoph and Lichterman 2003; Lichterman 2012; Edgell 2012.

21. Anderson 2010; Brubaker 2015; Hart 2001; Lichterman 2005; Markofski 2015b, 2019.

22. Lichterman 2005, 2012.

23. All personal and organizational names are pseudonyms unless otherwise stated.

24. On evangelical beliefs, practices, and relationship with God, see for example Smith 1998; Luhrmann 2012; Markofski 2015a; and Noll, Bebbington, and Marsden 2019.

25. Desmond 2014.

26. On strategic relocation, see Markofski 2015b and below.

27. Gordon and Perkins 2013.

28. Organizational Mission Statement, n.d.

29. Organizational Mission Statement, n.d. ; see also Chapter 2.

30. Chapter 6 includes further discussion of the failed community development venture involving PCDA in the 1990s to which Richard was referring.

31. Markofski 2015b.

32. 2012–2013 Annual Report.

33. IAF is not a pseudonym.

34. 11/02/11 fundraising letter, ABCD training material, p. 31.

35. Pein 2011.

36. Kretzmann and McKnight 1993.

37. CCG brochure, n.d.

38. CCG Background Information, n.d.

39. CCG brochure, n.d.
40. CCG brochure, n.d.
41. CCG brochure, n.d.
42. Harris 2011; Markofski 2015b.
43. 2014 Annual Report.
44. 2008 organizational mission statement.
45. Mitchell (CSJN Executive Director), August 2012 personal conversation, and "Lazarus at the Gate goes to the Slow Food Summit!" April 12, 2012.
46. E.g., Seim 2021; Tavory 2016.
47. Desmond 2014.
48. On ethnographic revisits, see Burawoy 2003. On longitudinal ethnography, see Lareau 2011:312–332.
49. Desmond 2016:325–326.
50. Desmond 2014.
51. Duneier 1999; Lubet 2018.
52. Desmond 2016; Lubet 2018.

References

Abbott, Andrew. (2016). *Processual Sociology*. Chicago: University of Chicago Press.

Addams, J. (2002 [1902]). *Democracy and Social Ethics*. Urbana: University of Illinois Press.

Alexander, Jeffrey C. (2004). "Cultural Pragmatics: Social Performance between Ritual and Strategy." *Sociological Theory 22*(4):527–573.

Alexander, Jeffrey C. (2006). *The Civil Sphere*. New York: Oxford University Press.

Allport, Gordon W. (1954). *The Nature of Prejudice*. Cambridge, MA: Perseus Books.

Anderson, Benedict. (1983). *Imagined Communities: Reflections on the Origin and Spread of Nationalism*. New York: Verso.

Anderson, Elizabeth. (2006). "The Epistemology of Democracy." *Episteme 3*(1–2): 8–22.

Anderson, Elizabeth. (2010). *The Imperative of Integration*. Princeton: Princeton University Press.

Andrews, Kenneth T. (2004). *Freedom Is a Constant Struggle: The Mississippi Civil Rights Movement and Its Legacy*. Chicago: University of Chicago Press.

Appiah, Kwame A. (2006). *Cosmopolitanism: Ethics in a World of Strangers*. New York: W.W. Norton.

Aristotle. (1980 [1925]). *The Nichomachean Ethics*. New York: Oxford University Press.

Arsenault, Mark. (2013a, October 1). "Clergy Try to Fend Off a Casino in East Boston." *The Boston Globe*. Retrieved from http://www.bostonglobe.com/metro/2013/09/30/clergy-organize-against-suffolk-downs-casino/tWoQ6EvkTmvdgHrxTv7AgL/story.html#.

Arsenault, Mark. (2013b, October 18). "Caesars Dumped from Suffolk Downs Casino Plan." *The Boston Globe*. Retrieved from http://www.bostonglobe.com/metro/2013/10/18/caesars-entertainment-dumped-from-suffolk-downs-venture/VvsDWIIzHvhnij61Akm6TJ/story.html.

Arsenault, Mark. (2013c, October 24). "Ceasars Signed Deal with Hotelier Accused of Having Tie to Russian Mob." *The Boston Globe*. Retrieved from http://www.bostonglobe.com/metro/2013/10/23/report-details-concerns-about-caesars/cK6K3OjC5ZeJ362QygGRvK/story.html.

Arsenault, Mark. (2013d, November 6). "East Boston Rejects Casino at Suffolk Downs." *The Boston Globe*. Retrieved from http://www.bostonglobe.com/metro/2013/11/05/suffolk-downs-defeated-boston-will-explore-revere-only-project/o2VK5haGBzosrwvu7mTLiI/story.html#.

Arsenault, Mark. (2013e, December 2). "Mass. Casino Foes Look to Rechannel Their Voices." *The Boston Globe*. Retrieved from http://www.bostonglobe.com/metro/2014/12/01/unbowed-ballot-defeat-anticasino-forces-seek-new-role/66VGX4qqjSbEkSpA43aXKM/story.html#.

Arsenault, Mark. (2014, June 20). "After Initial Fanfare, Skepticism on Casinos Grows." *The Boston Globe*. Retrieved from http://www.bostonglobe.com/metro/2014/06/19/seemed-like-sure-bet/GDKXqbkyGsZ7cIilZ061cM/story.html?comments=all&sort=HIGHEST_RATING.

Arsenault, Mark. (2015, January 5). "Boston Sues Panel to Try to halt Everett Casino." *The Boston Globe*. Retrieved from http://www.bostonglobe.com/metro/2015/01/05/bos ton-sue-gambling-commission-over-everett-casino-approval/a1lrirC4csg4ksLlGdD siI/story.html.

Arsenault, Mark and Andrea Estes. (2014, May 1). "Patrick Gets Gambling Panel to Pause." *The Boston Globe*. Retrieved from http://www.bostonglobe.com/metro/2014/05/01/decision-delayed-whether-boston-will-get-more-say-casino-proposals/TZJ 6Rk7LdENrUep6CLpGAN/story.html.

Asad, Talal. (2003). *Formations of the Secular: Christianity, Islam, Modernity (Cultural Memory in the Present)*. Palo Alto, CA: Stanford University Press.

Bakke, Ray. (1997). *A Theology as Big as the City*. Downers Grove, IL: InterVarsity Press.

Baldauf, Anette, Stefan Gruber, Moira Hille, Annette Krauss, Vladimir Miller, Mara Verlič, Hong-Kai Wang, and Julia Wieger. (Eds.) (2016). *Spaces of Commoning Artistic Research and the Utopia of the Everyday*. Berlin: Sternberg Press.

Balmer, Randall. (December 1, 2019). "Randall Balmer: The Other Evangelicals." *Concord Monitor*. Retrieved from https://www.concordmonitor.com/The-other-evangelicals-30772625/.

Balmer, Randall, Kate Bowler, Anthea Butler, Maura Jane Farrelly, Wes Markofski, Robert Orsi, Jerry Z. Park, James Clark Davidson, Matthew Avery Sutton, and Grace Yukich. (2017). "Forum: Studying Religion in the Age of Trump." *Religion and American Culture: A Journal of Interpretation* 27(1):2–56.

Banks, Adele M. (2020). "Multiracial churches growing, but challenging for clergy of color." *Religion News Service*. Retrieved from https://religionnews.com/2020/01/20/multiracial-churches-growing-but-challenging-for-clergy-of-color/

Barber, Leroy. (2016). *Embrace: God's Radical Shalom for a Divided World*. Downers Grove, IL: InterVarsity Press.

Baxter, Nathan A. (2006). "Bumping into Ourselves: Awaking from the Sound-Bite Stupor." *Cultural Encounters: A Journal for the Theology of Culture* 3(1):25–34. Portland: Institute for the Theology of Culture: New, New Wineskins of Multnomah Biblical Seminary.

Bayer, Patrick J. and Robert McMillan. (2005). "Racial Sorting and Neighborhood Quality." NBER Working Paper No. w11813. Retrieved from https://ssrn.com/abstract=875689.

Bean, Lydia. (2007). "New Wine in New Wineskins: Social Justice Evangelism in a Post-Christendom Era." Unpublished manuscript.

Bean, Lydia. (2014). *The Politics of Evangelical Identity: Local Churches and Partisan Divides in the United States and Canada*. Princeton: Princeton University Press.

Bean, Lydia and Brandon C. Martinez. (2014). "Evangelical Ambivalence toward Gays and Lesbians." *Sociology of Religion* 75(3):395–417.

Becker, Penny Edgell. (1998). "Making Inclusive Communities: Congregations and the 'Problem' of Race." *Social Problems* 45(4):451–472.

Bellah, Robert. (1967). "Civil Religion in America." *Journal of the American Academy of Arts and Sciences* 96(1):1–21.

Bellah, Robert N., Richard Madsen, William M. Sullivan, Ann Swidler, and Steven M. Tipton. (1996). *Habits of the Heart: Individualism and Commitment in American Life*. Berkeley, CA: University of California Press.

Bender, C., W. Cadge, P. Levitt, and D. Smilde, (Eds.) (2012). *Religion on the Edge: De-Centering and Re-Centering the Sociology of Religion*. New York: Oxford University Press.

Benford, Robert D. and David A. Snow(2000). "Framing Processes and Social Movements: An Overview and Assessment." *Annual Review of Sociology* 26:611–639.

Benhabib, Seyla. (1992). "Models of Public Space: Hannah Arendt, the Liberal Tradition, and Jurgen Habermas." 73–98 in *Habermas and the Public Sphere*. Craig Calhoun (Ed.). Cambridge, MA: MIT Press.

Benhabib, Seyla. (2006). *Another Cosmopolitanism*. New York: Oxford University Press.

Besbris, Max. (2020). *Upsold: Real Estate Agents, Prices, and Neighborhood Inequality*. Chicago: University of Chicago Press.

Besbris, Max and Jacob William Faber. (2017). "Investigating the Relationship Between Real Estate Agents, Segregation, and House Prices: Steering and Upselling in New York State." *Sociological Forum* 32(4):850–873.

Bhaskar, Roy. (1998 [1979]). *The Possibility of Naturalism: A Philosophical Critique of the Contemporary Social Sciences*. New York: Routledge.

Bhaskar, Roy. (2008 [1975]). *A Realist Theory of Science*. New York: Routledge.

Bielo, James S. (2011). *Emerging Evangelicals: Faith, Modernity, and the Desire for Authenticity*. New York: NYU Press.

"Black Americans who are Evangelical Protestants." (n.d.). *Pew Research Center*. Retrieved from https://www.pewforum.org/religious-landscape-study/religious-tradition/evangelical-protestant/racial-and-ethnic-composition/Black/.

Bohman, James. (2013). "Democratic Experimentalism: From Self-Legislation to Self-Determination." *Contemporary Pragmatism* 9(2):273–285.

Bonilla-Silva, Eduardo. (2003). *Racism without Racists: Color-Blind Racism and the Persistence of Racial Inequality in the United States*. Lanham, MD: Rowman & Littlefield.

Bonilla-Silva, Eduardo. (2004). "From Bi-Racial to Tri-Racial: Towards a New System of Racial Stratification in the USA." *Ethnic and Racial Studies* 27(6):931–950.

Bourdieu, Pierre and Loïc Wacquant (1992). *An Invitation to Reflexive Sociology*. Chicago: The University of Chicago Press.

Braunstein, Ruth. (2012). "Storytelling in liberal religious advocacy." *Journal for the Scientific Study of Religion* 51(1):110–127.

Braunstein, Ruth. (2017). *Prophets and Patriots: Faith in Democracy across the Political Divide*. Berkeley, CA: University of California Press.

Braunstein, Ruth, Brad R. Fulton, and Richard L. Wood. (2014). "The Role of Bridging Cultural Practices in Racially and Socioeconomically Diverse Civic Organizations." *American Sociological Review* 79(4):705–725.

Braunstein, Ruth and Grace Yukich. (2014). "Encounters at the Religious Edge: Variation in Religious Expression Across Interfaith Advocacy and Social Movement Settings." *Journal for the Scientific Study of Religion* 53(4):791–807.

Brayne, Sarah. (2014). "Surveillance and System Avoidance: Criminal Justice Contact and Institutional Attachment." *American Sociological Review* 79(3):367–391.

Bretherton, Luke. (2010). *Christianity and Contemporary Politics: The Conditions and Possibilities of Faithful Witness*. Hoboken, NJ: Wiley.

Bretherton, Luke. (2015). *Resurrecting Democracy: Faith, Citizenship, and the Politics of a Common Life*. New York: Cambridge University Press.

Bretherton, Luke. (2019). *Christ and the Common Life: Political Theology and the Case for Democracy*. Grand Rapids, MI: Wm. B. Eerdmans Publishing Co.

Brint, S. G. and J. R. Schroedel (Eds.). (2009). *Evangelicals and Democracy in America, Volume One: Religion and Society* and *Volume Two: Religion and Politics*. New York: Russell Sage Foundation.

Brooks, David. (February 4, 2022). "The Dissenters Trying to Save Evangelicalism From Itself." *The New York Times*. Retrieved from https://www.nytimes.com/2022/02/04/opinion/evangelicalism-division-renewal.html.

Brown, Wendy. (2017). *Undoing the Demos: Neoliberalism's Stealth Revolution*. Princeton: Princeton University Press.

Brubaker, Rogers. (2015). *Grounds for Difference*. Cambridge, MA: Harvard University Press.

Brummet, Q. and D. Reed. (2019). "The Effects of Gentrification on the Well-Being and Opportunity of Original Resident Adults and Children." Federal Reserve Bank of Philadelphia.

Burawoy, Michael. (1998). "The Extended Case Method." *Sociological Theory* 16(1):4–33.

Burawoy, Michael. (2005). "For Public Sociology." *American Sociological Review* 70:4–28.

Burke, Kelsy. (2014). "What Makes a Man: Gender and Sexual Boundaries on Evangelical Christian Sexuality Websites." *Sexualities* 17(1–2):3–22.

Burton, Johanna, Shannon Jackson, and Dominic Willsdon. (Eds.). (2016). *Public Servants: Art and the Crisis of the Common Good*. Cambridge, MA: MIT Press.

Butler, Anthea. (2021). *White Evangelical Racism: The Politics of Morality in America*. Raleigh, NC: UNC Press.

Burge, Ryan P. (March 21, 2019). "Evangelicals Show No Decline, Despite Trump and Nones." *Christianity Today*. Retrieved from https://www.christianitytoday.com/news/2019/march/evangelical-nones-mainline-us-general-social-survey-gss.html.

Campolo, Tony. (2008). *Red Letter Christians: A Citizen's Guide to Faith and Politics*. Ventura, CA: Regal.

Carlson, Kyogen. (2006). "All Wounds Are Our Own." *Cultural Encounters: A Journal for the Theology of Culture* 3(1):61–70. Portland: Institute for the Theology of Culture: New, New Wineskins of Multnomah Biblical Seminary.

Casanova, Jose. (1994). *Public Religions in the Modern World*. Chicago: University of Chicago Press.

Catholic Church and S. McDonagh. (2016). *On Care for Our Common Home: The Encyclical of Pope Francis on the Environment, Laudato Si'*. New York: Orbis Books.

"Center for Public Justice, About the Center." (n.d.) Retrieved from https://www.cpjustice.org/public/page/content/about_us/.

Chambers, Edward T. (2003). *Roots for Radicals: Organizing for Power, Action, and Justice*. London: Continuum.

Chastain, Blake. (August 28, 2021). "Evangelicals: You're Still Not Really Listening to What Exvangelicals Are Saying." *Religion News Service*. Retrieved from https://religionnews.com/2021/08/28/evangelicals-youre-still-not-really-listening-to-what-exvangelicals-are-saying/.

Christerson, B., K. L. Edwards, and M. O. Emerson (2005). *Against All Odds: The Struggle for Racial Integration in Religious Organizations*. New York: New York University Press.

Claiborne, Shane. (2006). *The Irresistible Revolution: Living as an Ordinary Radical*. Grand Rapids, MI: Zondervan.

Cohen, Joshua. (1986). "An Epistemic Conception of Democracy." *Ethics* 97(1):26–38.

Cohen, Joshua. (2009). *Philosophy, Politics, Democracy: Selected Essays*. Cambridge, MA: Harvard University Press.

Coley, Jonathon S. (2018). *Gay on God's Campus: Mobilizing for LGBT Equality at Christian Colleges and Universities*. Chapel Hill, NC: University of North Carolina Press.

Collins, Patricia Hill. (1986). "Learning from the Outsider Within: The Sociological Significance of Black Feminist Thought." *Social Problems* 33(6):S14–S32.

Collins, Patricia Hill. (1990). *Black Feminist Thought: Knowledge, Consciousness and the Politics of Empowerment*. New York: Routledge.

Collins, Patricia Hill. (2019). *Intersectionality as Critical Social Theory*. Durham, NC: Duke University Press.

Connolly, William E. (2002). *Identity/Difference: Democratic Negotiations of Political Paradox (Expanded Edition)*. Minneapolis: University of Minnesota Press.

Connolly, William E. (2005). *Pluralism*. Durham, NC: Duke University Press.

Cooper, Anna Julia. (2016 [1892]). *A Voice from the South by a Black Woman of the South*. Mineola, NY: Dover Thrift Editions.

Corbett, Steve and Brian Fikkert. (2014). *When Helping Hurts: How to Alleviate Poverty Without Hurting the Poor . . . and Yourself*. Chicago: Moody Publishers.

Cox, Daniel and Robert P. Jones. (2012). "Religion, Values, and Experiences: Black and Hispanic American Attitudes on Abortion and Reproductive Issues." *Public Religion Research Institute*. Retrieved from https://www.prri.org/research/african-american-and-hispanic-reproductive-issues-survey/.

Cox, Daniel and Robert P. Jones. (2017). *America's Changing Religious Identity. Public Religion Research Institute*. Retrieved from https://www.prri.org/research/american-religious-landscape-christian-religiously-unaffiliated/

Coy, Peter. (2021). "The 'Benefits Cliff' Discourages People From Making More Money." *The New York Times*. Retrieved from https://www.nytimes.com/2021/11/10/opinion/benefits-cliff-welfare.html.

"Creative Community for the Common Good." (n.d.) *Art House North*. Retrieved from https://www.arthousenorth.com/.

Dahl, Robert Alan. (1989). *Democracy and its Critics*. New Haven: Yale University Press.

Delahanty, Jack, Penny Edgell, and Evan Stewart. (2018). "Christian America? Secularized Evangelical Discourse and the Boundaries of National Belonging." *Social Forces* 97(3):1283–1306.

Desmond, Matthew. (2014). "Relational Ethnography." *Theory and Society* 43(5):547–579.

Desmond, Matthew. (2016). *Evicted: Poverty and Profit in the American City*. New York: Crown.

Desmond, Matthew. (May 9, 2017). "How Homeownership Became the Engine of American Inequality." *The New York Times Magazine*. Retrieved from https://www.nytimes.com/2017/05/09/magazine/how-homeownership-became-the-engine-of-american-inequality.html.

Desmond, Matthew, Carl Gershenson, and Barbara Kiviat. (2015). "Forced Relocation and Residential Instability Among Urban Renters." *Social Service Review* 89(2):227–262.

Desmond, Matthew and Kristin L. Perkins. (2015). "Housing and Household Instability." *Urban Affairs Review* 52(3):421–436.

Desmond, Matthew and Tracey Shollenberger. (2015). "Forced Displacement From Rental Housing: Prevalence and Neighborhood Consequences." *Demography* 52:1751–1772.

Dewey, John. (1980 [1916]). *Democracy and Education. Vol. 9 of John Dewey: The Middle Works, 1899–1924*. Boydston, J. A. (Ed.). Carbondale: Southern Illinois University Press.

Dewey, John. (1988 [1927]). *The Public and its Problems. Vol. 2 of John Dewey: The Later Works, 1925–1953*. Boydston, J. A. (Ed.). Carbondale: Southern Illinois University Press.

Dewey, John. (1988 [1929]). *The Quest for Certainty. Vol. 4 of John Dewey: The Later Works, 1925–1953*. Boydston, J. A. (Ed.). Carbondale: Southern Illinois University Press.

Dewey, John. (1934). *A Common Faith*. New Haven, CT: Yale University Press.

Dewey, John. (1988 [1939]). "Creative Democracy—The Task Before Us." *Vol. 14 of John Dewey: The Later Works, 1925-1953*. Boydston, J. A. (Ed.). Carbondale: Southern Illinois University Press.

Dewey, John. (1997 [1938]). *Experience and Education*. West Lafayette, IN: Kappa Delta Pi.

De Young, Curtis. P., Michael O. Emerson, George Yancey, and K. C. Kim. (2003). *United by Faith: The Multiracial Congregation as an Answer to the Problem of Race*. New York: Oxford University Press.

Dillon, Michele. (1999). "The Authority of the Holy Revisited: Habermas, Religion, and Emancipatory Possibilities." *Sociological Theory 17*(3):290–306.

Dillon, Michele. (2010). "Can Post-Secular Society Tolerate Religious Differences?" *Sociology of Religion 71*(2):139–156.

Doering, Bernard (Ed.) (1994). *Correspondence of Jacques Maritain and Saul Alinsky: "The Philosopher and the Provocateur*. Notre Dame: University of Notre Dame Press.

Dorf, Michael C. and Sabel, Charles F. (1998). "A Constitution of Democratic Experimentalism." *Columbia Law Review 98*(2):267–473.

Dreher, Rod. (2017). *The Benedict Option: A Strategy for Christians in a Post-Christian Nation*. New York: Sentinel.

Du Bois, W. E. B. (1999). *Darkwater: Voices from Within the Veil*. Mineola, NY: Dover.

Du Mez, Kristen Kobes. (2020). *Jesus and John Wayne: How White Evangelicals Corrupted a Faith and Fractured a Nation*. New York: Liveright.

Dumcius, Gintautas. (2015, April 2). "Revere Mayor Calls for Investigation into Sale of MBTA Land to Wynn Resorts for Everett Casino." *Masslive.com*. Retrieved from http://www.masslive.com/politics/index.ssf/2015/04/revere_mayor_calls_for_full_in.html.

Duncan, Greg J. and Katherine A. Magnuson. (2005). "Can Family Socioeconomic Resources Account for Racial and Ethnic Test Score Gaps?" *Future Child 15*(1):35–54.

Duncan, Greg J., Katherine A. Magnuson, and Elizabeth Votruba-Drzal. (2017). "Moving Beyond Correlations in Assessing the Consequences of Poverty." *Annual Review of Psychology 68*:413–434.

Duneier, Mitchell. (1999). *Sidewalk*. New York: Farrar, Straus and Giroux.

Earls, Aaron. (2016). "Evangelicals Remain Complicated." *Lifeway Research*. Retrieved from https://research.lifeway.com/2016/11/11/evangelicals-remain-complicated/.

Ecklund, Elaine H. (2008). *Korean American Evangelicals: New Models for Civic Life*. New York: Oxford University Press.

Edgell, Penny. (2012). "A Cultural Sociology of Religion: New Directions." *Annual Review of Sociology 38*:247–265.

Edin, Kathryn J. and H. Luke Shaefer. (2015). *$2.00 a Day: Living on Almost Nothing in America*. Boston: Mariner Books.

Edwards, Korie L. (2008a). *The Elusive Dream: The Power of Race in Interracial Churches*. New York: Oxford University Press.

Edwards, Korie L. (2008b). "Bring Race to the Center: The Importance of Race in Racially Diverse Religious Organizations." *Journal for the Scientific Study of Religion 47*(1):5–9.

Edwards, Korie L. (2016). "The Space Between: Exploring How Religious Leaders Reconcile Religion and Politics." *Journal for the Scientific Study of Religion 55*(2):271–287.

Edwards, Korie L., Brad Christerson, and Michael O. Emerson. (2013). "Race, Religion, and Integration." *Annual Review of Sociology 39*:211–228.

Elisha, Omri. (2011). *Moral Ambition: Mobilization and Social Outreach in Evangelical Megachurches*. Berkeley, CA: University of California Press.

Eliasoph, Nina and Paul Lichterman. (2003). "Culture in Interaction." *The American Journal of Sociology 108*(4):735–794.

Emerson, Michael O. (2011). [Review of the book *The Imperative of Integration* by Elizabeth Anderson.] *American Journal of Sociology 117*(1):317–319

Emerson, Michael O. and Christian Smith. (2000). *Divided by Faith: Evangelical Religion and the Problem of Race in America*. New York: Oxford University Press.

Emerson, Michael O. and Rodney M. Woo (2006). *People of the Dream: Multiractial Congregations in the United States*. Princeton, NJ: Princeton.

Emirbayer, Mustafa and Matthew Desmond. (2012). "Race and Reflexivity." *Ethnic and Racial Studies 35*(4):574–599.

Emirbayer, Mustafa and Matthew Desmond. (2015). *The Racial Order*. Chicago: University of Chicago Press.

Emirbayer, Mustafa and Molly Noble. (2013). "The Peculiar Convergence of Jeffrey Alexander and Erik Olin Wright." *Theory and Society 42*:617–645.

Emirbayer, Mustafa and Erik Schneiderhan. (2012). "Dewey and Bourdieu on Democracy." 131–157 in *Bourdieu and Historical Analysis*. Philip S. Gorski (Ed.). Durham, NC: Duke University Press.

Ermakoff, Ivan. (2014). "Exceptional Cases: Epistemic Contributions and Normative Expectations." *European Journal of Sociology 55*(2):223–243.

Ewoodzie, Joseph C., Jr. (2021). *Getting Something to Eat in Jackson: Race, Class, and Food in the American South*. Princeton: Princeton University Press.

Faber, Jacob William. (2013). "Racial Dynamics of Subprime Mortgage Lending at the Peak." *Housing Policy Debate 23*(2):328–349.

Faber, Jacob William. (2018). "Segregation and the Geography of Creditworthiness: Racial Inequality in a Recovered Mortgage Market." *Housing Policy Debate 28*(2):215–247.

Faber, Jacob William and Ingrid Gould Ellen. (2016). "Race and the Housing Cycle: Differences in Home Equity Trends Among Long-Term Homeowners." *Housing Policy Debate 26*(3):456–73.

Fiel, Jeremy. (2021). "Relational Segregation: A Structural View of Categorical Relations." *Sociological Theory 39*(3):153–179.

Finke Roger and Stark Rodney. (1988). "Religious Economies and Sacred Canopies: Religious Mobilization in American cities, 1906." *American Sociological Review 53*:41–49.

Flores, Edward Orozco. (2013). *God's Gangs: Barrio Ministry, Masculinity, and Gang Recovery*. New York: NYU Press.

Flores, Edward Orozco. (2018). *"Jesus Saved an Ex-Con": Political Activism and Redemption after Incarceration (Religion and Social Transformation)*. New York: NYU Press.

Fraser, Nancy. (1992). "Rethinking the Public Sphere: A Contribution to the Critique of Actually Existing Democracy." 109–142 in *Habermas and the Public Sphere*. Craig Calhoun (Ed.). Cambridge, MA: MIT Press.

Fraser, Nancy. (1995). "From Redistribution to Recognition? Dilemmas of Justice in a 'Postsocialist' Age." *New Left Review 212*:68–93.

Fulton, Brad R., and Richard L. Wood. (2017). "Achieving and Leveraging Diversity through Faith-Based Organizing." 29–55 in *Religion and Progressive Activism*. Ruth Braunstein, Todd Nicholas Fuist, and Rhys H. Williams (Eds).

Fulton, Brad R., Michelle Oyakawa, and Richard L. Wood. (2019). "Critical Standpoint: Leaders of Color Advancing Racial Equality in Predominantly White Organizations." *Nonprofit Management and Leadership 302*:255–276.

Fung, Archon and Erik Olin Wright. (2003). *Deepening Democracy Institutional Innovations in Empowered Participatory Governance*. New York: Verso.

Gadamer, Hans-Georg. (2013). *Truth and Method*. London: Bloomsbury Academic.

Gallagher, Sally K. (2003). *Evangelical Identity and Gendered Family Life*. Rutgers, NJ: Rutgers University Press.

Gallagher, Sally K. (2004). "The Marginalization of Evangelical Feminism." *Sociology of Religion 65*(3):215–237.

Gardner, Maria. (2011, October 13). "Landfill Proposal Draws Hundreds of Local Protestors." *The Poly Post*. Retrieved from http://www.thepolypost.com/landfill-propo sal-draws-hundreds-of-local-protestors/article_a96fbaf0-f5fe-11e0-b5db-0019bb30f 31a.html#.Tpgk2ObB8TQ.email.

Gasaway, Brantley W. (2014). *Progressive Evangelicals and the Pursuit of Social Justice*. Chapel Hill, NC: The University of North Carolina Press.

Gee, Alexander. (2013, December 18). "Justified Anger: Rev. Alex Gee Says Madison Is Failing its African-American Community." *The Capital Times*. Retrieved from http://host.madison.com/ct/news/local/city-life/justified-anger-rev-alex-gee-says-madison-is-failing-its/article_14f6126c-fc1c-55aa-a6a3-6c3d00a4424c.html.

Glaser, Barney G., & Anselm L. Strauss. (1967). *The Discovery of Grounded Theory*. Hawthorne, NY: Aldine de Gruyter.

Go, Julian. (2021). "Three Tensions in the Theory of Racial Capitalism." *Sociological Theory 39*(1):38–47.

Gordon, Wayne and John M. Perkins. (2013). *Making Neighborhoods Whole: A Handbook for Christian Community Development*. Downers Grove, IL: InterVarsity Press.

Gorski, Philip S. (2004). "The Poverty of Deductivism: A Constructive Realist Model of Sociological Explanation." *Sociological Methodology 34*(1):1–33

Gorski, Philip S. (2009). "Social 'Mechanisms' and Comparative-Historical Sociology: A Critical Realist Proposal." 147–196 in *Frontiers of Sociology, Annals of the International Institute of Sociology, Volume II*. Peter Hedström and Björn Wittrock. (Eds.) Leiden: Brill.

Gorski, Philip S. (2013a). "Bourdieusian Theory and Historical Analysis: Maps, Mechanisms, and Methods." 327–366 in *Bourdieu and Historical Sociology*. Philip S. Gorski. (Ed.) Durham, NC: Duke University Press.

Gorski, Philip S. (2017). *American Covenant: A History of Civil Religion from the Puritans to the Present*. Princeton: Princeton University Press.

Gorski, Philip S. (2020a, December 15). "Revisited: Why Do Evangelicals Vote for Trump?" *The Immanent Frame*. Retrieved from https://tif.ssrc.org/2020/12/15/revisi ted-why-do-evangelicals-vote-for-trump/.

Gorski, Philip S. (2020b). *American Babylon: Christianity and Democracy Before and After Trump*. New York: Routledge.

Gorski, Philip S., David K. Kim, J. Torpey, Jonathon VanAntwerpen. (Eds.) (2012). *The Post-Secular in Question: Religion in Contemporary Society*. New York: New York University Press.

Gorski, Philip S. and Ates Altinordu. (2008). "After Secularization." *Annual Review of Sociology 34*:55–85.

Gorski, Philip S. and Samuel L. Perry. (2020). "Practices of Relation: Gorski and Perry." *The Immanent Frame*. Retrieved from http://tif.ssrc.org/2020/04/02/gorski-and-perry/ ?source=relatedposts.

Gorski, Philip S. and Samuel L. Perry. (2022). *The Flag and the Cross: White Christian Nationalism and the Threat to American Democracy*. New York: Oxford University Press.

Greeley, Andrew and Hout, Michael. (2006). *The Truth about Conservative Christians: What They Think and What They Believe*. Chicago: University of Chicago Press.

Green, John C. (2013). "New and Old Evangelical Public Engagement: A View from the Polls." 129–156 in *The New Evangelical Social Engagement*. Steensland, B. and Goff, P. (Eds.) New York: Oxford University Press.

Green, Emma. (July 7, 2021). "The Vortex of White Evangelicalism." *The Atlantic*. https://www.theatlantic.com/politics/archive/2021/07/esau-mccaulley-black-christianity/619371/.

Griswold, Eliza. (December 26, 2018). "Evangelicals of Color Fight Back Against the Religious Right." *The New Yorker*. Retrieved from https://www.newyorker.com/news/on-religion/evangelicals-of-color-fight-back-against-the-religious-right/.

Gushee, David P. (2017). *Still Christian: Following Jesus Out of American Evangelicalism*. Louisville, KY: Westminster John Knox Press.

Habermas, Jürgen. (1991). *The Structural Transformation of the Public Sphere*. Cambridge, MA: MIT Press.

Habermas, Jürgen. (1992). "Further Reflections on the Public Sphere." 421–461 in *Habermas and the Public Sphere*. Craig Calhoun (Ed.). Cambridge, MA: MIT Press.

Habermas, Jürgen. (1995). "Reconciliation Through the Public Use of Reason: Remarks on John Rawls's Political Liberalism." *Journal of Philosophy* 92(3):109–131.

Habermas, Jürgen. (2006). "Religion in the Public Sphere." *European Journal of Philosophy* 14:1–25.

Habermas, Jürgen. (2008). "Secularism's Crisis of Faith: Notes on a Post-Secular Society." *New Perspectives Quarterly* 25:17–25.

Habermas, Jürgen and Joseph Ratzinger. (2006). *Dialectics of Secularization: On Reason and Religion*. San Francisco: Ignatius Press.

Habermas, Jürgen, M. Reder, J. Schmidt, N. Brieskorn, and F. Ricken. (2010). *An Awareness of What Is Missing: Faith and Reason in a Post-Secular Age*. Cambridge, MA: Polity Press.

Hale, Chad. (2019). *Forgive Us This Day Our Daily Bread: Can A Comfortable Church Remember Jesus?* Independently published.

Han, Hahrie and Maneesh Arora. (2022). "Igniting Change: An Evangelical Megachurch's Racial Justice Program." *Perspectives on Politics*, 1–15.

Han, Hahrie, Elizabeth McKenna, and Michelle Oyakawa. (2021). *Prisms of the People: Power and Organizing in Twenty-first-century America*. Chicago: University of Chicago Press.

Hardt, Michael and Antonio Negri. (2009). Commonwealth. Cambridge, MA: Belknap Press.

Hardt, Michael and Antonio Negri. (2012). *Declaration*. New York: Argo-Navis.

Harper, Brad. (2006). "The Scopes Trial, Fundamentalism, and the Creation of Anti-Culture Culture: Can Evangelical Christians Transcend Their History in the Culture Wars?" *Cultural Encounters: A Journal for the Theology of Culture* 3(1):7–16. Portland: Institute for the Theology of Culture: New, New Wineskins of Multnomah Biblical Seminary.

Harper, Lisa Sharon. (2008). *Evangelical Does Not Equal Republican . . . or Democrat.* New York: The Free Press.

Harper, Lisa Sharon. (2016). *The Very Good Gospel: How Everything Wrong Can Be Made Right.* Colorado Springs, CO: Waterbrook.

Harris, Dan. (2011, December 25). "Evangelicals Team with Portland's Gay Mayor for Charity." *ABC News.* Retrieved from http://abcnews.go.com/US/evangelicals-team-portlands-gay-mayor-charity/story?id=15218876.

Hart, Stephen. (2001). *Cultural Dilemmas of Progressive Politics Styles of Engagement among Grassroots Activists.* Chicago: University of Chicago Press.

Honig, Bonnie. (1993). *Political Theory and the Displacement of Politics.* Ithaca, NY: Cornell University Press.

Honig, Bonnie. (2017). *Public Things: Democracy in Disrepair.* New York: Fordham University Press.

Hunter, James Davison. (1987). *Evangelicalism: The Coming Generation.* Chicago: University of Chicago Press.

Hunter, James Davison. (1991). *Culture Wars: The Struggle to Define America.* New York: Basic Books.

Hunter, James Davison. (1994). *Before the Shooting Begins: Searching for Democracy in America's Culture War.* New York: The Free Press.

Hunter, James Davison. (2010). *To Change the World: The Irony, Tragedy, and Possibility of Christianity in the Late Modern World.* New York: Oxford University Press.

Hunter, James Davison. (2017, September 12). "How America's culture wars have evolved into a class war." Retrieved from https://www.washingtonpost.com/news/posteverything/wp/2017/09/12/how-americas-culture-wars-have-evolved-into-a-class-war/?utm_term=.06442c3d21f3.

Hunter, James Davison and Alan Wolfe. (2006). *Is There a Culture War? A Dialogue on Values and American Public Life.* Washington DC: Brookings Institution Press.

Hussain, Waheed. (2018). "The Common Good." *The Stanford Encyclopedia of Philosophy (Spring 2018 Edition).* Retrieved from https://plato.stanford.edu/entries/common-good/

Hwang, Jackelyn and Robert J. Sampson. (2014). "Divergent Pathways of Gentrification: Racial Inequality and the Social Order of Renewal in Chicago Neighborhoods." *American Sociological Review* 79(4):726–751.

Hymowitz, Kay S. (July 23, 2019). "Gentrification for Social Justice?" *City Journal.* Retrieved from https://www.city-journal.org/gentrification-for-social-justice/.

Inazu, John D. (2016). *Confident Pluralism: Surviving and Thriving Through Deep Difference.* Chicago: University of Chicago Press.

Jacobs, Alan. (2008). *Original Sin: A Cultural History.* New York: HarperCollins.

James, William. (1985 [1902]). *The Varieties of Religious Experience.* Cambridge, MA: Harvard University Press.

Jenkins, Philip. (2011). *The Next Christendom: The Coming of Global Christianity, Third Edition.* New York: Oxford University Press.

Jennings, William James. (2020). *After Whiteness: An Education in Belonging.* Grand Rapids, MI: William B. Eerdmans Publishing Company.

Johnson, Marcia. (2010). "Will the Current Economic Crisis Fuel a Return to Racial Policies that Deny Homeownership Opportunity and Wealth?" *The Modern American* 6(1):25–46.

Jonas, Michael. (2013, November 4). "Against All Odds, Casino Vote in Doubt." *Commonwealth.* Retrieved from http://commonwealthmagazine.org/uncategorized/558-against-all-odds-casino-vote-in-doubt/.

Jones, Robert P. (2020). *White Too Long: The Legacy of White Supremacy in American Christianity*. New York: Simon and Schuster.

Kamp, John. (2013, October 18). "Caesars Entertainment Exits Planned $1 Billion Boston Casino Project." *The Wall Street Journal*. Retrieved from http://www.wsj.com/articles/SB10001424052702304864504579144452311996252.

Keller, Tim and John Inazu. (Eds.) (2020). *Uncommon Ground: Living Faithfully in a World of Difference*. Nashville: Thomas Nelson.

Kight, Steph W. (September 19, 2021). "The Exvangelicals." *Axios*. Retrieved from https://www.axios.com/evangelical-exvangelicals-church-religion-christianity-100fc653-ef8f-4966-9653-6395cd30fb97.html.

Killian, Mark. (2017). *Religious Vitality in Christian Intentional Communities: A Comparative Ethnographic Study*. Lanham, MD: Lexington Books.

Kim, Rebecca Y. (2004). "Second-Generation Korean American Evangelicals: Ethnic, Multiethnic, or White Campus Ministries?" *Sociology of Religion* 65(1):19–34.

Kim, Rebecca Y. (2006). *God's New Whiz Kids: Korean American Evangelicals on Campus*. New York: NYU Press.

King, Martin Luther, Jr. (2019). *Strength to Love*. Boston: Beacon Press.

Klinenberg, Eric. (2020). "We Need Social Solidarity, Not Just Social Distancing." *The New York Times*. Retrieved from https://www.nytimes.com/2020/03/14/opinion/coronavirus-social-distancing.html.

Kretzmann, John P. and John L. McKnight (1993). *Building Communities from the Inside Out: A Path Toward Finding and Mobilizing a Community's Assets*. Evanston, IL: Institute for Policy Research.

Kymlicka, Will. (1996). *Multicultural Citizenship: A Liberal Theory of Minority Rights*. New York: Oxford University Press.

Labberton, Mark (Ed.) (2018). *Still Evangelical?: Insiders Reconsider Political, Social, and Theological Meaning*. Downers Grove, IL: InterVarsity Press.

Lamont, Michele Lamont and Virag Molnar. (2002). "The Study of Boundaries in the Social Sciences." *Annual Review of Sociology* 28:167–195.

Lampman, Jane. (March 12, 2008). "Rev. Jim Wallis Searches for Old-Time Justice." *The Christian Science Monitor*. Retrieved from https://www.csmonitor.com/The-Culture/Religion/2008/0312/p13s02-lire.html.

"Latinos Who Are Evangelical Protestants." (n.d.) *Pew Research Center*. Retrieved from https://www.pewforum.org/religious-landscape-study/religious-tradition/evangelical-protestant/racial-and-ethnic-composition/latino/.

Lareau, Annette C. (2011). *Unequal Childhoods Class, Race, and Family Life, Second Edition with an Update a Decade Later*. Berkeley, CA: University of California Press.

Lehman, Derek and Sherkat, Darren E. (2018). "Measuring Religious Identification in the United States." *Journal for the Scientific Study of Religion* 57:779–794.

Lichterman, Paul. (2005). *Elusive Togetherness: Church Groups Trying to Bridge America's Divisions*. Princeton: Princeton University Press.

Lichterman, Paul. (2012). "Religion in Public Action: From Actors to Settings." *Sociological Theory* 30(1):15–36.

Lichterman, Paul, Prudence L. Carter, and Michelle Lamont. (2009). "Race Bridging for Christ? Conservative Christians and Black-White Relations in Community Life." 187–220 in *Evangelicals and Democracy in America, Volume One: Religion and Society*. Brint, S. G. and Schroedel, J. R. (Eds.). New York: Russell Sage Foundation.

Lichterman, Paul and Nina Eliasoph. (1999). "'We Begin with Our Favorite Theory . . .': Reconstructing the Extended Case Method." *Sociological Theory* 17(2):228–234.

Lichterman, Paul and Nina Eliasoph. (2014). "Civic Action." *American Journal of Sociology* *120*(3): 798–863.

Lichterman, Paul and C. Brady Potts. (Eds.). (2009). *The Civic Life of American Religion*. Stanford: Stanford University Press.

Lichterman, Paul and Isaac Reed. (2015). "Theory and Contrastive Explanation in Ethnography." *Sociological Methods Research* 44(4):585–635.

Lichtman, Allan. (2008). *White Protestant Nation: The Rise of the American Conservative Movement*. New York: Atlantic Monthly Press.

Liebman, R. and R. Wuthow (Eds.) (1983). *The New Christian Right: Mobilization and 468 Legitimation*. Hawthorne, NY: Aldine Publishing.

Lindsay, D. Michael. 2007. *Faith in the Halls of Power: How Evangelicals Joined the American Elite*. NY: Oxford University Press.

Linthicum, Robert C. (2006). *Building a People of Power: Equipping Churches to Transform Their Communities*. Bletchley: Authentic Media.

Locke, John. (1988 [1698]). *Two Treatises of Government*. Peter Laslett (Ed.). Cambridge: Cambridge University Press.

Lubet, Steven. (2018). *Interrogating Ethnography: Why Evidence Matters*. New York: Oxford University Press.

Lupton, Robert D. (2005). *Renewing the City: Reflections on Community Development and Urban Renewal*. Downers Grove, IL: InterVarsity Press.

Lupton, Robert D. (2011). *Toxic Charity: How Churches and Charities Hurt Those They Help (and How to Reverse It)*. New York: HarperCollins.

Lynch, Michael P., Casey Rebecca Johnson, Nathan Sheff, and Hanna Gunn. (n.d.) "Intellectual Humility in Public Discourse: Literature Review." Retrieved from https://humilityandconviction.uconn.edu/blank/what-is-intellectual-humility/.

MacIntyre, Alisdair. (1988). *Whose Justice? Which Rationality?* Notre Dame: University of Notre Dame Press.

Mahmood, Saba. (2015). *Religious Difference in a Secular Age: A Minority Report*. Princeton: Princeton University Press.

Markofski, Wes. (2015a). *New Monasticism and the Transformation of American Evangelicalism*. New York: Oxford University Press.

Markofski, Wes. (2015b). "The Public Sociology of Religion." *Sociology of Religion* 76(4): 459–475.

Markofski, Wes. (2018a). "Rescuing Evangelicals," Feature Review Essay of *Growing God's Family: The Global Orphan Care Movement and the Limits of Evangelical Activism* [Samuel L. Perry]. *Sociology of Religion* 79(1):129–134.

Markofski, Wes. (2018b). "The Other Evangelicals." Series on American Religion, Humility, and Democracy. *The Immanent Frame*. [https://tif.ssrc.org/2018/01/11/the-other-evangelicals/].

Markofski, Wes. (2019). "Reflexive Evangelicalism." *Political Power and Social Theory* 36: 47–74.

Markofski, Wes, Brad R. Fulton and Richard L. Wood. (2020). "Secular Evangelicals: Faith-Based Organizing and Four Modes of Public Religion." *Sociology of Religion* 81(2):158–184.

Marsden, George M. (1997). *The Outrageous Idea of Christian Scholarship*. New York: Oxford University Press.

Marsden, George M. (2014). *The Twilight of the American Enlightenment: The 1950s and the Crisis of Liberal Belief*. New York: Basic Books.

Marsh, Charles. (2005). *The Beloved Community: How Faith Shapes Social Justice, from the Civil Rights Movement to Today*. New York: Basic Books.

Marti, Gerardo. (2012). *Worship across the Racial Divide: Religious Music and the Multiracial Congregation*. New York: Oxford University Press.

Marti, Gerardo. (2019). "The Unexpected Orthodoxy of Donald J. Trump: White Evangelical Support for the 45th President of the United States." *Sociology of Religion* 80:1–8.

Marti, Gerardo. (2020). *American Blindspot: Race, Class, Religion, and the Trump Presidency*. Lanham, MD: Rowman and Littlefield.

Marti, Gerardo and Emerson, Michael O. (2013). "The Rise of the Diversity Expert: How American Evangelicals Simultaneously Accentuate and Ignore Race." 179–99 in *The New Evangelical Social Engagement*. Brian Steensland and Philip Goff (Eds.). New York: Oxford University Press.

Marti, Gerardo and Gladys Ganiel. (2014). *The Deconstructed Church: Understanding Emerging Christianity*. New York: Oxford University Press.

Martinez, Jessica and Gregory A. Smith. (2016). "How the Faithful Voted: A Preliminary 2016 Analysis." *Pew Research Center*. Retrieved from https://www.pewresearch.org/fact-tank/2016/11/09/how-the-faithful-voted-a-preliminary-2016-analysis/.

Masci, David and Gregory A. Smith. (2016). "Exit Polls and the Evangelical Vote: A Closer Look." *Pew Research Center*. Retrieved from https://www.pewresearch.org/fact-tank/2016/03/14/exit-polls-and-the-evangelical-vote-a-closer-look/.

Masci, David and Gregory A. Smith. (2018). "5 Facts about U.S. Evangelical Protestants." *Pew Research Center*. Retrieved from https://www.pewresearch.org/fact-tank/2018/03/01/5-facts-about-u-s-evangelical-protestants/.

Massey, Douglas and Nancy A. Denton. (1993). *American Apartheid: Segregation and the Making of the Underclass*. Cambridge, MA: Harvard University Press.

Massey, Douglas S. and Jonathon Tannen. (2015). "A Research Note on Trends in Black Hypersegregation." *Demography* 52(3):1025–34.

McAlister, Melanie. (August 7, 2018). "A Kind of Homelessness: Evangelicals of Color in the Trump Era." *Religion & Politics*. Retrieved https://religionandpolitics.org/2018/08/07/a-kind-of-homelessness-evangelicals-of-color-in-the-trump-era/.

McCaulley, Esau. (2020). *Reading While Black: African American Biblical Interpretation as an Exercise in Hope*. Downers Grove: InterVarsity Press.

Mead, George Herbert. (1934). *Mind, Self, and Society*. Chicago: University of Chicago Press.

Meador, Jake. (2019). *In Search of the Common Good: Christian Fidelity in a Fractured World*. Downers Grove, IL: InterVarsity Press.

Menchik, Jeremy. (2015). *Islam and Democracy in Indonesia: Tolerance without Liberalism (Cambridge Studies in Social Theory, Religion and Politics)*. Cambridge: Cambridge University Press.

Mervosh, Sarah. (2021). "In Minneapolis Schools, White Families Are Asked to Help Do the Integrating." *The New York Times*. Retrieved from https://www.nytimes.com/2021/11/27/us/minneapolis-school-integration.html.

Mesh, Aaron. (2009). "Undercover Jesus." *Willamette Week*. Retrieved from http://www.wweek.com/portland/article-10543-undercover-jesus.html.

Merritt, Jonathon. (2016). "Donald Trump Exposes the Split Between Ordinary and Elite Evangelicals." *The Atlantic*. Retrieved from https://www.theatlantic.com/politics/archive/2016/02/donald-trumps-evangelical-divide/458706/.

Metzger, Paul Louis. (2006). "Mutuality and Particularity: Contours of Authentic Dialogue." *Cultural Encounters: A Journal for the Theology of Culture* 3(1): 51–60. Portland: Institute for the Theology of Culture: New, New Wineskins of Multnomah Biblical Seminary.

Miles, M. B. and A. M. Huberman (1994). *Qualitative Data Analysis: An Expanded Sourcebook.* Thousand Oaks, CA: SAGE Publications.

Miller, Donald E., Kimon H. Sargeant, and Richard Flory. (Eds.) (2013). *Spirit and Power: The Growth and Global Impact of Pentecostalism.* New York: Oxford University Press.

Monk, Ellis P., Jr. (2014). "The Cost of Color: Skin Color, Discrimination, and Health among African-Americans." *American Journal of Sociology* 121(2):396–444.

Monk, Ellis P., Jr. (2015). "Skin Tone Stratification among Black Americans, 2001–2003." *Social Forces* 92(4): 1313–1337.

Monk, Ellis P., Jr. (2022). "Inequality without Groups: Contemporary Theories of Categories, Intersectional Typicality, and the Disaggregation of Difference." *Sociological Theory* 40(1):3–27.

Moon, Ruth. (2014, November 13). "Segregated Surveys: How Politics Keeps Evangelicals White." *Christianity Today.* Retrieved from https://www.christianitytoday.com/ct/2014/november/segregated-surveys-how-politics-keeps-evangelicals-white.html.

Moon Dawne, Theresa W. Tobin, and J. E. Sumerau. (2019). "Alpha, Omega, and the Letters in Between: LGBTQI Conservative Christians Undoing Gender." *Gender & Society* 33(4):583–606.

Morehead, John W. (n.d.) "Evangelical Credibility and Religious Pluralism." Retrieved from: http://qideas.org/articles/evangelical-credibility-and-religious-pluralism/.

Morenoff, Jeffrey D., Robert J. Sampson, and Stephen W. Raudenbush. (2001). "Neighborhood Inequality, Collective Efficacy, and the Spatial Dynamics of Urban Violence." *Criminology* 39:517–58.

Morris, Aldon D. (1986). *The Origins of the Civil Rights Movement: Black Communities Organizing for Change.* New York: Free Press.

Morrison, Sara. (2014, July 14). "Casino Interests Have Spent Over $16.5m on Lobbyists Since 2007." *Boston.com.* Retrieved from http://www.boston.com/business/news/2014/07/14/casino-interests-have-spent-over-lobbyists-since/FmJgNYvtN2XyO9sVfmz1GN/story.html?p1=related_article_page.

Mouffe, Chantal. (2013). *Agonistics: Thinking The World Politically.* London: Verso.

Mouw, Richard J. (2011). *Abraham Kuyper: A Short and Personal Introduction.* Grand Rapids, MI: William B. Eerdmans Publishing Company.

Mouw, Richard J. (2016). *Adventures in Evangelical Civility: A Lifelong Quest for Common Ground.* Grand Rapids, MI: Brazos Press.

Mulder, Mark T., Aida I. Ramos, and Gerardo Martí. (2017). *Latino Protestants in America: Growing and Diverse.* Lanham, MD: Rowman & Littlefield.

Nemoianu, Virgil. (2006). "The Church and the Secular Establishment: A Philosophical Dialog Between Joseph Ratzinger and Jurgen Habermas." *Logos* 9:17–42.

Neuhaus, Richard. (1984). *The Naked Public Square: Religion and Democracy in America.* Grand Rapids, MI: William B. Eerdmans Publishing Company.

"National Association of Evangelicals, About Us." (n.d.) Retrieved from https://www.nae.org/about-us/.

"New Evangelical Partnership for the Common Good, About Us." (n.d.) Retrieved from http://www.newevangelicalpartnership.org/.

Noll, Mark A., David W. Bebbington, and George M. Marsden. (2019). *Evangelicals: Who They Have Been, Are Now, and Could Be*. Grand Rapids, MI: Wm. B. Eerdmans Publishing.

Nussbaum, Martha C. (2000). *Women and Human Development: The Capabilities Approach*. Cambridge: Cambridge University Press.

Offutt, Stephen. (2015). *New Centers of Global Evangelicalism in Latin America and Africa*. New York: Cambridge University Press.

Oldenburg, Gary. (1989). *The Great Good Place: Cafes, Coffee Shops, Bookstores, Bars, Hair Salons, and Other Hangouts at the Heart of a Community*. New York: Marlowe & Company.

Onishi, Bradley. (April 9, 2019). "The Rise of #Exvangelical." *Religion & Politics*. Retrieved from https://religionandpolitics.org/2019/04/09/the-rise-of-exvangelical/.

Pally, Marcia. (2011). *The New Evangelicals: Expanding the Vision of the Common Good*. Grand Rapids, MI: Wm. B. Eerdmans Publishing.

Patillo, Mary. (1998). "Church Culture as a Strategy of Action in the Black Community." *American Sociological Review* 63(6):767–784.

Patillo, Mary. (2008). *Black on the Block: The Politics of Race and Class in the City*. Chicago: University of Chicago Press.

Patillo, Mary. (2013). *Black Picket Fences, Second Edition: Privilege and Peril among the Black Middle Class, 2nd Edition*. Chicago: University of Chicago Press.

Patterson, Orlando. (1997). *The Ordeal of Integration*. Washington DC: Counterpoint.

Paxton, Pamela. (2002). "Social Capital and Democracy: An Interdependent Relationship." *American Sociological Review* 67(2):254–277.

Pein, Corey. (2011, October 11). "The Other Portland." *Willamette Week*. Retrieved from http://www.wweek.com/portland/article-18071-the-other-portland.html.

Perkins, John M. (2007). *With Justice for All: A Strategy for Community Development*. Ventura, CA: Regal.

Perrin, Andrew J. (2014). American Democracy: From Tocqueville to Town Halls to Twitter. Hoboken, NJ: Wiley.

Perry, Samuel L. (2017). *Growing God's Family: The Global Orphan Care Movement and the Limits of Evangelical Activism*. New York: NYU Press.

Perry, Samuel L. and Andrew L. Whitehead. (2019). "Christian America in Black and White: Racial Identity, Religious-National Group Boundaries, and Explanations for Racial Inequality." *Sociology of Religion* 80(3):277–298.

Perry, Samuel L., Andrew L. Whitehead, and Joshua T. Davis. (2019). "God's Country in Black and Blue: How Christian Nationalism Shapes Americans' Views about Police (Mis)treatment of Blacks." *Sociology of Race and Ethnicity* 5(1):130–146.

Pettigrew, Thomas F. and Linda R. Tropp. (2006). "A Meta-Analytic Test of Intergroup Contact Theory." *Journal of Personality and Social Psychology* 90(5):751–783.

Pettigrew, Thomas F. and Linda R. Tropp. (2008). "How Does Intergroup Contact Reduce Prejudice? Meta-analytic Tests of Three Mediators." *European Journal of Social Psychology* 38(6):922–934.

Pineo, Christopher S. (2013, October 25). "East Boston Faith Leaders Rally Against Casino." *The Boston Pilot*. Retrieved from http://www.thebostonpilot.com/article.asp?ID=16564.

Pitts, Leonard Jr. (September 13, 2007). "From Living Hell to Living Well: Atlanta Discovers What Works." *The Seattle Times*. Retrieved from https://www.seattletimes.com/opinion/from-living-hell-to-living-well-atlanta-discovers-what-works/.

Plantinga, Cornelius. (1995). *Not the Way It's Supposed to be: A Breviary of Sin.* Grand Rapids, MI: William B. Eerdmans Publishing Company.

Plato. (1991). *The Republic of Plato.* Allan Bloom (trans.), 2nd edition. New York: Basic Books.

Plummer, Robert L. (2012). *Journeys of Faith: Evangelicalism, Eastern Orthodoxy, Catholicism, and Anglicanism.* Grand Rapids, MI: Zondervan.

Putnam, Robert. (1993). *Making Democracy Work: Civic Traditions in Modern Italy.* Princeton: Princeton University Press.

Putnam, Robert. (2000). *Bowling Alone: The Collapse and Revival of American Community.* New York: Simon and Schuster.

Pyles, Rob. (2014, November 3). "Why I'm Voting for Casino Repeal (Question 3)." Retrieved from https://www.youtube.com/watch?v=eO49aGdk7nk&sns=fb.

Ragin, Charles C. and Howard S. Becker (Eds.) (1992). *What Is a Case? Exploring the Foundations of Social Inquiry.* Cambridge: Cambridge University Press.

Rah, Soong-Chan. (2009). *The Next Evangelicalism: Freeing the Church from Western Cultural Captivity.* Downers Grove, IL: InterVarsity Press.

Rawls, John. (1971). *A Theory of Justice.* Cambridge: Harvard University Press.

Rawls, John. (1985). "Justice as Fairness: Political not Metaphysical." *Philosophy & Public Affairs* 14(3):223–251.

Rawls, John. (1995). "Political Liberalism: Reply to Habermas." *Journal of Philosophy* 92:132–180.

Ray, Larry. (2004). "Pragmatism and Critical Theory." *European Journal of Social Theory* 7(3): 307–321.

"Reducing the Racial Homeownership Gap." (n.d.). The Urban Institute Housing Finance Policy Center. Retrieved from https://www.urban.org/policy-centers/housing-fina nce-policy-center/projects/reducing-racial-homeownership-gap/.

Reed, Isaac Ariail. (2011). *Interpretation and Social Knowledge: On the Use of Theory in the Human Sciences.* Chicago: University of Chicago Press.

Regnerus, M. D. and C. Smith. (1998). "Selective Deprivatization among American Religious Traditions: The Reversal of the Great Reversal." *Social Forces* 76(4):1347–1372.

Rehwaldt-Alexander, Jeremy. (2004). "Racial Reconciliation among Evangelicals: The Limits and Possibilities of Congregational Efforts." Ph.D. dissertation, Vanderbilt University.

Reilly, Adam. (2013, October 21). "After Caesars' Exit, Casino Opponents Rally In East Boston." *WGBH News.* Retrieved from http://news.wgbh.org/post/after-caesars-exit-casino-opponents-rally-east-boston#sthash.YMRwNDwu.dpuf.

Reynolds, Amy and Stephen Offutt. (2013). "Evangelical Action and Global Poverty." 242–257 in *The New Evangelical Social Engagement.* Brian Steensland and Philip Goff. (Ed.). New York: Oxford University Press.

Rice, Georgene. (2006). "Getting Along in the 21st Century: Building Beloved Community." *Cultural Encounters: A Journal for the Theology of Culture* 3(1): 41–46. Portland: Institute for the Theology of Culture: New, New Wineskins of Multnomah Biblical Seminary.

Rios, Victor. (2011). *Punished: Policing the Lives of Black and Latino Boys.* New York: NYU Press.

Roberts-Fronk, Julie and Lisa Engdahl. (2011, October 25). "Civic Engagement Requires Preparation." *Daily Bulletin.* http://www.dailybulletin.com/20111025/civic-engagem ent-requires-preparation/.

Robinson, Cedric. (2000). *Black Marxism: The Making of the Black Radical Tradition.* Chapel Hill, NC: University of North Carolina Press.

Rodriguez, Monica. (2012, July 17). "Pomona Council Gives Go Ahead to Building Waste Transfer Station." *Daily Bulletin.* http://www.dailybulletin.com/general-news/20120 717/pomona-council-gives-go-ahead-to-building-waste-transfer-station#f35f8bba74.

Rogers, Mary B. (1990). *Cold Anger: A Story of Faith and Power Politics.* Denton, TX: University of North Texas Press.

Robertson, Campbell. (March 9, 2018). "A Quiet Exodus: Why Black Worshipers Are Leaving White Evangelical Churches." *The New York Times.* Retrieved from https://www.nytimes.com/2018/03/09/us/blacks-evangelical-churches.html.

Roemer, John E. (1998). *Equality of Opportunity.* Cambridge, MA: Harvard University Press.

Rothstein, Richard. (2017). *The Color of Law: A Forgotten History of How Our Government Segregated America.* New York: Liveright.

Rousseau, Jean-Jacques. (1997). *"The Social Contract" and Other Later Political Writings, (Cambridge Texts in the History of Political Thought).* Victor Gourevitch (Ed. Trans.). Cambridge: Cambridge University Press.

Salomon, Noah. (2017). *For Love of the Prophet: An Ethnography of Sudan's Islamic State.* Princeton: Princeton University Press.

Sampson, Robert J., Stephen W. Raudenbush, and Felton Earls. (1997). "Neighborhoods and Violent Crime: A Multilevel Study of Collective Efficacy." *Science 227*:918–924.

Sampson, Robert J., Jeffrey D. Morenoff, and Felton Earls. (1999). "Beyond Social Capital: Spatial Dynamics of Collective Efficacy for Children." *American Sociological Review 64*:633–660.

Sampson, Robert J., Jeffrey D. Morenoff, and Thomas Gannon-Rowley. (2002). "Assessing 'Neighborhood Effects': Social Processes and New Directions in Research." *Annual Review of Sociology 28*:443–478.

Sater, Domyo and Matthew Farlow. (2006). "Dining with the 'Other.'" *Cultural Encounters: A Journal for the Theology of Culture 3*(1):71–74. Portland: Institute for the Theology of Culture: New, New Wineskins of Multnomah Biblical Seminary.

Seelye, Katharine Q. (2013, November 3). "End of Casino Partnership Leaves Fate of East Boston Racetrack in Doubt." *The New York Times.* Retrieved from http://www.nytimes.com/2013/11/04/us/end-of-casino-partnership-leaves-fate-of-east-boston-racetrack-in-doubt.html?_r=0.

Schelling, Thomas C. (1969). "Models of Segregation." *The American Economic Review 59*(2):488–493.

Schelling, Thomas C. (1971). "Dynamic Models of Segregation." *The Journal of Mathematical Sociology 2*(1):143–186.

Schneiderhan, Erik and Khan, Shamus. (2008). "Reasons and Inclusion: The Foundation of Deliberation." *Sociological Theory 26*:1–24.

Seim, Josh. (2021). "Participant Observation, Observant Participation, and Hybrid Ethnography." *Sociological Methods & Research.* https://doi.org/10.1177/004912412 0986209.

Seiple, Chris. (2018). "The Call of Covenantal Pluralism: Defeating Religious Nationalism with Faithful Patriotism (Templeton Lecture on Religion and World Affairs)." Retrieved from   https://www.fpri.org/article/2018/11/the-call-of-covenantal-pluralism-defeat ing-religious-nationalism-with-faithful-patriotism/.

Sen, Amartya K. (1980). "Equality of What?" 197–220 in *Tanner Lectures on Human Values, Vol. 1*. McMurrin, S. M. (Ed.) Cambridge: Cambridge University Press.

Sen, Amartya K. (1999). *Development as Freedom*. New York: Oxford University Press.

Shalin, D. N. (1992). "Critical Theory and the Pragmatist Challenge." *American Journal of Sociology* 98(2):237–279.

Shapiro, Thomas, Tatjana Meschede, and Sam Osoro. (2013). "The Roots of the Widening Racial Wealth Gap: Explaining the Black-White Economic Divide." *Institute on Assets and Social Policy* (IASP) Research and Policy Brief. Retrieved from https://heller.brand eis.edu/iere/pdfs/racial-wealth-equity/racial-wealth-gap/roots-widening-racial-wea lth-gap.pdf.

Sharkey, Patrick. (2013). *Stuck in Place: Urban Neighborhoods and the End of Progress Toward Racial Equality*. Chicago: University of Chicago Press.

Shellnutt, Kate. (September 16, 2021). "'Political Evangelicals'? More Trump Supporters Adopt the Label." *Christianity Today*. Retrieved from https://www.christianitytoday. com/news/2021/september/trump-evangelical-identity-pew-research-survey-preside ncy.html.

Shelton, Jason E. and Ryon J. Cobb. (2018). "Black Reltrad: Measuring Religious Diversity and Commonality Among African Americans." *Journal for the Scientific Study of Religion* 56(4):737–764.

Sheppard, Trent. (2014, October 31). "Faith for Casino Repeal." Retrieved from https:// www.facebook.com/FaithforRepeal?ref=profile.

Sherkat, Darren E. (2014). *Changing Faith: The Dynamics and Consequences of Americans' Shifting Religious Identities*. New York: NYU Press.

Sider, Ron. (2020, January 18). "Why I'm Still Evangelical in Spite of President Trump's Evangelical Supporters." Retrieved from https://www.redletterchristians.org/why-im-still-evangelical-in-spite-of-president-trumps-evangelical-supporters/.

Sider, Ronald J., John M. Perkins, Wayne L. Gordon, and F. Albert Tizon. (2008). *Linking Arms, Linking Lives: How Urban-Suburban Partnerships Can Transform Communities*. Grand Rapids, MI: Baker Books.

Sigurdson, Ola. (2010). "Beyond Secularism? Towards a Post-Secular Political Theology." *Modern Theology* 26(2):177–196.

Skillen, James W. (1994). *Recharging the American Experiment: Principled Pluralism for Genuine Civic Community*. Kentwood, MI: Baker Books.

Slade, Peter, Charles Marsh, and Peter G. Heltzel. (2013). *Mobilizing for the Common Good: The Lived Theology of John M. Perkins*. Jackson, MS: University of Mississippi Press.

Smidt, Corwin. (Ed.) (2003). *Religion as Social Capital: Producing the Common Good*. Waco, TX: Baylor University Press.

Smilde, David. (2007). *Reason to Believe: Cultural Agency in Latin American Evangelicalism*. Berkeley, CA: University of California Press.

Smith, Christian, with M. Emerson, S. Gallagher, P. Kennedy, and D. Sikkink. (1998). *American Evangelicalism: Embattled and Thriving*. Chicago: University of Chicago Press.

Smith, Christian. (2000). *Christian America? What Evangelicals Really Want*. Berkeley, CA: University of California Press.

Smith, Christian. (Ed.). (2003). *The Secular Revolution: Power, Interests, and Conflict in the Secularization of American Public Life*. Berkeley, CA: University of California Press.

Smith, Christian. (2011). *What Is a Person?: Rethinking Humanity, Social Life, and the Moral Good from the Person Up*. Chicago: University of Chicago Press.

Smith, Gregory A. (2021, September 15). "More White Americans Adopted Than Shed Evangelical Label during Trump Presidency, Especially His Supporters." Pew Research Center. Retrieved from https://www.pewresearch.org/fact-tank/2021/09/15/more-white-americans-adopted-than-shed-evangelical-label-during-trump-presidency-especially-his-supporters/.

Sparks, Paul, Tim Soerens, and Dwight J. Friesen. (2014). *The New Parish: How Neighborhood Churches Are Transforming Mission, Discipleship and Community.* Downers Grove, IL: InterVarsity Press.

Stavrides, Stavros and Mara Verlic. (2016). "Crisis and Commoning: Periods of Despair, Periods of Hope." 49–59 in *Spaces of Commoning Artistic Research and the Utopia of the Everyday.* Baldauf, Anette, Stefan Gruber, Moira Hille, Annette Krauss, Vladimir Miller, Mara Verlič, Hong-Kai Wang and Julia Wieger. (Eds.). 2016. Berlin: Sternberg Press.

Stears, Marc. (2010). *Demanding Democracy: American Radicals in Search of a New Politics.* Princeton: Princeton University Press.

Steger, Ted and Steger, Michele. (2014, October 28). "How our Faith Informs our Opposition to Casinos." Retrieved from http://www.macucc.org/blogdetail/466710

Steinmetz, George. (1998). "Critical Realism and Historical Sociology: A Review Article." *Comparative Studies in Society and History 40*(1):170–186.

Steinmetz, George. (2004). "Odious Comparisons: Incommensurability, the Case Study, and 'Small N's' in Sociology." *Sociological Theory 22*(3):371–400.

Stetzer, Ed. (November 2, 2016). "Evangelicals: This Is What It Looks Like When You Sell Your Soul For A Bowl Of Trump." *Christianity Today.*

Stetzer, Ed. (January 11, 2021). "Evangelicals Face a Reckoning: Donald Trump and the Future of our Faith." *USA Today.* Retrieved from https://www.usatoday.com/story/opinion/2021/01/10/after-donald-trump-evangelical-christians-face-reckoning-column/6601393002/.

Steensland, B., J. Z. Park, M. D. Regnerus, L. D. Robinson, W. B. Wilcox, and R. D. Woodberry (2000). "The Measure of American Religion: Toward Improving the State of the Art." *Social Forces 79*(1):291–318.

Steensland, Brian and Goff, Philip. (2013). *The New Evangelical Social Engagement.* New York: Oxford University Press.

Steensland, Brian, Robert D. Woodberry, and Jerry Z. Park (2018). "Structure, Placement, and the Quest for Unidimensional Purity in Typologies of American Denominations." *Journal for the Scientific Study of Religion 57*:800–806.

Stout, Jeffrey. (2010). *Blessed are the Organized: Grassroots Democracy in America.* Princeton: Princeton University Press.

Strauss, Anselm L. (1987). *Qualitative Analysis for Social Scientists.* New York: Cambridge University Press.

Swartz, David. (2012). *The Moral Minority: The Evangelical Left in an Age of Conservatism.* Philadelphia: University of Pennsylvania Press.

Swartz, David. (2020). *Facing West: American Evangelicals in an Age of World Christianity.* New York: Oxford University Press.

Taylor, Charles, with Kwame Anthony Appiah, Jürgen Habermas, Stephen C. Rockefeller, Michael Walzer, and Susan Wolf. (1994). *Multiculturalism: Examining the Politics of Recognition.* Princeton: Princeton University Press.

Thacher, David. (2006). "The Normative Case Study." *American Journal of Sociology 111*(6):1631–1676.

Tavory, Iddo and Stefan Timmermans. (2009). "Two Cases of Ethnography: Grounded Theory and the Extended Case Method." *Ethnography* 10(3):243–263.

Tavory, Iddo and Stefan Timmermans. (2012). "Theory Construction in Qualitative Research: From Grounded Theory to Abductive Analysis." *Sociological Theory* 30(3):167–86.

Tavory, Iddo. (2016). *Summoned Identification and Religious Life in a Jewish Neighborhood.* Chicago: University of Chicago Press.

Testa, Cynthia. (2011, September 25). "Waste Station Bad for Pomona." *Daily Bulletin.* Retrieved from http://www.dailybulletin.com/20110925/waste-station-bad-for-pomona.

"The Federal Bonding Program: A US Department of Labor Initiative." (2013). The United States Department of Justice. Retrieved from https://nicic.gov/federal-bonding-prog ram-us-department-labor-initiative.

The Inquirer Editorial Board. (2019). "Study on Gentrification's Benefits for Long-Time Residents Is Surprising and Useful." *The Philadelphia Inquirer.* Retrieved from https://www.inquirer.com/opinion/editorials/gentrification-study-federal-reserve-philadelp hia-research-20190721.html.

The Rutba House (Eds.). (2005). *School(s) for Conversion: 12 Marks of a New Monasticism.* Eugene, OR: Cascade Books.

Thomas, Todne. (2021). *Kincraft: The Making of Black Evangelical Sociality.* Durham, NC: Duke University Press.

Thurman, Howard. (1971). *The Search for Common Ground: An Inquiry into the Basis of Man's Experience of Community.* Richmond, IN: Friends United Press.

Tilly, Charles. (1998). *Durable Inequality.* Berkeley, CA: University of California Press.

Tisby, Jemar. (2020). *The Color of Compromise: The Truth about the American Church's Complicity in Racism.* Grand Rapids, MI: Zondervan.

Tocqueville, Alexis de. (1966 [1835/40]). *Democracy in America.* (G. Lawrence, Trans.). Mayer, J. P. (Ed.). New York: Harper and Row.

Tran, Jonathon. (2021). *Asian Americans and the Spirit of Racial Capitalism.* New York: Oxford University Press.

Tranby, Eric and Hartmann, Doug. (2008). "Critical Whiteness Theories and the Evangelical 'Race Problem': Extending Emerson and Smith's Divided by Faith." *Journal for the Scientific Study of Religion* 47(3):341–359.

Tucker, Robert C. (1978). *The Marx-Engels Reader.* New York: W. W. Norton & Company.

"Uncommon God, Common Good." n.d. Retrieved from https://www.patheos.com/blogs/uncommongodcommongood/.

Volf, Miroslav. (2011). *A Public Faith: How Followers of Christ Should Serve the Common Good.* Grand Rapids, MI: Brazos Press.

Volf, Miroslav. (2015). *Flourishing: Why We Need Religion in a Globalized World.* New Haven, CT: Yale University Press.

"Vote Common Good." (n.d.) Retrieved from https://www.votecommongood.com/.

Wacquant, Loïc. (2009). *Punishing the Poor: The Neoliberal Government of Social Insecurity.* Durham, NC: Duke University Press.

Wacquant, L. (2010). "Class, race & hyperincarceration in revanchist America." *Daedalus* 139(3):74–90.

Wald, K. D., D. E. Owen, and S. S. Hill, Jr. (1989). "Evangelical Politics and Status Issues." *Journal for the Scientific Study of Religion* 28(1):1–16.

Wallis, Jim. (2005). *God's Politics: Why the Right Gets It Wrong and the Left Doesn't Get It.* San Francisco: HarperOne.

Wallis, Jim. (2014). *The (Un)Common Good: How the Gospel Brings Hope to a World Divided.* Grand Rapids, MI: Brazos Press.

Walton, Emily. (2021a). "A culture of whiteness: How integration failed in cities, suburbs, and small towns." *Sociological Compass* 15(11):1–13.

Walton, Emily. (2021b). "Habits of Whiteness: How Racial Domination Persists in Multiethnic Neighborhoods." *Sociology of Race and Ethnicity* 7(1):71–85.

Walzer, Michael. (1983). *Spheres of Justice.* New York: Basic Books.

Warren, Mark R. (2001). *Dry Bones Rattling: Community Building to Revitalize American Democracy.* Princeton, NJ: Princeton University Press.

Warren, Mark R. (2010). *Fire in the Heart: How White Activists Embrace Racial Justice (Oxford Studies in Culture and Politics).* New York: Oxford University Press.

Warren, Mark R. and Karen L. Mapp. (2011). *A Match on Dry Grass: Community Organizing as a Catalyst for School Reform.* New York: Oxford University Press.

Weber, Max. (1949 [1904]). "Objectivity in Social Science and Social Policy." *The Methodology of the Social Sciences,* E. A. Shils and H. A. Finch (Ed. and Trans.). New York: Free Press.

Wehner, Peter. (January 14, 2016). "Why I Will Never Vote for Donald Trump." *The New York Times.* Retrieved from https://www.nytimes.com/2016/01/14/opinion/campaign-stops/why-i-will-never-vote-for-donald-trump.html.

Wehner, Peter. (December 24, 2020). "The Forgotten Radicalism of Jesus Christ." *The New York Times.* Retrieved from https://www.nytimes.com/2020/12/24/opinion/jesus-christ-christmas-incarnation.html.

Wehner, Peter. (October 24, 2021). "The evangelical church is breaking apart." *The Atlantic.* Retrieved from https://www.theatlantic.com/ideas/archive/2021/10/evangelical-trump-christians-politics/620469/.

West, Cornel. (1989). *The American Evasion of Philosophy: A Genealogy of Pragmatism.* Madison, WI: University of Wisconsin Press.

Whimster, Sam. (2004). *The Essential Weber: A Reader.* New York and London: Routledge.

White, Stephen. (2021). "Agonism, Democracy, and the Moral Equality of Voice." *Political Theory* 50(1):59–85. http://doi.org/10.1177/0090591721993862.

Whitehead, Andrew L., Samuel L. Perry, and Joseph O. Baker (2018). "Make America Christian Again: Christian Nationalism and Voting for Donald Trump in the 2016 Presidential Election." *Sociology of Religion* 79(2):147–171.

Whitehead, Andrew L. and Perry, Samuel L. (2020). *Taking America Back for God: Christian Nationalism in the United States.* New York: Oxford University Press.

Wilson, William J. (1987). *The Truly Disadvantaged: The Inner City, the Underclass, and Public Policy.* Chicago: University of Chicago Press.

Wilson, William J. and Taub, Richard P. (2007). *There Goes the Neighborhood: Racial, Ethnic, and Class Tensions in Four Chicago Neighborhoods and Their Meaning for America.* New York: Vintage Books.

Wolterstorff, Nicholas. (2010). *Justice: Rights and Wrongs.* Princeton: Princeton University Press.

Wong, Janelle S. (2015). "The Role of Born-Again Identity on the Political Attitudes of Whites, Blacks, Latinos, and Asian Americans." *Politics and Religion* 8(4):641–678.

Wong, Janelle S. (2018). *Immigrants, Evangelicals, and Politics in an Era of Demographic Change.* New York: Russel Sage Foundation.

Wong, Janelle S. (2018, November 1). "Evangelical Christians Hold Diverse Views on Immigration." *UPI*. Retrieved from https://www.upi.com/Top_News/Voices/2018/11/01/Evangelical-Christians-hold-diverse-views-on-immigration/6791541074482/.

Wood, Richard L. (2002). *Faith in Action: Religion, Race, and Democratic Organizing in America*. Chicago: University of Chicago Press.

Wood, Richard L. (2018, January 17). "Passion and Virtue in Public Life." *The Immanent Frame*. Retrieved from https://tif.ssrc.org/2018/01/17/passion-and-virtue-in-public-life/.

Wood, Richard L. and Brad R. Fulton (2015). *A Shared Future: Faith-Based Organizing for Racial Equity and Ethical Democracy*. Chicago: University of Chicago Press.

Wood, Richard L., Brad Fulton, and Kathryn Partridge. (2012). *Building Bridges, Building Power*. Boulder, CO: Interfaith Funders.

Woodberry, Robert D., Jerry Z. Park, Lyman A. Kellstedt, Mark D. Regnerus, and Brian Steensland. (2012). "The Measure of American Religious Traditions: Theoretical and Measurement Considerations." *Social Forces 91*(1):65–73

Wright, Erik O. (2010). *Envisioning Real Utopias*. New York: Verso Books.

Wuthnow, Robert. (2003). "Can Religion Revitalize Civil Society? An Institutional Perspective." 191–210 in *Religion as Social Capital: Producing the Common Good*. Smidt, C. (Ed.). Waco, TX: Baylor University Press.

Wuthnow, Robert. (2005). *America and the Challenges of Religious Diversity*. Princeton: Princeton University Press.

Wuthnow, Robert. (2021). *Why Religion Is Good for American Democracy*. Princeton: Princeton University Press.

Young, Iris M. (2011). *Justice and the Politics of Difference*. Princeton: Princeton University Press.

Yukich, Grace and Penny Edgell. (Eds.) (2020). *Religion Is Raced Understanding American Religion in the Twenty-First Century*. New York: NYU Press.

Zaman, Muhammad Qasim. (2004). "The 'Ulama of Contemporary Islam and their Conceptions of the Common Good." 129–155 in *Public Islam and the Common Good*. Armando Salvatore and Dale Eickelman. (Eds.) Leiden: Brill.

Index

For the benefit of digital users, indexed terms that span two pages (e.g., 52–53) may, on occasion, appear on only one of those pages.

Tables are indicated by *t* following the page number